Guide to the Hiking Areas of New Mexico

Guide to the Hiking Areas of New Mexico

Mike Hill

A COYOTE BOOK

University of New Mexico Press

Albuquerque

Library of Congress
Cataloging-in-Publication

Hill, Mike, 1944–
Guide to the hiking areas of New Mexico/ Mike
Hill.—1st ed.
    p.   cm.—(A Coyote Book)
Includes bibliographical references and index.
ISBN 0-8263-1557-7 (pbk.)
1. Hiking—New Mexico—Guidebooks.
2. New Mexico—Guidebooks.
I. Title.
II. Series: Coyote books (Albuquerque. N.M.)
GV191.42.N6H55 1995
796.5'1'09789—dc20
94–3202

Designed by Emmy Ezzell, and composed in
PageMaker in Aldus Roman type. Maps adapted
by Ron Stauber. Printed and bound in the United
States by Thomson-Shore, Inc.

Contents

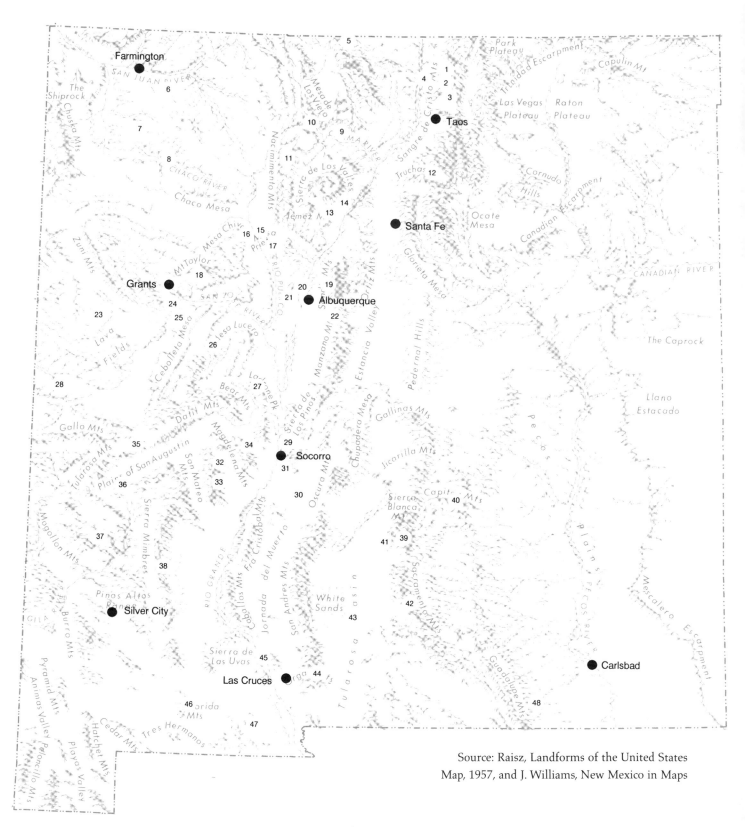

Farmington

The Shiprock

San Juan River

6

The Chuska Mts

7

8

Chaco River

Chaco Mesa

Zuni Mts

5

Park Plateau

Capulin Mt

Trinidad Escarpment

4 1
2
3

Las Vegas Plateau *Raton Plateau*

Taos

Sangre de Cristo Mts

Mesa de Los Viejo

10

9

SA RIVER

11

Nacimiento Mts

Truchas 12

Cornudo Hills

Sierra de Los Valles

14

Jemez M. 13

Canadian Escarpment

Ocate Mesa

Santa Fe

Mesa Chive 15
16
Prie 17

Mt Taylor

18

Rio Puebo Co

Glorieta Mesa

CANADIAN RIVER

Grants

24

23

Lava Fields

25

Cebolleta Mesa

Mesa Lucero

26

San Jo RIVER

Sandia Mts

20 19

21

Albuquerque

22

Ortiz Mts

Estancia Valley

Pedernal Hills

The Caprock

28

27

La-one Pk

Bear Mts

Datil Mts

Sierra de Los Pinos

Chupadera Mesa

Gallinas Mts

Llano Estacado

Gallo Mts

35

Tularosa Mts

Plains of San Augustin

34

San Mateo Mts

Magdalena Mts

29

Socorro

31

32

33

Jicarilla Mts

36

Sierra Mimbres

37

38

Mogollon Mts

30

Oscura Mts

Fra Cristobal Mts

Sierra Blanca Mt

Capitan Mts 40

Pecos Plains

41 39

Sacramento Mts

Pinos Altos Range

Silver City

GILA

Burro Mts

RIO GRANDE

Caballos Mts

Jornada del Muerto

San Andres Mts

White Sands

43

42

Pecos River

Mescalero Escarpment

Sierra de Las Uvas

45

Las Cruces

rga 44

Tularosa Basin

Carlsbad

Guadalupe Mts

48

Pyramid Mts

Animas Valley

Peloncillo Mts

46
orida Mts

47

Cedar Mts

Tres Hermanos

Hatchet Mts

Playas Valley

Source: Raisz, Landforms of the United States
Map, 1957, and J. Williams, New Mexico in Maps

Key to Hiking Areas

Hiking areas are listed here in the order of their appearance in the text. Numbers indicate the approximate location in New Mexico of each area. See Index to Maps, page 367, for additional details about specific hikes.

Preface

With my abiding companions of nature—the rocks, the trees, and the restless wind—I have counted the miles, noted the landmarks, and otherwise assembled these facts and figures. A fabric of numbers and words has been knitted into an informational resource: a guidebook. And yet there is something missing, something larger and more fundamental. More than just the physical beauty of the wilderness landscape, there is also that mysterious presence that stimulates our intellectual curiosity and draws us back again and again—an abstract power that compels us to sift the essential from the superficial and consider our purpose in the great cosmos. This is the final thread I wish to weave into the fabric, but the psychic rewards of the wilderness encounter form a nebulous concept not easily put into words, and the attempt is perhaps better left to others more capable than myself. So I simply wish to relate the following vignette—not a momentous happening, but a brief recollection that brings back some of the images, sensations, and reflections of a day spent in the New Mexico wilderness.

The year was 1978. The place, Chaco Canyon—a stepping stone along the eternal path of time and a place to which my memories return. In those days the whole of Chaco Canyon, save for a few prohibited sites, was open to backcountry hiking and I was on a solitary dayhike, walking where the ancients had walked through a small canyon far away from any road or trail. It was the rainy season and by mid afternoon the fleecy white clouds of the noon hour were beginning to darken and the gentle summer sky was rapidly giving way to an enormous, menacing wall of blue-gray storm clouds that spread across the entire width of the southwest horizon. Absorbed in aimless wandering, I suddenly became aware that things were developing much faster than I had realized. And as I began to think about retreating I knew it was too late: the brooding giant was moving relentlessly toward my little canyon and was closing with ominous speed. As a final shaft of sunlight played upon the tan walls of sandstone, an angry crash of thunder seemed to provide an urgency to the restless wind now stirring the dry grasses and the first scattered raindrops began to fall. The fragrant aroma of dampened earth tinged the air, and the steadily increasing drumroll of droplets disturbed the silence of the afternoon. I was almost resigned to a good soaking when I spotted it: a nearby cluster of large stone blocks that had broken away from the walls above sometime during the preceding millennia now provided a pocket large enough to shelter a single individual beneath a great horizontal slab. The small niche invited me in and I quickly accepted. As the storm raged about me and chocolate-colored rivulets of water drained past, I was reflecting upon my good fortune at finding this temporary sanctuary when I chanced to gaze up at the ceiling. There, pecked neatly into the sandstone, was a concise line-spiral design resembling a coiled rope, similar to many others in the area and probably placed there some 800 years before by an inhabitant of a nearby canyon. It occurred to me that the person who had created the petroglyph might also have been caught by a fast developing storm and had waited it out in this same spot just as I was doing. I could sense a feeling of human contact that spanned the ages, a spiritual fraternity with one long dead yet strangely present. Perhaps no one else had touched, or been touched, by this small artistic expression since it had been placed on its hidden panel. What was its meaning? Certainly, it had to be more than the furtive monuments to insensitive ego gratification that characterize modern rock graffiti. A stream of questions began to race through my mind as I wondered who the artist had been—what his name was, where he had lived, and how he had lived. Had he been a farmer, a warrior, a trader, or all of these? How had his society been organized? He may have made long journeys. Where might he have traveled, and of what did he dream along the way? Did he accomplish great things or die in obscurity? Perhaps there are those now walking the earth who are his great . . . great grandchildren. The stories he could tell if he were alive today!

As the storm passed over the high desert mesas and the distant rolling thunder echoed back to the small canyon, I walked back toward my truck through the cool fresh air of twilight. Civilization awaits! But my thoughts drifted back to my new friend from the rock shelter. I didn't know much about him but I knew that he had walked the same canyons and mesas that I have walked so many times before. His skin had felt the gentle breezes at the time when the yucca plant blooms, and he had wished for rain when the days grew long and the hot sun scorched the land. He had heard the lonely call of a distant coyote when the cottonwood leaves had turned to gold, and when the cold snow swept across the empty corn fields, he had huddled close to a fire of sagebrush and listened to the lyrics of ancient songs sung in a forgotten tongue. The land on which he had lived had been impartial and unforgiving, but he had seen its beauty, and by his wits, he had made the most of that which was offered. He had existed in harmony with the laws of nature , and in these he was well versed.

The memories of this ancient traveler who had taken respite, as I had, in that same small shelter, have been lost to time. His bones have lain under the sand for these many generations, but he will endure, for I shall think of him as I sit beside the lone campfire and reflect upon things that were. And I shall speak of him to my children.

And perhaps in the distant ages of yet unrecorded time a stranger will pass this way. He will walk the land where I have walked, and although I shall leave no mark on the rock to record my passing, he will know that I have stood there before him. He will know that I was a person who held dear the same things as he, and he will know that I have returned to the earth I loved where he must one day go as well. And as his shadow paints a fleeting image upon the ageless gallery of rock and soil, he will reflect upon things that were and upon generations yet unborn. And he will speak to his children, of a distant friend from long ago.

Introduction

If you have spent some time in New Mexico, then you probably have an appreciation for the remarkable diversity of the land's geology, climate, and life forms. If you are new to the state, then the popularly held image of sunbaked desert must eventually be amended to include towering alpine peaks with lush forests, lava flows, gentle meadows, broad grassy plains, deep river canyons, high mesa cathedrals, and much else in between. The one pervasive quality that all these areas have in common is solitude. Even the most heavily used hiking areas aren't really that crowded, and the out-of-the-way spots—well, they're downright lonely. New Mexico is the fifth largest state in the nation, with a population of about 1.5 million, a third of which is concentrated in and around Albuquerque. So there is a lot of empty space that helps to account for the sizable amount of designated and de facto wilderness. Of course, as we know, nature abhors a vacuum, and as a corollary it is known that industrial man abhors an undeveloped piece of land. And so, friends, it is my hope that you will get out and hike some of this magnificent country while it is still undeveloped. Walk in the beauty of the land and let its beauty inspire you; it will lower your blood pressure and make you a more tolerable person to be around when you get back to the city. And if you should be so inclined to do your part to see that these wild lands stay wild, I shall presume to speak for your grandchildren and say that it would be much appreciated.

On the following pages I have assembled the most comprehensive guide to New Mexico's hiking areas that is currently available. The areas covered range from the remote and little known to the ever popular. Large or small, rugged or manicured, with or without established trails, they all have something to offer.

I would like to express my gratitude to all those who have helped make this book a reality, and in that regard, a special thanks to Ilah Jones, Harless Benthul, and Cindy Hill.

The following section of the book, entitled "General Interest," contains a number of considerations concerning the peculiarities of New Mexico hiking, as well as general hiking tips intended to affect (positively, I hope) your comfort, safety, and enjoyment.

General Interest

Hiking Seasons

The most popular seasons for hiking in New Mexico are spring through fall, although the best times of year are largely a function of the latitude and elevation of the individual area. The more mountainous areas of the state tend to be snowbound through most of the winter with travel requiring cross-country skis or snowshoes, so it would normally be best to avoid planning hiking trips to forested areas above 7,000 feet in elevation from mid-November through March or April. Some of the very highest areas, such as Wheeler Peak or the Pecos Wilderness, might be impractical to hike until as late as early June, but these are particularly pleasant during the hottest months of summer and during the early fall. The lower lying areas of the state, particularly in the southern half, can be hiked year round but can be cold in winter and hot in summer; spring and fall are most comfortable. If you are unfamiliar with the state, try seeking advice for a particular area from a knowledgeable friend, a local hiking shop, or the appropriate governmental administrative field office. The latter are identified at the end of each hiking area description.

Weather

The weather in New Mexico begins to get quite pleasant for hiking in late winter or early spring, depending on the area, but can be rather unpredictable in March and April with the possibility of winter-like storms occurring into May. The weather begins to turn hot in May for the lower elevation areas and the heat persists through August or even later, although in the high elevations it can snow or sleet during any month of the year. The traditional thunderstorm season is July and August, with the typical scenario being a gradual cloud buildup during the course of the morning and a brief, sometimes violent, thundershower during mid- to late afternoon. Probably the most pleasant weather for hiking occurs during the fall months of September through mid-November. Days are warm, nights are cold, and there is a general lack of high wind and precipitation. Of course, trying to predict the weather is a notoriously risky undertaking, especially in this part of the country, so take no chances and be prepared for anything.

Altitude

Most of the hiking/wilderness areas in New Mexico are from about 5,000 to over 13,000 feet in elevation. If you are unfamiliar with hiking at these altitudes, there are several things you should know. First, you don't sit around in a T-shirt after the sun goes down. It gets cold at night, even in summer, and if there is any chance of your being caught out on the trail after dark, you should always carry some warm clothing in your daypack. A more immediately obvious affect of altitude, particularly if you live in a lower elevation part of the country, is an ego-deflating shortness of breath when hiking in the high country. Once you become acclimated (it takes a week or two), you may still suffer from shortness of breath, but then it will be a matter of physical conditioning rather than altitude (not that your heaving lungs will much care). Finally, it is not unusual to suffer mild altitude sickness in the form of a headache, a problem usually cured by a dose of aspirin. Also be aware of the more uncommon but much more serious altitude problems of cerebral and pulmonary edema. These require immediate evacuation of the victim to a lower elevation. Several mountain medicine publications deal with the symptoms and treatment of altitude sickness (see bibliography).

Map Coverage

I have provided a map for each of the hiking areas described in this book, so that you will be able to locate each area and find your way around. While the maps may show features such as trails and boundary lines that are not be shown on other available maps, and while some of the areas don't require much, if any, map coverage, you will undoubtedly want to obtain supplemental map coverage for some of the larger and more complex hiking areas. Since it is better to have too much information than not enough, I have listed for each hiking area the additional map coverage that is available and appropriate. The following paragraph outlines these map resources.

The most basic map coverage for any of the areas described in this book is provided by the U.S. Geological Survey (USGS) 7.5-minute topo or quadrangle (quad) maps. These maps generally cover an area approximately seven miles by ten miles, with a normal contour interval of 40 (sometimes 20) vertical feet. They also provide a declination diagram, specifying the discrepancy between true and magnetic north to help with compass work, distinguish forested areas, and provide excellent topographical detail. The drawbacks are that the trail information is often out of date, and because of the relatively small area covered, you may end up having to buy a lot of maps. Murphy's law of hiking states that the area you are interested in is always located where four maps come together. Topo maps on the 15-minute scale, which cover four times the area of the 7.5-minute maps, are sometimes available, but they are being phased out by the USGS. Another USGS alternative that proves to be the best option for some areas, at least until you feel the need for more detailed coverage, is the 1:100,000-scale map. These maps cover an area approximately 58 miles by 34 miles and provide the same basic topographical and surface feature information as the smaller-scale maps. This results in a smaller number of maps, but the detail is quite a bit coarser, which may present a problem. Another drawback for those of us who are not yet well integrated into the metric system is that elevations are shown in meters, which results in a certain amount of mental number crunching (1 meter = 3.2808 feet) and a deceptive 164-foot (50-meter) contour interval. The 1:100,000-scale maps come in a standard version and a Bureau of Land Management (BLM) edition showing surface management status that identifies the ownership status or governmental administering agency for the land covered by the map. The BLM version is occasionally useful when you are uncertain of the land ownership status of a potential hiking area. USGS maps can be purchased from various sporting goods and book stores, or from the USGS supply centers in Denver, Colorado (80225) and Reston, Virginia (22092). BLM edition maps are sold at several of the BLM district offices.

For hiking areas located within the national forests, the Forest Service has prepared maps that are most useful for identifying roads, trails (which are frequently out of date), campgrounds, and other man-made features. However, the standard national forest maps are without topographical information, and because of their broad scale and general clutter, I find them to be most useful as a supplement to the USGS topo maps. In addition to the national forest maps, the Forest Service has produced maps for most of the wilderness areas located on national forest land, and these are excellent. The topography is shown, the scale is reasonable, the trails are complete and (usually) accurately located, and many of the maps are now being printed on a durable, water-resistant paper. Forest Service maps can be purchased locally at the regional office in Albuquerque (517 Gold Avenue SW), at most of the district offices and ranger stations, and at some of the local hiking shops.

In addition to the various maps described above, you will need a basic road map of the state to help you get to the hiking area of your choice. For even better road coverage, you may want to invest in a copy of *The Roads of New Mexico* (see bibliography). In addition to providing quite a bit of regional information, this publication shows not only the major road system but also the usually confusing tangle of county roads and other minor back roads and jeep trails. Several other map resources that I have found to be useful are the *Highroad Map Series* (revised edition, published by Highroad Publications), *Guide to Indian Country* (published by the AAA Automobile Club of Southern California), and the *State of New Mexico Wilderness Status Map* (published by the U.S. Department of the Interior, Bureau of Land Management).

Wilderness Study Areas

A number of hiking areas discussed in this book are currently designated as Wilderness Study Areas (WSAs), with most under the administration of the Bureau of Land Management. The WSA designation gives these areas certain kinds of protection from further development until they are either upgraded to the status of a Wilderness Area or dropped from consideration. The WSAs tend to be remote and undeveloped, without established hiking trails. Even though some of these areas may not make the final cut to Wilderness Area and the WSA status may not apply by the time you visit the area, it is my belief that, barring some unforeseen land-use travesty, these areas will continue, whatever their status, to provide opportunities for solitude and offer valuable primitive hiking alternatives to the better developed and more popular areas.

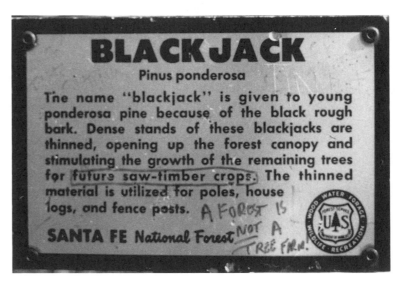

A Disgruntled Hiker Makes an Addition to a Santa Fe National Forest Sign.

Indian Reservations

Some of the prime wildlands in New Mexico are located on Indian reservations, but hikers generally aren't welcome. Trespassing on the backcountry parts of the reservations is prohibited without special permission from the appropriate tribal authorities. None of the hiking areas covered in this book involve reservation land.

Military Reservations

The above comments on Indian reservations also apply to military and restricted governmental installations. Places such as White Sands Missile Range, Los Alamos Labs, Kirtland Air Force Base, as well as others, contain some nice hiking areas, but without special permission you had better forget it.

Private Land

The receptivity of private landowners to the presence of hikers on their land varies considerably, but the rule should always be to obtain permission before hiking on private land except for short easement situations on established trails. These landowners have had to put up with a seemingly never-ending supply of slobs and vandals who, without permission, cut firewood, hunt game (and livestock), dump trash, cut fences, etc., to the point that it's a wonder any trespassing is allowed at all. However, it has been my experience that if you ask permission and explain what you are doing, the landowner usually doesn't object to your hiking on his or her land. There is a sizable amount of public land, usually BLM land, for which grazing allotments have been issued. This is public land and you don't need permission to hike it. And occasionally, you will find yourself in a situation where you just can't distinguish what is public land and what is private land. If the land is privately owned and trespassing is not allowed, the landowner has a responsibility to post this information, and in this case you should definitely keep off the land. If you believe the land to be public and there is nothing to indicate otherwise, proceed accordingly. Finally, when driving on a publicly maintained county road, you will sometimes encounter no trespassing notices at fence lines. These signs apply to the land on either side of the road but not the road itself, and unless the road is identified as a private road, you may open closed gates (and reclose them again) in order to proceed.

Access Road Conditions

I have tried to give accurate directions for reaching the hiking areas, and also some indication as to the condition of the access roads, what type of vehicle is adequate or inadequate, and at which times of year the roads may be impassible due to snow or mud. On occasion, your choice of a hike may be dictated by the condition of the access roads and the kind of vehicle you are driving. Since the information on road conditions is rather subjective or may not have been included, it would be a good idea to check with the appropriate administrative agency (included at the end of the area description) if you are in doubt.

Geology

One of the fascinating aspects of hiking in the Southwest is the vividly revealed geological record often on display as part of the local landscape. Just as knowledge of the plant and animal life you encounter on a hike adds to the experience for you and your companions, a basic understanding of the land forms and natural history of an area opens up a new field of interest. For those who can read them, the walls and slopes around you are like a book, documenting the millions of years of geologic processes and telling of ancient seas, deserts, meandering rivers, eroding mountain ranges, forests, and much more. Geologists have unraveled the complex sequence of geologic events that occurred in this part of the country, and the information can be found in several of the publications listed in the bibliography.

Hiking Clubs

If the idea of a group hiking experience appeals to you, then you should consider joining one of the outdoor clubs that sponsor hikes around the state. Not only do these clubs or organizations tend to have knowledgeable members who enjoy leading hikes, but they usually serve to promote and galvanize support for pro-hiking and pro-wilderness issues in the local community. It is a great way to experience local hiking areas with other outdoors-oriented individuals much like yourself. To locate hiking clubs that are active in your area, inquire at a local retail shop specializing in hiking equipment.

Hiking Equipment

The idea here is to bring along the items you will need for your safety and comfort without loading down your pack any more than necessary. Since necessity is a rather subjective determination, you will eventually want to assemble your own equipment checklist as you gain experience, and I do urge you to maintain and use a checklist. This idea will be reinforced each time you inconvenience yourself by forgetting to bring along lunch, raingear, toilet paper, or some other basic. When you end up wanting an item on a hike that you didn't bring along, remember to add it to your list, and eliminate the stuff that proves to be unnecessary or inappropriate. Keep your equipment lightweight and be willing to part with enough money to get a daypack that is comfortable, well made, and large enough to carry what you will need. If you don't already have a hiking equipment checklist, one is provided at the back of this book.

Hiking Speed

Many of the trails described in this book will specify a range of average hiking times required to complete the hike. These times assume a hiker of capable, though not extraordinary, hiking ability. For planning purposes, however, it is preferable for each individual to get a feel for his or her own typical time requirements needed to cover trail distances on a per-mile basis. Your rate of hiking speed will be influenced by elevation gain, physical conditioning, frequency and duration of rest stops, and time spent for plant identification, etc. Once you become familiar with your typical hiking speed for trails of various difficulty, you will be able to plan with reasonable accuracy the time required to hike a particular distance, as well as estimate distance covered based on time elapsed. When hiking with a group, realize that the rate of speed for the group is both inversely proportional to the size of the group and directly tied to the hiking ability of the slowest member of the group. For an individual hiker, I would offer the following general guidelines: for an average but well-conditioned hiker on fairly level terrain, three to four miles per hour is about the best you will be able to do, and an average speed of over three miles per hour is very difficult to maintain. An elevation gain of 500 or more feet per mile results in strenuous hiking with increased rest stops, and with elevation gains of 500 to 1,000 feet per mile your speed will drop dramatically. Since trails typically don't ascend at a constant rate, you will need to learn to use the contour lines on your topo map to get an accurate estimate of the elevation situation. For an average hiking trail, you can probably count on averaging 1.5 to 2.5 miles per hour, with the downhill segment being somewhat faster than the uphill part. Pay attention to your hiking times on the trail and budget enough time to make the return trip. Knowledge comes from experience and observation.

Using the Topo Map

The topo map is one of the most useful items on your list of necessities, and for some hiking areas, it is absolutely indispensable. To get the most out of it, it is necessary to understand what information is presented on the map and how to use the information to your advantage. A topo map is basically a two-dimensional presentation of a three-dimensional land surface. The horizontal component of the land surface is shown as with any other map, complete with distance scale and features such as roads, trails, rivers and streams, towns, boundaries, and man-made structures. The third, or vertical, dimension of the land surface is shown by means of contour lines which represent lines of constant elevation across the landscape and which can be visualized as the lines of intersection of a series of horizontal planes with the surface of the land (40 vertical feet apart is standard for the 7.5-scale maps). By studying the contour lines, it is possible to discern the location and shape of mountains, valleys, ridges, and other terrain features by visualizing both the horizontal and vertical component of the land. Every hiker should eventually attain at least a minimal level of proficiency using map and compass, and it would be worthwhile to obtain a publication dealing specifically with the subject (see bibliography). The best way to get started is to begin using a topo map to follow your progress on hiking trips. Don't depend upon the expertise of a hiking companion. Become involved as if you alone were responsible for route finding—because some day you might be. Purchase a topo map for your next outing and get the salesperson to explain to you the map symbols for paved roads, improved roads, unimproved roads, trails, bridges, houses, or whatever else appears on the map that you don't understand (a USGS pamphlet is available that provides a key to the topo map symbols). Notice that the forested areas have green overprint, unforested areas have none, and swamps and areas of scattered forest cover have special patterns of green overprint. Locate the trail you intend to hike and study the landmarks and terrain features that trail passes through. Does the trail follow valley bottoms or ridgelines? Where are the points of reference such as wilderness boundaries, lakes, stream crossings, or trail intersections? Places where the contour lines are close together indicate steep terrain, while widely spaced contour lines indicate mesas, meadows, or other areas of flat relief. The contour lines for hollows and ridges look very similar on a topo map, but in time you will be able to distinguish them. Figure the elevation gradient over a particular stretch of trail by counting the number of contour lines that the trail cuts across. Once on the trail, fold your map to fit inside a medium to large ziplock bag in order to keep it dry and prolong its usefulness, and refer to it often as you hike up the trail. Try to keep track of exactly where you are by paying attention to landmarks and whatever points of reference that are available. Notice how the topography of the terrain and obvious landmarks around you are depicted in the contour lines of the map. You can't become adept in the use of a topo map if it stays in your daypack, and there will come a time when map-reading skills are something you will surely need to have. As with many other wilderness skills, good map work comes only with experience.

Getting an Early Start

In the high country where the weather can change rapidly, getting started early in the day often makes the difference between reaching a hiking objective and having to turn back in the face of thunderstorms or approaching darkness. Because of the typical pattern of afternoon storms during the rainy season, an early start not only makes walking through the rain less of a possibility but it also decreases a potential safety concern. You will have more time to hang out and take rest stops and more time to deal with unplanned delays.

Group Hiking

There are two important considerations when hiking with a group. First, as mentioned earlier, the hiking performance of the group will be dictated by the slowest member of that group, and you should plan your rate of progress accordingly. Even with a strong group of hikers, the group will move at a slower rate than the individuals would on their own. Secondly, you must realize the importance of staying together on the trail. When the stragglers are out of sight from the rest of the group, it is far too easy for them to wander off on a side path or game trail, and the leaders won't know if the others are lost, injured, or simply taking longer. The result can be a lot of lost time and anxious moments. If the hiking speeds within the group are too divergent to comfortably stay together, then the people in front need to stop frequently and let the others catch up. Finally, if the group includes inexperienced hikers, stick a little extra moleskin in your pack and help see that they come properly equipped for the hike.

Backpacking Tent with Lightweight Cooking Gear

Backpacking

Overnight backpacking is a logical extension of dayhiking but with additional considerations, including more complex equipment requirements that would fill too many pages to adequately cover in this book. You can find various publications on the subject at a local hiking shop or bookstore (See *Backpacking One Step at a Time* in bibliography) and a sample equipment checklist has been included at the back of this book. There are many fine backpacking areas in New Mexico, including many of the areas discussed in this book, although some are impractical usually for reasons of small size, lack of drinking water, or governmental prohibition. The suitability for backpacking of the various hiking areas is generally discussed as part of the individual hiking area descriptions.

Car Camping

The accessibility of public lands for car camping and the facilities available, if any, vary according to the land status. On BLM lands camping is allowed so long as you keep your vehicle on existing roads. In national forests car camping is allowed in the designated campgrounds but not in picnic areas. The campgrounds are shown on the national forest maps and are listed in the Forest Service publication, *Recreation Sites in Southwestern National Forests*, available free where Forest Service maps are distributed. Most state parks have camping facilities, as do some of the national parks and monuments, but the latter will only allow camping in designated camping areas. Many of the individual hiking area descriptions include information on car camping in the vicinity. If your plans include camping out of your car, it would be prudent to inquire ahead of time

One caveat on theft and vandalism: an unpleasant fact of life concerning automobiles, no matter where they happen to be parked, is that they occasionally get broken into. The potential threat varies with the campsite or trailhead, and to a large extent is beyond your control. Just be aware of the possibilities when you leave your car and make it a less-tempting target by not leaving expensive gear in plain view.

Horse Travel

From an administrative standpoint, horses are generally allowed on all the Forest Service and BLM trails open to hiking, including wilderness areas, unless specifically excluded. From a practical standpoint, some trails are unsuitable for horses due to steep, dangerous sections, or other reasons, and since this book is concerned mainly with foot travel, this distinction may not always be made clear in the trail descriptions. If you want to take livestock on the trails, you should first check with the administering agency specified at the end of the trail sections of the book. When on foot and encountering livestock on the trails, hikers should yield the right of way, preferably by climbing to the uphill side of the trail, and give the animals plenty of room.

Campfires

A camping trip seems somehow incomplete without the ritual of sitting around a campfire to ward off the chill of night. But campfires do have their drawbacks as well. They tend to scar the landscape and they present a potential fire hazard. If there is an old campfire ring near your camp, reuse it rather than making a new one and be especially careful not to let the fire get out of hand. Clear away forest litter down to ground level around the campfire ring, and make certain all the coals are out before you leave the fire. In dry weather conditions when fire danger is high, you have no business making campfires, and the Forest Service will usually restrict campfires in this situation anyway. A lightweight campstove is therefore one of the essentials on your checklist of backpacking equipment. Some final suggestions: leave the hatchet and saw at home, as you can break up all the wood you need by hand; place your tent out of range from wind blown sparks; and don't place your wet boots too close to the fire to dry them out, a procedure that has wasted many a pair. If it's too hot for your skin, it's too hot for the boots. When wood is scarce, the always present dried cow chip will provide fuel in a pinch.

Car Shuttles

A number of the hiking trail descriptions in this book suggest that you consider a car shuttle as a means of facilitating a one-way hike without having to retrace your route back to the trailhead. This can be accomplished when there are two or more automobiles in your hiking group (if the group is small enough to fit into one car) simply by dropping off one vehicle at the point where you intend to end the hike and using the other vehicle(s) to ferry the group back to the start of the hike.

Drinking Water

The basic rule for naturally occurring water in lakes, streams, and springs is not to drink it unless you purify it. Although there are potentially several unsavory organisms lurking in untreated water, the tiny giardia organism that has become so widespread over the past 20 years or so is by itself adequate reason for purifying naturally occurring drinking water. The giardia organism is not life threatening, but exposure does result in moderate to severe gastrointestinal discomfort and is well worth avoiding. Perhaps the most certain method of treating the water is to boil it for five minutes or more, but the road to intestinal mayhem is paved with good intentions and chances are you're just not going to go to the trouble. Chemical treatments such as halazone and iodine tablets are a traditional and inexpensive alternative, but they make the water taste weird and effectiveness depends on exposure time. Treating water overnight is preferred, if you can wait that long. The best of the chemical treatments is a system marketed as the "Sierra Water Purifier," which is effective and eliminates most of the drawbacks associated with the other chemical products. A third popular alternative is the water filter, of which there are several versions on the market. These devices work by pumping water through a filter to strain out unwanted organisms. They have the advantage of producing drinking water on demand, but they are also relatively more expensive, somewhat bulky, have the potential for mechanical failure, and clog up easily in silty water. Even with these drawbacks, some people consider filters to be the best alternative. If you decide to go for the unstated option of drinking the water without treating it, then do so as close to the water's source as possible, such as at a spring. For day hikes, it is a good idea to plan on bringing along with you the water you will need. For moderate dayhikes, one quart per person is usually sufficient. For long hikes, especially in hot weather, take along two quarts per person, and if your pack can stand it, carry along a little extra just in case. For multiday trips in hot weather, you will need at least a gallon of water per person per day. These quantities are impractical to carry with you, so plan accordingly.

Sanitation

Locate toilet sites well away (at least 150 feet) from any streams, lakes, or other water drainages, and also well away from potential campsites and rest areas. It is highly irritating to discover that the perfect spot to pitch your tent is already occupied by a small dump of you know what. Human waste and toilet paper should be buried six to eight inches deep under the soil. If that proves impossible (and some ground just can't be dug into with a plastic trowel), then at least bury the result of your efforts under whatever loose dirt you can scrape together and cover it all with some heavy rocks to discourage scatter by the local critter population.

Hiking with Dogs

Taking your dog along on a hike can be a great opportunity for both pet and master to share in some fresh air and exercise, but unless your dog is well mannered and responsive to commands it is better to either keep him on a leash or leave him at home. Most hikers find it annoying to be barked at and hassled by dogs when this may be one of the very aspects of city living they are trying to escape. Similarly, the local wildlife shouldn't have to put up with being chased by dogs. Also note that the national parks and monuments, as well as some of the other areas, generally either prohibit or restrict hiking with dogs, so it is a good idea to check and see if any dog regulations apply to the area you intend to visit. If you do take your dog along, see that you bring along adequate food and water (if unavailable on the trail), and consider getting him a dog pack to carry it in.

Hunting Seasons

Large tracts of New Mexico's public lands have hunting seasons for a variety of game animals, and these lands include many of the areas covered in this book. For obvious reasons—not being shot at is near the top of the list—you may wish to time a hiking trip so as not to coincide with these hunting seasons, particularly the rifle hunts for deer and elk. This hunting activity is most intensive in the forested areas of the state and tends to occur from late October through early November. The actual hunt dates vary for the many different sectors of the state but are spelled out in a complex but comprehensive big game hunting proclamation available free at various Forest Service and BLM offices and at stores that sell hunting equipment and firearms. You can also get hunting information from the source, at the Department of Game and Fish. The main office is at the Villagra Building, 408 Galisteo, Box 25112, Santa Fe, NM 87504, (505) 827-7911. There are also Game and Fish offices located in Albuquerque, Las Cruces, Raton, and Roswell. You can also report any poaching activity to these locations. If you do go hiking in an area where hunting may be in progress, it is a good idea to wear bright colors, preferably as much blaze orange as you are able to stand.

Hiking Permits

I am not aware of any national forest or BLM areas that currently require hiking permits, but this has not always been the case and could change. If you are making inquiries into a particular area, ask about the permit situation as well. A number of other hiking areas, including Bandelier and Chaco Canyon, do require backcountry hiking permits. Inquire at the area Visitor Centers for details.

Search and Rescue

There are a number of search and rescue organizations in the state, both civilian and military, comprised of dedicated individuals who volunteer their time when necessary to search for and extricate lost and injured backcountry trekkers. These groups are coordinated under the direction of the New Mexico State Police, and their task is greatly simplified when they know where to look. It is a simple and prudent precaution before taking off on a wilderness outing to leave word with someone as to where you intend to go hiking, when you plan to return, and when to initiate a search if you fail to do so. To initiate a search and rescue effort, you should contact the state police, the local county sheriff's office, or the nearest national forest ranger station.

Survival

Experienced hikers are rather sheepish about admitting to having been lost while in the woods (or temporarily disoriented, as most would prefer to call it), but you can bet that plenty of them have been seriously disoriented more than once. If it can happen to an experienced hiker, it can certainly happen to a beginner. A misdirected off-trail shortcut or wander usually results in nothing more than a bit of anxiety and a lot of wasted time and energy before your objective is eventually relocated. But there is that possibility that someday you may become caught by darkness, injured, or disoriented enough that you'll have to spend one or more unplanned nights in the wide open spaces before you can find your way out. It is the kind of eventuality you should plan for anytime you hike into the kind of country where it might happen. Forget about such nonsense as learning to chip out flint points or set rabbit snares. The overriding considerations to surviving a few unplanned nights in the wilderness where serious injury is not a primary factor (and maybe even if it is) revolve around two major points. First, it is absolutely imperative that you get things into perspective and avoid panic. This cannot be overstated, so I will say it again: Don't Panic! You will have some decisions to make, and everything revolves around your ability to think rationally. Even though the thought of being the object of a search and rescue operation may be too ignominious to bear, you need to know when to press on, when to slow down, and when to call it a day. The other major consideration is that you have the things with you that will allow you to keep warm, stay dry, and start a fire. If you have planned properly, you will have these things with you in your pack, and your physical needs will automatically be taken care of. If you have also included extra food, water, and map and compass, you will be that much better off. Learn something about constructing emergency shelters. You may never need to construct one, but it is good to have put some thought into it if you do. If you are mobile and unimpeded by snow, a logical search should allow you to find the trail on which you were originally traveling. Alternatively, locate a drainage system and continue following it downhill until you eventually come to a trail or road, or if on flat terrain, pick out a likely compass heading and stick to it. In any case, decide on a logical course of action rather than randomly wandering about. If you are injured, get caught in snow, or find yourself in especially rough terrain, your best course of action may be to stay put and wait for help to arrive. In this kind of situation, the search is greatly facilitated if the victim stays in one place where he can be seen from the air and has left word with someone as to the intended vicinity of the outing. A smoky fire and signal mirror are your best means of attracting attention from airborne search craft. Lost hunters and hikers are located safely in the great majority of instances, but a little common sense and prior planning helps a lot. And remember—don't panic.

Rockfall

In backcountry hiking it is not uncommon to have to negotiate a steep, rocky
section where one of the primary safety concerns is being struck by a rock dislodged
by one of your companions from above. Some of the high mountains also contain
natural debris chutes where rockfall is particularly dangerous and where you should
spend as little time as possible. In an area where rockfall is a hazard, it is best to either
have the group travel closely together so that dislodged rocks won't have time to
gather momentum before reaching the rest of the group or, if possible, for the group to
ascend individually while the other members seek a sheltered spot. Probably the only
serious injury I have ever sustained in backcountry hiking occurred as I walked too
near the edge of a small undercut cliff, only to have it all collapse in a shower of large
boulders—a situation I could have avoided had I used a bit more caution. On vertical
terrain proceed with care and expect the unexpected.

Rock Climbing

Most people have a natural fear of vertical exposure which prevents them from
climbing out on rock faces from which a fall would have disastrous consequences, yet
every year there are a number of deaths and serious injuries from people doing exactly
that. Rock faces, particularly sandstone, can be misleading in their difficulty, and it is
always easier to climb up than to climb back down. Use some judgement and don't
climb out on anything that you can't afford to fall off of. Leave rock climbing for
properly trained and equipped rock climbers.

Stream Crossings

Hiking trails that follow streams or rivers inevitably result in a certain number of
stream crossings that are mostly uneventful, with bridges, logs, or handy rocks in place
to facilitate the effort. From time to time, though, no such aids will be present and

you'll just have to wing it and get across as best you can. In this case, be cautious of slippery rocks and logs, and when you have to walk through water a foot or more deep, use a sturdy wood staff or stick placed downstream for a tripod effect to aid in balance. When crossing deep water, unfasten the waist belt on your pack so you can quickly shed it if you fall in, and if you know ahead of time that you will be doing a lot of stream crossings, bring along a pair of lightweight running shoes in order to keep your hiking boots dry. Keep in mind that a stream that you can practically jump across in mid-summer may look like something more appropriate for whitewater rafting in spring when the snows are melting out of the high country, so plan accordingly.

Blisters

One of the unfortunate realities of hiking is that the feet are not generally conditioned to the punishment of thousands of repetitions up and down on a rocky hiking trail. Unless you hike frequently, a long trek will result not only in sore feet but perhaps a nice blister or two as well, and a blister can turn into a very serious handicap. Even boots that are well fitted and well broken in are no guarantee against blisters, but new or ill-fitting boots are certain trouble. Avoiding blisters is one of the more worthwhile things you can do on a hike, and the time to give some thought to the situation is before you begin your hike, not while sitting by the side of the trail with your boot off gazing forlornly at your heel. The boots you hike in should be comfortable and should be snug enough to eliminate unnecessary slippage but not tight enough to pinch your feet. They should have plenty of toe room but shouldn't slip at the heel. Experiment with a pair of thin neoprene insoles, if necessary, to alter the fit, and have your boots well broken in by doing a series of shorter hikes. It is often good insurance to bring along a pair of lightweight running shoes to change into if your primary hiking boots aren't working out. A medium to thick pair of socks is usually sufficient, but avoid cotton as it has a tendency to hold moisture and wrinkle. A pair of thin liner socks next to your skin made of a wicking material such as polypropylene or thermax will help keep your feet dry and reduce friction. The combination of socks that you wear will be determined partly by the amount of space available inside your boot, and you shouldn't try to cram more socks in than are comfortable. Take along one or two extra pairs of socks to change into when the ones you are wearing become damp. Once on the trail, it is absolutely preferable to deal with a potential blister problem before the blister develops. You should have with you a package of moleskin, an adhesive-backed, felt-like material (available at a drugstore or hiking shop) and a roll of adhesive tape an inch or more wide. As soon as you feel an uncomfortable friction spot developing on your foot, remove your boot and sock and cut a generous size piece of moleskin to be taped on your foot over the trouble spot. Tape the edges down well with the adhesive tape so they will not curl up. Heels are the worst trouble spot, and if you know beforehand that you are prone to heel blisters, tape up your heels with moleskin before you start out. Another technique that has gained in popularity and also seems to work well is to tape your heels with duct tape before starting out. If you have waited too long to deal with the situation and a blister has already developed, there is a product manufactured by Spenco Corporation called second skin, and should you have some with you, you can substitute it for the moleskin. Otherwise, cut the moleskin into strips and build up several layers around the periphery of the blister to help force the boot away from the blister and reduce friction between the blister and your sock. The best prevention, however, is to stop and treat the problem while it is still relatively easy to do so. Since there may be others in your hiking group who won't have brought along moleskin and tape, it is a good idea to take along an extra supply and to encourage your companions to sound off as soon as one of them begins to feel a blister coming on.

Sunburn

By now there should be a reasonably high awareness as to the effects of excessive ultraviolet radiation on the skin, but still you see a lot of reddened noses on the hiking trail. Incident ultraviolet radiation increases with elevation, and a hat with a brim or bill to shade the face is a near necessity, as is a sunscreen with a sun protection factor (SPF) of 15 or more to apply to exposed skin. The exception, as long as you have an appropriate hat, is to avoid putting sunscreen on the forehead in order to avoid having PABA-laden sweat running down into your eyes.

Hypothermia

Hypothermia is the process that occurs when the temperature of the body core is gradually lowered below that which is required to sustain it, ultimately resulting in death. Hypothermia progresses in its effect on the body through stages, beginning with intense but manageable cold, followed by uncontrollable shivering, followed by incoordination and mental disorientation, and finally unconsciousness. The process is insidious in that the victim is unable to think clearly in the advanced stages, and unless the victim's companions recognize what is happening, the process may be irreversible. The underlying causes of hypothermia are almost always wind, moisture, and cold, often aggravated by exhaustion and hunger. When hiking in cool and inclement weather it is important to avoid becoming damp and exhausted due to overexertion and to have rainwear to protect against precipitation and wind chill. Additional garments for extra warmth should also be carried. Once a person becomes hypothermic, it is necessary to replace the victim's wet garments with dry ones, get him out of the wind, and warm him up by whatever means—body heat, campfire, or warm drinks. A classic reference on the subject is included in the bibliography.

Lightning

People are killed and injured every year by being on ridges and localized high spots during the course of a lightning storm, and New Mexico is one of the leading states in both incidence of lightning strikes and resulting deaths. When you know that thunderstorms are likely to occur during the course of the day, get started early and plan to be off the high spots before the action starts. If you are unable to avoid getting caught in a lightning storm, distance yourself from ridges, peaks, or other localized high spots, and avoid lone trees, clearings, or other locations where you or something near you is the highest thing around. A further precaution is to stash metal gear such as pack frames, fishing rods, hiking staffs, and tripods in another location until the danger is over.

Flash Floods

This is flash flood country. Don't camp in the floodplain of a dry water drainage.

Poison Ivy

Some of the canyon bottoms and river banks have occasional patches of poison ivy. Teach your children to identify and avoid this plant.

Cactus

If you tend to do much off-trail hiking, you might want to get a pair of all-leather hiking boots. The fabric kind don't stop cactus spines. Despite your best precautions, however, a set of tweezers in your Swiss army knife or first-aid kit will occasionally prove to be a useful item to have along.

Back Country Injury

The remoteness of many of the hiking areas of the state makes an injury a very serious possibility for the solo hiker. If you like to hike alone, recognize the risks and leave your itinerary and expected time of return with someone. Some emergency first aid is a great thing to know in the field. Several good references are included in the bibliography.

Plague

In past years there have been a number of isolated cases of bubonic plague as a result of rodent or flea bites. Your chances of ever contracting plague are extremely remote, and the disease is treatable, yet the consequences of neglecting it are serious. Don't attempt to handle wild animals , dead or alive, and if you do suffer an animal bite, seek medical attention. If you take pets into plague areas, take the precaution of dusting them with flea powder.

Ticks

Tick bites are relatively rare in New Mexico, and I have not experienced one in all my years of hiking in the state.

Western Diamondback Rattlesnake in Ojito Wilderness Study Area

Marmot at Wheeler Peak Summit

However, tick bites are known to occur and ticks are known to transmit both Rocky Mountain spotted fever and lyme disease, although I am not aware of any cases of the latter being contracted within the state as of this time. Suffice to say that if you should suffer a tick bite and develop fever or other unusual symptoms, then you should get it checked out.

Mosquitos

Significant parts of New Mexico are characterized by a dry climate and are largely free of mosquitos, but don't assume this to always be the case. The wetter areas in the state may have a reliable presence of these pests, and I can recall one memorable hike during a period of wet weather on the seemingly dry lava beds when the hordes of mosquitos resembled something out of a nature documentary on the arctic tundra. A small bottle of insect repellent in your backpack may be a handy essential to have along.

Fishing

If you plan on hiking in an area with streams and lakes, you might want to consider doing some trout fishing as a side activity. Check in ahead of time with the local ranger station to get a reading on the fishing situation, and don't forget that a current New Mexico fishing license will be required.

Anasazi Pottery Fragments, Often Found near Prehistoric Dwelling Sites

Mountain Bikes

The recent popularity of mountain bikes has led to the sharing of some trails by hikers and bike riders, although few hiking trails receive significant bike traffic, if any at all. The general rule is that mountain bikes are permitted on roads and trails within lands open to the public, with the exception of designated wilderness areas or where otherwise specifically prohibited. For more information on suggested areas for mountain biking, refer to the publication by Hayenga and Shaw listed in the bibliography.

Fossils and Artifacts

New Mexico is richly endowed with both archaeological and paleontological sites. In hiking around the state, you will frequently encounter prehistoric pottery fragments, an occasional arrowhead, and possibly items even more exotic. It is against the law to remove any of these artifacts, no matter how insignificant they

Prehistoric Rock Art at
Three Rivers
Petroglyph Site

may seem, from public lands. There are unexcavated prehistoric dwelling sites around the state by the thousands, and you will undoubtedly "discover" one on occasion. Many of these have already been looted and had their archaeological value compromised by people digging for artifacts. Never dig into a site—it's incredibly irresponsible. With respect to collecting fossils, it is more a matter of scale. Picking up an occasional fossil such as a sea shell or a shark tooth is probably tolerated although probably not encouraged, but excavating a fossil skeleton is not. A sample of petrified wood is one thing, a trunkful is another. For a more exacting definition on what kind of collecting is permissible, you should contact the government office administering the land in question.

Prehistoric Rock Art

The native inhabitants of the Southwest had no written language as we know it prior to contact with European peoples, but they did produce innumerable examples of rock inscriptions throughout the area, some spare and simple and some grand and complex. These artistic renderings were scratched, pecked, or painted onto panels of sandstone and basalt to depict various items—some recognizable as human figures and indigenous flora and fauna and some as inscrutable geometric symbols. Despite at least one article having been published which purports to have unlocked the secrets of the ancient rock art, it is obvious to most people that even the most knowledgeable individuals can do no more than guess at the meaning of most of the symbolism or how it related to the culture of the people who created it. The mystery will undoubtedly endure. When you encounter a panel of Native American rock art, ponder it, photograph it, but please don't touch it. This is a resource that is deteriorating fast enough, due to the natural forces of nature and senseless vandalism, not to need any further help to accelerate the process. Areas with excellent examples of Native American rock art include the Petroglyph National Monument west of Albuquerque, the Three Rivers Petroglyph Site near Tularosa, Bandelier National Monument, and Chaco Canyon National Historical Monument.

Spanish Placenames

You can have a great time hiking around New Mexico without knowing a word of Spanish, but one look at a typical New Mexico topo map and you will know that you are missing out on something. The Spanish culture is a big part of the heritage of the state, and a good many placenames were given by the early Spanish that settled the area. Some of the placenames were given in honor of family surnames and Catholic saints, but most involve a physical description of the feature or location, and understanding the meaning behind the name adds interest and insight. For the non-Spanish speaking majority, I have included in this book a partial dictionary of many of the Spanish words you will encounter.

Hiking Areas

You have read the information in the preceding sections of the book and your trusty backpack is loaded and at the ready. All that is left now is to select a hike and go do it. From a number of standpoints the spectrum of potential hikes is indeed broad, and you will need enough information to select and locate a hike that is appropriate for your interests and abilities, with additional information such as seasonal considerations and special features and hazards thrown in for good measure. I begin by attempting to characterize each area as to its size, geographical location, topography, and its general nature in terms of climate, geology, plant life, and solitude. Also included is information dealing with water availability, best time of year to visit, and any other special considerations that seem pertinent. In addition to the maps provided in the book, the appropriate topo maps are listed for each hiking area, and a detailed access description is provided for locating the area. Note that many of the hiking areas do not have established hiking trails. These areas are for the solitude-loving hiker who prefers to make his or her own way through an undeveloped wilderness setting. For the hiking areas that do have established trails, there are directions for locating the individual trailheads, information on trail length and elevation gain, and a trail description that will vary in detail according to the individual trail. Finally, the appropriate government office administering the area is identified should you want additional information.

All the trails and areas in this section have been hiked recently enough so that the information should be accurate as of this writing. However, although I have tried hard to avoid it, the hand of Murphy will almost surely swing into action when I state west when I meant to say east, or something of that nature. And predictably, trail signs will disappear, trails will be rerouted, and road access will change. So, to a certain extent, you may occasionally be left to your own instincts in overcoming these obstacles. Depending upon the kind of hiking you do, you will need to develop some route-finding skills and have a feel for when to keep going and when to turn back and retrace your steps. A guidebook can be a helpful asset, but it cannot substitute for your own good judgment, and it shouldn't be any other way. A guidebook will merely facilitate the opportunity for a hiking adventure, but the outcome of that adventure will depend upon you and your companions and the decisions you make.

I bid you many safe and enjoyable wilderness outings.

Latir Mesa

Latir
Peak
Wilderness

GENERAL DESCRIPTION

The Latir Peak Wilderness is a 20,506-acre Forest Service-administered Wilderness Area along the crest of the Sangre de Cristo Mountains, about 4 miles northeast of the town of Questa and 10 miles south of the Colorado border. This is in the heart of the northern New Mexico high country, with dense forests, mountain lakes, and peaks above 12,000 feet in elevation. The Latir Peak area is just north of the Wheeler Peak and Columbine-Hondo areas, with scenery that is unexcelled anywhere in the state, and hiking and horsepacking pressure that is low to moderate. Both dayhiking and overnight backpacking are appropriate for this area—there are plenty of potential campsites with nearby water, and there is fishing in the streams and lakes. The Wilderness is characterized by extensive forests of ponderosa, fir, and aspen in the lower elevations (10,000-foot range), with scattered grassy meadows located among the aspen and spruce stands in the mid-range elevations. Latir Peak is the high point of the range at 12,708 feet and overlooks the high alpine part of the area, which includes rugged peaks, steep cirques, and high, rolling mesa country with grass and tundra vegetation. The views from the top of the range are exceptional. The area north of Latir Peak, including Latir Lakes is on private property and not included in the Wilderness. Hiking and fishing is only permitted in that area with a permit from the Rio Costilla Co-op Livestock Association in Costilla, New Mexico.

The best time to hike the Latir Peak Wilderness is from June, when the snow cover has melted, through about mid-October, when temperatures begin to get uncomfortable and the snow begins to fall. During the rainy season in late summer, afternoon rain showers are almost automatic, but if you get started hiking early in the day, you can get a lot of hiking done before it clouds up. There are hunting seasons for deer and elk in October that you may want to find out about if you are planning a fall trip. For car campers, there is a small Forest Service campground by Cabresto Lake at the entrance to the Wilderness, and several larger ones nearby along Highway 38 between Questa and Red River.

Map Coverage

Probably the best map to get for the Latir Peak Wilderness is the special Carson National Forest map for the Latir Peak and Wheeler Peak Wilderness Areas. It shows topography and trails in pretty good detail. For more detailed topographic coverage, the USGS 7.5-minute scale Latir Peak map is adequate for the area covered by the hike described below. To cover the entire Wilderness Area, you would also need the 7.5-minute scale Cerro, Questa, and Red River maps.

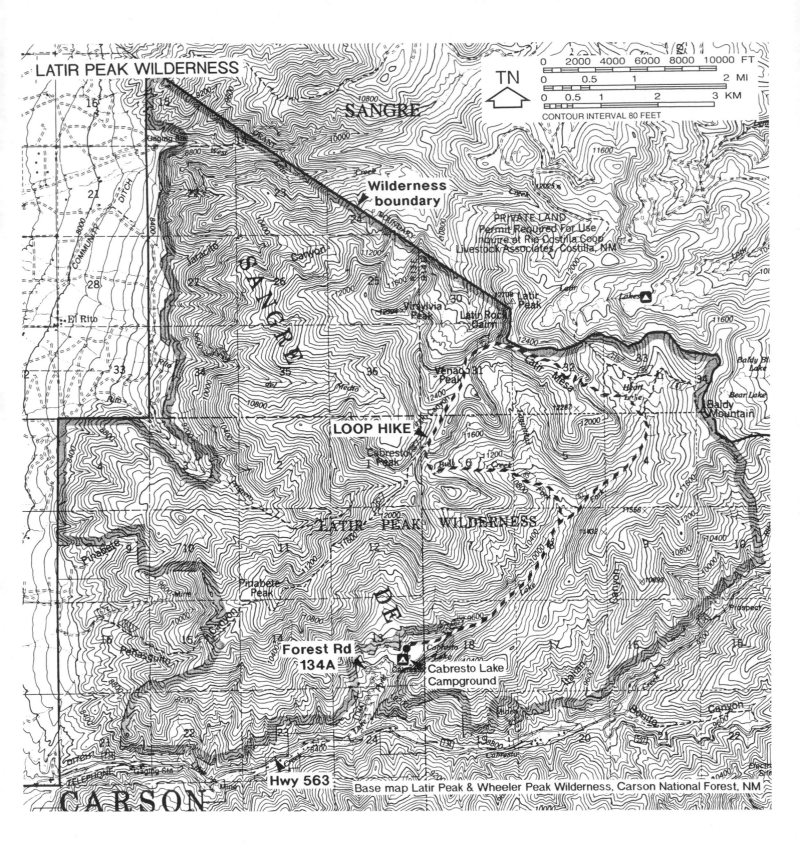

LATIR PEAK WILDERNESS

SANGRE

0 2000 4000 6000 8000 10000 FT
0 0.5 1 2 MI
0 0.5 1 2 3 KM

TN

CONTOUR INTERVAL 80 FEET

Wilderness boundary

PRIVATE LAND
Permit Required For Use
Inquire at Rio Costilla Coop
Livestock Associates, Costilla, NM

LOOP HIKE

Forest Rd 134A

Cabresto Lake
Campground

Hwy 563

Base map Latir Peak & Wheeler Peak Wilderness, Carson National Forest, NM

CARSON

Access

Travel north from Taos to the town of Questa and turn east at the traffic light on to Highway 38. After making the turn, go 0.25 miles and then turn back sharply to the north on Highway 563. This road is paved for the first 2.2 miles to the forest boundary, after which it becomes a wide gravel road that continues for another 3.4 miles to a road sign for Forest Road 134A and Cabresto Lake. Turn north on Road 134A and follow it 2.2 miles to Cabresto Lake and a small parking area by the trailhead at the north end of the campground. This road is rough and narrow and is not suitable for standard passenger cars.

Hiking Trails

The primary entry point for the Latir Peak Wilderness is from Cabresto Lake just outside the south boundary, with most of the Wilderness traffic running along the Lake Fork Trail from Cabresto Lake north to Heart Lake. This section of trail, along with the route up and over Latir Mesa and the trail back down Bull Creek, makes a pretty comprehensive introduction to the Latir Peak Wilderness; a loop hike, past streams and lakes through the heart of the high part of the Wilderness, goes through some great alpine terrain with some beautiful scenery. This makes a long day hike or a backpack of two or three days, and is a good route to take for your first trip into

the area, although there are several other trails to choose from as well. The Baldy Mountain Trail enters on the east side of the Wilderness, and the Rito Primero and Pinabete Peak trails enter on the west side. I have not hiked these trails, but they are definitely less travelled and are probably used mostly by hunters and horsepackers. From a base camp on the upper part of Lake Fork or Bull Creek, these other trails would make interesting day hikes. Also, Lagunitas Basin would be interesting to explore, and if the weather was nice, you could spend a whole dayhiking around on top of Latir Mesa. The trails tend to be easy to follow in the canyon bottoms, but when hiking through large open areas, particularly on Latir Mesa, the trails get faint and disperse, and you will need to look for rock cairns and be prepared to do some map and compass work. Bring your fishing gear along (including fishing license), but remember that the Latir Lakes are off-limits without a special permit.

TRAIL DESCRIPTION

Lake Fork/Bull Creek Loop Hike

This hike combines the Lake Fork Trail (#82) to Heart Lake with the Bull Creek Trail (#85), which climbs over Latir Mesa and drops down through the Bull Creek Fork drainage for a 14-mile loop that ranges between 9,180 and 12,560 feet. Hiking time to complete the hike with a daypack is 6 to 12 hours, but if you do it as a backpacking trip you will enjoy it that much more. The hiking is strenuous, with trails that are sometimes rugged but generally easy to follow, except for places on Latir Mesa. It is best to traverse the part of the trail above timberline before noon, if possible, as thunderstorms can move in fast.

Lake Fork/Bull Creek Loop Hike

Distance: 14 miles round trip
Net elevation gain: 3,380 feet
Difficulty: Strenuous

From the trailhead at the south end of Cabresto Lake, the trail begins by skirting the west edge of the lake and following the creek up Lake Fork Canyon. For the first 2 miles the trail is closed in with foliage before the canyon begins to open up a bit and permit an occasional meadow. At about the 3-mile point you will come to a trail sign indicating the junction with the Bull Creek Trail; cross the log footbridge to the right and continue up toward Heart Lake. The trail steepens a bit in some sections, but the meadows become more expansive. At 0.3 miles below Heart Lake you will pass the junction for the Baldy Mountain Trail, which turns off to the right. Continue left up the final steep trail segment to the lake, with rock cairns in some of the open areas to help with navigation. There are numerous camping spots along the upper part of Lake Fork Creek and in the vicinity of Heart Lake, but if you camp near the lake, pitch your tent at least 100 feet back from the shoreline.

To continue the hike past Heart Lake, walk west from the lake past the trail sign to Latir Mesa on the steep section of trail which leads to jumbled talus slopes. This talus is the terminal moraine of a small glacier that formed in the cirque above during relatively recent geological times, perhaps about 10,000 years ago. It is the line along which the glacier began to recede and dropped its load of rock and debris, and as you follow the trail, which switchbacks up the north side of the cirque, you can see the terminal moraines of successive glaciers that pushed down the cirque. The steep set of switchbacks terminates at the edge of Latir Mesa with a nice view of Heart Lake and the mountain country beyond. Once on top of Latir Mesa, the map and compass need to come out of your pack—there are initially a few rock cairns to help guide you but these

Looking North into Latir Lakes Basin during Winter

begin to diminish. The trail heads north-west across the mesa and skirts above the head of the next large basin (Lagunitas) on your left. You want to head toward the obvious rocky outcrop to the west on the upper rim of the basin, on which the trail once more becomes defined (if energy, time, and weather permit, you may also want to make a short detour north to the summit of Latir Peak). As you pass behind and beyond the rocky outcrop, now heading southwest, you should stay on the high grassy mesa and head down the gentle valley which is formed to the right of the ridge of small peaks on your left. There is nothing to mark the trail along this section, but about 1 mile past the rocky outcrop, at the bottom of the valley,

you will see a trail sign indicating Rito del Medio down to the west and Cabresto Peak up to the southwest. Take the latter branch, and follow the now-defined trail that angles up the south side of the valley and gains the top of the ridge. A little farther on is a saddle in the ridge with a trail sign indicating the trail down Bull Creek drainage to the south. The Bull Creek Trail follows a steep path down the canyon and intersects the Lake Fork Trail at the junction you passed on the way up. There are good campsites along Bull Creek, both near the top of the canyon and 0.5 to 0.75 miles up from the bottom. Complete the hike by returning back down Lake Fork to Cabresto Lake.

For Further Information

Carson National Forest
Questa Ranger
District
P.O. Box 110
Questa, NM 87556
(505) 586-0520

Carson National Forest
Supervisor's Office
Forest Service
Building
P.O. Box 558
Taos, NM 87571
(505) 758-6200

Columbine-Hondo
Wilderness Study Area

GENERAL DESCRIPTION

Columbine-Hondo is a Forest Service wilderness study area (WSA) located southwest of the town of Red River and situated between the Wheeler Peak Wilderness to the south and the Latir Peak Wilderness to the north. Columbine Campground is the primary entry point on the north side of the area, and Hondo is the canyon bordering the south side, thus the resulting hyphenated title of Columbine-Hondo. Personally, I would have chosen Gold Hill, the most prominent feature of the WSA, as a namesake, but I wasn't consulted on the matter, so Columbine-Hondo it is. By whatever name you want to call it, this is an area that has some great dayhiking potential but really requires a backpacking trip to best see and enjoy it. This is a steep area, and a hike that penetrates deep into the high interior and returns in one day may turn out to be more of a death march than a meditative, interpretive hike. The combination of stately forests, high rugged peaks and ridges with scenic vistas, broad grassy cirques and meadows, water, campsites, trout streams, and low hiker density make it a backpacking destination that is unsurpassed in the state. It is not, however, for especially light-duty hikers as most of the trails involve significant elevation gain; a maximum net elevation differential of about 4,900 feet exists within the area. In addition, some of the trails are rather faint, or even nonexistent, in spots, and some of the trail junctions are not well signed, so the area would probably most appeal to the hiker with a bit more experience. Most of the dayhiking that is done is on the lower part of the trail leading out of Columbine Campground, and on the Gold Hill Trail from the Twining side.

The WSA is approximately 7 miles by 11 miles in area and gets about 45 inches of annual precipitation, making for plenty of water and lush vegetation. The hiking season is from early June when the snows melt out to late October when they return. Summer temperatures are comfortable by day and chilly at night. The rainy season is from July through August with afternoon thunderstorms common. Keep in mind that the high part of the range can see just about any kind of weather, anytime. No permits are needed to hike or backpack the area, and there are good campgrounds for car camping along Highway 38 between Questa and Red River. The trailheads are about a three-hour drive from Albuquerque.

Map Coverage

The best map to carry is the Latir Peak and Wheeler Peak wilderness map with water resistant coating, produced by the Forest Service and available at the Forest Service offices in Questa and Taos, or at other distribution centers for Forest

Service maps. The Columbine-Hondo area is shown on the map, sandwiched between the Wheeler Peak Wilderness to the south and the Latir Peak Wilderness to the north. USGS maps in the 7.5-minute scale which cover the area are the Red River and Wheeler Peak maps for the east side, and the Questa and Arroyo Seco maps for the west side.

Access

Each of the three hikes described in this section begins from a different trailhead, so access directions are included with the individual trail descriptions. Note that the Columbine Campground and Twining trailheads are accessed by paved roads, while the primitive dirt road leading to the San Cristobal trailhead requires, as a minimum, high vehicle clearance.

Hiking Trails

The hiking trails in Colombine-Hondo generally tend to follow either ridge lines or valley bottoms. Along the ridges the trails are usually easy to follow with cairns and posts occasionally marking the vague areas. The trails that follow the drainages are also easy to follow for the most part, but you may have to do some searching in some of the meadows where the hiking traffic tends to disperse, and you will have to avoid intersecting game trails put in by the local deer, elk, and cows, which crisscross through the forests. It is worth making a special effort to stay on the trail because the combination of thick forest cover and steep terrain can make for difficult off-trail bushwhacking. If you do try an off-trail shortcut, you will probably get to experience the dynamics of stepping on wet aspen logs that are pointed downhill, and the strenuous maneuver that involves trying to limbo under a low tree branch

with your backpack on. The usual result of the latter is that the backpack snags on the tree branch arresting forward progress, and you get to see how long you can support the weight of your pack with your legs flexed at a 90-degree angle. A dozen or more separate trails are designated by the Forest Service, providing the flexibility of everything from short dayhikes to longer trips using various combinations of trails and trail segments. The hikes described below fall into the latter category, but you can just as well come up with your own combination. There are additional trails entering the WSA from the south along Hondo Canyon, and from the east and west sides, with the Latir Peak and Wheeler Peak wilderness map (see the map coverage section) providing a good overview of the trails available.

TRAIL DESCRIPTIONS

Hike #1. Loop Hike from Columbine Campground to Gold Hill

This is a nice three-day backpack through spectacular alpine and subalpine peaks and forests, which loops through the heart of the wilderness on one of several route options. The total length of the hike is 17 miles using the Placer Creek Trail option or 19.5 miles using the loop through the upper end of the Columbine Trail. Net elevation gain is 4,890 feet, much of it gained on the first day of the hike. Water is plentiful at the campsites and in the canyons.

To locate the trailhead at Columbine Campground, drive east from the town of Questa (or west from Red River) on Highway 38 to the campground entrance 4.7 miles east of Questa. If you have questions concerning trail conditions, etc., you may first want to drop by the Questa ranger station, which is located 1.5 miles along the highway east of Questa. At the

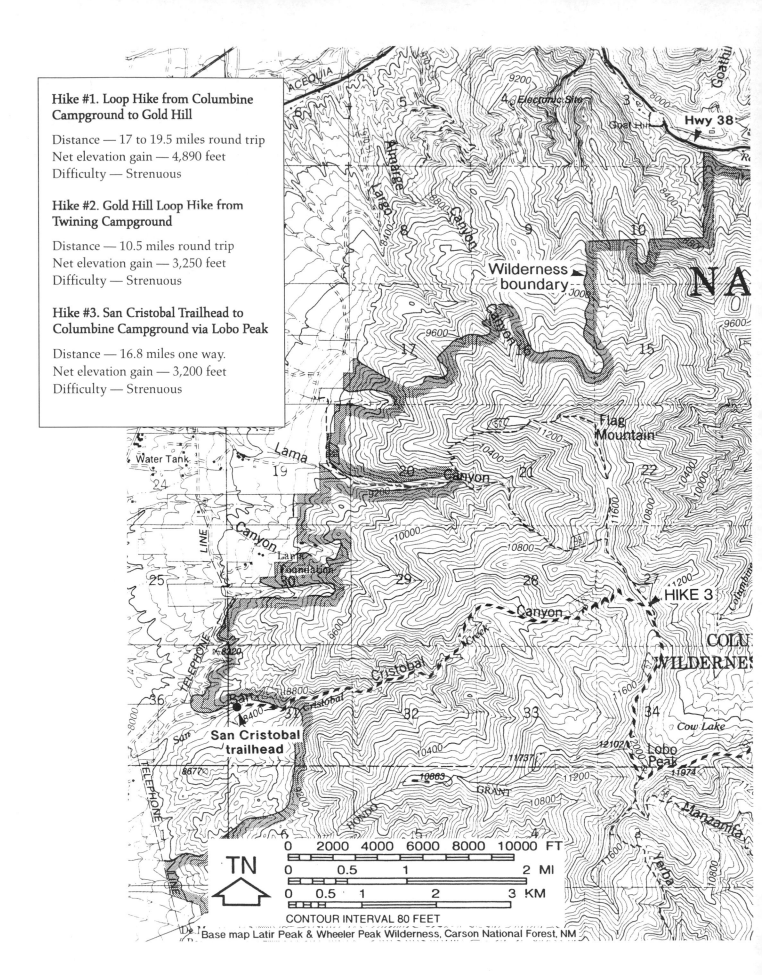

Hike #1. Loop Hike from Columbine Campground to Gold Hill

Distance — 17 to 19.5 miles round trip
Net elevation gain — 4,890 feet
Difficulty — Strenuous

Hike #2. Gold Hill Loop Hike from Twining Campground

Distance — 10.5 miles round trip
Net elevation gain — 3,250 feet
Difficulty — Strenuous

Hike #3. San Cristobal Trailhead to Columbine Campground via Lobo Peak

Distance — 16.8 miles one way.
Net elevation gain — 3,200 feet
Difficulty — Strenuous

CONTOUR INTERVAL 80 FEET
Base map Latir Peak & Wheeler Peak Wilderness, Carson National Forest, NM

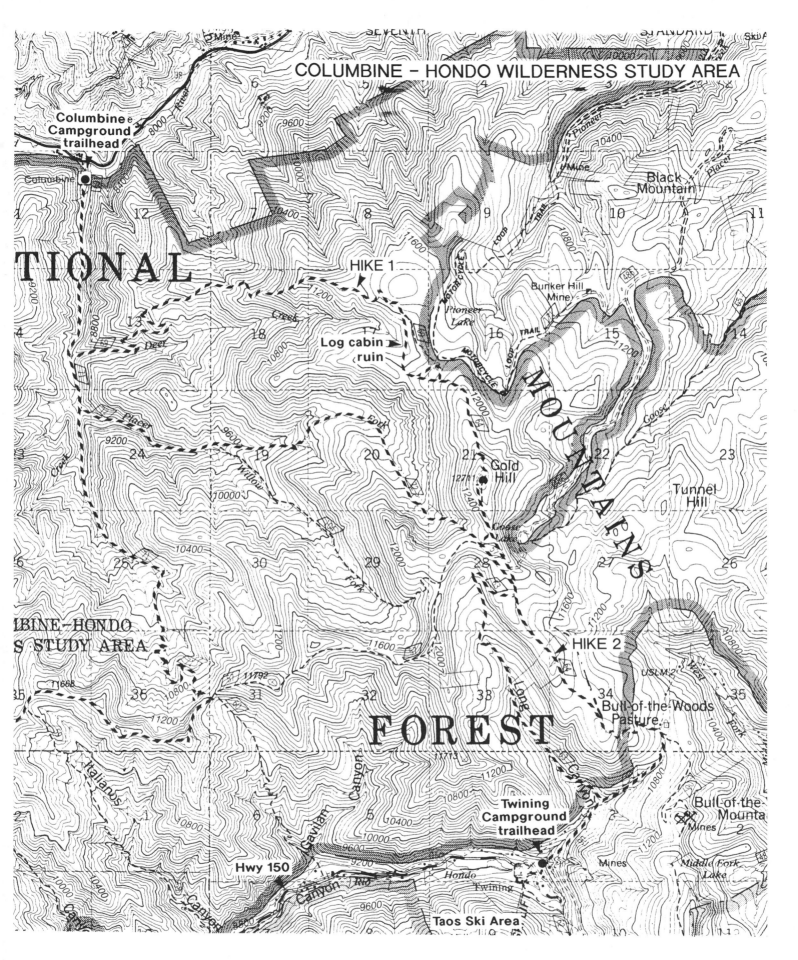

campground, proceed to the south end, where a parking area is provided just north of the trail entrance. The first part of the hike is an easy walk up Columbine Trail with foot bridges over the stream crossings and lots of day hikers. About a half-hour up the trail, just before a bridge crossing to the west side of the creek, is a trail sign marking a trail heading to the east. This is part of the Columbine-Twining National Recreation Trail, which goes from Columbine Campground over Gold Hill to the Twining area, and which is better maintained than the other trails in the WSA. Head east at the trail sign on what is now the Deer Creek Trail as it follows Deer Creek for 0.6 miles and then crosses on a footbridge and begins a long series of switchbacks as it climbs up the north side of the canyon. The trail is good and the hiking is steep. At about 7 miles and 3,700 vertical feet after the start of the hike, the trail levels out and reaches a

small clearing with a log cabin ruin. The trail reenters the forest on the other side of the clearing near the ruin, and since the trail is imperceptible across the clearing, there is a rock cairn to mark the entry points at both ends of the clearing. This is a good place to camp, with a nearby spring that is the first dependable water supply since leaving Deer Creek. This clearing is not far below the Gold Hill Summit Ridge, and if you still have time and energy you may want to explore the area further.

From the rock cairn by the cabin ruin the trail leads up into the forest for perhaps 0.3 miles until you find yourself just below a grassy ridge. Proceed directly up to the ridge, passing a small rock cairn (which will serve as a landmark if you return by this route), and on up to the crest of the ridge at the bottom of a saddle. This ridge forms the divider between the Deer Creek and Placer Fork

Log Cabin Ruins on Upper Deer Creek in Columbine-Hondo Wilderness Study Area

drainages. At this point the trail is obscure, but turn left, heading up the ridge at tree line. The trail reenters the forest about halfway up the ridge, joins the Gold Hill Trail from Red River, and turns back south again, ending up on the broad slopes of the Gold Hill summit ridge as the trail switchbacks up and over the summit of Gold Hill. A more direct alternative is to proceed up the Deer Creek/Placer Fork ridge from the saddle, avoid the loop back through the woods, and follow the tree line up through small bristlecone pines until you intersect the Gold Hill Trail. Gold Hill is the large, bald peak that can be seen above the head of Placer Fork. At 12,711 feet elevation it well deserves to be called a mountain rather than a hill, and it provides a spectacular view from the top in all directions. In case you should want to avoid the climb over Gold Hill, a further alternative exists from the saddle on the

ridge between the Deer Creek and Placer Fork drainages: continue over the low point in the saddle, dropping down the other side into the Placer Fork drainage. You will pass a dead tree with a faded yellow sign and shortly thereafter pick up a faint trail which leads down, then contours to the left, eventually ending up near the head of Placer Fork below the broad cirque beneath Gold Hill. The trail plays out near the end, and you will have to bushwhack over to Placer Fork (you would probably have trouble picking up this trail in the opposite direction on the Placer Fork side). Back to the main route on the summit of Gold Hill, the trail continues south along the summit ridge making its way toward Twining. About a mile past the summit you will intersect the Lobo Peak Trail, which comes in from the west. Turn on to the Lobo Peak Trail and hike for about 0.25 miles, at which point the Placer Fork Trail branches off to

Looking Southeast toward Gold Hill (at Left) from Deer Creek Trail

Beaver Pond on Placer Fork

the right and drops steeply down into the Placer Fork drainage. An alternative route is to continue 0.5 miles farther along the Lobo Peak Trail and drop down instead into the Willow Fork drainage. Both Placer Fork and Willow Fork have scenic, high meadows below the initial steep sections, which provide good campsites. Both drainages have places where the trails are difficult to locate, but the trails generally follow the canyon bottoms that come together about 1.3 miles east of Columbine Creek. A trail sign marks this junction, from which the trail follows Placer Fork west on down to the Columbine Creek Trail. Complete the hike by turning north on the Columbine Creek Trail and returning to the campground.

One final route alternative is worth mentioning in addition to those described above: from the summit of Gold Hill, catch the Lobo Peak Trail as before, but pass by both the Placer Fork and Willow Fork cutoffs. The trail follows the high ridge line to the west with nice views to both sides until you come to a sharply defined saddle in the ridge 4.5 miles beyond Gold Hill. Trails drop down off the ridge on both sides. Take the north trail, which leads toward Columbine Creek and, eventually, Columbine Campground. There are good campsites beginning about a mile down this trail from the ridge, and continuing intermittently for the next 2 miles.

Hike #2. Gold Hill Loop Hike from Twining Campground

This hike begins at the Twining pseudo-Campground at the Taos Ski Area and completes a fairly popular (though not by Wheeler Peak standards) loop hike to Gold Hill, a major peak north of the Rio Hondo. The hike is a steep 10.5 miles round trip with 3,250 feet of elevation gain. It can be done as a dayhike but makes a nice overnight backpack. The loop route as described here takes the Gold Hill Trail up from Bull of the Woods pasture and returns on the Long Canyon Trail branch, or it can be done in the reverse order. This is a hike up the highest peak in the immediate vicinity, with conifer forests, high alpine meadows, and great views.

Reach the trailhead by driving to the blinking light at the north edge of Taos and turning east on Highway 150, which leads about 15 miles to the Taos Ski Area. Proceed to the uppermost gravel parking area and park below the picnic units that constitute Twining Campground. At the northeast corner of the parking lot a gravel road continues up, with a trail sign a short distance up the road on the left. The trail sign points the way to Bull of the Woods pasture and Old Mike Peak Trail #90. Start up the trail (this trail is more fully described in the Wheeler Peak section), taking the left fork a short distance up, and follow the steep path that continues above the stream along the north bank. Go left at the red arrow on the aspen tree about 20 minutes up the trail, and cross the stream a little farther up. At the 0.8-mile point is the Long Canyon Trail on which the hike will return, and a little farther beyond is a sign pointing toward Bull of the Woods Pasture. Higher up, the trail intersects a jeep road, and the most straightforward choice here is to turn north on the jeep road and stay on it as it curves back to the south and then back east, following the canyon the rest of the way up to Bull of the Woods Pasture, 1.8 miles from the start of the trail. If the hike up to this point has not rated inclusion in your list of top-ten hiking experiences, you can take comfort in knowing that you have knocked off nearly half the net elevation gain and that the most scenic and enjoyable part of the hike is still ahead. When

you come to the small pond at the bottom of the meadow (Bull of the Woods Pasture), the Wheeler Peak Trail continues below the pond to the right. Hike, instead, on the left trail fork which goes north, to the west of the pond, to a trail sign a short distance beyond, marking the start of the Gold Hill Trail. Take this trail and follow a series of steep switchbacks up wooded slopes, 670 vertical feet up to the crest of a broad ridge, where the trail levels out and begins to follow the ridge to the northwest. This ridge connects to Gold Hill and leads directly to its summit. As you proceed up the ridge, the trail breaks into broad meadows with nice views and continues up near an old miner's cabin. From here on up, the trail gets faint in spots and you will occasionally have to look for trail markers, but since Gold Hill is about 1 mile directly up the ridge, it is easy enough to just make your way up the steep but easy ridge line directly to the top. There is a large rock cairn to mark the summit of Gold Hill, and you will want to linger a while, weather permitting, and take in the scenery. If you happen to be doing a one-way hike, the trail continues north along the ridge from the summit and on to Columbine Campground. To complete the loop hike described here, return back to the south along the summit ridge on the trail, which is now apparent, in case it wasn't on the way up, passing the Lobo Peak Trail sign on the way down, followed by the sign for the trail to Goose Lake, and on down to the Long Canyon Trail sign. A short walk down and to the right on the Long Canyon fork leads to the head of Long Canyon, where the trail drops into the canyon and follows the stream down until it pulls away and joins the Bull of the Woods Trail at the trail junction you passed on the way up.

If you are backpacking, the best places to camp are the area below the cabin ruins on the way up and the area in Long Canyon just below the upper steep section. There is no dependable water above these points. Bull of the Woods Pasture is also a nice campsite, but you will compete for space with the Wheeler Peak hikers.

Hike #3. San Cristobal Trailhead to Columbine Campground via Lobo Peak

Starting at the San Cristobal Trailhead on the west side of the WSA, this hike climbs to the head of San Cristobal Canyon, follows a long ridge line around Lobo Peak, and joins the Columbine Trail, which is taken all the way to Columbine Campground. The trail length one way is 16.8 miles with 3,200 feet in elevation gained up to Lobo Peak and 4,000 feet lost from Lobo Peak to Columbine Campground. This is a one-way hike requiring a vehicle to be located at each trailhead. Since the road from the community of San Cristobal to the trailhead on the west side is quite rough in spots, each vehicle should have high road clearance. If there has been snow or a lot of wet weather, this trailhead might be tough to reach, and because of the long ridge exposure on the trail, this is not a good hike to choose if you expect thunderstorms. A good time to plan to do this hike would be around mid- to late June or mid- to late September, although you will have to determine this for yourself depending upon the current weather situation. This could be done as a long, strenuous dayhike with a light pack or as a backpack of one or more nights. Don't depend on finding water above the upper sections of Cristobal Canyon and Columbine Canyon.

To begin the hike, first convoy to the Columbine Campground trailhead (see Hike #1) and drop off a vehicle(s). Return to the town of Questa and drive south on Highway 522 for 7 miles to the highway sign for San Cristobal. If you happen to

be driving north from Taos, it is the second San Cristobal sign (San Cristobal Post Office) that you want. Turn off the highway and drive east on the gravel road for 0.7 miles to the sign for Forest Road 493 pointing up San Cristobal Canyon. Ignore this sign and continue for 0.1 miles farther on the main gravel road, turning east on to the well-used dirt road. Drive 2 miles east past this turnoff and take a right at the fork in the road. Over the next stretch of road you will encounter several small side roads, but you generally keep to the east as the road stays atop the mesa above the valley and heads toward the mountains. About 1 mile past the road fork mentioned above, you will come to another fork, with the right-hand branch identified as Forest Road 111. Turn off on this fork as it drops steeply to the south on a contour down the hillside to a small, undeveloped parking area by a stream. The trailhead is located at the east end of the parking area, with the road bermed to prevent further entry by motor vehicles. A trail sign directs you east up the remaining stretch of the old road, which leads east up San Cristobal Canyon toward Lobo Peak. The parking area by the trailhead makes an adequate car camping site.

From the trailhead, follow the old road until it ends and continue on the trail, which makes a rather steep ascent up the canyon along the stream. At about the 4-mile point there are some flat areas with good campsites just below the final steep ascent, which climbs the last mile out of the canyon on to the ridgeline. Once on the ridgeline, the route goes south along the top of the ridge to Lobo Peak. (The trail that goes north along the ridge line toward Flag Mountain and Lama Canyon would appear to be a good alternative route for a shorter, one-way hike keeping to the west side of the Columbine-Hondo area, but I have not hiked this trail nor have I been to the Lama Trailhead.) From the trail junction on the ridge above San Cristobal Canyon, approximately the next 6 miles of trail will continue south and follow the high system of ridges. There will be no water, and lightning will be a potential danger, but if the weather is clear there will an uninterrupted panorama to enjoy. Upon reaching Lobo Peak there will be another trail junction, with the branch that goes down the ridge to the south leading to the Yerba and Manzanita Trails. Continue instead on the trail branch that leads down the ridge to the east toward Gold Hill. The final section of the ridge line continues to the east, passing the Italianos Trail junction,

until a steep descent into a well-defined saddle (with a trail sign at the bottom) marks the turnoff to the north for the Columbine Trail. After a steep descent of about a mile, you will begin to encounter good campsites as the trail begins to level out. The trail joins Columbine Creek and continues the rest of the way down Columbine Canyon heading north to Columbine Campground. As a further option for a backpack campsite, the Cow Lake Basin just northeast of Lobo Peak near the Italianos Trail junction is a nice area. It would also make a good overnight destination via the Italianos Trail from the south.

For further information:

Questa Ranger District Office
Box 110
Questa, NM 87556
(505) 586-0520

Carson National Forest
Box 558
Taos, NM 87571
(505) 758-6200

Wheeler Peak Wilderness

GENERAL DESCRIPTION

Wheeler Peak Wilderness is a mountainous alpine environment of about 20,000 acres located in the vicinity surrounding Wheeler Peak, the highest summit in the state. Located northeast of Taos and south of Red River in an area of prime attraction for camping, fishing, skiing, and general mountain tourism, Wheeler Peak Wilderness receives relatively heavy attention, especially from out-of-state hikers. Few experienced hikers living in New Mexico have not visited the area to climb the highest point in the state or to backpack through the dramatic scenery marked by high, rugged peaks, clear mountain lakes, and pleasant glacial cirques. Most of the wilderness area lies above 10,000 feet in elevation, with Wheeler Peak cresting at 13,161 feet.

The area about Wheeler receives from 35 to 40 inches of annual precipitation and supports dense forests of aspen and conifers and lush slopes of grasses, tundra vegetation, and wildflowers. Small stands of bristlecone pine grow near the upper limit of the tree line. It sometimes takes until mid-June for the snow to sufficiently melt out in the highest elevations to accommodate hiking, and the snow begins to accumulate again in mid- to late October, resulting in a hiking season of about five months in most years. During the rainy months of July and August, day hikers need to start early and travel at a steady clip to avoid the afternoon thunderstorms that are a regular occurrence. Definitely don't get caught on the high ridges during a lightning storm. If you have your choice, the best month to hike the area is probably September, but hiking is potentially good any time the absence of snow permits. Summer brings T-shirt hiking conditions that can change in a hurry, so always carry along some warm clothing in addition to rainwear. Water is available to varying degrees on all the trails, so 1 liter of water to start out with along with means to purify more should be sufficient. In addition to the standard mountain fauna population, which includes deer, elk, black bear, and mountain lion, the Wheeler Peak area also supports a lively population of marmots in the high areas above timberline. One particularly bold group hangs out near the summit of Wheeler Peak and has adopted the dietary routine of freeloading off handouts provided by hikers lunching on top. Permits are not now required by the Forest Service for hiking or backpacking in the wilderness. The best car camping spots are in the Forest Service campgrounds located along Highway 38 between Questa and Red River. If you wish to camp closer to the trails leading from the Twining area, there is a pseudo-campground at the Taos Ski Area, but you may prefer camping at the trailhead for one of the trails leading north off the highway to the ski area. The nearest

Forest Service ranger station is the Questa ranger station located about 2 miles east of the town of Questa along Highway 38.

Map Coverage

The best map to get is the Latir Peak and Wheeler Peak Wilderness Area map, produced by the Forest Service. It is available with a durable, water resistant treatment that is well worth the small additional cost. The appropriate USGS maps are the Wheeler Peak and Eagle Nest 7.5-minute scale quads. If you are using the 7.5-minute Wheeler Peak map, note that there are several trail reroutings and omissions that apply to several of the trails described in this book.

Access

The hiking trails described in the following section for the Wheeler Peak Wilderness begin either at the Taos Ski

Area or near the town of Red River. General directions for reaching these two locations are given below. More specific directions for reaching the individual trailheads will be included with the trail descriptions.

Taos ski area. Drive north through the town of Taos on the main highway to the intersection with Highway 150 at a blinking yellow light on the north side of town. Turn east and follow the paved road for about 15 miles until it dead ends at the ski area. The only possible tricky spot is a jog that you have to make at the small community of Arroyo Seco. The final ascent into the ski area, also known as Twining (a turn of the century gold mining town), passes the trailheads for a number of trails that climb north into the Columbine-Hondo Wilderness. The road is paved all the way to the ski area.

Red River. Drive north through Taos to

Below Frazer Mountain on Bull of the Woods Trail

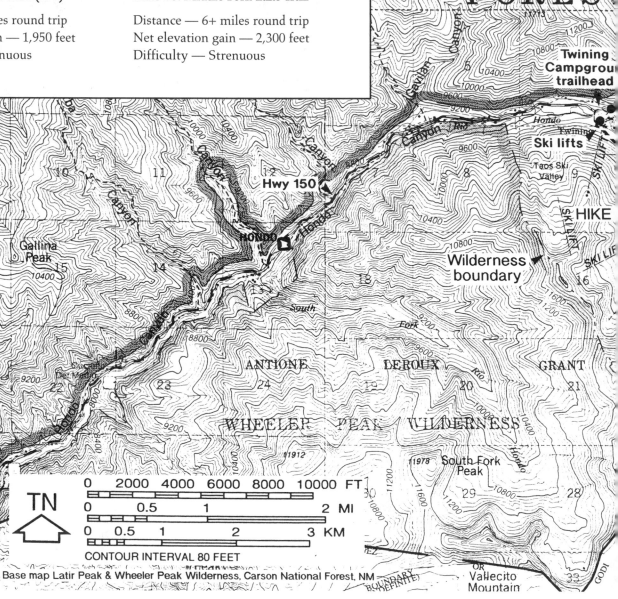

Hike #1. Bull of the Woods Trail (#90)

Distance — 14 miles round trip
Net elevation gain — 3,720 feet
Difficulty — Strenuous

Hike #2. Williams Lake Trail (#62)

Distance — 6.4 miles round trip
Net elevation gain — 1,600 feet
Difficulty — Moderate to strenuous

Hike #3. Lost Lake Trail (#91)

Distance — 8 miles round trip
Net elevation gain — 1,950 feet
Difficulty — Strenuous

Hike #4. East Fork Trail (#56)

Distance — 12 miles round trip
Net elevation gain — 1,940 or 2,400
feet to alternate destinations
Difficulty — Strenuous

Hike #5. Sawmill Park Trail (#55)

Distance — 8 to 9 miles round trip
Net elevation gain — 1,400 feet
Difficulty — Moderate to strenuous

Hike #6. Middle Fork Lake Trail

Distance — 6+ miles round trip
Net elevation gain — 2,300 feet
Difficulty — Strenuous

WHEELER PEAK WILDERNESS

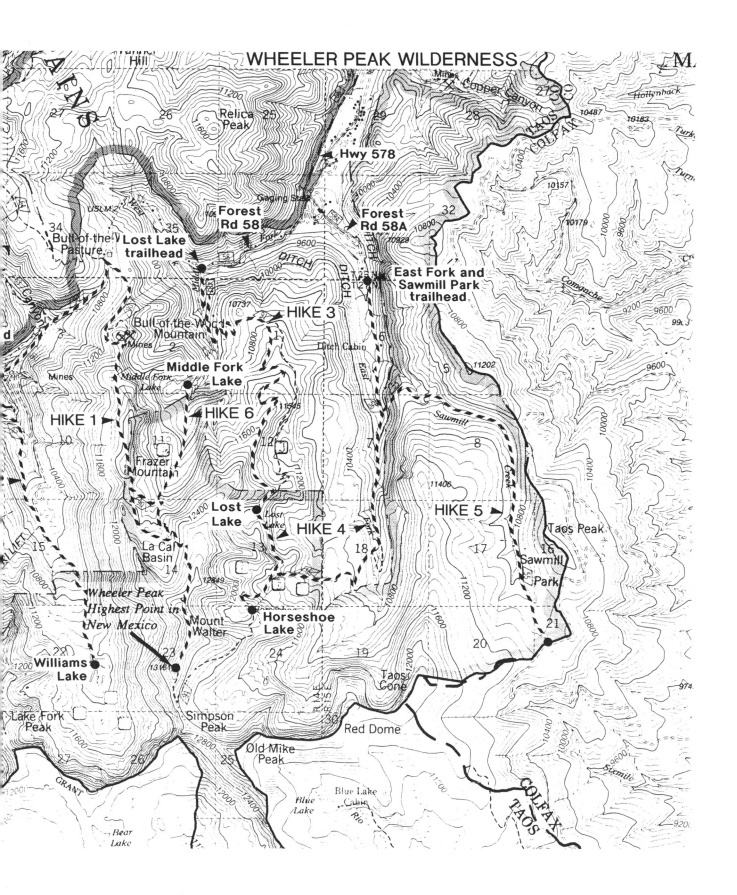

the town of Questa and turn east on Highway 38. This is a paved highway that continues east directly to the town of Red River, passing a number of Forest Service campgrounds along the way.

Hiking Trails

Wheeler Peak hiking trails are generally steep and the air is thin, so if you haven't acclimated don't overestimate your hiking abilities. Plan on taking it slow and enjoy the scenery. Also, don't underestimate the ability of the weather to change quickly. These trails get a fair amount of use and many of the popular camping sites are without firewood, particularly, as you might expect, above timberline. If you are backpacking, carry along a campstove. Even though you won't need to carry much water, you will need to purify that which you find. There is a rather busy network of trails and old mining roads, so be sure to bring a map.

TRAIL DESCRIPTIONS

Hike #1. Bull of the Woods Trail (#90)

This is probably the primary route to Wheeler Peak, and it has the advantage of an all-weather road to the trailhead. The first mile of the trail has the potential for some confusion, with a number of intersecting jeep roads and side trails, but it is really not difficult to follow, and the balance of the trail is in good condition and pleasant to hike. The round-trip distance to Wheeler Peak is 14 miles, and the net elevation gain is 3,720 feet. If you are in decent hiking condition, this is a very manageable though strenuous day hike. A strong hiker can reach the top in 3.5 hours, so plan on a total round trip hiking time of from 7 to 15 hours. If you want to spend more than one day and backpack the trail, the best sites with

water are at Bull of the Woods Pasture or at La Cal Basin.

To locate the trailhead, follow the access directions to Taos Ski Area and drive to the uppermost gravel parking area (the RV Only signs apply during ski season). Park below the informational sign and several nearby picnic units that constitute Twining Campground. At the northeast corner of the parking lot a gravel road continues up, with a trailhead a short distance up the road on the left. A trail sign points the way to Bull of the Woods Pasture and Old Mike Peak Trail (#90). Old Mike Peak is a point along the summit ridge south of Wheeler Peak and a namesake that has now generally fallen into disuse. The first 1.8 miles to Bull of the Woods Pasture and a little over a mile beyond crosses private land, and you will have to contend with a number of intersecting routes.

A short distance up from the start of the hike, take the left trail fork and climb up the obvious, steep path that follows above the north bank of the stream. Go left at the red arrow on the aspen tree about 20 minutes up the trail and cross the stream a little farther up. At the 0.8-mile point is an intersection with the national recreation trail that follows Long Canyon north toward Gold Hill and Columbine Campground, and a little farther beyond is a sign pointing toward Bull of the Woods Pasture. Continuing on up, you will come to a jeep road. You can either go north on the jeep road or continue up the very steep trail segment on the other side of the road, which again intersects the road higher up. Either way, this jeep road is what you will end up following all the rest of the way to Bull of the Woods Pasture. Once you reach Bull of the Woods Pasture the drudgery part of the hike is behind you as the trail levels out some and you start to get some scenic views. Cross below the small pond, take the uphill branch at the next trail fork, and follow the double track road that turns south and begins to wind up the side of Bull of the Woods Mountain. Ignore the major switchback to the left at the 2.8-mile point and continue on around until you crest out at a saddle overlooking the Red River drainage to the east. Take the footpath that heads south along the ridge a short distance to a vehicle obstruction made of logs and a sign pointing to Wheeler Peak. The wilderness area effectively begins at this point, and from here on you will be hiking mostly above timberline with outstanding views. Take care not to veer off onto the crude road that crosses the trail below Frazer Mountain, particularly easy to do on the way back. At about the 4.5-mile point you will come to the north edge of La Cal Basin where the trail drops down across the mouth of the basin, up through the timber on the other side, and switchbacks up the broad east side of the basin heading for the saddle at the southeast corner. As an alternative, my preference is to hike to the first signpost (sign presently missing) you come to when entering the basin and head south, contouring around the basin and intersecting the trail again on the east slope, thus losing less of your hard-earned elevation. There is good camping both at the lower end of La Cal Basin in the trees and at the high south end of the basin. Once at the saddle above the basin it is a short distance to Mount Walter, which is commonly mistaken for Wheeler on the hike up, and another 0.5 miles south down the ridge to the real Wheeler Peak. On the summit of Wheeler Peak you will have unsurpassed views, but you may need some wind gear to hang around very long. If you find yourself beset by imminent lightning storms, or if you want an alternative route back, you can scramble down the steep slopes to the

west into the Williams Lake Basin and take the Williams Lake Trail back to the ski area.

Hike #2. Williams Lake Trail (#62)

Williams Lake is located in a huge glacial cirque with towering walls, permanent snowfields, and great slopes of granite boulders. Wheeler Peak is located atop the east wall of the cirque, and the lake at the bottom is a remnant left from the last glacial activity, which ended about 10,000 years ago. The hike is most often done as a day hike but also makes a good backpack, although you are not allowed to camp near the shores of the lake. The total round-trip hiking distance is a little over 6 miles, with an elevation gain of 1,600 feet, which is steep, but not particularly so by Wheeler Peak standards. There is abundant water at numerous points along the trail.

To find the trailhead, follow the access directions for Taos Ski Area and park at the upper parking lot. Make your way south to the center of the ski village and head for the two main ski lifts. Hike up from the east chairlift until you find a road coming in from the left. This is a return ski trail, located on private land and closed to uphill travel during the ski season, which bends to the south and follows the stream on its west side as it heads up Lake Fork Canyon. Follow this ski trail for about 1.5 miles, paralleling the stream until you come to the base of the Kachina Chairlift #4. At the chairlift and restaurant, cross to the east side of the river and continue on the dirt access road until it forks before the main road recrosses the river. Take the left fork and follow the sign toward Williams Lake. The wilderness boundary is 0.3 miles farther on. There is no way to get lost the rest of the way to the lake (someone will undoubtedly prove me wrong), as the trail steadily gains altitude, confined by the

topography of the canyon. Once at the lake you will want to spend some time hanging out admiring the grand scenery and exploring the upper end of the cirque, where there are some good campsites. There is a faint trail, which is difficult to follow very far, ascending the east walls of the basin toward Wheeler Peak. It is very steep with lots of loose rock, but it is quite feasible to work your way to the top. If the slopes are covered in snow, don't try it; this is prime avalanche country. Williams Lake also makes a nice ski tour in the winter, with the alternative route to Kachina Lift being the access road, which begins at the top of the residential area above and east of the ski village. The lake freezes solid in winter and is thus incapable of supporting a population of fish.

Hike #3. Lost Lake Trail (#91)

Lost Lake is one of several glacially formed lakes that are located in a series of cirques on the east side of the Wheeler Peak massif. This trail follows a route up through forests alternating with meadows and occasional scenic vistas to Lost Lake, situated at an elevation of 11,495 feet in a compact glacial cirque at tree line. The total trail length is about 8 miles round trip from the trailhead at the Forest Road 58 junction, and the net elevation gain is 1,950 feet. The trail is rather steep but reasonable either as a day hike or a backpacking trip. Water is available at both ends of the trail and sometimes at one or two points in between.

To reach the trailhead, follow the access directions to Red River and drive to the east end of town. Turn south on Highway 578 and continue for 6.2 miles until the pavement ends. Take the right road fork (Forest Road 58), which heads west toward the West Fork of the Red River and Middle Fork Lake. After about 1.5 miles the road is blocked and a jeep road

At the Summit of Wheeler Peak Ridge with a North View

that leads to Middle Fork Lake continues to the south. Park in the parking area at this intersection. The jeep road is very rough and suitable only for motorcycles and short wheelbase, four wheel drive vehicles, with no further parking areas before the lake. Hike up the jeep road for a little less than 1 mile along the east side of the stream until the road crosses over to the west side of the river. At this point, a trail sign will direct you to the east toward Lost Lake on a foot trail that climbs steeply up the forested slope to a saddle where the rate of climb eases somewhat. As the trail swings south through more open country, the hiking becomes more enjoyable, with numerous meadows and aspen groves to complement the scenery. A final steep section of trail completes the climb into the Lost Lake Basin. This is a lovely area and a nice place to camp, but you are not permitted to camp within 300 feet of the lake. The lake is periodically stocked with trout and can be fished. There is also a 1.4-mile segment that continues south to Horseshoe Lake, which positions you for a short but steep summit approach to Wheeler Peak.

Hike #4. East Fork Trail (#56)

This is a popular hiking trail that leads to some of the same area as is accessed by the Lost Lake Trail. The upper end of the trail intersects the connector trail between Lost Lake and Horseshoe Lake, leaving you with a decision to make as to your final destination. The trail length is 12 miles round trip to either Lost Lake or Horseshoe Lake, with a net elevation gain to Lost Lake of 1,940 feet as compared to a 2,400-foot gain to Horseshoe Lake. It is another 1 to 1.5 miles, depending on your route, and 1,200 vertical feet, to continue from Horseshoe Lake to the summit of Wheeler Peak. Plenty of water is available along the trail, which is often done as a

day hike, but this trip also makes a nice backpack of one or more nights. Once again, don't camp near the lake shores, and use a camp stove for cooking.

One factor to consider when planning this hike is that the access road has a stretch that is sometimes muddy enough to require four wheel drive, particularly during wet weather. To access the trailhead, drive to the east side of Red River on the main highway and take Highway 578 south 6.2 miles to the end of the pavement. At this point, go left on Forest Road 58A, across the bridge, and then turn right, going up the hill. There are a number of road forks and private drives to avoid, but the road you want is the better traveled gravel road going up the hill to the east. During the next 1.2 miles you will go through one or more gates that you may have to open and close, and there will be numerous private drives to add confusion. But if you persevere and are able to make it through the muddy sections, you will come to a Forest Service parking area built to accommodate wilderness users where the trail begins.

Begin hiking on the now-blocked road for 0.8 miles to the Ditch Cabin Site on easy terrain and continue across a bridge. At this point, a trail sign confirms that you are on Trail #56 and the trail proceeds another 2.2 miles, past the Sawmill Park cutoff on the left, to another foot bridge where the trail bends to the west and begins to climb up out of the valley. The trail continues to ascend the slopes to the west until it reaches a "T" intersection, with one trail segment going toward Lost Lake 1 mile to the north and another to Horseshoe Lake 1 mile to the south. Level areas above and below this trail intersection provide good campsites. If your ultimate hiking objective is to reach Wheeler Peak, an alternative to the Horseshoe Lake route is to ascend the ridge to the west of the trail intersection and join the Bull of the Woods Trail near the head of La Cal Basin.

Hike #5. Sawmill Park Trail (#55)

This is a moderate hike of 8 to 9 miles round trip which leads into a gentle valley at the extreme southeast corner of the wilderness area. In addition to being scenic, this is a good hike if you are interested in stream fishing for trout. The net elevation gain is 1,400 feet. To find the trailhead follow the directions for the East Fork Trail. After you have walked down the East Fork 0.6 miles past the Ditch Cabin Site, the Sawmill Park Trail branches off to the east, crosses the wilderness boundary, and climbs steeply for a short stretch before leveling off and following Sawmill Creek all the way into the upper reaches of the valley. If you are camping in Sawmill Park or have time for exploring, you may want to ascend the ridge to the south and make your way to Taos Peak to the north, or to Taos Cone and points beyond along the ridge to the west.

Hike #6. Middle Fork Lake Trail

The trail up from Middle Fork Lake is not an official Forest Service trail, but it receives regular use and is the shortest route to Wheeler Peak. It is also the steepest, gaining 2,300 feet to Wheeler Peak over a round trip distance of just over 6 miles. From La Cal Basin on, the trail incorporates the final stretch of the Bull of the Woods Trail.

The trail begins at Middle Fork Lake, which is accessed by way of a truly horrendous jeep road. Some of the switchbacks are sharp enough to exceed the turning radius of a long wheelbase pickup, making jeeps and motorcycles the vehicles of choice. To locate this final access road, read the access directions for the Lost Lake Trail and ascend the jeep road referred to at the end of Forest Road 58. Once having reached Middle Fork Lake, follow the foot trail that ascends the drainage heading south. After about 1 mile of steep climbing, the trail intersects the Bull of the Woods Trail at the lower end of La Cal Basin. At this trail junction, turn east (left) on to Bull of the Woods Trail, although the trail you are joining is descending at this point and it may not seem like the logical direction to head. The trail will bottom out a short distance farther to the east and then proceed to switchback up through the trees and up the east side of La Cal Basin to the saddle above the southeast corner of the basin. A short but strenuous climb gains the summit ridge of Wheeler (beyond Mt. Walter) and a final push down the ridge completes the ascent.

For Further Information:

Questa Ranger District
P.O. Box 110
Questa, NM 87556
(505) 586-0520

Carson National Forest
Service Building
P.O. Box 558
Taos, NM 87571
(505) 758-6200

Wild Rivers Recreation Area

GENERAL DESCRIPTION

The Wild Rivers Recreation Area is a BLM recreation site situated on the mesa above the confluence of the Rio Grande and Red River, 17 miles south of the Colorado state line. The area offers camping in developed camping areas, hiking trails, interpretive displays, guided hikes, and scenic views of the Rio Grande and Red River canyons. In addition, the rivers below offer excellent trout fishing. The 800-foot-deep river canyons are the product of faulting and river erosion. The canyon walls offer a cutaway view of the alternating layers of volcanic basalt and gravel sediments that make up the geology of the Taos Plain. Several ancient volcanoes can be seen across the north horizon, which hint at the unsettled natural history that occurred along the great Rio Grande Rift, which runs north and south along the entire length of the state. During the Cretaceous period, 66 to 144 million years ago, the North American continent broke away from Europe and began its drift to the west. Partly as a result of this still developing drift some 25 to 35 million years ago, the Rio Grande Rift began to sink between two sets of faults, creating a series of sinks and basins later accompanied by volcanic activity, the results of which are still in evidence today. Some 2 to 5 million years ago, as the basins began to fill in with volcanic material and the gravel from

Wild Rivers
Recreation Area, Taos
Plain

eroded mountain ranges, the Rio Grande was formed by creating a path through the low lying areas of the rift, a process of erosion that continues today. The campgrounds in the recreation area are located to take advantage of the scenery afforded by the great eroded river canyons and are open year round. The weather most of the year offers pleasant temperatures, except in winter, when you should expect the possibility of uncomfortably cold conditions. A small fee is charged for use of the campgrounds. The trails down to the rivers are primarily used for dayhiking and fishing but can be backpacked as well, with camping areas located at river level at the base of all the trails north of the confluence. There are six trails that lead down to the rivers, all excellently constructed with help from the Volunteers for the Outdoors, a local nonprofit organization. There is also a trail to the top of nearby Guadalupe Mountain. The semiarid plant ecology of the Taos Plain with the towering Sangre de Cristo Mountains to the east and the deep river canyons to the west and southeast provide a great variety of scenic contrast. The sections of the Rio Grande above and below the confluence area offer good whitewater boating, but the stretch in the vicinity of the confluence includes some extremely challenging Class 6 whitewater. When the river is running high, these are probably the most awesome rapids anywhere along the entire river.

Map Coverage

Map coverage for this area includes the USGS 7.5-minute scale Guadalupe Mountain quad and a trail map on the back of the Wild Rivers Recreation Area brochure (see "For Further Information").

Access

The primary access to the Wild Rivers Recreation Area, and the one to be used for all but the Cebolla Camping Area, is to drive north from Taos on Highway 522 to the town of Questa and continue north from the traffic light another 2.6 miles to the intersection with Highway 378. Turn west on Highway 378 and continue for 5.5 miles to the entrance of the recreation area. This highway has been designated as a back country scenic byway, chosen for the scenic overlooks along the rim of the Rio Grande Canyon. From the recreation area entrance sign it is another 1.7 miles to the turnoff for the Guadalupe Mountain Trail on your left, and another 3.8 miles to the Visitor Center turnoff. Except for the Cerro Chiflo Campground, which was passed farther back on the road, the remaining campgrounds are strung along the rim to the right of the road. The highway is paved all the way to the campground area.

The Cebolla Campground is reached by driving 16.5 miles north from Taos, or 3.5 miles south of Questa, on Highway 522 and turning west on Forest Road 9 at a road sign indicating the Rio Grande Wild River. Follow the gravel road for 3.4 miles to the campground. In contrast to the all-weather road to the other campgrounds, the gravel access road to Cebolla Campground may be difficult to negotiate in passenger cars during wet or snowy conditions.

Hiking Trails

The trails in the recreation area include the trails that lead from each of the six campgrounds at the canyon rim down to river level, the river trails along the Rio Grande and Red River which connect the campground trails at their lower ends, the La Junta Point Nature Trail, and the Guadalupe Mountain Trail. The trails leading down to the river are short but steep, and you should hike at least one of them to experience firsthand the ecosystem at river level. The ponderosa and

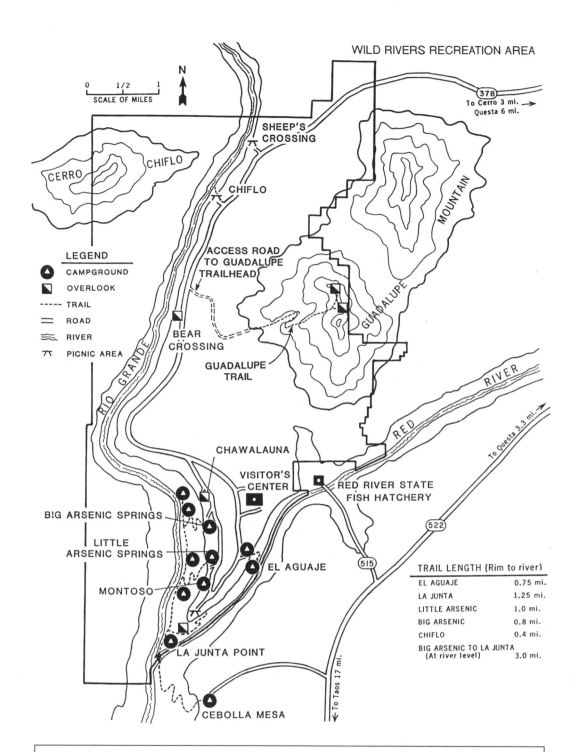

WILD RIVERS RECREATION AREA

N

0   1/2   1
SCALE OF MILES

378
To Cerro 3 mi. →
Questa 6 mi.

SHEEP'S CROSSING

CERRO   CHIFLO

CHIFLO

ACCESS ROAD
TO GUADALUPE
TRAILHEAD

LEGEND

⊘ CAMPGROUND
◨ OVERLOOK
---- TRAIL
═ ROAD
≋ RIVER
⅄ PICNIC AREA

BEAR
CROSSING

GUADALUPE
TRAIL

GUADALUPE   MOUNTAIN

RED   RIVER

To Questa 3.3 mi. →

RIO GRANDE

CHAWALAUNA

VISITOR'S
CENTER

RED RIVER STATE
FISH HATCHERY

BIG ARSENIC SPRINGS

LITTLE
ARSENIC SPRINGS

EL AGUAJE

522

MONTOSO

515

TRAIL LENGTH (Rim to river)

EL AGUAJE	0.75 mi.
LA JUNTA	1.25 mi.
LITTLE ARSENIC	1.0 mi.
BIG ARSENIC	0.8 mi.
CHIFLO	0.4 mi.
BIG ARSENIC TO LA JUNTA (At river level)	3.0 mi.

LA JUNTA POINT

To Taos 17 mi.

CEBOLLA MESA

Hike #1. Campground Trails to River Level
Distance — 0.8 to 3 miles round trip
Net elevation gain — Approximately 800 feet
Difficulty — Moderate

Hike # 2. River level trails
Distance — 3 miles one way
Net elevation gain — negligible
Difficulty — easy

Hike #3. La Junta Point Nature Trail
Distance — 0.5 mile round trip
Net elevation gain — negligible
Difficulty — Easy

Hike #4. Guadalupe Mountain Trail
Distance — 4.2 miles round trip
Net elevation gain — 350 feet
Difficulty — Easy to moderate

broadleaf trees along the edge of the rivers contrast with the sagebrush-covered slopes higher up, and in late summer and early fall the pleasant green waters flow past smooth, water-polished boulders, creating an idyllic river scene. In spring the swollen, turgid waters of the Rio Grande thunder with the sound of rapids and hydraulics, particularly impressive in the vicinity of Big and Little Arsenic Springs. There are a number of campgrounds at river level, complete with three-sided shelters, toilets, and wood-fire cooking units. Permits are required to camp in these river-level sites but not for hiking and day use. Don't go swimming in the river without a life jacket, and carry drinking water with you on the hiking trails.

TRAIL DESCRIPTIONS

Hike #1. Campground Trails to River Level

Six trails have been constructed from campgrounds on the canyon rim to the river below, and they are collectively described since they are all fairly similar in terms of distance, elevation gain, trail quality, and type of terrain. These trails, with round-trip mileage in parentheses, are Chiflo (0.8), Big Arsenic (1.6), Little Arsenic (2.0), La Junta (2.5), El Aguaje (1.5), and Cebolla Mesa (3.0). The average elevation differential is about 800 feet. To use the Little Arsenic Trail as a typical example, the trailhead is marked by a trail sign on the river side of the campground. The trail length is 1 mile in each direction, and a strong hiker with day pack can descend the trail to its end on a bench just above river level in 15 minutes and hike back up in 20 to 25 minutes. If the legs are a little bit rusty, you should double or triple those times. At the bottom of the canyon, the Little Arsenic Trail intersects the trail that runs along the side of the

river with another trail sign to mark the intersection. Little Arsenic Spring (I don't know the origin of the name, but the water won't poison you) lies north of the trail junction, and camp shelters are to the south. A spring is also located at the bottom of Big Arsenic Trail and campsites at the bottom of all the trails except Chiflo. You can spend all day wandering along the edge of the river, go fishing, or just hang out. If you want to camp, don't forget the permit.

Hike #2. River Level Trails

There is a maintained trail that runs along the Rio Grande from somewhat north of the lower end of Big Arsenic Trail south to La Junta Point at the Red River confluence. The length of this trail is about 3 miles one way and is easy to follow with insignificant elevation change. This trail connects the Big Arsenic, Little Arsenic, and La Junta Point trails at their lower ends. The Cebolla Mesa Trail comes in just across the Red River at La Junta Point. From the confluence at La Junta Point, there is a non-maintained fishermen's trail that follows the north bank of the Red River for about 2 miles up to the lower end of El Aguaje Trail. Farther up the river, you can see the road leading to the Red River State Fish Hatchery. The Red River begins its journey about 30 miles away, high in the Sangre de Cristo Mountains to the east, and its German brown and rainbow trout make it a well-regarded fishing destination.

Hike #3. La Junta Point Nature Trail

This trail is a short path, somewhat less than 0.5 miles in length, that starts at the La Junta Point Picnic Area, loops along the canyon rim behind the picnic area, and ends not far from its starting point. It is an easy trail with negligible elevation differential. The trail begins at a trail sign located at the east end of the large parking area in front of the picnic facility. A box at the trailhead contains interpretive booklets to be used during the hike which correspond to numbered markers along the trail dealing with various examples of geology, plant life, and animal life of the region. The trail first follows the canyon rim above the Red River, rounds the point with some great vistas of the confluence, and continues back along the Rio Grande Canyon to the west end of the parking area. The trail that drops down the side of the canyon at the point is La Junta Point Trail and not part of the nature trail. If you have children along, keep an eye on them while along the canyon rim, and don't let them throw rocks over the edge.

Hike #4. Guadalupe Mountain Trail

This is a short trail that ascends Guadalupe Mesa, one of the small extinct volcanoes in the confluence region. Start by driving the road leading into the Wild Rivers Recreation Area to a point 1.7 miles south of the entrance sign, where a dirt road branches off to the east and travels another 1.7 miles to a small parking area by a sign at the trailhead. The trail follows the old road, now blocked, which continues up the canyon to the northeast and switchbacks up to a saddle near the summit of Guadalupe Mountain. From the saddle a foot trail leads back to the west to an overlook opposite Cerro Chiflo, with some excellent vistas of the Taos Plain and Rio Grande Canyon below and several of the extinct volcanoes off in the distance. The trail length to the saddle is 1.5 miles with an additional 0.6 miles to the overlook, for a total round-trip distance of 4.2 miles. The elevation gain of about 350 feet is not unpleasant, and the trail is easy to follow. Even with this relatively small

elevation gain, it is interesting to observe how the plant life at the trailhead, predominantly piñon pine, juniper, rabbit brush, and sagebrush, quickly gives way with increasing altitude to other species including ponderosa pine, Douglas fir, oak, mountain mahogany, and currant and gooseberry bushes. There are undeveloped camping spots at the summit saddle, but no water is to be found along the trail.

The Rio Grande in Wild Rivers Recreation Area

For Further Information:

Bureau of Land
   Management
Taos Resource Area
224 Cruz Alta Road
Taos, NM 87571
(505) 758-8851

Visitor Center, Wild
   Rivers Recreation
   Area

Wild Rivers Recreation
   Area Brochure,
   published by the
   Bureau of Land
   Management and
   available from the
   Taos Resource Area
   Office and the
   Recreation Area
   Visitor Center

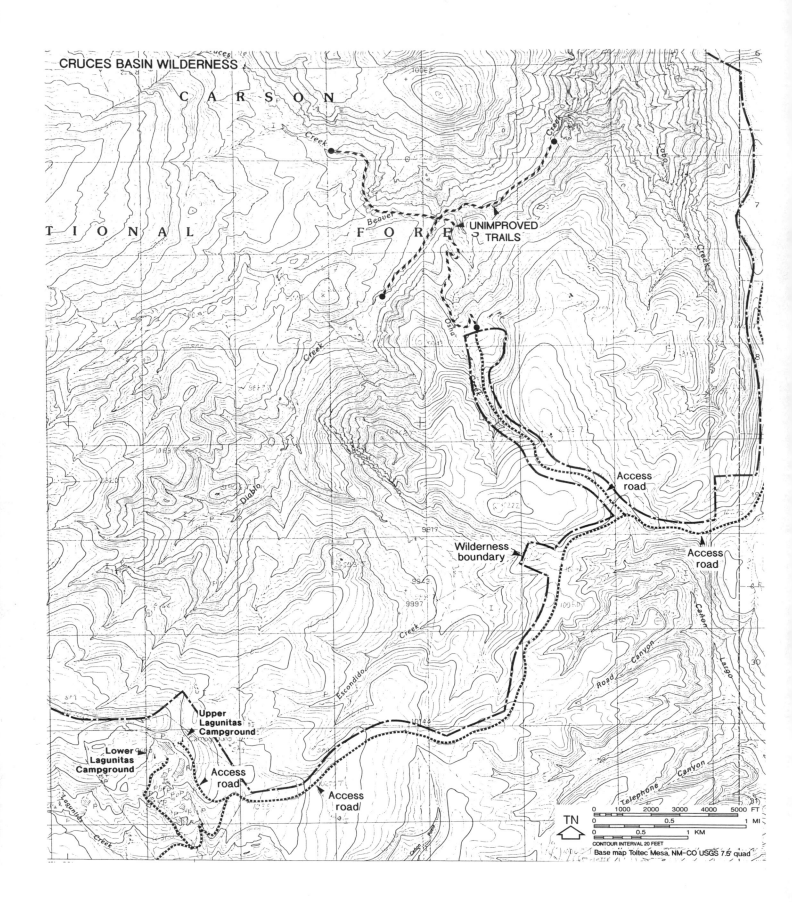

CRUCES BASIN WILDERNESS

CARSON

TIONAL   FORE

UNIMPROVED
TRAILS

Access
road

Wilderness
boundary

Access
road

Upper
Lagunitas
Campground

Lower
Lagunitas
Campground

Access
road

Access
road

TN

1000 2000 3000 4000 5000 FT
0   0.5   1 MI
0   0.5   1 KM
CONTOUR INTERVAL 20 FEET
Base map Toltec Mesa, NM-CO USGS 7.5' quad

Cruces Basin Wilderness

GENERAL DESCRIPTION

The Cruces Basin Wilderness, in far north-central New Mexico less than a mile south of the Colorado border, is one of the lesser known, but also one of the more lovely Wilderness Areas in the state. It is a smallish area of 18,902 acres set among the rolling hills and ridges of the high mesa country in the Carson National Forest, with an elevation that ranges between 8,600 and 10,900 feet. It is roughly circular in shape, about 6 miles in diameter, and is defined mostly by a series of forest roads and a small strip of private land along the Rio de los Pinos on the northeast. The central feature for which the area is named is the basin that drops down from the gently sloping Brazos Ridge to the west and Toltec Mesa to the north—an area of wide, grass-covered slopes and bottom lands, with scattered stands of aspen, spruce, and fir. A number of small, placid trout streams provide clear flows of water which meander through open grasslands and course down through forest groves and around occasional rock outcrops. The Wilderness is well off the beaten path, and while not undiscovered, it gets only light to moderate use and seems to be mostly visited by hunters and fishermen, and a few of the people staying in the local campgrounds. There are no designated trails in the area, although several have been beaten in, mostly along the creeks. The area is ideal for dayhiking, but although small, it also

Cruces Basin Wilderness Looking North from the Access Road

has potential for overnight backpacking, with plenty of spots to camp, adequate forest cover, and running water. The weather should be very pleasant from spring through fall, but cold weather and heavy snow cover will hamper access from about early to mid-November through March or April. And because of the long gravel access roads, a period of heavy rainfall is a good time to plan a trip somewhere else. Besides a number of informal campsites occasionally located along the scenic access roads, there are Forest Service campgrounds located in the vicinity, including the Lagunitas Campground just outside the southwest corner of the Wilderness, and the Los Pinos Campground several miles to the east. This area is a major elk summer range and you may have an opportunity to observe some of the elk herds, although if you visit during the last week in October, you will have an opportunity to observe the herds of elk hunters that may be even more numerous than the elk. If you plan to visit around this time, call the Tres Piedras Ranger Station for the deer and elk hunt dates in this region.

Map Coverage

The Wilderness is shown on the USGS 7.5-minute scale Toltec Mesa quad map. The Carson National Forest map is also good to have for a larger picture of the area surrounding the Wilderness.

Access

Drive north on Highway 285 from Española to the town of Tres Piedras and continue another 10.6 miles north of the Highway 64 intersection to the junction with Forest Road 87, just south of San Antonio Mountain. Forest Road 87 is identified by a road sign, and after turning west onto the road, another sign will announce 16 miles to Laguna Larga and 28 miles to Lagunitas. This is a good quality gravel road, and it continues past a number of other road junctions along the 21.7-mile distance to the primary turnoff to the Wilderness. This is a short spur road labeled as Forest Road 572, which turns off Forest Road 87 to the north at a sign indicating 2 miles to the Cruces Basin Wilderness. This road continues north past a sign that proclaims the road to be a limited use road, not

suited for wet weather or low clearance vehicles (maybe a bit overstated, unless the weather has really been bad), and drops down a little under 2 miles to a parking area at the end of the road on a large clearing. There are several nice, unimproved camping areas at the edges of this clearing. Another entrance to the Wilderness can be located by continuing west on Forest Road 87 for 3.7 miles past the Forest Road 572 turnoff to the junction with Forest Road 87DD, which leads north .3 miles to a gate on the high southwest corner of the Wilderness. A faint trail leads down from the gate toward Diablo Creek. This entry point is immediately east of Upper Lagunitas Campground, with the primary campground in the area, Lower Lagunitas, a little farther to the west.

Hiking Trails

There are no designated trails established in the area, but several unofficial trails exist. The best hiking introduction to the Wilderness is to drive to the bottom of Forest Road 572 and park at the end of the road. A well-worn trail continues on down Osha Canyon from the end of the road for 0.9 miles (550 vertical feet) to the junction of Beaver Creek and Diablo Creek. This is a very scenic spot and worth the hike down, even if you go no farther. From the creek junction, an intermittent trail continues along Beaver Creek in both directions about 3 miles downstream to the Rio de los Pinos, or 4.5 miles up to the head of the creek near the Wilderness boundary. Diablo Creek also makes a good pathway, leading up to the Wilderness entry point near Upper Lagunitas Campground. Otherwise, the Wilderness is untracked, but although the terrain is steep in some areas, it is also open, and ideal for cross-country travel.

For Further Information:

Carson National Forest
Tres Piedras Ranger District
P.O. Box 728
Tres Piedras, NM 87577
(505) 758-8678

GENERAL DESCRIPTION

Kutz Canyon is a shallow basin of colorful eroded badlands located a few miles south of Bloomfield in northwest New Mexico. It is often associated with Angel Peak, a nearby prominent landmark that provides the namesake for a BLM recreation area located on the mesa top overlooking the canyon on the south side. The distinctive geology, similar to that of the Bisti and De-Na-Zin Wilderness areas, was formed as hundreds of feet of organically rich sediments were deposited beneath ancient seas some 40 million years ago and later eroded into interesting formations of sandstone, shales, and compacted mud. Unfortunately, from a hiking standpoint, Kutz Canyon overlies extensive oil and gas resources, and the wilderness values of the area are compromised somewhat by a number of well sites and access roads in the canyon. Even so, the rugged nature of the area and generally low visitation results in decent-sized tracts where hours of solitude can be spent scrambling through the picturesque badlands. The main canyon runs about 10 miles in length, beginning below the heavily eroded escarpment across the south end, and continuing as a shallow sandy wash crossing Highway 44 on the northwest end. There are no designated trails through the area, although several possible entry points provide access.

The elevation for the Kutz Canyon area ranges from about 5,900 feet at the canyon bottom to 6,600 feet at the south rim of the canyon. The canyon bottom slopes rather gently, with most of the elevation differential coming from scrambling up and down the escarpment to the south and the hills and ridges within the canyon. The local vegetation is sparse, with scattered junipers and

Kutz Canyon

KUTZ CANYON

Access road

Access road

Highway 44

Angel Peak

Angel Peak Recreation Area

TN

CONTOUR INTERVAL 40 FEET
Base map Bloomfield, NM USGS 15' quad.

associated high desert grasses and shrubs, resulting in an area that is open and easy to walk through—except when conditions are damp, when each boot will quickly be encased in a tenacious blob of wet mud the approximate size and weight of an adobe brick. The canyon is accessible year round, although recent rain or snow may hamper access on the dirt roads within the canyon, and you may want to have an alternate destination in late summer when thunderstorms are common. This part of the state can get uncomfortably cold during the winter months but is generally pleasant the rest of the time. Camping is available at the BLM campground on the south rim, although drinking water is unavailable and you will need to bring along your own supply.

Map Coverage

USGS topo map coverage of Kutz Canyon is best shown on the 15-minute scale Bloomfield map if you can still find it. Otherwise, the 1:100,000-scale Navajo Reservoir map or the 7.5-minute scale East Fork Kutz Canyon and Huerfano maps also show the area.

Access

You can either drop down from the Angel Peak Campground on the south rim and make your way over to the upper east fork of Kutz Canyon or drive directly to the midpoint of the main canyon from an access road off Highway 44. To reach the campground, drive 71 miles north of the town of Cuba or 15 miles south of Bloomfield on Highway 44 and turn east on an improved gravel road at the BLM

road sign directing you to the Angel Peak Recreation Area. Follow the road for 6.5 miles to the campground. To reach the lower main canyon, continue 7 miles north of the campground turnoff on Highway 44 to a good gravel road that turns off to the east. After about 4 miles you will come to the bottom of the canyon, where a road turns off following the canyon in both directions. The most interesting terrain is found by taking the road that continues up the canyon to the south. A network of roads continues for several miles, providing numerous spots to pull over and hike. In wet weather it would be a good idea to avoid these roads entirely, but if conditions are dry, they are readily accessible.

Hiking Trails

There are no formal trails in the canyon but there is a rough path that leads from the campground on the south rim and drops several hundred feet to the upper end of the canyon floor. To locate this trail, walk a short distance from the campground to the canyon overlook and find the obvious path that follows a ridge system down over loose rock bearing north and west. This trail is steep and rough in places but not particularly difficult. Once in the canyon, by whichever access you took, the best dayhiking consists of short wandering routes, scrambling about through the colorful and scenic side canyons in the upper south branches of the main canyon. If you park your car down in the canyon, pay close attention to landmarks so you won't have trouble relocating it.

For Further Information:

Bureau of Land
    Management
    Farmington
    Resource Area
1235 La Plata
    Highway
Farmington, NM
    87401
(505) 327-5344

Bisti
Wilderness

GENERAL INFORMATION

The Bisti Wilderness is a 3,946-acre area in the northwestern part of the state whose name is taken from a Navajo word that translates as "badlands." While the area is a badlands if your measure involves water and vegetation, it is at the opposite extreme in terms of scenic values—a stunning landscape of eroded spires, hoodoos, mushroom formations, colorful banded mounds and ridges, great petrified logs, and a plethora of fossils. The geology of the area began to form about 70 million years ago during the Upper Cretaceous period near the end of the dinosaur era when it lay at the margin of a great inland sea in a setting of coastal swamps, meadows, and tropical forests. It was covered by lush vegetation and a rich variety of animal life, which swam, crawled, and stalked about what must have been a boggy and fertile ecosystem. The players in this Darwinian survival epic included fish, turtles, lizards, primitive mammals, and of course, that most dominant of life forms, the dinosaur.

As the interior of the continent began to rise and great mountains were formed, the seas retreated and the massive uplifted blocks of the earth's crust underwent the process of being leveled at the hands of the slow but steady effects of wind, rain, frost, and flowing streams. When mountains erode, the debris has to go somewhere, and that somewhere was the lower lying areas of the continent on either side of the mountain ranges such as the Bisti area, which were gradually filled in by vast plains of particulate matter ranging in size from fine silt to gravel. This covering of debris acted to preserve the remains of the plant and animal life, now once again exposed in fossil form as the overlying deposits have been subsequently stripped away. The two major geological formations found in the Wilderness are the Fruitland Formation and the Kirtland Shale. The Fruitland Formation makes up most of the local geology, including interbedded sandstone, shale, mudstone, silt, and coal. The Kirtland Shale caps the mushroom-shaped landforms of the area, with the red colors resulting from the shale being baked at high temperatures produced by the ancient oxidation of the surrounding coals.

The area covered by the Wilderness lies directly to the east of the Gateway Mine, a strip mine for coal to supply nearby power plants, and permission had been sought to expand the mine to the east. Fortunately, significant opposition to the expansion developed and instead of being strip mined, as very well might have happened had no one bothered to speak up, Wilderness designation was established for the area in 1986. This is an excellent example of the fact that the efforts of various far-sighted individuals, both in and out of government, can be influential in preserving a unique and irreplaceable natural treasure such as the Bisti. The present wilderness area is an arid and barren depression about 35 miles south of Farmington, set in an area of eroded topography as previously described. It is a remote setting, nearly bordering the large Navajo Indian Reservation, and although various displays and other developments are planned, it currently has no established trails and only a small parking area on the west boundary, with a sign to identify the area as the Bisti Wilderness. Partly because of ongoing paleontological research and for

benefit of future visitors, no collecting of petrified wood and vertebrate fossils is allowed. Other prohibitions include motorized travel, mountain biking, open fires, and discharging of firearms. Climbing on delicate geological features is also frowned upon. The area is accessible year round, but it can get very cold in the winter and too muddy to hike when it has been raining. The best times to visit are in the dry parts of spring and summer, and in the fall. Water is nowhere to be found, and you will need to bring along all that you will need. There are no established campgrounds nearby, but you can car camp on any of the BLM land in the vicinity. Some hikers camp near the undeveloped parking area on the west side of the Wilderness, but my favorite camping spot is on the mesa just to the south of the area. If you want to carry in the water and other necessary gear, you are allowed to backpack and camp anywhere within the wilderness area.

Map Coverage

The area covered by the Bisti Wilderness is mostly represented by the USGS 7.5-minute scale Alamo Mesa West map, with a small sliver of the west end shown on the Bisti Trading Post map, and a similarly small sliver of the south end on the Tanner Lake map. For a larger scale view of the entire region, get the 1:100,000-scale Toadlena map, but on my copy the main approach highway is not shown. A crude but marginally adequate map of the Wilderness is also shown on the BLM Bisti Wilderness brochure.

Access

The Bisti Wilderness is most commonly accessed by paved highway, either from Farmington to the north or from Interstate 40 from the south. There are currently no highway signs to help locate the area and it is not easy to find without

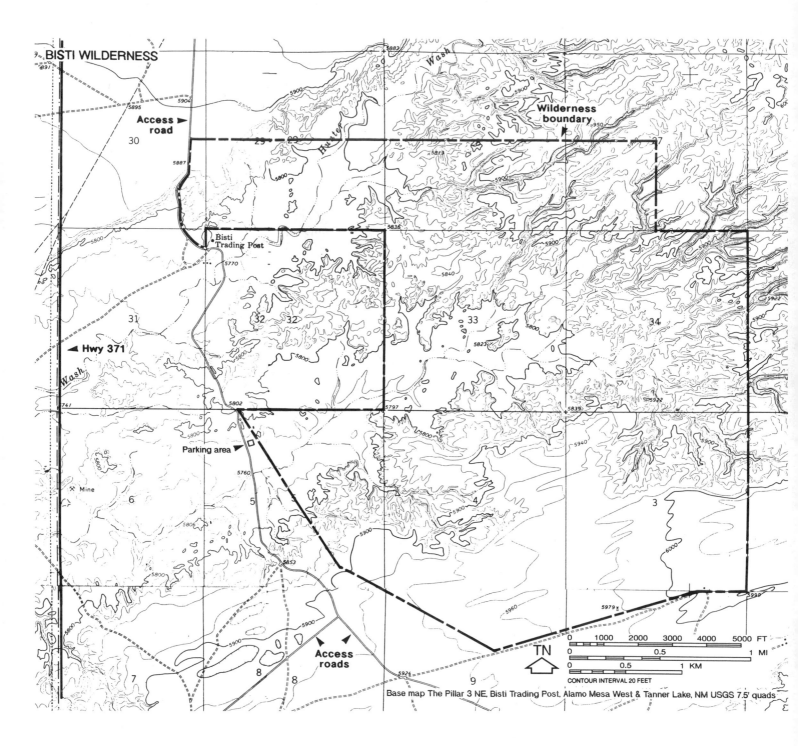

BISTI WILDERNESS

Access road

30

Access road

Wilderness boundary

5895
5904
5887
29
5883
Wash
Wash
Hunter
5800
5895
5900
5950
5900
27

Bisti
Trading Post
5770
5800
5836
5900
5900

31
5800
32
32
33
5840
5823
5800
34
5922

Hwy 371

Wash
741
5802
5797
5835
5922

Parking area
5760
5900
5940
5900

Mine
6
5800
5
5
4
3
6000

5806
5900
5900

5853
5900

5900
5958

5960
5979
5998

Access roads

7
8
8
5924
9

TN

0   1000   2000   3000   4000   5000 FT
0   0.5   1 MI
0   0.5   1 KM
CONTOUR INTERVAL 20 FEET

Base map The Pillar 3 NE, Bisti Trading Post, Alamo Mesa West & Tanner Lake, NM USGS 7.5' quads

directions. Although highway signs will probably be erected to make the process easier, the directions provided below assume the more obscure access situation as it presently exists.

South Access. Drive west on Interstate 40 from Grants and take the Thoreau exit, proceeding north on Highway 371. Pass the turnoff for Crownpoint and continue approximately another 45 miles to the Don Gleason Bridge, which is identified by a road sign. Another 0.9 miles past the bridge, or 0.2 miles past mile marker 70, is a well-traveled gravel road that goes east for 1.8 miles, ending in an intersection with another gravel road. Turn north on this road (south leads back toward Crownpoint) and continue for another 1.2 miles to the parking area for the Bisti Wilderness on the east side of the road.

North Access. Drive south from Farmington on Highway 371 for 28 miles until you get to a scenic marker by the highway for the Bisti Badlands. Opposite this marker on the east side of the road is the junction with County Road 7290. Turn onto this gravel road and drive south for several miles, past the old Bisti Trading Post, and continue as the road drops down to the Bisti Wilderness parking area, which will be on the east side of the road.

From either access direction on Highway 371, you will begin to see the unusual eroded landscape as you approach the Bisti area. If you come to the broad obvious arroyo that drains out of the Bisti with two small bridges in succession, you have missed your turnoff. If road conditions are dry, the gravel approach roads are suitable for any vehicle, but if muddy, approach with caution.

Hiking Trails

There are currently no established trails within the wilderness area. However, something of a crude trail has been worn in, starting at the parking area at the west boundary and continuing east up the main wash that leads into the badlands. Here the erosional effects of water runoff have etched down through the geographical strata to reveal the natural history of the ancient wetlands, and it is magnificently revealed in a discordant assemblage of sculpture. Weird landforms and improbably balanced rocks contrast with gently rounded slopes and hillocks in a blaze of earth-hued pastels. After about a mile the main wash begins to divide into smaller branches, which continue to subdivide, and each path leads into a separate fantasy scene, with the occasional animal fossil or petrified log inviting the curiosity for a life form that preceded us long ago. I have made several trips to the Bisti Badlands and have never walked the same route twice—I think it would be almost impossible. If you venture in very far, and you can easily go 3 or 4 miles before turning around, just keep track of your general heading and a few prominent landmarks so you will have no trouble filtering your way back to your starting point. You can also hike across the mesa to the south and drop into the Wilderness from the south rim (where you get a great overview of the area), but this will involve a more challenging route-finding problem in locating your way back. However you do it, don't forget to bring drinking water and don't forget your camera. And to be considerate of others who will follow, don't further erode delicate formations or hack up fossil remains trying to remove them from the surrounding matrix.

For Further Information:

Bureau of Land
  Management
Farmington Resource
  Area Office
1235 La Plata Highway
Farmington, NM 87401
(505) 327-5344

Bisti Wilderness, a BLM
  brochure available at
  the BLM area resource
  offices in Farmington
  and Albuquerque.

Chaco Canyon National Historical Monument

GENERAL DESCRIPTION

One of the peculiar charms to hiking in New Mexico is the ubiquitous evidence in the form of ruins, rock art, and artifacts left behind by the prehistoric Indians who inhabited the area. The first visitors to the area may have arrived as early as 20,000 years ago, possibly much earlier, and have endured to the present time through a long series of migrations, cultural infusion, and ecological adaptation. Around

900 A.D., the cultural traits of the early Pueblo Indians living in the Four Corners region had evolved into those that define the group now broadly referred to as the Anasazi, a name which derives from a Navajo term meaning "the ancient ones" or something to that effect. All of the great stone ruins that abound throughout the Southwest were built by the Anasazi or their contemporaries, and to visit Chaco Canyon is to visit the site of the pinnacle of Anasazi cultural achievement. The architecture is the most impressive to be found, including the more often visited Mesa Verde. Sophisticated solar calendars and irrigation works were in use at Chaco. Extensive trade patterns existed, with trade goods from as far away as Central America and the Pacific Coast. Broad roadways, some still visible, radiated out in every direction. They were laid out in straight lines and were up to 20 and 30

Prehistoric Ruins at Pueblo Alto, Chaco Canyon

feet wide; their use remains a mystery. Thousands of huge pine beams were carried in from over 30 miles distant. One can only imagine what forms of social, economic, and religious organization were in effect, although the structure of modern Pueblo societies, which have apparently descended from Anasazi groups, provides tantalizing hints. Perhaps the most perplexing question is how such a sophisticated culture was able to survive for 300 to 400 years or more in such a difficult setting, so apparently devoid of natural resources, and then vanish. At about 1250 A.D. to 1300 A.D. there occurred an abrupt decline of the civilization at Chaco Canyon, and indeed throughout the entire Southwest. A great drought was probably a factor, and many other theories have been put forth, including a breakdown of the social order, disease, overuse of natural resources, warfare, and a combination these factors. Whatever the explanation, the pueblo dwellers left Chaco Canyon and the other Anasazi villages great and small and began a gradual migration that brought them to the Rio Grande drainage and the mesas of present-day Acoma, Zuni and the Hopi mesas. The dwelling places of the ancient ancestors now lie empty, and the dry desert winds blow across the works of a civilization left unfulfilled by the mysterious forces of the past.

Chaco Canyon is set about a deep arroyo system running east-west, located in the sandstone mesa country of northwest New Mexico. In the vicinity of the largest ruins, bounded by towering sandstone cliffs on both sides of the canyon, the Chaco Culture National Historic Park of some 21,500 acres has been established. The length of the segment of canyon within the park that you are permitted to visit runs about 9 miles. The setting is that of a semi-arid desert steppe region typical of the sandstone canyon country of the southeast Colorado plateau and the San Juan Basin, of which Chaco Canyon is a part. The sandstone and shale rock is mostly of Upper Cretaceous origin, and it tends to step back from the canyon bottom in a series of steep cliffs. Precipitation in the area averages less than 9 inches per year, with a typical vegetation mix including desert shrubs and grasses such as sage, rabbit brush, tumbleweed, saltbush, Mormon tea, and Indian rice grass, with yucca, cacti, and occasional junipers and piñon pines in some areas. Along the bottom of the arroyo there is also cottonwood, willow, and tamarisk. The elevation of the canyon bottom is slightly over 6,000 feet. Winters are cold and summers are hot and dry, making spring and fall the most comfortable times of year to visit.

There is a Visitor Center located at the park headquarters, with a small interpretive museum and a ranger during duty hours to answer questions. Overnight camping is provided at an established campground, but other than drinking water, no supplies or services are available. Talks by the park staff concerning various aspects of Chaco prehistory are conducted in the evenings at the campground, and tours of some of the major ruins are scheduled each day. A one-way loop road runs up and down the canyon in the vicinity of the largest ruins, and you will undoubtedly want to spend some time walking through these magnificent works.

Map Coverage

Topographical map coverage for the Chaco Canyon area is provided by the USGS 7.5 scale Pueblo Bonito, Kin Klizhin ruins, and Sargent Ranch maps. 1:100,000-scale coverage is shown on the Chaco Canyon and Toadlena maps.

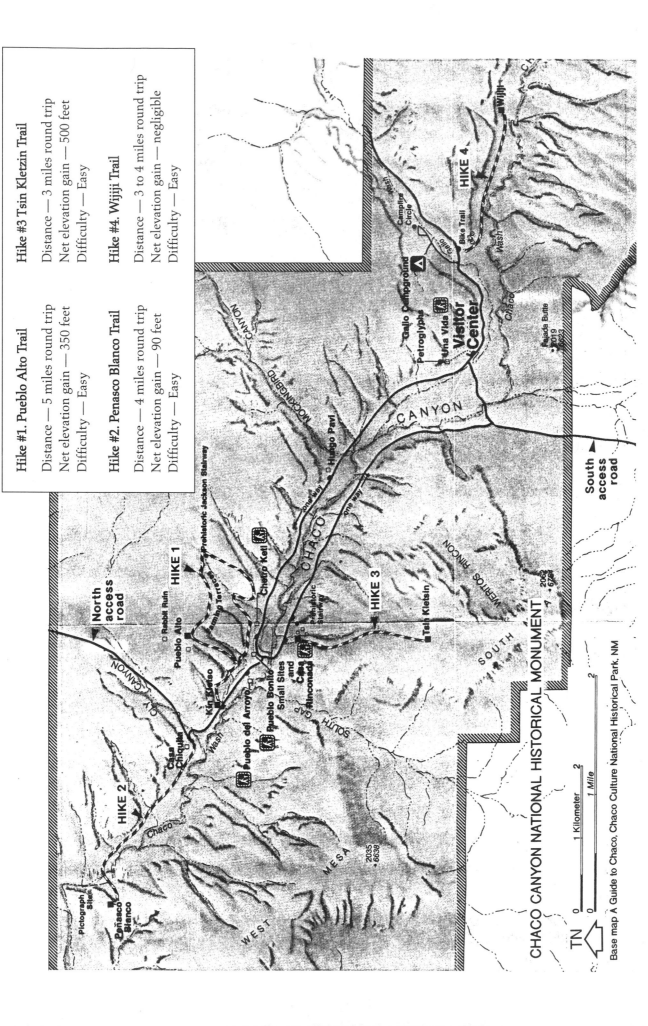

Hike #1. Pueblo Alto Trail

Distance — 5 miles round trip
Net elevation gain — 350 feet
Difficulty — Easy

Hike #2. Penasco Blanco Trail

Distance — 4 miles round trip
Net elevation gain — 90 feet
Difficulty — Easy

Hike #3 Tsin Kletzin Trail

Distance — 3 miles round trip
Net elevation gain — 500 feet
Difficulty — Easy

Hike #4. Wijiji Trail

Distance — 3 to 4 miles round trip
Net elevation gain — negligible
Difficulty — Easy

CHACO CANYON NATIONAL HISTORICAL MONUMENT

Base map A Guide to Chaco, Chaco Culture National Historical Park, NM

Access

You can access Chaco Canyon either from the north or the south, with both approaches involving a long final stretch of gravel road that is easily negotiable by passenger cars under most conditions, but not after heavy rains. The heavy clay content of the roads make them very difficult when wet, and when this is the case you should consider visiting another area. Phone the park headquarters for road conditions if you are concerned. The total one-way driving time from Albuquerque is about 3 to 3.5 hours either way you approach.

To approach Chaco Canyon from the north, take Highway 44 north from Bernalillo to the town of Cuba and continue northwest on 44 about another hour past Cuba to either Nageezi or Blanco Trading Post; both are shown on the roadmaps. From either of these points, both of which have signs at the highway announcing the turnoff to Chaco Canyon, turn south on gravel roads (that connect farther south) and continue for about 30 miles, until you drop down into the west end of Chaco Canyon. Follow the canyon road 3 miles to the east to reach the Visitor Center. To approach from the south, take Interstate 25 west past Grants and turn north on to Highway 371 (formerly Highway 57) at the small community of Thoreau. Continue north past the turnoff for the town of Crownpoint, and go another 4 miles and turn east on Highway 9 (Highway 9 also used to be designated as Highway 57, but I believe the road signs have been changed to reflect the redesignation). Follow Highway 9 east for approximately 15 miles to a road junction, where you turn north on a gravel road with a highway sign pointing the way to Chaco Canyon. Drive the final 20 miles on the gravel road, which enters Chaco Canyon on its south side. Follow the signs to reach the Visitor Center and the campground, both a short drive to the east.

Hiking Trails

Because of concerns by the Park Service for the many prehistoric cultural sites in the area, you are no longer allowed to wander about the Chaco backcountry, but are restricted to the immediate vicinity of the large ruins along the loop drive and the several designated backcountry hiking trails. Each of the trails leads to a major ruin, and all give access to a Chaco backcountry that is scenic and interesting to hike. For these trails a backcountry hiking permit must first be obtained at the Visitor Center. No overnight backpacking is allowed within the park boundaries, and you are warned to keep off ruin walls and not to collect artifacts.

TRAIL DESCRIPTIONS

Hike #1. Pueblo Alto Trail

Pueblo Alto is the major ruin at the terminus of this trail, the name meaning "high village" in Spanish (where the adjective refers to the topography of the village rather than the emotional state of the inhabitants). The ruin is, in fact, high up on the mesa top north of the canyon, and it served as the starting point for most of the ancient roadways that radiated out from the north side of Chaco Canyon and connected to various outlier pueblos. These roadways, which are now discernable only by subtle differences in vegetation and sometimes only by aerial observation, had prepared surfaces, were up to 30 feet wide near the canyon, were laid out in straight lines, and have been traced for distances of over 60 miles.

While these roadways were evidently intended for travel, their extensive and seemingly overbuilt engineering features indicate that there is much we do not know about them. Pueblo Alto Ruin is an unusual one-story design that is thought to have been a center for trading or redistribution of market goods. It is also thought to have been one of a number of sites located on high points that formed a visual communication system, utilizing signal fires, that covered a rather large geographical area. Analysis of pollen samples excavated from the ruin have corroborated the theory that the flora in the area, and therefore the climate, have changed very little since the ruin was inhabited nearly a thousand years ago.

The hiking trail follows a loop that is 5 miles round trip, with a 350-foot elevation gain. To locate the trailhead, drive west from the Visitor Center on the main loop road to Kin Kletso Ruin, about 0.5 miles west of Pueblo Bonito. Find the trail that ascends the crack in the sandstone cliff behind the ruin and climb to the top of the cliffs and continue east 0.5 miles to a trail junction. A short spur to the south leads to an overlook above Pueblo Bonito. The other two trail branches form the start of the trail loop, and it doesn't really matter on which fork you start. The north branch goes directly to the Pueblo Alto ruins. From the ruins, the trail continues along the upper mesa top to the east and passes above prehistoric farming terraces and an access feature named Jackson's Staircase. The latter is an impressive set of steps that were cut by the Indians into the rock face of the topmost set of cliffs, providing a route up and down. Don't try to descend the steps; the edges have rounded with time, and they are not only dangerous to climb on, but doing so is also prohibited by park regulations. From the staircase the trail turns southwest, passes an ancient road alignment along

the way, and follows the top of the lower cliffs past an overlook for the Chetro Ketl ruins to the original trail junction. Allow several hours to do the entire loop hike.

Hike #2. Penasco Blanco Trail

This hike leads to Penasco Blanco, a medium-size pueblo ruin, which was up to four stories high and located on the south rim of the canyon with a nice view of the surrounding canyon area. The trail is 4 miles round trip, with less than 100 feet in elevation gain to the ruin. One of the outstanding features of this hike is the abundance of prehistoric rock art to be seen along the way, including both petroglyphs (pecked in) and pictographs (painted on).

Find the trailhead by driving to the far west end of the canyon road and parking in the parking lot for Casa Chiquita Ruin. The trail starts on the west side of the ruin and continues west on the dirt road below the sandstone cliffs. There is rock art all along these cliffs, some of it in high, seemingly inaccessible locations. Some of the more subtle rock art panels have work that requires diligent searching, and each time you do this hike you will see things that you missed on previous trips. If you are photographing, you will want to take along a tripod and a long lens. About 1.5 miles down the canyon the trail turns south and crosses the arroyo. The main trail continues up to the south canyon rim and on to Peñasco Blanco Ruins a short distance farther. Just on the south side of the arroyo, before the trail ascends the mesa, there is also a short side trail, which leads west along the base of the cliffs to the Supernova Pictograph, probably the best-known example of rock art in the entire area, with the possible exception of the solar calendar on Fajada Butte. The Supernova Pictograph is painted on the underside of a rock roof perhaps 25 feet above the trail

and depicts a crescent moon, a star shape, and a human handprint. It is thought to represent an astronomical supernova event (expanding star) that occurred in 1054 A.D. and was recorded by Chinese astronomers. The phase of the moon and relative position to the star would have been correct for the event. After seeing the pictograph and climbing to the ruins on the mesa top, complete the hike by retracing the same trail back to your car.

Hike #3. Tsin Kletzin Trail

This is a 3-mile round-trip hike that begins at Casa Rinconada ruins on the south side of Chaco Canyon and gains 500 feet in elevation in reaching the destination of the hike at Tsin Kletzin ruins on the mesa south of Chaco Canyon. Tsin Kletzin was a "D"-shaped pueblo of about 75 ground-floor rooms with two tower kivas. The pueblo was another of the conspicuous vantage points that was in

visual contact with other far-flung sites and may have been part of a visual communication network.

The trailhead is located by taking the paved loop road to the Casa Rinconada ruins, located on the south side of Chaco Wash. The trail begins up the low sandstone cliffs to the south, but before starting out you will probably want to walk the short trail that winds among the ruins. The central feature of the ruins is Casa Rinconada, a huge kiva 63 feet across that is the largest in the canyon. The kiva was undoubtedly an imposing structure, and one can almost imagine the ancient ceremonies that were conducted in it—ceremonies that were handed down in the oral tradition over many generations, and which must have been an integral part of the social and religious infrastructure of the pueblo society. After you have finished browsing the ruins, climb up on the Tsin Kletzin Trail to the

Jackson's Staircase, Visible along the Pueblo Alto Trail

south canyon rim and follow the sandy trail leading to the Tsin Kletzin Ruin 1.5 miles distant. Except for the ruin, there are no notable attractions to see along the trail, just some nice views and lots of fresh air and sunshine. This hike is a good opportunity to identify the various native plants growing along the mesa top.

Hike #4. Wijiji Trail

The Wijiji Trail is a 3 to 4 mile round-trip walk down a Park Service access road that leads up the canyon on the east end of the park. The hike includes some rock art on the cliffs along the approach and some nice ruins at Wijiji on the east end of the hike. The Wijiji Ruin was a pueblo community of about 100 rooms, constructed relatively late during the period of prehistoric Chacoan civilization. As with the other ruins, you can't help but imagine the life stories played out in this small community; the events and the drama of forgotten times played out by people now known only to God. It is a place to let your imagination soar and to ask questions that can never be answered.

Locate the trailhead by driving on the paved road a short distance north from the campground, or just walk across from the campground. A short segment of road turns back to the south to a small parking area where the trail begins. Continue east on the dirt road, noticing the occasional rock art on the lower walls of the cliffs to the north. Of special interest are the painted handprints, which are relatively unusual for Chaco Canyon but common in certain other parts of the Anasazi domain. Perhaps the artists were immigrants from another area. Upon reaching Wijiji you will have to turn back to complete the hike. There is another ruin farther up the road, which predated the Chaco culture, but travel to it is not permitted.

For Further Information:

Chaco Culture National Historical Park Box 6500 S.R. 4 Bloomfield, NM 87413 (505) 988-6716.

A Guide to Chaco, A pamphlet produced by the National Park Service (available at the Visitor Center), U.S. Department of the Interior.

Chaco Canyon, Archaeology and Archaeologists, by Robert H. Lister And Florence C. Lister, University Of New Mexico Press, Albuquerque, NM, 1981.

New Light on Chaco Canyon, edited by David Grant Noble, School Of American Research Press, Santa Fe, NM, 1984.

Backcountry Trail Guide, a Booklet by Rob Eaton, National Park Service, Chaco Culture National Historical Park, 1982.

Ghost Ranch

GENERAL DESCRIPTION

Ghost Ranch is a unique center owned by the Presbyterian Church in northern New Mexico, north of Abiquiu Reservoir along Highway 84. It is a 21,000-acre parcel of the old Spanish Piedra Lumbre land grant that has been developed over the past 30-plus years into a nationally known complex hosting a wide range of educational seminars, craft development programs, and religious retreats, with housing and support facilities for up to 350 guests. Included on the grounds are two museums and a bookstore. There are also archaeological and paleontological projects, and diverse experimental programs in such subjects as range management, erosion control, alternative housing design, irrigation techniques, and small acreage farming. The ranch is located in a majestic setting at an elevation of 6,500 feet, below colorful cliffs and mesas that were a favorite subject of the artist Georgia O'Keeffe, who lived in nearby Abiquiu.

Several hiking trails have been constructed, which lead from the conference center and extend into the multihued red and cream-colored sandstone cliffs and formations behind the center. Visitors are invited to hike these trails but should first check in at the Ghost Ranch office at the conference center, where informed staff members can answer questions about the area. An all-weather road leads to the conference center and, unless precluded by snow accumulation, hiking can be done year round. Summers can be hot but bearable, and winters can range from pleasantly crisp to uncomfortably cold. During the thunderstorm season from late summer to early fall, it is best to get started early and avoid the potential afternoon rain and lightning. Water is unavailable along the trails. Car camping in the vicinity is available at campgrounds in the Santa Fe National Forest south of Highway 96, at the Forest Service Echo Amphitheater Site a few miles up Highway 84, and along the Monastery road by the nearby Chama River Canyon Wilderness. Ghost Ranch is set in one of the most scenic and picturesque areas of the state, and it's worth the drive just to view the scenery; once you have viewed it, you will want to hike it.

Map Coverage

The Ghost Ranch is shown on the USGS 7.5-minute scale Ghost Ranch quad map. For a larger scale overview of the area, get the 1:100,000-scale Abiquiu map. The Santa Fe and Carson National Forest maps are also useful if you plan to explore some of the surrounding national forest.

Access

From Albuquerque or Santa Fe, travel north on Highway 84/285 to Española (if you need instructions for getting through

Española, see the Cañones Creek access description). From the intersection 6 miles north of Española where Highway 285 splits off, travel 28.8 miles north on Highway 84, 6.2 miles past the Abiquiu Dam turnoff, to a highway sign directing you north to Ghost Ranch. One mile past the turnoff, the road forks, with the left fork leading another 0.4 miles to the conference center office. Travel time to the center is about 1.5 hours from Santa Fe or 2.5 hours from Albuquerque.

Hiking Trails

There are three short to medium-length trails that lead from the conference center to the colorful sandstone cliffs north and east of the center. All the trails involve some elevation gain in ascending sandstone formations, but they are not difficult to hike and are generally easy to follow. Bring water and sun protection, and remember your camera.

TRAIL DESCRIPTIONS

Hike #1. Kitchen Mesa Trail

This trail ascends the large sandstone mesa east of the conference center. The trail length is about 4.5 miles round trip, with an elevation gain of 580 feet and a hiking time of 2 to 3 hours. The trail is easy to follow and not strenuous, except for the steep climb to gain the mesa top.

To find the trailhead, begin at the conference center office and drive east on the road that runs along the front of the complex. After the road widens out just past the swimming pool, make a sharp left around the Piñon Social Center and continue northeast to a small parking area with signs marking the trailhead. Begin hiking north from the trailhead for a short distance until a trail sign directs you

to the right, across the arroyo. From here on, the trail is easy to follow, but to make sure, there are occasional coffee cans nailed to posts to mark the route. The trail bends around into a cul de sac and then switchbacks up the side of the mesa and through a final narrow passage to gain the top. The route then follows the center of the mesa around to the right to a point overlooking the conference center. Here you will want to spend some time taking in the fantastic views before turning around and retracing the approach route. Be careful of loose or slippery rock on the way back down.

Hike #2. Box Canyon Trail

The Box Canyon Trail is 5.0 round-trip miles in length, with a net elevation gain of 800 feet. The elevation gradient is not unpleasant, making a nice 2 to 3 hour hike. The trailhead is the same as for the Kitchen Mesa Trail, but instead of turning off to the right just past the trailhead, continue straight on the old dirt road, which leads past some hogans (Navajo-style dwellings) and out across the level area above the creek bottom. The road presently ends, as the trail drops down into the creek drainage and follows it to the east. After perhaps 0.5 miles, the trail climbs up out of the drainage, and up a fairly steep ridge to an area where the trail levels out and crosses open slopes to the entrance to a box canyon. A final steep scramble leads to the scenic canyon where the trail ends. This trail has fairly steady elevation gain after the first part, but is easy to moderate in difficulty. It provides a good outing for identifying some of the native plant life.

Hike #3. Chimney Rock Trail

This hike is about 2.5 miles round trip, with 630 feet of net elevation gain. Total time to complete the hike is 1.5 to 2

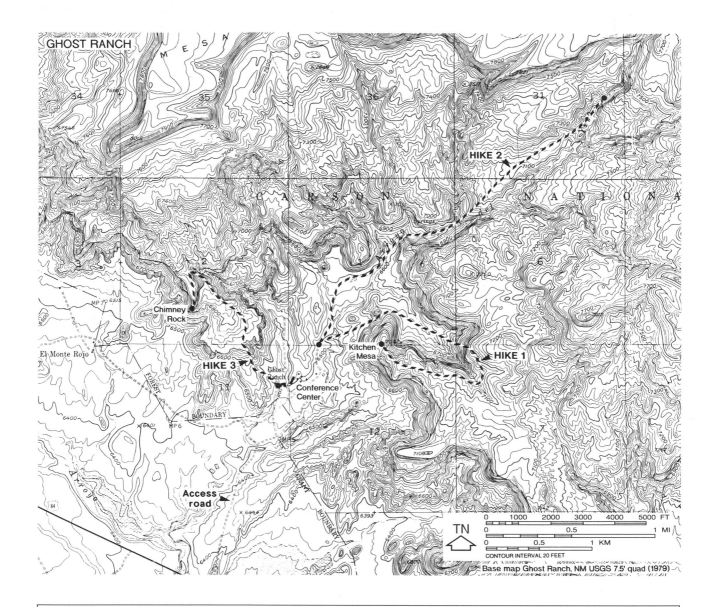

Hike #1. Kitchen Mesa Trail

Distance — 4.5 miles round trip
Net elevation Gain — 580 feet
Difficulty — Easy to moderate

Hike #2. Box Canyon Trail

Distance — 5.0 miles round trip
Net elevation gain — 800 feet
Difficulty — Easy to moderate

Hike #3. Chimney Rock Trail

Distance — 2.5 miles round trip
Net elevation gain — 630 feet
Difficulty — Easy to moderate

Chimney Rock

hours. Although the steep part of the trail is moderately strenuous, overall it is short, easy to follow, and easy to moderate in difficulty. The trail ends at the tip of the mesa opposite Chimney Rock, a picturesque spire that has been separated from the mesa by erosion, and there is a wonderful view of a broad stretch of the Chama River valley with Cerro Pedernal in the distance.

To locate the trailhead, drive west from the conference office on the road running in front of the complex and take the first road heading north, following the sign to the "Mesa." Just after making the turn, make another turn to the left and park at the west end of the gravel area behind the Ruth Hall Museum of Paleontology. A

small trail sign directs you to a path that ascends the steep slope to the west to the top of a low mesa. The trail continues northwest along the broad mesa as Chimney Rock comes into view at the line of cliffs ahead. Along this stretch of trail, numbered steel posts provide reference points for an interpretive trail guide that can be purchased back at the office. The steep part of the trail lies ahead, as you climb up to the level above the set of cliffs to the north. Once above the cliffs, the final segment of trail runs back south to the mesa point opposite Chimney Rock. The edge of the mesa here is very sheer, so avoid getting too close and keep a close watch on children.

For Further Information:

Ghost Ranch
    Conference Center
    Abiquiu, NM 87510
    (505) 685-4333

Ghost Ranch Living
    Museum
    Carson National Forest
    Highway 84
    Abiquiu, NM 87510
    (505) 688-4312

The Rio Chama, a Wild
and Scenic River

Chama River Canyon Wilderness

GENERAL DESCRIPTION

This Wilderness is located in north-central New Mexico on 50,300 acres of national forest, situated on either side of a segment of the Chama River between El Vado Reservoir and Abiquiu Reservoir. The Chama River Canyon Wilderness is but one component of a group of contiguous, publicly administered recreation areas, which are grouped under the common umbrella called the Rio Chama Corridor. The other members of this group are the Rio Chama Wild and Scenic River, a 24.6-mile stretch of the Chama River below El Vado Dam; and the Rio Chama Wilderness Study Area, an 11,985-acre BLM area located along the river to the north of the Chama River Canyon Wilderness. Parts of the Rio

Chama Corridor are administered by several different government agencies, and an overall management plan for the area, which has the impossible sounding requisite of coordinating and ranking the requirements of the Santa Fe and Carson National Forests, the Bureau of Land Management, and the U.S. Army Corps of Engineers, has been established, and is currently providing for such things as trail and campground improvements. The most popular attraction, by far, in the Rio Chama Corridor is the wild and scenic part of the Chama River, a stretch of the river that is popular for whitewater boating and fishing. Less used, but of more interest for hiking, is the adjacent Chama River Canyon Wilderness.

The Chama River Canyon Wilderness is an area of forested canyons that cuts through high mesas with towering cliffs of sandstone, shale, and limestone. In addition to the Chama and Gallina rivers, which trisect the Wilderness, there are a number of springs and streams with running water, as well as plentiful wildlife and lots of nice forest landscape and scenic vistas. Despite the popularity of the Chama River, the trail system in the surrounding Wilderness is not heavily used at present. The elevation gradient of the area goes from a little less than 6,200 feet at river level to over 8,600 feet at the mesa tops, which results in a range of flora that includes piñon pine, juniper, cottonwood, and associated species at the lower elevations, up through the firs and aspens at the higher elevations. This region of the state gets plenty of snow in the winter, which usually melts out sufficiently for hiking by mid-April to mid-May, depending on the trail. The hiking season extends through late October or early November when the snows return. There are campgrounds at Cooper's Ranch, a private facility just below El Vado Dam, which charges a small fee, and at the Rio Chama Campground, 6.0 miles up the Chama River from the southern access point at Big Eddy, on Forest Road 151. Numerous other Forest Service campgrounds within reasonable driving distance are situated in the adjacent Carson and Santa Fe National Forests, and can be located on the National Forest maps or by contacting one of the ranger stations listed at the end of the section.

Map Coverage

The Carson and Santa Fe National Forest maps are good for general coverage of the national forests surrounding the area, showing forest roads and other access roads, campgrounds, and trails, but not topography. For more detailed topographic coverage to supplement the map in this book, the USGS Laguna Peak and Echo Amphitheater 7.5-minute scale quad maps cover the trails described in this section. If you are going to explore the far north end of the Wilderness, you will also need the Navajo Peak map. Large scale topographic coverage of the area is shown on the USGS 1:100,000-scale Abiquiu map or the 15-minute scale Tierra Amarilla map.

Access

The primary access to the Chama River Canyon Wilderness is via Forest Road 151, which is also the approach used to reach the southern portion of the Rio Chama Corridor. To reach this access, drive north from Española on Highway 84 to a point 1 mile north of the Ghost Ranch Living Museum (just north of mile marker 227), where Forest Road 151, marked by a Rio Chama access sign, turns west from the highway. Forest Road 151 is a gravel road that is easily negotiated by passenger car when conditions are dry, but having significant clay composition, the road is notoriously difficult to drive,

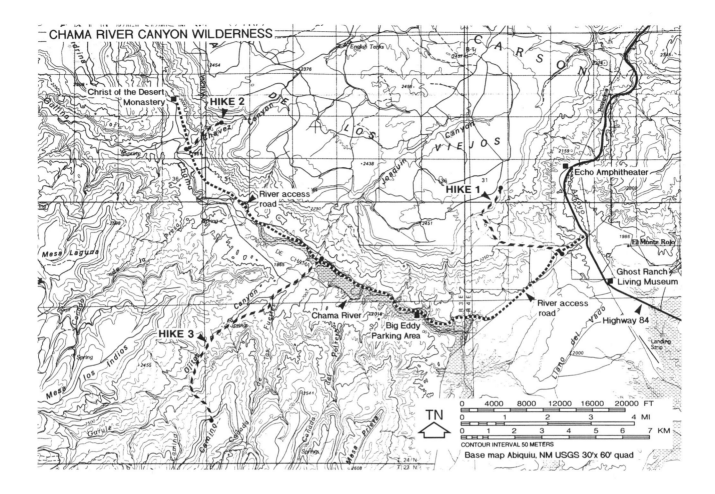

with or without four wheel drive, when the road surface is muddy. The road continues west for 5.4 miles, reaching the river and a large parking area at what is known as Big Eddy Takeout, which is the primary exit point off the river for whitewater boaters running the Wild and Scenic stretch. From Big Eddy, Forest Road 151 continues north along the east bank of the river for about 8 miles, ending at the Christ of the Desert Monastery.

The Wilderness is also accessible at a number of other points along its periphery by a tangle of obscure forest roads, which I cannot begin to describe here, and which are unnecessary for any of the trails described in this section. The final access route into the Wilderness, though definitely not the most straightforward

Hike #1. Rim Vista Trail (#15)

Distance — 4.6 miles round trip
Net elevation gain — 1,250 feet
Difficulty — Easy to Moderate

Hike #2. Chavez Canyon Trail

Distance — 1.6 miles round trip
Net elevation gain — 250 feet
Difficulty — Easy

Hike #3. Ojitos Trail (#298)

Distance — 12.0 miles round trip
Net elevation gain — 1,740 feet
Difficulty — Moderate

Trailhead at
river bridge

HIKE 3

Dirt road

Mesa del Camino

TN

| 0 | 1000 | 2000 | 3000 | 4000 | 5000 FT |

| 0 | | 0.5 | | 1 MI |

| 0 | 0.5 | 1 KM |

CONTOUR INTERVAL 20 FEET

Base map Laguna Peak, NM USGS 7.5' quad

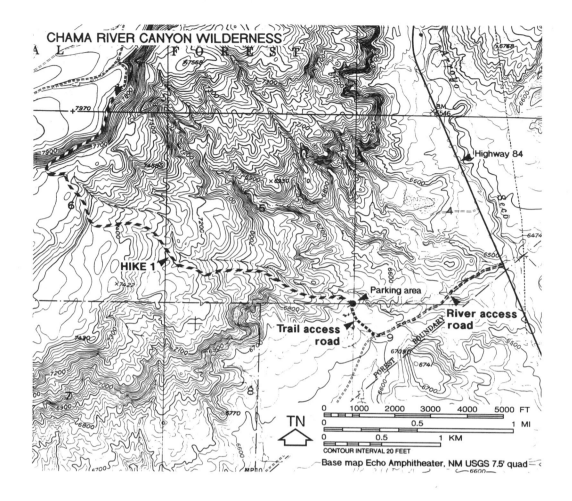

CHAMA RIVER CANYON WILDERNESS

Hiking Trails

access to the trailheads, is by river travel from the egress point below El Vado Dam at El Vado (Cooper's) Ranch. Boating down this stretch of the Rio Chama is strictly controlled by permit; contact the Taos BLM office for more information. Should you want to reach the river from the Cooper's Ranch access point, begin by driving north on Highway 84 toward the town of Chama. Several miles north of the blinking traffic light at the community of Tierra Amarilla, you will see a sign directing you west on Highway 112 to El Vado Dam. About 0.5 miles before reaching the dam, turn west on a short dirt road to El Vado Ranch on the east bank of the river.

The Wilderness trails described in this section include two trails located in the Santa Fe National Forest, and one, in the Carson National Forest, that is technically located just outside the Wilderness boundary by virtue of the curious process in which boundaries are located. All these trails are accessible by Forest Road 151. Although not presently posted as such, the Ojitos Trail serves as a portion of the Continental Divide National Scenic Trail, which will eventually tie in with trails to the north and south. In addition to the trails described here, there is a trail that drops down into Hart Canyon, which I have not hiked, and plans for some 14 additional miles of trails. These planned additions include a 0.75 to 1.0 mile interpretive nature trail along the "Big Bend" area of the river, several miles north of Big Eddy, as well as trails in the vicinity of Navajo Peak, Cebolla Canyon, and a Hart Canyon Loop Trail.

TRAIL DESCRIPTIONS

Trail #1. Rim Vista Trail (#15)

The Rim Vista Trail takes a 4.6-mile round trip path up through scattered piñon/juniper forests to a lookout point atop Mesa de Los Viejos, with a spectacular view of the scenic landscape in the vicinity of Ghost Ranch and Abiquiu Reservoir. The trail is located to the east of the Chama River Canyon, just outside the Wilderness boundary—although the surroundings are as wild as for any of the trails within the boundary. It gains 1,250 feet to the top, with easy to moderate hiking on a well-marked trail. With no water available along the trail, this is more suited as a day hike than an overnight backpack. The total time required to do the hike, including lunch break, is about 2.5 to 5 hours. The area covered is shown on the USGS 7.5-minute scale Echo Amphitheater map.

Begin by turning west off of Highway 84 on to Forest Road 151 as previously described, and drive 0.7 miles to a dirt road that turns off to the north, with the entrance marked by a sign for the Rim Vista Trail. Follow this road perhaps 0.2 miles north to a fork, where you take the right branch and continue a short distance farther to an informal parking area and a sign marking the trailhead. The trail follows a ridge system to the north and west, gradually gaining elevation to a level area below the final steep rim of Mesa de Los Viejos. At this point, the trail turns back to the east and begins a long gradual contour up the rim to the top of the mesa at the Rim Vista Lookout. There is also a spur road off Forest Road 131 on top of the mesa, which leads to the lookout. The trail is easy to follow all the way to the top, with blue diamonds nailed to trees to mark the path most of the way up.

Hike #2. Chavez Canyon Trail

This is a short, easy hike of 1.6 miles round trip which takes a path up Chavez Canyon to the east from the Rio Chama to the base of some of the colorful rock walls that help define the river canyon. The trail has some scenic views of the cliffs and of the river canyon to the west. Locate the trailhead by turning off of Highway 84 on to Forest Road 151 and following the road to the river, then north up the river to within about 0.5 miles of the end of the road at the Monastery. At this point, on the river side of the road, you will see a river access area with parking and picnic facilities where you can park your car. Opposite all this, on the east side of the road, you will find the Chavez Canyon Trail leading up an old road into the canyon. The trail continues on up into the canyon after the road ends and follows the canyon until you come to the first set of cliffs. The trail is easy to follow, with a round trip hiking time of 1 to 1.5 hours.

Hike #3. Ojitos Trail (#298)

The Ojitos Trail makes a moderately long day hike through some splendid forest scenery in the Wilderness west of the Rio Chama, but it is also the trail to take for a backpacking trip of two or more days, with running water and plenty of potential campsites along the route in Ojitos Canyon, and lots of other interesting terrain in the area to explore. The trail takes a 12-mile round trip path up Ojitos

Canyon, ending at a forest road on a ledge below the summit of Mesa del Camino, with most of the 1,740 feet of net elevation gain on the final ascent of the mesa. As previously mentioned, this trail is slated to become a link in the Continental Divide National Scenic Trail, although it is located miles to the east of the actual Continental Divide. The Ojitos Trail is well laid out and generally easy to follow, with the possible exception of one spot mentioned below. Allow a minimum of 6 to 7 hours to do the hike, and if possible, budget a full day. Better yet, budget about three days and see some more of the remote country back in the upper part of the canyon. The USGS 7.5-minute scale topo map for this area is the Laguna Peak quad, but the trail is not shown on the map.

Find the trailhead by driving on Forest Road 151 to the Big Eddy parking area and then continuing north on the road for another 2.8 miles to Skull Bridge, a bridge across the river that is now blocked to vehicular traffic. Park at a small parking area with a Forest Service information display just south of the bridge. Walk across the bridge, where a trail sign marks the trailhead. The trail goes west up the broad canyon entrance on an old road, continues west at the 0.25 point where the road turns north, and follows a series of posts with pointed tops that periodically mark the trail over the next several

miles. At about 0.7 miles beyond the second Wilderness boundary sign, a road forks south off the road leading up the canyon. Take this south fork and continue to follow the marker posts as the trail bends west again and skirts behind a small hill, returning again to the canyon bottom at the edge of a large clearing with a log maze, or gate, to admit pedestrian traffic. To the south of this point is the site of a former homestead near a growth of cattails marking the *ojitos* (springs) for which the canyon is named. Just past the log pedestrian gate is the tricky spot referred to above. There is a fork in the trail, with the south fork leading to a dead end about 0.5 miles beyond; instead, take the fork that continues west at the log gate and crosses a couple of deep arroyos not far beyond as it runs southwest along the main branch of the canyon. The trail surface is occasionally a bit faint but not hard to follow; the path crosses the stream a number of times, but the water flow is small enough to hop across without getting your feet wet. At about the 5-mile point, the trail leaves the gentle elevation gradient of the canyon bottom and begins a series of broad switchbacks, ending at the forest road below Mesa del Camino. A trail sign marks this intersection. Complete the hike by returning back along the same route.

For Further Information:

Coyote Ranger Station
Santa Fe National
Forest
Coyote, NM 87012
(505) 638-5526

Carson National Forest
P.O. Box 558
Taos, NM 87571
(505) 758-6200

Taos Resource Area
Bureau of Land
Management
P.O. Box 1045
Taos, NM 87571
(505) 758-8851

Ghost Ranch Living
Museum
Carson National
Forest
Highway 84
Abiquiu, NM 87510
(505) 688-4312

El Vado Ranch
P.O. Box 129
Tierra Amarilla,
NM 87575
(505) 588-7354

*Rio Chama
Management Plan*,
published by USDA
Forest Service,
Santa Fe National
Forest; USDI
Bureau of Land
Management,
Albuquerque
District; U.S. Army
Corps of Engineers,
Albuquerque
District; November
1990.

San Pedro Parks Wilderness

GENERAL DESCRIPTION

The San Pedro Parks Wilderness consists of 41,132 acres located about 5 miles northeast of the town of Cuba, on a high plateau in the small range known as the San Pedro Mountains, at the northwest corner of the Jemez Mountains. The landscape is characterized by rolling terrain covered in forests of aspen, ponderosa pine and other conifers, and broad open meadows with streams, marshes, and beaver ponds. The central features of the area are the large meadows, or parks, which are scattered through the high interior of the wilderness, and which generally provide the destination for most of the trails that enter around the perimeter. These scenic and expansive parks, strewn with wildflowers and cloaked in a sea of grass, are a delight to hike through. A tent site at the edge of one of these meadows and a moonlit walk through the soft grass on a clear night help produce an unforgettable camping trip. There is abundant wildlife in the area, including large populations of elk and mule deer, and the streams and ponds are habitat for native Rio Grande cutthroat trout. And then, of course, there is the cow—less intensively grazed here than in some of the other hiking areas of the state, but occasionally seen none the less. Even so, people who have hiked and backpacked here usually rate San Pedro Parks Wilderness as one of their favorite areas in the state.

Located within two to three hours driving time from Albuquerque or Santa Fe, San Pedro Parks is conveniently located for most of the population of the state, but not heavily hiked. The weather is comfortable any time of year except winter when the area is snowbound. Even during summer, however, the weather should not be underestimated. The typical elevation is around 10,000 feet, with 35 inches of annual precipitation, and much of the rainfall occurs during the months of July and August. Considering the elevation, it can get uncomfortably cold any time of year for the unprepared. So make sure you put some rain gear and extra clothing for warmth in your pack before starting out on a hike. The access roads to the area are generally good, and there are several Forest Service campgrounds around the perimeter of the Wilderness for car campers. Although wilderness permits were required in the past, they are not currently being used.

Map Coverage

The best map to get is the *Visitors Guide to the San Pedro Parks Wilderness*, a special map of the area produced by the Forest Service showing trails and topography, along with brief descriptions of the various trails and other basic information. This map is available from Forest Service map distribution centers and offices and ranger stations of the Santa Fe National Forest. Finer topographic detail is shown on the USGS 7.5-minute scale Nacimiento Peak and Gallina quads.

Access

There are trailheads distributed around the entire perimeter of the Wilderness. They are generally reached by short access roads that branch off a perimeter road system that is initiated either through the town of Coyote to the northeast of the area, or Cuba to the

southwest. More detailed access directions in the individual trail descriptions will reference this perimeter road system, which is described as follows:

West and North Sides of the Wilderness from Cuba. Highway 96 is the road that loops around the west and north sides of the area and can be initiated either from Cuba or Coyote. From Cuba, travel 4.5 miles north of town on Highway 44 and turn north on Highway 96 toward Regina. Highway 96 continues north, skirting the west side of the mountains, until 2 miles north of the county line where it turns to the east, while Highway 112 continues north. Stay on Highway 96 as it runs along the north side of the mountains and continues 21 miles to Coyote.

South and East Sides of the Wilderness from Cuba. A route consisting primarily of Forest Roads 70 and 103 circumscribes this part of the Wilderness. From Cuba, drive north on Highway 44, 1 mile past the Cuba Ranger Station at the south edge of town, to a right (east) turn on Highway 126 near the center of town. Highway 126 is a paved road that wanders east up into the mountains for

9.7 miles, where the pavement turns to gravel. After driving 0.3 miles past the end of the pavement, turn north on Forest Road 70. Drive 2.5 miles up the road past the Forest Road 267 turnoff, and another 0.3 miles to the trailhead for the Vacas Trail, where you will find good parking and toilet facilities. This is also the access to San Gregorio Lake. Continuing on Forest Road 70 to the east, you will pass the Palomas Trailhead, the intersection with Forest Road 69 (stay on Forest Road 70), and the Peñas Negras Trailhead, before arriving at the Forest Road 103 intersection 14.7 miles past the Vacas Trailhead. Turn north on Forest Road 103 and continue past Teakettle Rock and the Forest Road 316 intersection to the Rio Puerco Campground, 10.4 miles north of the turnoff, and another 6.6 miles to the intersection with Forest Road 172. Bear north on Forest Road 172 and follow it 4 miles to Highway 96.

South and East Sides of the Wilderness from Coyote. Reach the town of Coyote by driving north on Highway 84 from Española, turning south on Highway 96 at the road sign for Abiquiu Dam, and continuing 12.2 miles to the turnoff for the Coyote Ranger Station on the east side of town (Highway 96 continues through town and loops around the north and west sides of the Wilderness all the way to Highway 44). Continue through Coyote on Highway 96, 5.1 miles past the ranger station to a south turn onto Forest Road 172, just before mile marker 29. After turning on Forest Road 172, take the right fork at the road junction just south of the turnoff and continue 4.0 miles, merging left onto Forest Road 103. You will then reverse the route described from Cuba, traveling 17 miles south to Forest Road 70, and then west on Forest Road 70 for 17.3 miles to Highway 126. Highway 126 leads west to Cuba or east toward Jemez Springs or Los Alamos.

Hiking Trails

San Pedro Parks Wilderness is well covered by about a dozen different trails, most of which originate from different trailheads located around the periphery of the Wilderness on all sides. The trails tend to gain elevation most steeply for the first several miles, then level out as they approach the parks in the high interior. The trails form, in effect, a network of interconnecting trail segments that can be pieced together to form any number of different hiking routes. The trailheads are well marked, and the trails are reasonably well worn and easy to follow along the wooded stretches, marked by blazes cut into and painted on trees, but often not well defined across open meadows. On these stretches, look for marker posts and rock cairns and the point on the far side of the meadow where the trail reenters the forest. The trail junctions are usually well marked, but because these trail junctions are numerous, and because the trails are obscure in some areas, you should definitely carry along a trail map. The routes I have chosen to describe in this section include one trail entering the Wilderness from each of the major compass headings, and I have arbitrarily described each hike with the same end point, at the heart of the large system of parks (San Pedro Park) in the central part of the Wilderness. Each trail can be done round trip in a day (in some cases, a long day), but you may want to alter the route to make a loop hike or to spend several days exploring different parts of the Wilderness.

TRAIL DESCRIPTIONS

Hike #1. Vacas Trail (#51)

This is the most popular trail in the Wilderness and has one of the smallest net elevation gains to the San Pedro Parks. The round trip distance is 17 miles, with a net elevation gain of 1,180 feet. This is a well-worn trail that runs through pleasant terrain, with running water available at a number of points along the way. The hiking is easy, but if done as a day hike, it takes a long day and the trail length may factor the difficulty rating up a notch. The trailhead is most easily approached from Cuba as described above under directions to the south and east sides of the Wilderness. The trail begins at the parking area by the road.

The first mile of the trail follows the Clear Creek Drainage to San Gregorio Reservoir, a smallish lake stocked with trout that is the object of most of the traffic on this part of the trail. The trail skirts the east side of the lake, turns east through a small saddle, and then continues to follow Clear Creek to the north. After a little more than an hour, the trail climbs northeast out of the Clear Creek drainage and runs through forests and meadows to a stream crossing at the Rio de las Vacas, where the Palomas Trail joins. This junction is a little more than 5 miles from the trailhead. The trail then follows the Rio de las Vacas north, passing the Los Piños trail junction 0.2 miles farther, and joining the Peñas Negras Trail after another 2.2 miles. For dayhikers, this section of trail goes through some spacious parks that may make you wish you had done the hike as a backpack trip, instead of trying to see it all in one day. From the Peñas Negras Trail junction, the Vacas Trail turns west away from the stream and continues about another mile to the terminus at San Pedro Park. If you are doing the hike as a backpacking trip, there are numerous places to camp in the system of parks in the large interior, preferably within the treeline at a place already used by previous campers. While I wouldn't term the camping activity here as heavy, there is enough so that it is worth the effort to avoid scarring the area with additional campfire rings, particularly in the open parks. Don't forget to bring along some insect repellent, as you will probably have to contend with mosquitos. You can complete the hike by returning the way you came or by adding a loop, using segments of Trails #46 and #435, adding 2 miles to the return leg.

Hike #2. Vega Redonda and Upper Rio Puerco Trails (#43 & #385)

The Vega Redonda Trail is easiest to reach from the town of Coyote and is named for the beautiful meadow or park that is located at the upper terminus of the trail, 3 miles beyond the Wilderness boundary, or 3.5 miles beyond the lower trailhead. The elevation gain to Vega Redonda is 1,100 feet, making the trail somewhat steeper than it seems. From Vega Redonda, sections of the Rio Puerco and Vacas Trails can be followed another 3.1 miles to reach San Pedro Park, with an additional net elevation gain of 380 feet. The total round-trip hiking distance to and from San Pedro Park is 13.2 miles. Water is abundant along the trail.

To find the trailhead from Coyote, follow the access directions above to the intersection of Forest Roads 172 and 103. Continue south on Forest Road 103 from this intersection, and drive 5.1 miles to the junction with Forest Road 93. Turn west on Forest Road 93 and travel about 2 miles to the spacious Resumidero Campground, on your right just as the road bends to the south. Park in the campground and locate the trailhead a short distance south of the campground on Road 93. The route heads west from the trailhead up the rough double track road, which becomes a trail at the Wilderness boundary, and continues up along the stream through mixed conifer forest until turning south away from the stream at a small meadow. About another mile of hiking leads to a beaver pond at the north tip of Vega Redonda. Enjoy the grand scenery as you walk south along the edge of this meadow, following marker posts to the junction with the Rio Puerco Trail and a set of trail signs with suspect trail

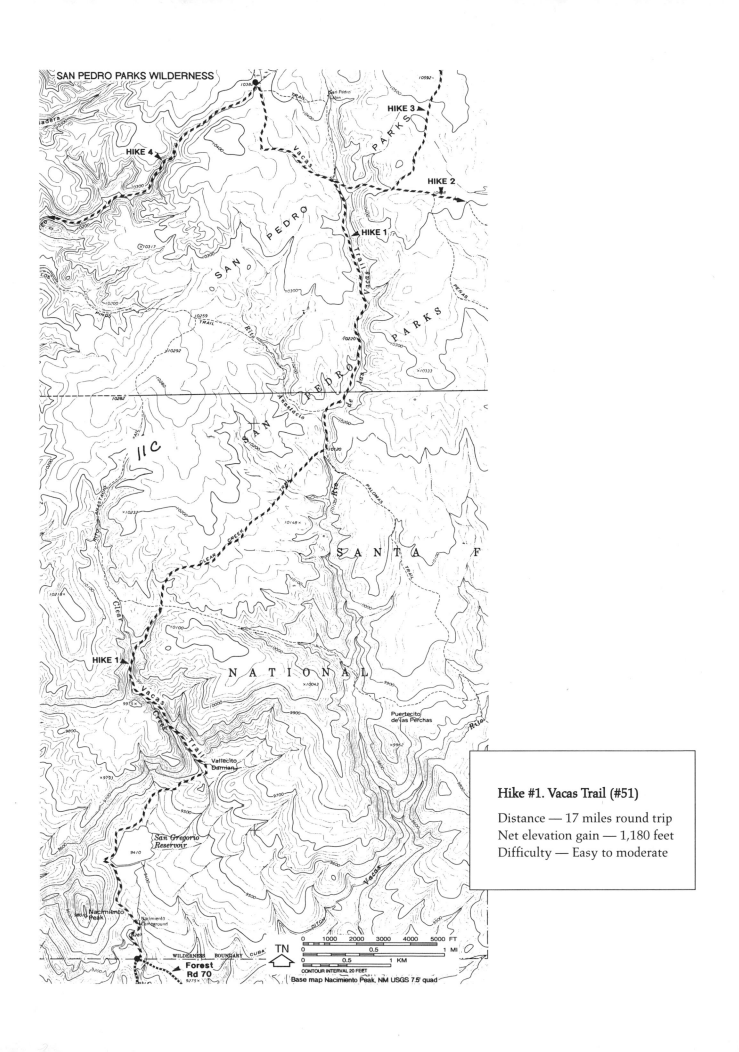

Hike #1. Vacas Trail (#51)

Distance — 17 miles round trip
Net elevation gain — 1,180 feet
Difficulty — Easy to moderate

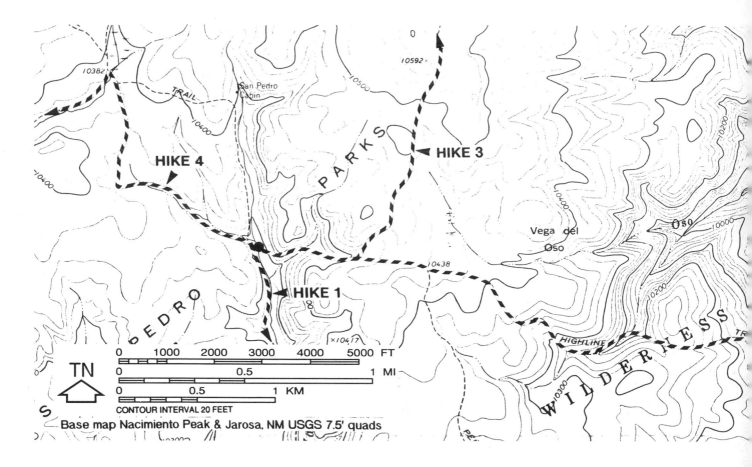

Base map Nacimiento Peak & Jarosa, NM USGS 7.5' quads

distance information. From this trail junction, head west on the Rio Puerco Trail to the far west side of the meadow and through more forest, down and out of the Oso Creek drainage, to another set of broad meadows beginning with Vega del Oso. At this point, the trail will join the Peñas Negras Trail (#32), which continues west and passes the junction with Trail #31 a short distance farther. Another stretch of beautiful scenery leads to the Rio de las Vacas, followed immediately by the Vacas Trail (#51). Follow the Vacas Trail a little under a mile to San Pedro Park, where it joins Trails #33 and #46. There are good camping spots at numerous points along the hike.

Hike #3. Red Rock and Upper Rio Capulin Trail (#30 & #31)

The Red Rock Trail (#30) is the primary access from the north side of the

---

Hike #2. Vega Redonda and Upper Rio Puerco Trails (#43 & #385)

Distance — 13.2 miles round trip
Net elevation gain — 1,100 feet
Difficulty — Easy to moderate

Wilderness, and when combined with the upper section of the Rio Capulin Trail (#31), leads to the area around San Pedro Peaks, the rounded ridge that forms the highest part of the Wilderness. The distance to San Pedro Peaks is 12.4 miles round trip, with 2,280 feet in net elevation gained. To continue all the way to San Pedro Park adds 5 additional round-trip miles, with insignificant additional elevation change, for a total round-trip hiking distance of 17.4 miles. The total

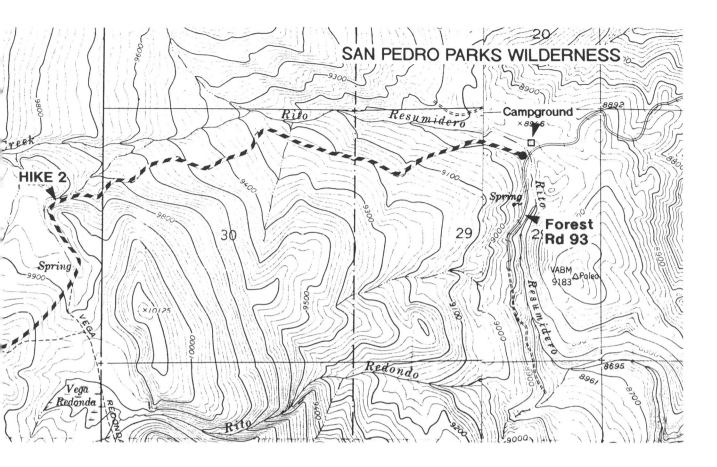

hike makes a long, rather strenuous day hike. Water is unavailable above Rio Capulin until you come to the streams in the central parks south of San Pedro Peaks, if you hike that far.

Locate the trailhead by driving on Highway 96 from either Cuba or Coyote and turning south on Forest Road 76, 4.6 miles east of the intersection with Highway 112, just west of the town of Gallina. Continue on Forest Road 76 for 4.3 miles to a sharp bend in the road, where Forest Road 14 branches off to the south and continues 1.5 miles to the trailhead. This last section of road is rough and ungraveled, and during wet weather, requires a vehicle with high clearance, if not four wheel drive. If there is snow on the ground, find another area to hike, as the snow in the north-facing timber above is certain to get considerably deeper.

From the trailhead, the trail climbs up along the Rio Gallina to the south for 1.2 miles to a junction with the Gallina Trail (#36), which cuts steeply up the slope to the right. Stay on Trail #30, which branches off to the east and levels off momentarily before taking a steep ascent to the southeast through conifer and aspen forest and passing below the red cliffs for which the trail is named. The aspen stands not only provide a pleasant hiking environment, but present one of the classic scenery attractions of the mountains in fall when the foliage turns a bright golden yellow—a time of year no doubt eagerly awaited by many a film processing lab. From the Trail #36 junction, it is another 2 miles to a crossing of the Rio Capulin (and the last source of water along the trail for a long stretch) and an intersection with Trail #31 a short distance farther on. Turn south on Trail

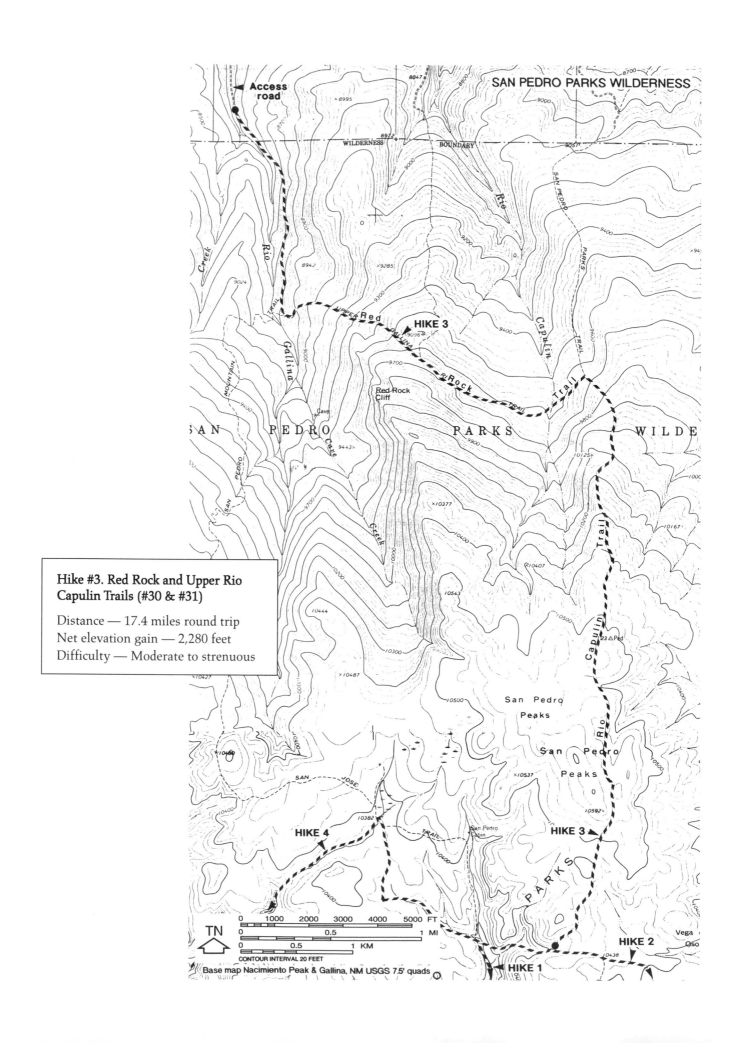

SAN PEDRO PARKS WILDERNESS

Hike #3. Red Rock and Upper Rio Capulin Trails (#30 & #31)

Distance — 17.4 miles round trip
Net elevation gain — 2,280 feet
Difficulty — Moderate to strenuous

HIKE 3

HIKE 4

HIKE 3

HIKE 2

HIKE 1

TN

| 0 | 1000 | 2000 | 3000 | 4000 | 5000 FT |

| 0 | | 0.5 | | 1 MI |

| 0 | | 0.5 | | 1 KM |

CONTOUR INTERVAL 20 FEET

Base map Nacimiento Peak & Gallina, NM USGS 7.5' quads

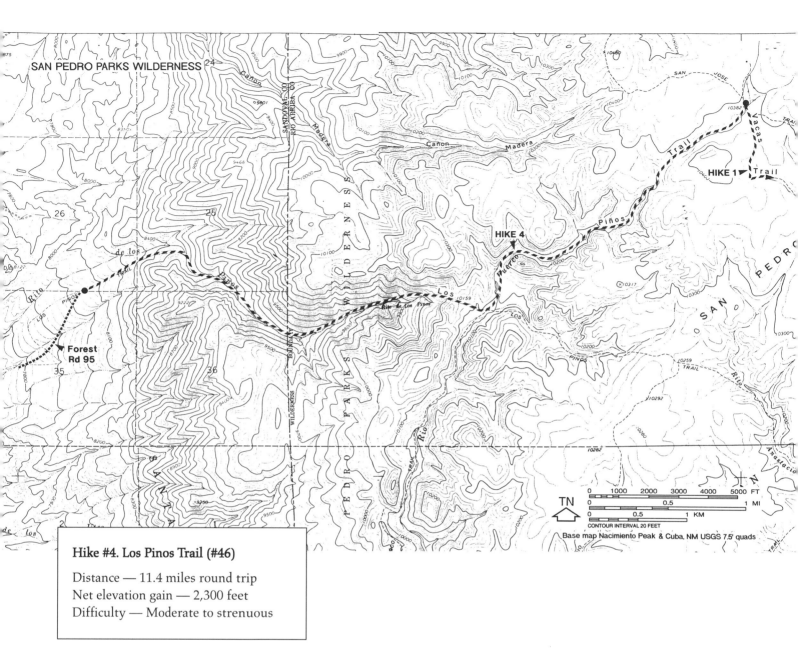

Hike #4. Los Pinos Trail (#46)

Distance — 11.4 miles round trip
Net elevation gain — 2,300 feet
Difficulty — Moderate to strenuous

#31 and begin another steep section, as the trail climbs toward the high ridge that constitutes San Pedro Peaks, reaching the high point along the ridge about 1.5 to 2 hours from the trail junction. At this point, it is worth a short climb to a vantage point for a scenic look around. One thing that sets this area apart from the other mountain areas of the state is the lack of rugged peaks with steep cirques and ridges, and the view from the high point will confirm the gentle nature of the landscape. For many day hikers, this will be the turnaround point of the hike. For those hikers continuing on to San Pedro Park, some route finding is in order, and the trail map needs to come out of the pack. As the trail breaks into the open areas in the vicinity of San Pedro Peaks, the traffic tends to disperse to the point that the trail becomes faint and hard to follow. Look for a route that continues just to the east of the highest part of the ridge and heads approximately south to join Trail #32 at the treeline along the south edge of Vega del Oso. When searching for a landmark such as this, when you aren't precisely sure of your location, take frequent mental notes of the route behind you, in case you find it necessary to return along the same line. Once on Trail #32, note your entry point to be sure of your bearings on the return leg, and continue west, joining Trail #51 for the final leg to San Pedro Park. From San Pedro Park you can reverse the route to return, or you have the further option of returning via a loop, using segments of the San Jose (#33) and Upper Gallina (#36) trails. I have not used this optional return loop, but it appears to offer a shorter and more direct return leg.

Hike #4. Los Piños Trail (#46)

The Los Piños Trail ascends the forests of the steep western slopes of the range that can be seen from Highway 44, rising up from the valley floor to the northeast of Cuba. The total trail distance to San Pedro Park is 11.4 miles round trip. The total elevation gain is 2,300 feet, with over 2,000 feet of the total in the first 3 miles of the trail. It is one of the shorter routes to San Pedro Park, but also one of the steepest. Water is plentiful along the trail.

To locate the trailhead, take Highway 44 to Cuba and turn east on Forest Road 95 at an intersection 0.5 miles north of the Highway 126 intersection. Stay on Forest Road 95, passing numerous side roads, for 6.7 miles until the road ends at a turnaround with a trail sign for the Los Piños Trail. The trail starts out on moderately sloping terrain, heading west into a small canyon that confines the Rio de los Piños. After crossing the stream, the trail begins to climb in earnest, as it continues to follow the drainage up the side of the mountain. The mountain stream and occasional small meadows provide scenery, with forests of mixed conifers interlaced with stands of aspen rising up on both sides. At 1.9 miles past the trailhead, the wilderness boundary is crossed, and 1.2 miles farther, above the headwaters of the Los Piños, is the junction with the Anastacio Trail (#435), which provides a link with the popular Vacas Trail, 2.6 miles to the east. At the trail junction, take the left fork, keeping on the Los Piños Trail. The elevation levels out at this point, and the trail assumes a northeasterly heading, following a drainage system for 2.6 miles to the upper terminus at San Pedro Park. At San Pedro Park, you may want to make a loop hike out of your return leg by hiking back down the Vacas Trail to the Anastacio Trail junction, and back to the Los Piños Trail via the Anastacio Trail. The total round trip distance is increased by 3.3 miles using this loop option, but either way it is a reasonably strenuous trip if done as a day hike, requiring 6 to 10 hours to complete the hike. On this hike, you stand a good chance of getting your feet immersed in water, making an extra pair or two of dry socks a good accessory.

For Further Information:

Santa Fe National Forest
 Cuba Ranger District
 P.O. Box 130
 Cuba, NM 87013
 (505) 289-3264

Santa Fe National Forest
 Coyote Ranger District
 Coyote, NM 87012
 (505) 638-5547

GENERAL DESCRIPTION

The Pecos Wilderness is located in northern New Mexico northeast of Santa Fe at the southern end of the Sangre de Cristo Mountains in the Santa Fe and Carson National Forests. It is a heavily forested mountain area of 223,667 acres, with elevations ranging from about 8,400 feet to 13,102 feet at Truchas Peak, the second highest point in the state. The Wilderness is characterized by dense forests, towering peaks with sheer granite walls, grassy meadows and ridges, mountain streams, and glacial lakes. Its alpine features and beautiful scenery have long made it one of the premier outdoor destinations in the state. It probably competes with the Sandia Wilderness as the most heavily used hiking area in the state but is clearly the most popular for overnight backpacking. Because of its large size there is a large, well developed system of trails to choose from, a few of which are relatively lightly used. But this is not an undiscovered hiking area; during the peak summer hiking season, it receives a lot of use from both in-state and out-of-state visitors, and you can expect to have company on many of the trails. Annual precipitation in the Pecos Wilderness averages 35 to 40 inches per year, with half of that coming from winter snows. Due to the high elevation and long, cold winters, the snowpack is sometimes not sufficiently melted out to permit unimpeded travel until early to mid-June at some elevations. Summer daytime temperatures average a pleasant 70 degrees F, but at night it can dip into the 30s. May and June are relatively dry, and afternoon showers and thunderstorms are common in July and August, although it can rain, sleet, or snow any month of the year. Rain protection and warm clothing are a must in the Pecos

Looking Northeast from Hamilton Mesa

Pecos Wilderness

Wilderness, and hypothermia is something to be aware of. Winter storms start in mid- to late October and typically continue through April and sometimes into May.

Hiking in the Pecos Wilderness is done primarily through the forested slopes that are typical of the mountain environment. This includes numerous species of conifer trees, along with extensive stands of Aspen. The latter are especially apparent in the fall, when the foliage turns a brilliant yellow-gold, adding a splash of color to the scenery.

Grassy clearings are scattered about the lower to mid-elevation levels, and at the higher elevations above the tree line, peaks and ridges are covered with arctic tundra, and this is where the really great vistas are located. Wildflowers are common at all levels. Water sources are fairly abundant in the Pecos Wilderness, but water should be purified before drinking, as it is not otherwise considered safe. Streams and lakes are natural attractions for back country camping, and some of these areas have received such heavy use that some camping restrictions are in effect (more about this in the Trail Descriptions that follow). If you enjoy trout fishing, there are various opportunities to fish the streams and lakes for fish that tend to be small but fun to catch; just make sure you have your fishing license. Hiking permits were once a requirement but are not in use at this time. Car camping is available at a number of Forest Service campgrounds around the periphery of the Wilderness. These are shown on the Pecos Wilderness and Santa Fe National Forest maps.

Map Coverage

All the Pecos Wilderness trails described in this section, as well as those that aren't, are shown on the Pecos Wilderness Map, which is produced and distributed by the U.S. Forest Service. This is the best overall map to get, showing topography and trails, as well as access points and campgrounds. The USGS 7.5-minute scale topo maps covering the area are numerous and are thus referenced in the individual trail descriptions. The USGS topo maps give better topographical detail, but since some of the trails are missing or not accurately shown, it is still a good idea to carry the Wilderness Map or to update your topo maps from the maps in this book.

Access

There are a number of different entry points on all sides of the Wilderness, and the access directions to each of these is included with the individual trail descriptions. Most of the Pecos Wilderness entry points are accessible by paved road and standard passenger car. One important development that has occurred recently and exists as of this writing is that the road to Jacks Creek and Panchuela Campgrounds is presently closed, due to unsafe levels of lead in the old mine tailings that were used to surface the road. Jacks Creek and Panchuela are two of the most popular entry points for the Wilderness, and I would assume that they will eventually be reopened. However, the timetable is not definite, and you should check with the Forest Service Ranger Station in the town of Pecos (see "For Further Information" at end of section) before planning a hiking trip leaving from one of these trailheads. Otherwise, "plan B" may go into effect shortly after you reach the road closure signs.

Hiking Trails

There are more designated trails in the Pecos Wilderness than I care to try and count, and a look at the Pecos Wilderness Map will indicate the extent of this trail system. To try and describe all of the trails is well beyond the scope of this book. Some of the trails are somewhat redundant in terms of destination and area traversed, some are merely segments connecting other trails, and in any case, I haven't hiked them all anyway. The hikes described in this book, some of which include parts of several trails, include many of the classic Pecos Wilderness hikes that are still among the most popular. They traverse the most scenic parts of the Wilderness, they are widely located, the trailheads are easy to reach, and, because of their popularity (or in spite of it), they provide a good group to choose from if you are unfamiliar with the area. If you want to try some of the more out of the way hikes, consult your map or the trail guides listed at the end of this section. Take note of the road closure mentioned under "Access" above, which temporarily eliminates from consideration several of the hikes described in this section. Also note that to protect the scenic beauty and fragile environment of the Wilderness, the Forest Service has closed several areas to camping because of overuse. These include the area around Pecos Falls and Beatty's Flats, as well as all the lake basins. Also excluded in these areas are campfires, although in some cases, you would have to walk so far to find enough firewood for a campfire that it wouldn't be worth it. But don't despair; there are still plenty of good places to camp, and for dayhiking it won't matter anyway.

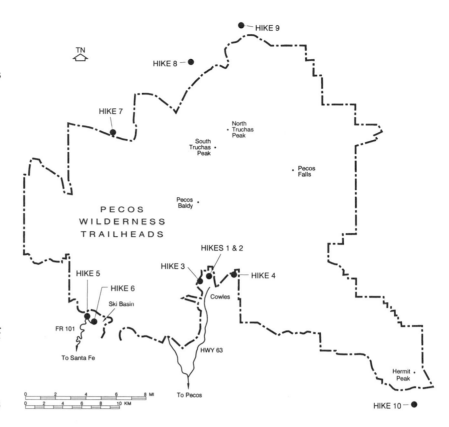

TRAIL DESCRIPTIONS

Hike #1. Jacks Creek Campground to Beatty's Cabin and Pecos Falls

This hike takes you into the heart of the Pecos Wilderness through lots of nice scenery. Beatty's Cabin, no longer standing, is the site of a 19th-century prospector's cabin on a pretty stretch of the Pecos River called Beatty's Flats. Pecos

Falls, several miles farther up the river, is a stepped series of waterfalls. Both destinations are among the most popular in the Wilderness—so much so that camping is not permitted at either location. In addition to these attractions, there are scenic views along the way in the vicinity of Round Mountain. The round trip distance to Beatty's Flats is 10 miles, with an additional 7 miles of round trip hiking if Pecos Falls in included in the plan. Net elevation gain is 560 feet to Beatty's Flats and 1,360 feet to Pecos Falls, but an additional 640 feet should be added to these totals for elevation lost on the north side of Round Mountain. This is a moderate or maybe harder hike, depending upon how far you go. If you go all the way to Pecos Falls and back in a day, it will be a long, tiring hike. Water is plentiful along the hike at the Pecos River in the vicinity of Beatty's Flats and Pecos Falls. USGS topo map coverage for this hike requires the 7.5-minute scale Cowles, Pecos Falls, and Truchas Peak maps.

To reach the trailhead at Jacks Creek Campground, take the Pecos/Glorieta exit off Interstate 25 southeast of Santa Fe, and continue east to the town of Pecos. Turn north at Pecos on Highway 63, and continue until Highway 63 ends about 2 miles north of the community of Cowles at the entrance to the campground. In case Jacks Creek Campground is not accessible because of the road closure, an alternative starting point for reaching Beatty's Cabin and Pecos Falls is at Iron Gate Campground (see hike #4). The route out of Iron Gate, which begins with Trail #249 heading north across Hamilton Mesa, has about 300 feet less elevation gain and is also a popular hike.

Begin the hike at Jacks Creek Campground by taking Trail #25 up the east slope of the canyon. The trail is steep at first but gradually eases up as it follows the ridge up toward Round Mountain. At the trail fork with Trail #257 below Round Mountain, take the east branch and continue almost another 2 miles to a trail junction with Trail #26 on the east side of the mountain. Much of this area lacks tree cover, and you will have some nice views across the Wilderness. At the second trail junction, stay on Trail #25 by again taking the east trail branch, which begins to contour down the side of the Pecos River Canyon, reaching river level at Beatty's Flats. The best route for continuing on to Pecos Falls is to follow the trail on up the river for another 0.5 miles to the junction with Rito del Padre, and then take the east branch at the trail fork (Trail #24), which climbs up along the west slope of the canyon. At the junction with Trail #239, the segment of the intersecting trail leading to the east drops down to Pecos Falls. If you are backpacking, the Pecos Falls area puts you

---

Hike #1. Jacks Creek Campground to Beatty's Cabin and Pecos Falls

Distance — 10.0 miles round trip to Beatty's Cabin; 17.0 mile round trip to Pecos Falls
Net elevation gain — 1,360 feet
Difficulty — Moderate to strenuous

Hike #2. Jacks Creek Campground to Pecos Baldy Lake and Truchas Peaks

Distance — 16.0 miles round trip to Pecos Baldy Lake; 27.0 mi round trip to Truchas Peaks
Net elevation gain — 2,460 feet to Pecos Baldy Lake; 4,063 feet South Truchas Peak
Difficulty — Strenuous

Hike #3. Panchuela Campground to Horsethief Meadow

Distance — 11.0 miles round trip
Net elevation gain — 1,600 feet
Difficulty — Moderate

Hike #4. Iron Gate Campground to Mora Flats

Distance — 6.0 to 8.0 miles round trip
Net elevation gain — 320 feet
Difficulty — Easy

(See map on page 99 for Hike #7)

---

in position to continue on into the far northeast part of the Wilderness; it is steep and rugged, but remote and uncrowded.

Hike #2. Jacks Creek Campground to Pecos Baldy Lake and Truchas Peaks

This hike is a backpack of two or more nights that leads into the heart of the Pecos high country and includes sparkling glacial lakes, towering alpine peaks, and tundra-clad slopes above timberline with scenic vistas in all directions. From Jacks Creek Campground at an elevation of 9,040 feet, it is a 16-mile round trip hike to Pecos Baldy Lake (11,320 feet, or a 27-

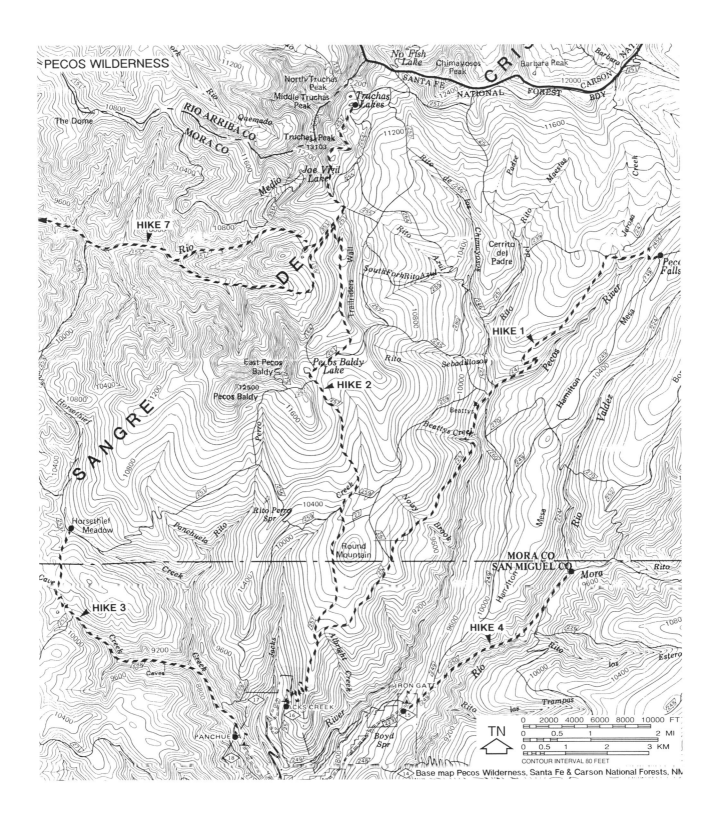

mile round trip hike to Truchas Lakes (11,720 feet). Pecos Baldy Peak and the Truchas Peaks tower above their respective lakes and present the opportunity for summit climbs that are nontechnical but steep, and may be challenging for those who are not acclimated or are bothered by vertical exposure. South Truchas Peak, at 13,103 feet elevation, is the second highest point in the state. The trails covered by this hike are among the most popular in the Wilderness, particularly the section to Pecos Baldy Lake, which can also be done as a long day hike. The USGS 7.5-minute scale topo maps covering this area are the Cowles and Truchas Peak maps.

There are several things to be aware of on this hike. First, as previously mentioned, no camping is permitted in the Pecos Baldy and Truchas Lake basins. Also, the weather tends to be more extreme at the higher elevations, and any hiking on the high peaks and ridges should be started early in the day, if possible, to allow for the contingency of fast developing thunderstorms, which typically occur in the afternoons. It is particularly important not to get caught on high terrain if lightning is in the area, and this applies not only to the big peaks but also to the segment of trail along Trailriders Wall. If weather is a problem, there is a lower elevation trail alternative to Trailriders Wall (check your map). When scrambling on the high peaks, keep in mind that this is serious terrain that requires caution in places. Watch for loose rock, stay off vertical faces, and avoid traversing steep snow gullies, especially when you can't see the bottom of the runout.

Follow the same approach route as for Hike #1 to locate the trailhead at Jacks Creek Campground. The first 2.5 miles of the hike is also the same as for Hike #1, as you follow Trail #25 on a steep ascent up the forested east side of the canyon to a trail junction on the broad grassy ridge south of Round Mountain. Take the west fork at this intersection (Forest Trail #257), following several marker posts around the west side of Round Mountain, and drop down into the trees to Jacks Creek. The trail continues along the creek for a distance, then begins a steep ascent that ends at the cirque or basin containing Pecos Baldy Lake below the east face of East Pecos Baldy. The cirque was gouged out 10,000 to 12,000 years ago by a glacier moving down off the peak. If you are inclined to scramble up to the summit of East Pecos Baldy, the best route is to gain the ridge on the north side and continue up the ridge to the top. From the top of East Pecos Baldy, another ridge leads southwest to the summit of Pecos Baldy at 12,500 feet. From the lake below, the most straightforward route to the Truchas Peaks area is Forest Trail #251, which runs north from the lake and ascends the smooth ridge to the north known as Trailriders Wall. The trail stays more or less on the crest of Trailriders Wall and continues north, passing a couple of trail intersections along the way, and drops down into the small basin containing the paired Truchas Lakes. From the lakes, a crude path winds up through the talus slopes to the west and gains a saddle on the summit ridge. From this point, Truchas Peak, the tallest summit to the south, and Middle Truchas Peak can be easily reached; North Truchas Peak is a bit more of a scramble. There is also an informal trail leading down the west side of the ridge into the Truchas Amphitheater. The views from the summits are unexcelled. From the lakes, you can return back to Jacks Creek Campground by way of the approach route, or complete a loop trip by taking one of the trail routes that leads to the east and return back down the Pecos River drainage.

Hike #3. Panchuela Campground to Horsethief Meadow

This is a moderate hike that climbs up along a creek with interesting limestone caves and ends at a large picturesque meadow. The trails are heavily used, mostly by day hikers, but there are also good camping spots, with water plentiful along much of the route. The total round trip distance covered is 11 miles, with 1,600 feet of elevation gain. If you want to bring along the USGS 7.5-minute scale topo maps of the area, get the Cowles and Truchas Peak maps.

To access the trailhead at Panchuela Campground, travel on Interstate 25 southeast of Santa Fe to the Pecos/Glorieta exit and then continue east to the town of Pecos. Turn north at Pecos on Highway 63 and continue north to the community of Cowles and turn west on Forest Road 121 toward the Windsor Creek Campground. Immediately after turning off toward the Windsor Creek Campground, turn north on Forest Road 305, which leads a little over a mile to Panchuela Campground. From the parking area at the campground, walk upstream until you find the small bridge across the creek that marks the start of the trail. Continue up the creek for 1 mile to a trail junction at the Wilderness boundary. Take the west fork (Trail #288) and follow an easy path up Panchuela Creek until the trail crosses the creek and turns west, leading up along Cave Creek. You will begin to encounter the caves for which the creek was named shortly after turning up the creek. At the 4-mile point, the trail climbs steeply up the north branch of the drainage, passes the Trail #251 turnoff to Stewart Lake, and leads north to the high point of the hike on a ridge. From here, the trail (now Trail #253) drops down to Horsethief Meadow, a pleasant, open area with good camping. From Horsethief Meadow, you can return the way you came, or continue northeast to Pecos Baldy Lake or Northwest toward the Rio Medio drainage.

Hike #4. Iron Gate Campground to Mora Flats

Iron Gate Campground is a good jumping-off point for destinations along the Pecos River drainage, as well as some of the area in the eastern and southeastern part of the Wilderness. The hike described here is an easy day hike or overnight backpack that climbs 160 feet to the high elevation point of the hike on Hamilton Mesa, a broad, smooth ridge with nice views to the east and west, and then drops 320 feet down to the Rio Mora. The stretch of river above and below the point where the trail joins is called Mora Flats. It is a flat, pleasant length of river bottom that is a favorite camping area and also a decent area for trout fishing, although the fish tend to be small. The round trip hiking distance is 6 to 8 miles, depending upon how far along the Rio Mora you walk. The route to Mora Flats is heavily used and is only the initial part of a more complex system of trails that penetrate farther into areas to the north, east, and south, so if you want to extend the trip into more solitary parts of the Wilderness, there are a number of route possibilities. The USGS 7.5-minute topo map covering this hike is the Elk Mountain quad.

To reach the trailhead at Iron Gate Campground, take Interstate 25 southeast of Santa Fe and take the Pecos/Glorieta exit and continue east to the town of Pecos, turning north on Highway 63. After you cross the bridge at Terrero, continue north about 5 miles to the intersection with Forest Road 223, which leads north and east for several miles to Iron Gate Campground. The forest road is rough but adequate for passenger car traffic if it isn't too muddy. The trailhead

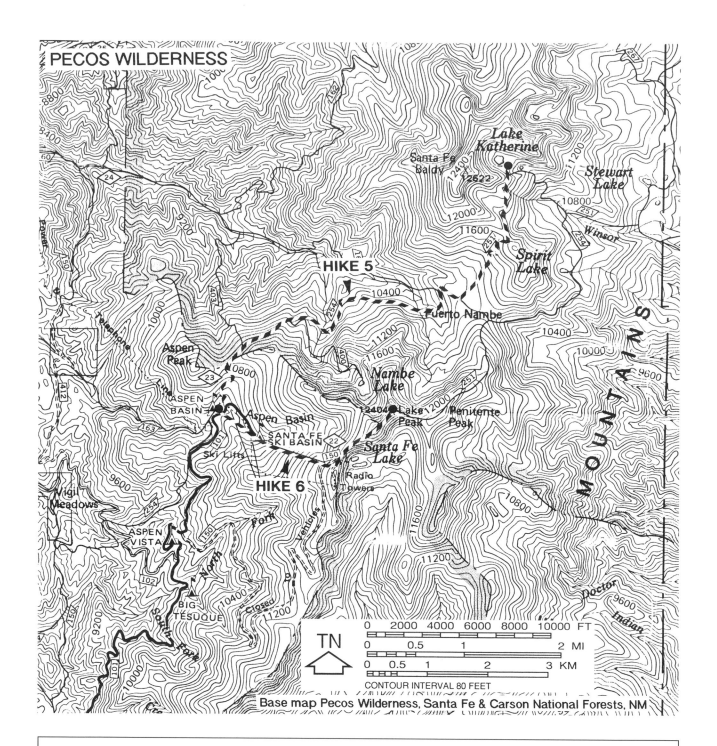

Hike #5. Aspen Basin to Puerto Nambe and Lake Katherine

Distance — 8.0 miles round trip to Puerto Nambe; 14.0 miles round trip to Lake Katherine
Net elevation gain — 830 feet to Puerto Nambe; 1,490 feet to Lake Katherine
Difficulty — Moderate to strenuous

Hike #6. Santa Fe Ski Basin to Lake Peak

Distance — 5.0 miles round trip
Net elevation gain — 2,010 feet
Difficulty — Moderate to strenuous

is at the north end of the campground, from which Trail #249 climbs through the trees for 0.6 miles to a trail junction on Hamilton Mesa. The trail branch you want to take is Trail #250, which branches off to the east, but if you have the time, include as a side hike the segment of Trail #249 that continues north of the trail junction for about a mile to the top of Hamilton Mesa. This area along the mesa is covered in grass and wildflowers, and there are great views of the Pecos Baldy and Truchas Peak massifs, separated by Trailriders Wall, off to the west. This also provides a popular alternative route to Beattys Flats and Pecos Falls. Back to the trail junction, follow Trail #250 as it drops down the side of the canyon to the Rio Mora and Mora Flats. There are good camping spots all along the Rio Mora to the junction with the Rio Valdez. If you want more seclusion, continue upstream along either tributary.

Hike #5. Aspen Basin to Puerto Nambe and Lake Katherine

This is a moderate to strenuous day hike or backpack, which begins at the parking lot west of the Santa Fe Ski Area and takes a route through the forest cover to Puerto Nambe, a broad mountain pass with nice views, and on to Lake Katherine, nestled below the 12,622-foot Santa Fe Baldy. Many hikers also include a scramble up to the summit of Santa Fe Baldy. The hiking distance is 8 miles round trip to Puerto Nambe, or 14 miles round trip if you go all the way to Lake Katherine. The trailhead is at 10,250 feet, and the trail gains almost 600 feet before a long descent followed by a steep climb to Puerto Nambe at 11,080 feet, and an additional 660-foot elevation gain to Lake Katherine. This is a heavily used route year round, although in winter it is a ski or snowshoe trail. The scenery is espe-

cially nice when the Aspens are changing color in the fall. The USGS 7.5-minute scale topo maps for the area are the Aspen Basin and Cowles maps.

To reach the trailhead, travel to Santa Fe and drive north on St. Francis Avenue (from the St. Francis exit off Interstate 25) to the second intersection with Paseo de Peralta, north of the intersection with Alameda Road. Drive east on Paseo de Peralta to Washington Avenue, just beyond the distinctive pink-colored Masonic Temple, and turn north on Washington. Continue north a few blocks and turn east on Artist Road, which is the start of a 17-mile paved route leading to and terminating at the Ski Area, located in a large bowl called Aspen Basin. Once you reach the Ski Area, continue to the northwest corner of the lower parking area, where the trail begins, and park.

The hike to Puerto Nambe is on the Windsor Trail (Trail #254), which begins with a steep ascent of the north side of the basin to an open area at the top of the ridge, where the Wilderness boundary begins. Continue on a long descending contour to the east, passing several trail junctions over the next 3 miles, but stay on Trail #254 to Puerto Nambe/Lake Katherine until you have made the steep climb up to Puerto Nambe, a scenic meadow area on a high shelf in the upper Nambe drainage. Here you will come to the Skyline Trail (Trail #251), which leads to Lake Katherine. This provides the most direct access to the lake, although you can also get there by continuing on the Windsor Trail and taking a longer path past Spirit Lake. Hike up the Skyline Trail as it takes a steep route up the slope to the northeast and crests on a saddle at the top of the divide. From here, you can either continue on the trail as it drops down across a cirque to Lake Katherine or climb up the ridgeline to the northwest for a 900-foot ascent to the summit of Santa Fe Baldy. This makes a long, tiring day hike, but the views are outstanding.

Hike #6. Santa Fe Ski Basin to Lake Peak

This hike begins at 10,400 feet at the base of the downhill ski area in Aspen Basin and climbs about 2.5 miles (5 miles round trip) to the summit of Lake Peak at 12,409 feet. It is a short but strenuous route that provides quick access to the top of one of the high Pecos Wilderness peaks, with inspirational vistas in all directions. It is most often done as a day outing and can be extended into a longer loop hike using the west end of the Windsor Trail. No water is available along the hike, and wind and rain protection should be taken along to provide for the typical difference in weather conditions that may exist between the upper and lower elevations. The appropriate USGS 7.5-minute topo map for the area is the Aspen Basin quad.

To reach the hike, follow the access directions for Hike #5, and upon reaching the parking area west of the ski facility, proceed to the east end and park your vehicle. Walk east from the parking area past the ski lodge to the base of the ski runs at the north end of the ski bowl. Begin the hike by ascending one of the ski runs that lead east up to the ridge that tops the ski area on the east side; there is no trail to follow here other than the ski runs, but it is a straightforward matter to make your way up the steep slopes to the high ridge. Once on top of the ridge, you will have most of the elevation gain out of the way and you should end up somewhere in the vicinity north of the radio towers, from which Trail #251 runs north along the ridge. Continue north along the trail as it follows the ridge about 0.5 miles to the summit of Lake Peak. From the summit, an additional 0.25-mile hike north along the continuation of the ridge leads to a nice overlook of the Rio Nambe

drainage, although this last stretch requires a moderately exposed traverse to the right, below a steep rocky section of the ridge. The other option for extending the hike from the summit of Lake Peak is to follow Trail #251 about 0.5 miles along the ridge to the east, down across the saddle, and up to Penitente Peak. From Penitente Peak, the trail drops down to the north and connects with the Windsor Trail. Other alternatives for reaching Trail #251 on the ridge above the east end of the ski area include a hike of several miles along the Aspen Vista road (Forest Road 150) or purchasing a ride up on the ski lift.

Hike #7. Borrego Mesa Campground to Trailriders Wall via the Rio Medio Trail

If this hike is followed as far as Trailriders Wall or beyond, it will be done as a backpacking trip of one or more nights. Since the trail follows the Rio Medio for nearly its entire length, there are numerous spots to camp with nearby running water, or you can day hike as far up the stream as you want and return. If done in its entirety, this hike is a moderately strenuous trip of 21 miles round trip, with 3,060 feet of elevation gain. The trail climbs up through forest cover, with occasional meadows and numerous stream crossings; if you want to keep your boots dry you will probably need to take along a pair of running shoes for wading. Once on the broad slopes below Trailriders Wall, you will encounter extensive high alpine meadows, a couple of small lakes, and a nice view back down the Rio Medio drainage. The crest of Trailriders Wall, which is actually a broad grassy ridge, gives access to the high parts of the Wilderness around Truchas and Pecos Baldy Peaks and provides an encompassing view of much of the area. The trail is not as heavily hiked as many of the Pecos trails, and you probably

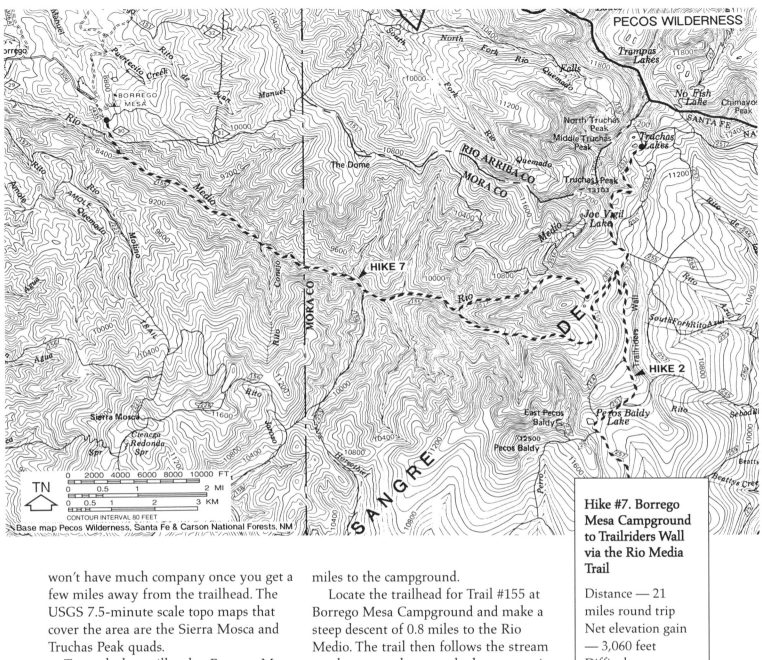

CONTOUR INTERVAL 80 FEET

Base map Pecos Wilderness, Santa Fe & Carson National Forests, NM

TN

HIKE 7

HIKE 2

Hike #7. Borrego Mesa Campground to Trailriders Wall via the Rio Media Trail

Distance — 21 miles round trip
Net elevation gain — 3,060 feet
Difficulty — Strenuous

---

won't have much company once you get a few miles away from the trailhead. The USGS 7.5-minute scale topo maps that cover the area are the Sierra Mosca and Truchas Peak quads.

To reach the trailhead at Borrego Mesa Campground, drive north from Santa Fe on Highway 84 for about 16 miles to just after the Los Alamos turnoff, and turn east on to State Highway 503. Continue for 11 miles to the village of Cundiyo. After crossing a bridge just past the village, the road continues for another 2.5 miles to a junction with Forest Road 306. Turn on to Road 306 and continue several

miles to the campground.

Locate the trailhead for Trail #155 at Borrego Mesa Campground and make a steep descent of 0.8 miles to the Rio Medio. The trail then follows the stream southeast on a long, gradual ascent, as it switches back and forth between both banks. At the 6-mile point, you will pass the junction for Trail #158 on the right and the Brazos Cabin site (nice campsite) a short distance beyond at a meadow where the stream splits. About 1 mile farther, the trail splits at another fork in the stream, with Trail #351 following the north fork of the stream and Trail #155 following the south fork. Each trail fork makes a steep 2 to 3 mile loop around to the east side of the obvious peak between the stream forks, rejoining again near two small lakes on a bench to the east of the peak on the lower slopes of Trailriders Wall. The trails are obscure in spots, and you may have to do some searching. A final short, steep climb up from the lakes leads to the crest of Trailriders Wall and a junction with Trail #251.

Hike #8. Trampas Canyon Campground to Trampas Lakes and Hidden Lake

The Trampas Lakes, looking like twin footprints, and the somewhat lower-elevation Hidden Lake, are glacially formed lakes located in a high cirque at the head of Trampas Canyon. This hike climbs up the canyon to the lakes in a 13 to 14-mile round trip route that gains about 2,500 feet in elevation. It is a moderate to strenuous hike that can be done either as a day hike or an overnight backpack, with abundant water available along the route. The USGS 7.5-minute scale topo maps covering the area are the El Valle and Truchas Peak quads.

To reach the trailhead at Trampas Canyon Campground, drive north from Santa Fe on Highway 84 for about 16 miles to just after the Los Alamos turnoff and turn right onto State Highway 503. Follow Highway 503 through the village of Cundiyo, then north to the intersection with Highway 76, and continue east on Highway 76 past the villages of Truchas and Las Trampas. About 1 mile past Las Trampas, turn right on Forest Road 207 and continue for 9 miles to the campground.

The trail (Trail #31) begins at 8,900 feet at the Trampas Canyon Campground and follows the Rio de Las Trampas up a steep canyon to the southeast. After a little over a mile, the trail crosses the Wilderness boundary, and as the canyon walls steepen, you will notice perennial avalanche chutes coming down the south side of the canyon, now populated mostly by shrubs and small aspens. One particularly monstrous snow avalanche during the winter of 1972/1973 swept down the canyon and gave vivid testimony to the power of the event by depositing great amounts of broken and twisted timber for several hundred feet along the trail. And during the same winter, San Leonardo Lake in the next canyon to the south was filled with avalanche debris; it serves as a reminder that this rugged mountain area demands respect and can harbor a potential for danger for the unwary and ill-prepared. The trail continues up the canyon in straightforward fashion, with switchbacks on the steep sections, to a trail junction about 6 miles from the trailhead. The trail that drops down to the west leads 1 mile down to Hidden Lake, and the trail branch that continues straight leads 0.5 miles up to the Trampas Lakes. These mountain lakes are a pleasant destination, nestled in the forest cover surrounded by towering walls that were shaped by deep glaciers. Further hiking possibilities at this point will be limited by the steep terrain, but a nice addition to the hike is to scramble up the steep slopes south of the Trampas Lakes to the high ridge on the south side of the cirque. Sheeps Head is the high point on the ridge to the south and west of the lakes, and the strenuous climb up is rewarded by a fine view on top, including the Truchas Amphitheater to the south and the Truchas Peaks to the south and east. Camping at the lakes is not permitted, but there are decent spots a little farther down along the stream.

Hike #9. Santa Barbara Campground to the Santa Barbara Divide via the West Fork of the Santa Barbara River.

This hike enters the Pecos Wilderness from its north end and follows Trails #24 and #25 up the West Fork of the Santa

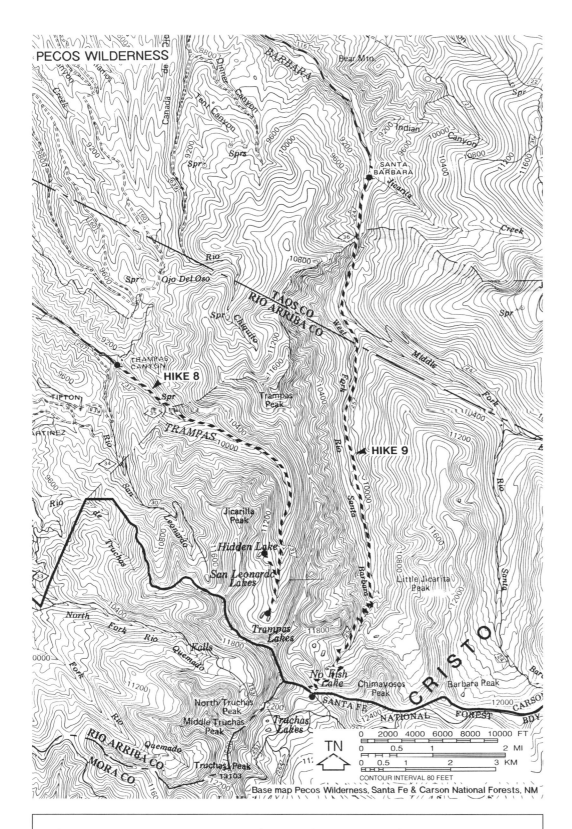

PECOS WILDERNESS

Base map Pecos Wilderness, Santa Fe & Carson National Forests, NM

CONTOUR INTERVAL 80 FEET

Hike #8. Trampas Canyon Campground to Trampas Lakes and Hidden Lake.

Distance — 13.0 to 14.0 miles round trip
Net elevation gain — 2,500 feet
Difficulty — Moderate to strenuous

Hike #9. Santa Barbara Campground to the Santa Barbara Divide via the West Fork Trail

Distance — 17.0 miles round trip
Net elevation gain — 2,900 feet
Difficulty — Strenuous

Barbara River south to the massif of peaks and ridges called the Santa Barbara Divide, which cuts east/west across the Wilderness. The round trip distance to the top of the Divide between Chimayosos and North Truchas Peaks is 17 miles. The starting elevation is 8,900 feet, and the elevation at the saddle atop the divide is 11,800 feet, making it a fairly strenuous hike, although most of the trail along the river is an easy walk, with available water and lots of camping spots. It can be done either as an overnight backpack or a day hike, which is long and strenuous if hiked the full distance, but less challenging and still enjoyable without including the final steep section up the Divide. The hike has plenty of nice forest and meadow scenery along the river and spectacular views from the alpine-like terrain of the Divide, and although it is the most popular route on the north end of the Wilderness, it receives much less hiking pressure than most of the trails entering on the south side.

To reach the Santa Barbara Campground, take Highway 68 between Española and Taos to the Highway 75 junction at La Cienega. Drive east on Highway 75 to the village of Peñasco, where you turn south on to Highway 73 at a bend in the road. Continue south to Forest Road 116, which follows the Santa Barbara River for 3 miles to the campground.

Begin the hike at the Santa Barbara Campground by heading south on Trail #24, which follows the river 1 mile to the Wilderness boundary and then another mile to a fork in the trail. At this point, our route continues south on Trail #25, which continues to follow the West Fork of the river. However, it is worth digressing a moment to briefly discuss the alternative trail branch (Trail #24), which turns east and heads up the Middle Fork of the Santa Barbara River. This trail

climbs steeply at first as it follows the Middle Fork up into the high and relatively remote area that drains the north slopes of the Santa Barbara Divide. The trail splits again where the East Fork of the river joins the Middle Fork, with each trail branch continuing up the respective river forks. There are good areas for camping along both forks, and this region of the Wilderness is a good choice to consider for a backpacking trip if solitude is important to you; it is a sizable area with nice wilderness scenery and low hiker density. Both trail branches eventually climb to the top of the Divide, with the Middle Fork Trail continuing on over the Divide and down to the Pecos Falls area and beyond. Getting back to the trail junction on the West Fork, continue the hike by walking south on Trail #25, which crosses the Middle Fork and follows the West Fork for several miles of easy elevation gain through forest cover and occasional meadow areas with wildflowers. As the trail reaches a point west of Little Jicarita Peak, the elevation steepens abruptly, and it is here that most day hikers turn back. The remaining distance of just over 2 miles to the top of the Divide gains about 1,400 feet as the trail switchbacks up the head of the West Fork, past No Fish Lake, and up a final steep section to the saddle on the ridge between Chimayosos Peak and North Truchas Peak. Here your exertions will be rewarded by some spectacular alpine scenery, and you can either turn back to complete the hike or continue on over the pass into the center of the Wilderness.

Hike #10. El Porvenir Campground to Hermit Peak

This moderate to strenuous hike in the extreme southeast corner of the Pecos Wilderness has as its objective Hermit Peak, a prominent landmark west of the town of Las Vegas which is regularly

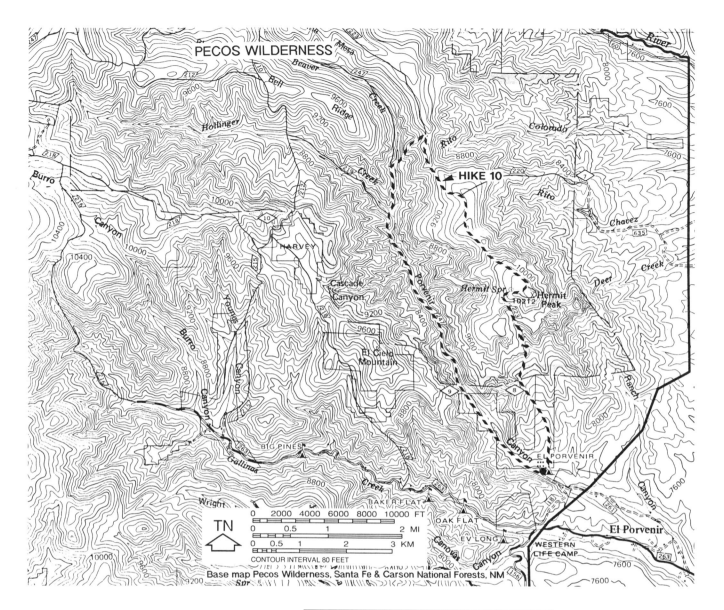

Base map Pecos Wilderness, Santa Fe & Carson National Forests, NM

CONTOUR INTERVAL 80 FEET

viewed by thousands of motorists traveling along Interstate 25. From a starting elevation of 7,500 feet at the trailhead, the trail gains 2,700 feet to the summit of the peak over a round trip distance of 8 miles. The peak immortalizes an Italian missionary named Juan Maria Agostini, who came to the area and lived as a hermit in a cave near the top of the mountain in the 1860s. The mountain still attracts followers of the obscure religious brotherhood with which he was associated, but today mainly attracts a

Hike #10. El Porvenir Campground to Hermit Peak

Distance — 8.0 miles round trip
Net elevation gain — 2,700 feet
Difficulty — Moderate to strenuous

steady procession of hikers who are drawn by the forest wilderness and the spectacular views from the top of the peak. In his time here on earth, the mountain must have provided an inspirational sanctuary for the hermit who was apparently killed by Apache Indians in 1869 while leading a similar life of seclusion near Las Cruces. This hike can be done as a day hike or, if extended into the area north and west of Hermit Peak, it is suitable for overnight backpacking. The USGS 7.5-minute scale topo maps of the area are the El Porvenir and Rociada quads.

To reach the trailhead at El Porvenir Campground, exit Interstate 25 at Las Vegas and drive northwest on Highway 65. As the road passes the United World College, it turns west and follows Gallenas Creek up to Gallenas, where Forest Road 261 turns off to the north and leads the remaining 3 miles to the campground.

From the parking area at El Porvenir Campground, begin hiking on Trail #223, which soon climbs north out of Porvenir Canyon and steadily ascends the broad, forested slopes toward Hermit Peak. As the terrain steepens near the base of the mountain, a strenuous set of switchbacks continues up through the walls on the south face to a level area not far below the summit. A final steep push leads past Hermit Spring on the west side of the summit, and a pleasant walk east over the rounded top of the peak leads to an overlook with spacious views off to the east. As an alternative to retracing the route up the peak, a loop hike can be done which add 10 miles to the distance already covered. Continue the loop hike alternative by hiking north from Hermit Peak on Trail #223 toward Beaver Creek. The trail descends a broad ridge to the northwest until a trail junction is reached at 3.5 miles past the summit, with the left trail branch descending steeply down to Beaver Creek. Upon reaching the creek, follow the trail that leads back down the Beaver Creek and Porvenir Canyon drainages, ending at the road shortly below the campground. Numerous stream crossings on the final leg of the loop suggest the need for a pair of lightweight wading shoes to be included as part of your equipment.

For Further Information:

Santa Fe National Forest
  Pecos Ranger District
  P.O. Drawer 429
  Pecos, NM 87552
  (505) 757—6121

Santa Fe National Forest
  Las Vegas Ranger
  District
  1925 North 7th Street
  Las Vegas, NM 87701
  (505) 425—3535

Santa Fe National Forest
  District Office
  1220 St. Frances Drive
  P.O. Box 1689
  Santa Fe, NM 87504
  (505) 988—6940

Pecos Wilderness Trail Guide, by Southwest Natural and Cultural Heritage Association in cooperation with Patty Cohn and the staff of Santa Fe National Forest, published by Southwest Natural and Cultural Heritage Association, Albuquerque, NM, 1991.

Day Hikes in the Santa Fe Area, by the Santa Fe Group of the Sierra Club, National Education Association Press, Santa Fe, NM, 1981.

Trail Guide to the Upper Pecos, by Arthur Montgomery and Patrick K. Sutherland, New Mexico State Bureau of Mines and Mineral Resources, Socorro, NM, 1967.

Pecos Wilderness Trails for Day Walkers, by Carl Overhage, William Gannon Press, Santa Fe, NM, 1984.

Jemez
Mountains

GENERAL DESCRIPTION

In a state with such a wide diversity of scenery, no part is more scenic or more interesting than the Jemez Mountains. It is a large area of approximately 2,500 square miles, the center of which is located about 60 miles northwest of Santa Fe, and is mostly contained within the Santa Fe National Forest. To generally define the area, it begins on the south side with the mountainous uplift starting on a line between Jemez Pueblo and Cochiti Pueblo, and continues north to the Chama River Valley. It extends to the Naciamento Mountains on the western edge, and on the eastern side to the hills and mesas north and south of Los Alamos. Contained within these boundaries are an abundance of gentle peaks, rolling valleys, mesas, canyons, trout streams, hot springs, and a high concentration of prehistoric Indian sites. It is a favorite area for hiking and camping, fishing, cross-country skiing, mountain biking, and general sightseeing. The high point of the mountains is 11,254 feet at Redondo Peak, and a total of four climatic zones are represented. The most common vegetation types encountered on the hiking trails are those associated with the pleasant ponderosa forests that cover the area. In winter, the Jemez Mountains receive a significant covering of snow, but the high country begins to open up for hiking in early spring, and the hiking remains good until the snows begin in late fall. Temperatures are generally pleasant all through the summer. Lower parts of the area can be hiked almost year round.

To begin to understand and appreciate the Jemez Mountains, you have to understand something of the relatively recent geologic events that formed the region. Some 15 million years ago the continent began to stretch or expand in an east-west direction, creating ground faults such as that followed by the Rio Grande. This was accompanied by vigorous volcanic activity, which for millions of years uplifted highlands such as the Jemez area and created numerous volcanos and lava vents that reached down into the earth's mantle and gradually built up tremendous volumes of lava and basaltic rock. A little over one million years ago, a large volcano, which may have been similar in size and shape to Mt. St. Helens before it erupted, stood at the center of the present Jemez Mountain area. Then, in one of the most incredible and massive volcanic events ever to occur on earth, two successive eruptions obliterated the mountain, dumping 50 to 75 cubic miles of ash and debris into the atmosphere and leaving a crater about 14 miles in diameter where the mountain had previously stood. The human imagination is ill-equipped to grasp the scale of such an event, but imagine, if you will, an area 40 miles by 40 miles piled 200 to 300 feet deep with a layer of volcanic ash, in addition to the uncounted cubic miles of volcanic rock previously deposited. Imagine also, a million years of slow erosion, with the falling rain and flowing streams rounding the landscape, carving deep canyons and broad valleys, and nurturing a complex ecosystem of forests and grasses. This is the present-day Jemez Mountains. The great lake that once occupied the old caldera has long since been drained by a major canyon that was gradually formed by the waters that fed the lake, and the lava dome that formed in the collapsed caldera is now known as Redondo Peak.

Because of the natural resources, climate, and scenic beauty there, the Jemez Mountains have long attracted human occupation. A number of large prehistoric Indian ruins, and thousands of smaller ones, are sprinkled across the canyons and mesas as silent reminders of the hundreds of years of human presence before European man arrived. Nearly a dozen present-day Pueblo Indian tribes inhabit areas on the periphery of the Jemez Mountains; some were in place when the Europeans first arrived, and most trace their ancestry to the inhabitants of the ancient ruins. These modern descendants return periodically to conduct religious ceremonies at the old sites. The many faint roads and trails that cover the area are a legacy of the later Spanish and Anglo inhabitants, who also had an appreciation for the abundant resources and made full use of them to farm and mine the land, graze livestock, and log the forests. The extinct caldera (Valles Caldera) in the center of the region is located in a large 12.5-square mile block of privately owned land, which is off-limits to trespassing, and numerous other small, privately owned parcels also exist within the surrounding national forest. The national forest includes campgrounds and picnic areas, trails, and old roads, which are variously traversed by foot, horseback, bicycle, four wheel drive, or in the winter by ski, snowshoe, and snow-mobile. If you are unfamiliar with the Jemez Mountains, an excellent introduction is to drive through the area on the paved loop route described in the subsequent access section. This scenic route includes several historic, prehistoric, and natural history attractions, as well as several campgrounds and picnic areas.

Map Coverage

The Jemez Mountains cover a large area, so the USGS 7.5 scale map coverage is included as part of the individual hiking trail descriptions. If you can still find them, the 15-minute scale Jemez and Jemez Springs maps show much of the area. A good large-scale overview of the Jemez Mountains is shown on the 1:100,000-scale Los Alamos and Abiquiu maps, and on the 1990 Santa Fe National Forest map.

Access

All the hiking trails later described here begin at different trailheads, so access directions are included with the trail descriptions. Since several of the trailheads are accessed via the Highway 4 loop route that traverses through the heart of the Jemez Mountains, directions for this route are included here. Highway 4 can be approached either from the north (Santa Fe) or from the south (Albuquerque). From Santa Fe, drive north on Highway 84/285 toward Española, but at Pojoaque turn west on Highway 502 toward Los Alamos. You will begin to see plenty of the characteristic volcanic tuff by the time you reach the junction with Highway 4, which you take south through White Rock. After passing through White Rock, the highway passes the Bandelier National Monument turnoff, and then the south turnoff for Los Alamos, as it climbs to the west, up through ponderosa forests. Several miles after passing the Los Alamos turnoff, you will see part of the Valles Caldera, as the highway skirts the southeast corner of the part called Valle Grande. As the highway continues to the west, you will pass several national forest campgrounds and will eventually come to the junction with Highway 126, about 21 miles west of the Los Alamos turnoff. Turn south, staying on Highway 4 toward Jemez Springs. The highway drops down to the south passing through Jemez Springs 8 miles from the Highway 4/126 junction, and continues another 16 miles to San Ysidro, where you stand a good chance of making a cash contribution to the village economy as a result of the local speed trap, if you don't stay well within the posted speed limits.

To approach from the south, take the Bernalillo/Placitas exit off Interstate 25 and drive west through Bernalillo on Highway 44 until you get to San Ysidro. At San Ysidro, drive north on Highway 4 and reverse the route described above. In winter, the section of Highway 4 between Jemez Springs and White Rock is often snowpacked, making it dangerous or impassible. Otherwise, it is a good paved road that is suitable for any passenger car. One-way travel time to reach the area from Albuquerque or Santa Fe is 1 to 1.5 hours.

Hiking Trails

The trails described below include long and short, some well marked and frequently traveled, and some unmarked and not often hiked. Some are suitable for backpacking and others more suitable for dayhiking. Water is sometimes present but should be treated. If you encounter prehistoric ruins when hiking in the Jemez, don't climb on the ruins and don't collect artifacts. Some of the present-day Pueblo Indians maintain links to the old ruins and claim ancestry to the people buried therein; oral traditions still identify some of the important ancestors by name. Even though these sites are on national forest land, the tribe members get very emotional about any desecration. After having tried some of the trails described in this book, there are other trails and old roads in the area that you may want to search out on your own. If you like the area, you will also want to hike some of the trails in the adjoining Dome/Bandelier Wilderness.

TRAIL DESCRIPTIONS

Hike #1. East Fork Trail (#137)

The East Fork Trail is an 8.9-mile series of trail segments, with the east end at the East Fork of the Jemez River near Las Conchas Campground, and the west terminus at the Battleship Rock picnic area. Two additional trailheads are located along the route of the trail at the East Fork and Jemez Falls picnic areas, providing a variety of entry points. The stretch of trail between Jemez Falls and Battleship Rock is usually hiked independently of the rest of the trail and is described separately under Hike #2. The segment of trail described here is the 4.5-mile stretch that runs between the East Fork trailhead on the west side and the Las Conchas trailhead on the east side. It is described here as starting from the East Fork trailhead (you can start from either end) and traverses the ponderosa and aspen slopes and grassy meadows atop the south side of the river canyon, and eventually drops down to follow the river the rest of the way to the Las Conchas trailhead. The trail gains 520 feet of elevation to the high point of the trail, just before dropping down into the canyon, and then loses 200 feet to Las Conchas. It is a 9-mile round trip hike, but can be hiked one way with an easily done car shuttle. This is a very pretty hike and a good one to do in summer when it turns hot. The segment of trail between the East Fork picnic area and Jemez Falls picnic area can either be worked into the hike described thus far, or it can be done as a short individual hike. The USGS 7.5-minute topo map for this area is the Redondo Peak quad, but the trail is not shown on the current version of the map. Also, the Jemez Falls picnic area is labeled on the map as the Banco Bonito Campground. Refer instead to the map in the book.

To locate the East Fork trailhead, drive to a point 6.2 miles east of the Highway 4/126 junction (see "Access" above) on Highway 4, where you will see a turnoff on the east side of the road with a sign for the East Fork Trail. This is not the small parking area just past the river, but 0.4 miles on east up the hill (if you are doing a car shuttle or starting from the east end, the Las Conchas trailhead is another 3.5 miles east along Highway 4 and 0.5 miles west of Las Conchas Campground). Drive to the east end of the picnic area and park in a small parking area by the pit toilets. Begin at the pedestrian gate and walk past the trail sign on the old four-wheel-drive road. The old road is used as a cross-country ski trail in winter, and you will notice the blue diamonds marking it as such. After going 0.25 miles, the trail splits off from the road and traverses to the north. The trail and the road both continue east over more or less the same route, and at a number of spots where the ridge narrows, they join briefly before pulling apart again, with the trail staying north of the road when they aren't coinciding. You should keep to the trail rather than the road to keep from missing the place where the trail drops down into

the canyon. After hiking 1 mile from the trailhead, a short side trail drops down to the west end of the East Fork Box, a stretch of canyon that forms a small gorge but cannot be hiked up without wading up the river. Continuing east on the main trail from the trail junction, the path follows along the canyon rim, as it joins and departs the old road several times more with occasional views of Redondo Peak to the north before reaching the high elevation point of the hike and dropping down the canyon on a contour to join the river. The remaining segment of perhaps 1.5 miles follows the river the rest of the way to the Las Conchas trailhead. The river bottom is lovely and refreshing, and the water is stocked with trout. You will probably have trouble keeping your feet dry on the river trail, so you may want to have some wading shoes. The round-trip hiking time for this trail is 2.5 to 4 hours.

To hike the 1-mile trail segment between the East Fork trailhead and the Jemez Falls trailhead, you can pick up the east trailhead directly across the highway from the East Fork picnic area. The trail heads down the forested slopes to the west before dropping down into the East Fork Canyon, crossing the river on a log bridge, and climbing up to the Jemez Falls picnic area on the other side of the canyon. Locate the Jemez trailhead by turning off Highway 4, 5.4 miles east of the Highway 4/126 intersection, and following the gravel road south until it ends. The trail is easy to hike, with a 160-foot elevation differential.

Hike #2. McCauley Hot Springs Trail (#137)

This 3.4-mile segment of trail has a trailhead at either end and has as its main attraction a popular hot spring along the way. It is officially the western end of East Fork Trail #137, but it is most often hiked from one trailhead or the other to

Battleship Rock

the hot springs, and rehiked to the same trailhead. McCauley Hot Springs consists of a nice, spacious pool formed by a small rock dam, with water that is more warm than hot. It is located on a bench in the ponderosa forest 200 feet above the east fork of the Jemez River and about midway between the two trailheads: Battleship Rock picnic area on the west end and the Jemez Falls campground (shown on the 7.5-minute scale Redondo Peak map as Banco Bonito Campground) on the east end. It can be approached with equal effort from either end and is an easy day hike either way, with no obvious camping spots except in the vicinity of the springs. The water in the pool is comfortable to soak in any time of year. Winter hiking should be done from the lower-elevation Battleship Rock trailhead, but recent snows will make the trail impassible on foot. Judging by the elevation gradient of the lower part of the

trail, skiing it could be a fearsome ordeal. If you use the Battleship Rock trailhead, note that this is a day use picnic area only. If you arrive back at your car after 10:30 p.m., it may not be there.

To locate the Battleship Rock trailhead, drive on Highway 4 either 4.3 miles north of the town of Jemez Springs or 3.2 miles south of the Highway 4/126 intersection, to a turnoff for the Battleship Rock recreation area. Continue to the east end of the picnic area and park. Cross the bridge where a trail sign marks the start. From this end, the trail is a 3.2-mile round trip hike to the springs, with a net elevation gain of 580 feet. The trail starts up the north bank of the river for about 0.5 miles and then switchbacks up the side of the canyon to a fairly level contour, with a steep finish near the end just before reaching the springs. The trail is well worn in and easy to follow. The only tricky spots are at one or two

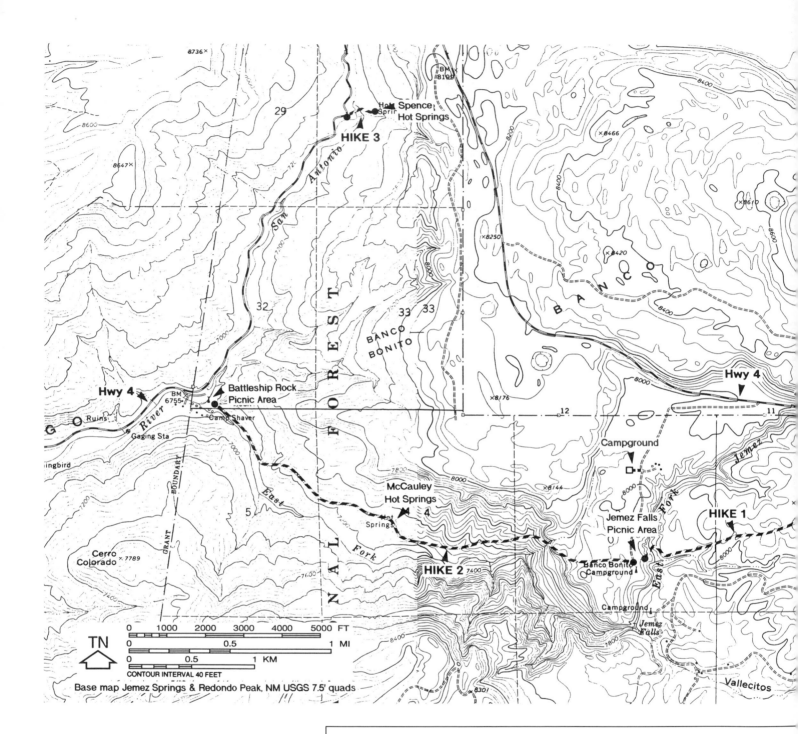

Hike #1. East Fork Trail (#137)

Distance — From east fork trailhead, 4.5 miles one way or 9 miles round trip to Las Conchas; 2 miles round trip to Jemez Falls
Net elevation gain — From east fork trailhead, 320 feet to Las Conchas, plus 200 feet lost from high point in trail; 160 feet to Jemez Falls
Difficulty — Easy

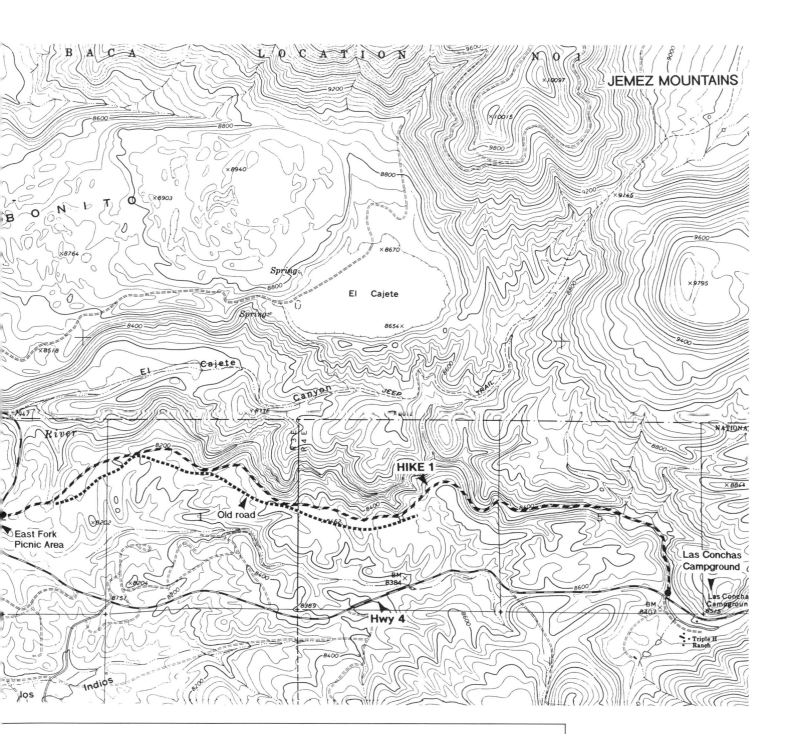

Hike #2. McCauley Hot Springs Trail

Distance — 3.2 miles round trip from
Battleship Rock; 3.6 miles round trip from
Jemez Falls
Net elevation gain — 580 feet from Battle-
ship Rock; 560 feet from Jemez Falls
Difficulty — Easy

Hike #3. Spence Hot Springs Trail

Distance — 0.4 miles round trip
Net elevation gain — 165 feet
Difficulty — Easy

switchbacks, where a faint false trail keeps going straight.

The Jemez Falls trailhead is reached by driving east on Highway 4, 5.4 miles from the Highway 4/126 intersection, and turning south toward the Jemez Falls campground on a 1.4-mile paved road that continues past the campground to the end of the road at a picnic area. Walk to the west side of the privies and locate a sign for Trail #137. The trail makes a short initial climb and then levels off for a distance before dropping fairly steeply on a path that eventually intersects the stream coming down from the hot springs. A short climb up ends at the springs. A round-trip hike to the hot springs from the Jemez Falls side covers 3.6 miles, with a net elevation drop to the springs of 560 feet. Besides the hot springs, a couple of other features of this hike that I find interesting are the huge blocks of volcanic glass along the trail and the prehistoric Indian ruins located just to the west of the springs. Perhaps this was a prehistoric health spa. From the Jemez Falls picnic area, you may also want to do the short 0.6-mile roundtrip hike down to the Jemez Falls overlook. From the east side of the parking area, take the road-sized trail down toward Jemez Falls, but as you approach the creek, take the well-worn trail that angles up to the right. A short distance farther is a viewing area from which you can see the falls. The trails described in this section are missing from the Redondo Peak map, but the map in this book is sufficient.

Hike #3. Spence Hot Springs Trail

Although the great volcano of the Valles Caldera ceased to be active, or even exist, nearly a million years ago, the earth's crust under the area continues to seethe with geothermal activity. A major project near Fenton Lake which proposed to tap this great energy source using geothermally heated steam was abandoned only a few years ago due to technological limitations in the recovery process. But the existence of a number of hot springs in the region provides evidence of the elevated temperatures below the surface. Naturally, these hot springs have long attracted human visitation, and never more so than with our own culture. Almost any hot spring is guaranteed visitation, and Spence Springs is probably the most accessible and most visited of the hot springs in the area. It can be hiked to year round, and the moderately sized pool below the springs is hot but tolerable. I like the springs best in winter, when a short trek through the snow is required to gain access, but even then it is necessary to occasionally exit the water to keep from overheating. Although bathing suits are the norm, particularly during daylight hours, nudity is also common and may in fact be the prevailing mode after dark; other than to state the facts on the subject, I cannot advise you. If you enjoy sipping bottled spirits while in the heated pool, make it a plastic bottle. And as a precaution, it is a good idea to wear some kind of footwear while at the springs.

The trail is a short climb of about 0.4 miles roundtrip, which leads up to the pool below the springs, which are located 165 feet up the side of the canyon above the river. The area is shown on the 7.5-minute scale Jemez Springs map, but forget it—you won't need a map for this hike. To locate the trailhead, drive 6 miles north of Jemez Springs (1.7 miles north of the Battleship Rock turnoff) on Highway 4 and pull off on to a parking area that has been bladed out on the east side of the road. Locate a well-worn trail that descends to the river below. After crossing the river on a log, the trail takes a steep, rather direct path to the springs above. There is some dangerously sheer rock on this side of the canyon so don't wander

East Fork of the Jemez River

onto something where you shouldn't be. If you aren't on a trail where a lot of people have walked, retrace your steps until you find the trail. Take along a flashlight if you plan to stay until after dark, and don't forget the towel and warm clothes.

Hike #4. Tent Rocks

At the eastern border of the Jemez Mountains, set in layers of volcanic tuff deposited about a million years ago, lie the peculiar formations known as Tent Rocks. Situated in a half-mile-long cluster, these conically shaped pillars were formed by the processes of wind and water erosion, which wore away the softer tuff and pumice around hard stone caprocks that came to be located at the apex of the cones as the formations were gradually shaped. The Tent Rocks vary in size from a few feet to over 90 feet in height, and according to the BLM, which administers the site as an area of critical environmental concern, comparable formations are only known to occur in the country of Turkey. Also abundant in the area are raisin-sized beads of black volcanic glass known as Apache tears. The striking cone formations and the delicate stratified layering of the tuff deposits have been a popular theme with photographers for many years. Colorful Indian paintbrush, chamisa, manzanita, and Apache plume, as well as the stately ponderosa pines, add a nice vegetative contrast.

This is an area for dayhiking without designated trails. Round-trip hiking distances are in the 1 to 3-mile range, with negligible elevation gain if you stay down in the canyons. The area can be hiked year round, although fresh snow in the winter will limit access. Water is generally unavailable. Driving time to reach the area is about one hour from

either Albuquerque or Santa Fe. The area is shown on the USGS 7.5-minute scale Canada quad.

To reach the trailhead, travel south from Santa Fe or north from Albuquerque on Interstate 25, take the Cochiti Pueblo exit (Exit 264), and travel west on Highway 16 to a junction with Highway 22, 7.9 miles past the Interstate. Turn north on Highway 22 and continue for 2.5 miles, passing below Cochiti Dam, until Highway 22 turns south toward Cochiti Pueblo. Follow this branch of the road south for another 1.6 miles. The Cochiti Indians are famous for the quality of their ceremonial drums, and you will notice a water tower on a hilltop which is painted to look like a drum. A second, more slender tower is encountered shortly beyond and it is here, at the 1.6-mile mark mentioned above, that you turn west on a gravel road just beyond the second tower. The road is marked both as

Forest Road 266 and Route 92. If there is a graveyard on your right after you have made the turn, you are on the right road. Continue west on this road for 4.5 miles until you come to a BLM sign indicating a parking area on the north side of the road. The Tent Rock formations will be clearly visible from the parking area.

After a welcome sign that lists all the things that you aren't allowed to do, there is an informational sign at the north end of the parking area. An informal but well-worn trail begins past the sign, ascends a small ridge, and climbs around the east end of the Tent Rocks formation. After about 0.4 miles the trail drops down and merges with a dry stream bed, where the visible trail more or less ends. From this point, you can walk in any direction and it will all be scenic and enjoyable. You can continue up the stream bed to the west for another 0.6 miles until you come to a fence, with most of the interesting stuff

McCauley Hot Springs. Feel free to take a dip, but respect the sensibilties of others who may join you. And please, keep the area clean.

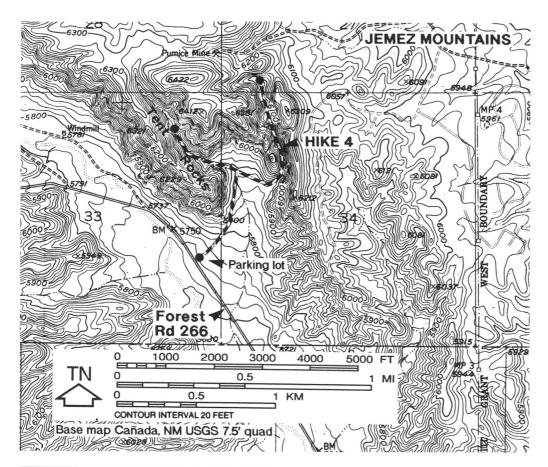

Base map Cañada, NM USGS 7.5' quad

CONTOUR INTERVAL 20 FEET

Hike #4. Tent Rocks

Distance — 1 to 3 miles round trip
Net elevation gain — Negligible
Difficulty — Easy

---

behind you, or you can walk to the north and examine the small cave, apparently of prehistoric origin, that is carved into the base of the tuff wall. But the most scenic hiking, and the heart of the Tent Rocks area, is a magnificent canyon located farther to the east around the corner in a steep, narrow cleft hidden from view on your approach hike from the parking area. To locate this canyon, walk to the east below the steep tuff wall that contains the cave that can be clearly seen from the approach trail. Keep to the north wall but stay low, walking across small gullies for several hundred feet east of the cave until you come to a broad, sandy stream bed that leads north into the narrow canyon. If you have to climb up slopes to enter the canyon, you turned north too soon. Once in the canyon, you will be treated to a wonderful natural sculpture that extends for perhaps another 0.5 miles through a winding passageway set between towering palisades of layered tuff, which at times is narrow enough to simultaneously touch each opposing wall. You will occasionally have to surmount small ledges and obstructions before the path is finally blocked, although for the determined hiker it is possible to hike out of the canyon and up to the top. One word of caution however: the BLM warns you not

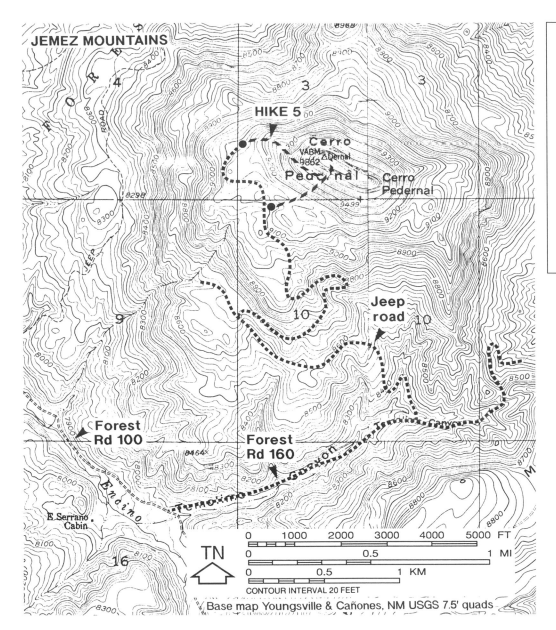

JEMEZ MOUNTAINS

HIKE 5

Cerro
Pedernal

VABM
9862

Cerro
Pedernal

Jeep
road

Forest
Rd 100

Forest
Rd 160

E. Serrano
Cabin

TN

| 0 | 1000 | 2000 | 3000 | 4000 | 5000 | FT |

| 0 | | 0.5 | | 1 | MI |

| 0 | | 0.5 | | 1 | KM |

CONTOUR INTERVAL 20 FEET

Base map Youngsville & Cañones, NM USGS 7.5' quads

Hike #5. Cerro
Pedernal

Distance — about
2 miles round
trip if you drive
up four wheel
drive access road
Net elevation
gain — about 740
feet
Difficulty —
Moderate

to climb the tuff formations and it is good advice, not only for the sake of the rock. The tuff is loose and crumbly, and if you get any higher than you are willing to fall, you could be in real danger. Bring your camera along and budget some time to spend admiring the unusual scenery.

Hike #5. Cerro Pedernal

Cerro Pedernal, also known as Pedernal Peak, is the northernmost of the Jemez Mountain peaks. Its flat-topped shape is a well-known landmark across a wide area of northern New Mexico. Meaning "flint hill" in Spanish, the peak is actually crowned by a basalt ridge but named for a flint outcrop located in a band of tuff, deposited during the tertiary period, near the base of the mountain, which was quarried for thousands of years by prehistoric Indians as a material for stone tools and projectile points. The view from the top of the peak includes the Chama River and Rio Puerco canyons to the north and west, with brightly hued rock of red, yellow, cream, and tan, the blue waters of Abiquiu Lake to the north, and green forests and meadows to the south and east. While the steep cliffs of the summit ridge appear formidable from below, the route to the top is regularly done by people of little or no rock climbing accomplishment or potential. Even if you decide against climbing the final steep section, the pleasant ponderosa forests, green meadows, and expansive views on the way up will make the hike worthwhile.

The hike up Cerro Pedernal varies in distance according to how far up you drive your vehicle. The maximum round-trip hiking distance is 8.5 to 9 miles and the minimum from 1 to 2 miles. If you are driving a four wheel drive vehicle, the latter set of distances is more likely to apply. The elevation at the start of the four wheel drive road (Forest Road 160) is 8,000 feet, the large meadows below the peak and near the top of the road are at about 9,140 feet, and the summit is at 9,862 feet. The typical time required to hike to the top and return can vary from 3 hours to 7 hours. The best time of year to hike the area is spring through fall. Winter is impractical, due to cold temperatures and snowpack on the roads. During the rainy season of July and August, get started early and be prepared to back off if thunderstorms threaten. Bring your drinking water with you, as you probably won't find any on the way up, and be careful not to dislodge rocks onto your companions while on the final steep section below the summit. Map coverage of Cerro Pedernal is shown on the USGS 7.5-minute scale maps of Youngsville and Cañones, and the 1:100,000-scale Abiquiu map.

To access the hike from Albuquerque

Hiking through the Tent Rocks

or Santa Fe, take Highway 84/285 north into Española and turn west at the first traffic light, where Highway 84/285 branches off from Highway 68. Continue west across the river and turn north at the next traffic light. Follow Highway 84 north toward Chama, 28.6 miles from this intersection, to the Highway 96 turnoff, just west of mile marker 218, and drive south toward Abiquiu Dam. Continue across the dam and on to the junction with Forest Road 100, 11 miles past the Highway 96 turnoff. Along this stretch of highway, you will see Cerro Pedernal as the truncated peak off to the south. Forest Road 100 turns off to the south just past mile marker 38 and opposite the Youngsville sign. It is a good quality gravel road that runs south and east past colorful geologic formations toward Cerro Pedernal, which now appears as a rocky spire when viewed from the northwest direction. After driving 5.6 miles up

Forest Road 100, look for a double-track dirt road that turns off to the east and heads up Temoline Canyon. This is Forest Road 160 and it leads to a network of jeep roads that cover about 3.5 miles from the Forest Road 160 turnoff to the large meadows below the steep slopes at the top of the peak. These jeep roads can be driven, walked, or both, in proportion to how much punishment you are willing to let your vehicle absorb. If you want to drive to the meadows at the top of the jeep road, you will need some combination of high vehicle clearance, four-wheel drive, and dry road conditions.

After turning off on to Forest Road 160, drive east for 1.2 miles, where a well-worn dirt road turns north, crosses the canyon bottom, and climbs increasingly steep terrain. At 0.4 miles past the Forest Road 160 turnoff, you will come to the obvious flint outcrop, with colorful pieces of flint or chalcedony littering both sides of the road. At a fork in the road 0.1 miles past the flint outcrop, take the left fork and continue 0.7 miles to the next road fork, taking the right fork that cuts up sharply to the right and contours back to the east. If you are apprehensive about driving past the fork, there is a small, level area where you can park just up and west of the fork. The road above gets even rougher, but the view begins to open up until you come to a series of wide, pleasant meadows about a mile past the last road fork. From these meadows, some 700 to 800 feet below the summit, you will be able to see an obvious cave at the base of the summit headwall above, toward the west end of the peak. Your objective will be the broken area in the cliffs, just to the west of the cave, which provides a feasible path to the top and can be reached from the meadows by one of two different routes. The most gradual, and I think preferable, ascent is to continue walking north through the series of meadows, heading for the ridge that drops down from the west end of the peak across the skyline. Once you reach the crest of the ridge at its base, where you may see a large cairn, continue up the center of the ridge over faint trail segments to the base of the summit cliffs. Make your way along the base of the cliffs to the south until you come to another large rock cairn below a negotiable-looking section of the cliff where the final ascent begins. The first 10 feet of the final section are steep but not really difficult, although you should test all hand and foot holds before committing your weight (basic rule of Rock Climbing 101). An obvious and easy path leads the rest of the way to the top. If you traverse all the way to the large cave before beginning your final ascent to the top, you need to return about 75 feet back to the west and look for the route.

The other approach up from the meadows below the summit is to hike across to the bottom of the steep slopes below the cave area and look for one of the steep trails that ascend directly up to the route through the summit cliffs. These approach trails climb up loose sand and rock and are better for descending than ascending. From the top of Cerro Pedernal you have one of the better summit panoramas in the state. You can walk the trail that runs along the top and take it all in, but take note of the rock cairn at the spot where you gained the summit plateau; it marks the only safe way back down. Once again, be careful not to dislodge rocks on your friends below as you start back down.

Hike #6. Cañones Creek Trail (#82)

Cañones Creek is a drainage of about 20 miles in length beginning in the high country just north of the Valles Caldera in the Jemez Mountains. It flows to the north, skirts the Cerro Pedernal massif,

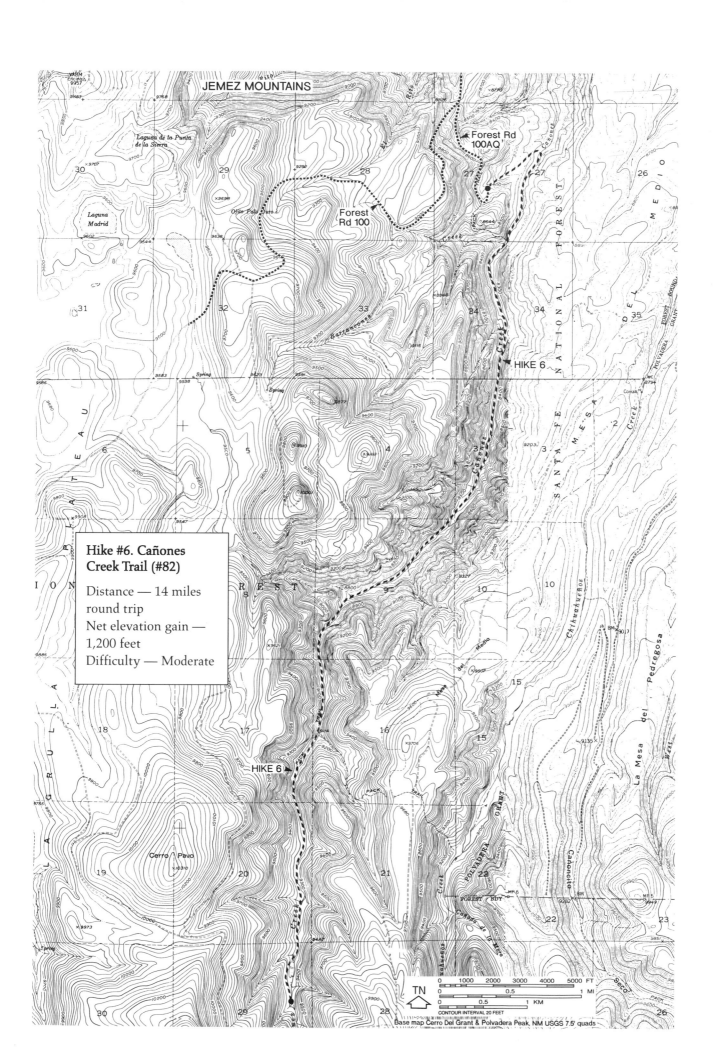

JEMEZ MOUNTAINS

Forest Rd
100AQ

Forest
Rd 100

HIKE 6

Hike #6. Cañones
Creek Trail (#82)

Distance — 14 miles
round trip
Net elevation gain —
1,200 feet
Difficulty — Moderate

HIKE 6

TN

CONTOUR INTERVAL 20 FEET

Base map Cerro Del Grant & Polvadera Peak, NM USGS 7.5' quads

continues past the village of Cañones, and empties into Abiquiu Reservoir on the Chama River. The hiking trail, which follows the upper part of the creek in the Santa Fe National Forest, winds through an area of open grassy meadows mixed with forest of pine, spruce, fir, and aspen. The access road is graveled and well maintained but may require a high-clearance vehicle in wet conditions, particularly on the final stretch of road. Numerous unimproved sites for car camping are located along Forest Roads 100 and 99, with designated Forest Service campgrounds located farther to the west (see the Santa Fe National Forest map). The Cañones Creek Trail runs along the entire length of the creek down to the village of Cañones, but the trail described here travels the upper section of the creek, which is more scenic and has less population pressure from the village. The trail is 7 miles one-way from the trailhead to the upper end of the creek to the north. After an initial drop of 250 feet to reach the creek, the trail gains 1,200 feet to the north end for a very comfortable hiking gradient. There are several side trails, which branch away from the creek and appear to climb up out of the canyon and join one of the Forest Roads that travel above the rim of the canyon. However, none of these are marked at the upper end, so the best plan seems to be to hike as far up the creek as you want and then return by the same route. The trail along Cañones Creek is suitable for either dayhiking or backpacking, with water flowing along the entire length of the creek. Much of what relatively little hiking the trail sees is from local fishermen. During winter the entire area receives plenty of snow, making mid-May through late October the best time of year to visit. The air temperature is especially pleasant during summer and fall. The Cañones Creek Trail is shown on the

USGS 7.5-minute scale Cerro del Grant map. For a broader perspective of the area refer to the 1:100,000-scale Abiquiu map or the Santa Fe National Forest map. Driving time from Albuquerque is about 2.5 hours; from Santa Fe about an hour less.

The approach for Cañones Creek is the same as that for Cerro Pedernal and is repeated here: Take Highway 84/285 north into Española and turn west at the first traffic light, where Highway 84/285 branches off from Highway 68. Continue west across the river and turn north at the next traffic light. Follow Highway 84 north toward Chama, 28.6 miles past this intersection to the Highway 96 turnoff, just west of mile marker 218, and drive south toward Abiquiu Dam. Continue south across the dam and on to the junction with Forest Road 100, 11 miles past the Highway 96 turnoff. Forest Road 100 turns off to the south just past mile marker 38 and opposite the Youngsville sign. Drive up the road for 7.2 miles (passing the Pedernal turnoff at the 5.6-mile point) to a dirt road that angles down to the left. This road is marked as Forest Road 100AQ, and it takes a steep path down into the Cañones Creek drainage. At 1.3 miles past the turnoff from Road 100, you will come to a road junction where you will turn left on to the better-traveled road and go another 0.3 miles down to a parking area at a log vehicle obstruction. The trail begins here at the entrance provided through the barrier.

The trail drops down toward the creek (this section is not currently shown on the topo map) and goes 0.5 miles to a junction with Trail #82 on the east side of the creek. Turn south and follow the trail that runs along the creek, crossing at several points; you should be able to keep your feet dry unless the water is running high. The canyon is narrow and thickly wooded for the first mile before small meadows begin to be encountered. After another 1 or 2 miles along the creek, the canyon begins to open up somewhat and the meadows become more expansive. The farther up the canyon you hike, the more beautiful the scenery becomes. There are numerous places to camp, with nice views and little likelihood of encountering other hikers. At about the 7-mile point, the upper end of the canyon terminates in a broad, grassy bowl, and you will either have to climb up out of the canyon or return back down the creek. This would be a good trip to bring your fishing pole and spend a few days camping in the broad meadows toward the upper end of the creek. Along with some cows, there is also a lot of wild game in the area, so if you are hiking during hunting season in late fall, plan to wear some bright colors.

For Further Information:

U.S. Forest Service
Santa Fe National Forest
Jemez Ranger District
Jemez Springs, NM 87025
(505) 829-3535

U.S. Forest Service
Santa Fe National Forest
Coyote Ranger District
Coyote, NM 87012
(505) 638-5526; (505) 988-6999

BLM District Office (for the Tent Rocks Area)
435 Montaño NE
Albuquerque, NM 87107
(505) 761-8700

Exploring The Jemez Country, By Roland A. Pettitt, revisions by Dorothy Hoard, published by the Los Alamos Historical Society, Los Alamos, NM, 1990.

Tent Rocks, Area Of Critical Environmental Concern, a pamphlet distributed by The Albuquerque BLM Office.

Bandelier Wilderness

GENERAL DESCRIPTION

Approximately one million years ago a great volcano, which had been formed through successive eruptions over the ages, stood about 40 miles northwest of present-day Santa Fe. As the pressure within the earth's crust built to a final irresistible level, the great volcano exploded in two successive eruptions of unimaginable power, releasing some 50 to 75 cubic miles of volcanic debris. Some of the incandescent material was blasted into the atmosphere and drifted as far as the American Midwest, and some flowed down the sides of the volcano in the form of glowing ash avalanches that deposited in layers hundreds of feet thick over many square miles atop a base of basalt remaining from even more ancient volcanic activity. The ash particles welded together to form a porus rock called tuff, into which deep canyons have been carved by flowing streams, with flat mesa tops forming between the canyons where the softer top layer has been eroded down to a harder inner layer. The original volcano finally spent itself and collapsed into a vast caldera 14 miles across. Into this setting came man. The first visitors probably passed through several thousand years ago, by which time a million years of erosion had left the area much as it is today. Around 1100 A.D., significant groups of Indians began settling and farming the canyons and mesa tops, and

Painted Cave, Bandelier

for the next five centuries they built stone dwellings, carved rooms out of the soft tuff in the canyon walls, established still-recognizable trails, put in irrigation systems, and in many ways left their mark on the land. Today, thousands of ruins left by the ancient inhabitants dot the area, and the most spectacular part has been set-aside as Bandelier National Park, with the Dome Wilderness, a small contiguous Forest Service wilderness area, established on the western edge. I shall jointly refer to these as the Bandelier Wilderness.

The Bandelier Wilderness is an area of about 37,000 acres which is characterized by deep canyons carved into the tuff and basalt, with perennial streams of water flowing through pleasant bottoms past tall ponderosa and species of broad leaf riparian vegetation. Between the canyons are rolling mesa tops of high desert vegetation, featuring densely packed forests of juniper and piñon pine alongside open stretches of grassland. At the western border, where the elevation is higher, stand a series of small basaltic peaks. The trails in the Bandelier Wilderness tend to run along the relatively flat canyon bottoms and mesa tops, with abrupt interruptions as they ascend and descend the steep canyon sides. In the hot part of summer the hiking tends to be uncomfortably warm, while in winter the area receives frequent snowfalls, making the best time to visit from spring through early summer and from fall through early winter. Both dayhiking and backpacking are popular, but a permit is required to hike in the Wilderness backcountry. These can be obtained at the Visitor Center or by contacting the Superintendent, Bandelier National Monument, Los Alamos, NM, 87544, (505) 672-3861. Reliable water sources in the Wilderness are present, but only in the deep canyons, and you should treat any such water you

use. There are two established campgrounds in the park to accommodate overnight car camping and a number of National Forest campgrounds located in the nearby Jemez Mountains farther to the west. Outstanding features of the area include the many ruins, artifacts, and prehistoric rock art panels, along with the unusual and scenic geology. Remember that it is forbidden to remove any of the potsherds or other artifacts that you may find. Special hazards, in addition to getting caught removing artifacts, include trying to climb up the steep and deceptively easy-looking tuff slopes, and the danger of lightning during thunderstorm season on the mesa tops.

Map Coverage

The appropriate map coverage depends on the specific hike and is included as part of the individual hike descriptions.

Access

The trails described in this section depart from the Visitor Center, the Juniper Campground, the Eagle Canyon Pumice Mine, and the St. Peter's Dome trailhead in the Dome Wilderness. The individual trail descriptions will refer to these trailheads, and the access to each is described below. The Tsankawi Trail is considered separately.

Juniper Campground. The Juniper Campground is reached by driving north from Santa Fe on Highway 285 and turning west on Highway 4 at Pojoaque. Take the branch toward White Rock and continue a few miles past the town to a turnoff leading south toward Bandelier National Monument. This turnoff is marked by a prominent sign. Follow the signs directing you to Juniper Campground, located on the mesa above the north rim of Frijoles Canyon. The Bandelier turnoff can also be reached by traveling north on Highway 4 at San Ysidro and making the loop through Jemez Springs. This section of road is more scenic and pleasant in summer but is often snowpacked in winter.

Visitor Center. To reach the Visitor Center at Bandelier, follow the directions for Juniper Campground, but continue on past the campground turnoff to the park headquarters at the bottom of Frijoles Canyon. There is a small fee to enter the park, but the road is paved all the way to the Visitor Center.

Eagle Canyon Pumice Mine. To reach the Eagle Canyon Pumice Mine trailhead, take the Cochiti Dam exit off Interstate 25 just south of La Bajada Hill (39 miles north of Albuquerque) and travel west on Highway 16 to a "T" intersection with Highway 22. Turn north and travel several miles, crossing the bridge below the large dirt berm that is Cochiti Dam, and continue straight on the paved road, past the community of Cochiti Lake to the end of the pavement. Just over a mile farther on the dirt road is Forest Road 289, a gravel road which turns north. After driving about 4 miles north on Forest Road 289, you will come to a sharp bend in the road, which turns back to the left just below a steep section. Here you can pull off to the right and park. You will pick up the trailhead (no trail marker currently exists), which heads north on the west side of a shallow canyon in the vicinity of several white-colored pumice slides. Because of the stream crossing about a mile north of the Forest Road 289 turnoff, which can be running high in the springtime, and because the road gets progressively rougher from this point on (particularly during wet weather), a vehicle with high clearance may be needed to reach this trailhead.

St. Peter's Dome Trailhead. The St. Peters Dome trailhead is reached by following the directions to the Eagle Canyon Pumice Mine trailhead, but continuing north on Forest Road 289 another 4 miles to the junction with Forest Road 142, which leads 3.5 miles east to the trailhead for the Picacho Trail near the St. Peter's Dome lookout. The trailhead for the Capulin Canyon and Boundary Peak Trails, not described in this book, is located about a mile back down the road from St. Peter's Dome.

Hiking Trails

The Bandelier Wilderness has a rather extensive trail system, out of which I have selected seven hikes, including both day hikes and multiday backpacking trips. The hikes described vary from easy to strenuous, cover most geographical parts of the wilderness, and visit most of the popular attractions. There are other trails not described in this book, and should you want to find out more about them, a good source is *A Guide to Bandelier National Monument* by Dorothy Hoard (see bibliography). The park ranger at the Visitor Center can also help direct you.

TRAIL DESCRIPTIONS

Hike #1. Frijoles Ruins Trail

Frijoles ("beans" in Spanish) Canyon was apparently named for one of the staple crops of the prehistoric inhabitants and was a particular focus of Adolph Bandelier, the Swiss-born historian and anthropologist for whom the area is named, in his studies there in the 1800s. It contains the most-concentrated and spectacular set of ruins and cliff dwellings, carved into the soft volcanic tuff, that the area has to offer. The ruins, which are within easy walking distance of the

Visitor Center, belonged to the Indians who grew corn, beans, and squash in the wide canyon bottom during the time period surrounding 1100 A.D. A self-guiding booklet is available at the Visitor Center.

Begin by walking west on the trail from the Visitor Center. The trail is very easy to walk, and there are several minor variations as the trail winds its way past the ruins and along the north canyon wall for about 1 mile up the canyon. The end point for the hike is Ceremonial Cave, a small dwelling group with a restored kiva located 140 feet up the canyon wall, which is reached with the aid of an airy but secure wood ladder. At Ceremonial Cave you may turn back and return the way you came back to the Visitor Center. The total round trip distance is 2 miles or a little more, and the elevation gain is about 200 feet. This is the standard tourist walk and a good hike to start with. The topo map covering this area (you won't need it for this hike) is the USGS 7.5-minute Frijoles quad.

Hike #2. Lower Frijoles Canyon Trail

This hike takes you from the Visitor Center down Frijoles Canyon, past two scenic waterfalls, and ends at the Rio Grande. If you go all the way to the river, the trail is 2.4 miles in each direction on an easy-to-follow path. The elevation of the Visitor Center is 6,060 feet and the trail drops to 5,400 feet at river level, for a 660-foot gradient. The area is shown on the USGS 7.5-minute Frijoles quad.

Begin at the east end of the picnic area at the Visitor Center on the south side of the stream, and walk east on a trail that leads down the canyon. This hike is an excellent way to observe the various layers of volcanic tuff and other igneous rock through which the stream has cut. In addition to the colorful geology of the canyon walls, you may, on the first part of the hike, notice the distinctive rock formations known as tent rocks. Between the first and second mile of the hike, you will also come to what is perhaps the primary feature of the hike, the upper and lower falls. These waterfalls were created by bands of basalt that were resistant to the eroding stream of water. The trail continues to work its way down the final stretch of the canyon as it exits the east border of the monument boundary and joins the Rio Grande a few miles north of Cochiti Dam. This is along a stretch of river that provides a popular whitewater boating run in the spring. In years of high runoff, the reservoir has backed up past the entrance to Frijoles Canyon, killing trees along the river and creating a world class patch of cockleburs. Finish the hike by returning back up the canyon the way you came and regaining all the elevation you lost on the way down.

Hike #3. Upper Frijoles Canyon Trail

This hike begins at the Visitor Center and heads west up Frijoles Canyon, incorporating the Frijoles Ruins Trail for the first mile. One-way hiking distance to the upper Frijoles crossing is 5.5 miles, with 940 feet of net elevation gain. If you want more, you can continue for 2 miles and 600 vertical feet farther up the canyon to the Apache Spring Trail. This can be done either as a day hike or a backpack, with a reliable supply of water in the canyon bottom. The appropriate USGS topo map is the 7.5-minute Frijoles map, and if you hike up-canyon past the upper crossing, the 7.5-minute Bland map as well.

Start the hike at the Visitor Center and follow the trail west up the canyon past the ruins, continuing past Ceremonial Cave. The trail stays down in the canyon, crossing the stream in a number of places under cool riparian foliage, and occasion-

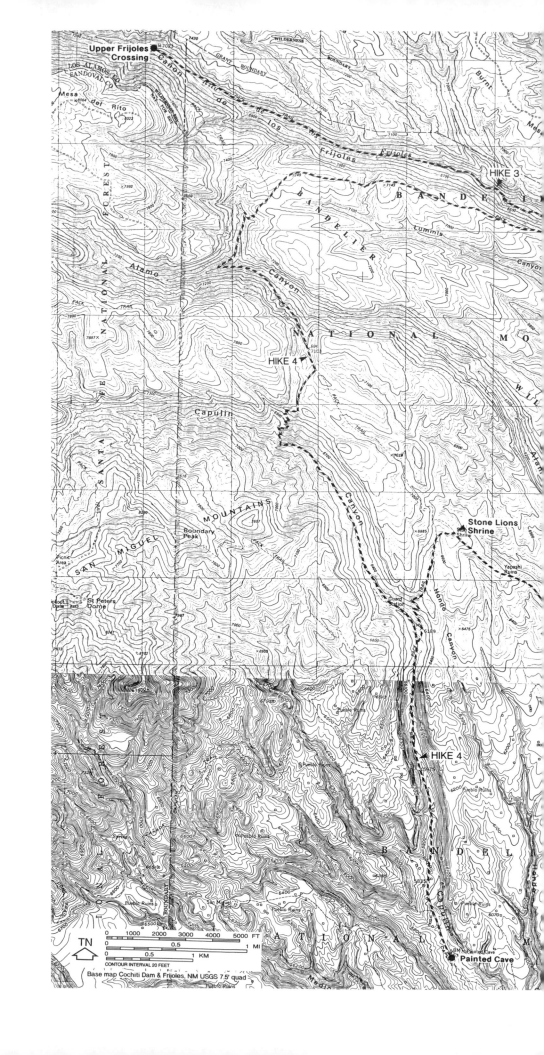

Upper Frijoles
Crossing

HIKE 3

HIKE 4

Stone Lions
Shrine

HIKE 4

TN

Painted Cave

| 0 | 1000 | 2000 | 3000 | 4000 | 5000 FT |

| 0 | | 0.5 | | 1 MI |

| 0 | 0.5 | 1 KM |

CONTOUR INTERVAL 20 FEET

Base map Cochiti Dam & Frijoles, NM USGS 7.5' quad

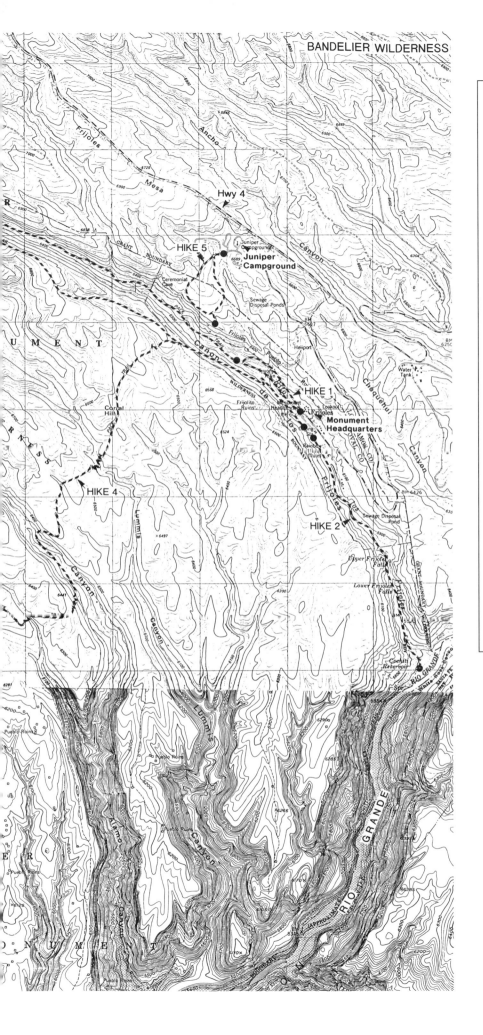

BANDELIER WILDERNESS

Hike #1. Frijoles Ruins Trail

Length — 2 miles round trip
Net elevation gain — 200 feet
Difficulty — Easy

Hike #2. Lower Frijoles Canyon Trail

Length — 4.8 miles round trip
Net elevation gain — 660 feet
Difficulty — Easy

Hike #3. Upper Frijoles Canyon Trail

Length — 11 miles round trip
Net elevation gain — 940 feet
Difficulty — Moderate

Hike #4. Backcountry Loop Hike to Stone Lions and Painted Cave

Length — 21.5 miles round trip
Net elevation gain — 1,170 feet; total is much higher
Difficulty — Strenuous

Hike #5. Tyuonyi Overlook Trail

Length — 2 to 2.5 Miles
Net elevation gain — Negligible
Difficulty — Easy

ally climbs up on the south side of the canyon. At the 5.5-mile point, Upper Frijoles crossing is reached. If you turn north on the crossing trail, the trail climbs out of the canyon and continues about a mile across the mesa to the Ponderosa Campground. This hike is sometimes done as a one-way hike between the Visitor Center and Ponderosa Campground or, more commonly, in the reverse direction with a car shuttle in place. If you turn south at the Upper Frijoles crossing intersection, you climb out of the canyon and head south into the wilderness area (this requires a backcountry hiking permit). Continuing straight up the canyon leads, after 2 additional miles, to the Apache Spring Trail, which climbs out of the canyon to the north and ends at a Forest Service road. It is also possible to continue past the Apache Spring Trail to the upper reaches of the canyon.

This trail receives a fair amount of hiking traffic (most within a few miles of the Visitor Center) and is easy to follow, with a good trail surface. The difficulty is rated moderate primarily because of the distance involved, with an elevation gain that is not much of a factor unless you climb out of the canyon. It is a pleasant and scenic hike.

Hike #4. Backcountry Loop Hike to Stone Lions and Painted Cave

This is a strenuous backcountry backpack usually done in two or more days, with a total length as described below of about 21.5 miles. The net elevation gain is 1,170 feet, but this figure is fairly meaningless because you gain and lose much more than that climbing in and out of steep canyons. Map coverage for this hike requires the USGS Frijoles and Cochiti Dam 7.5-minute quad maps. A backcountry hiking permit is required.

The Stone Lions Shrine and Painted Cave are two of the most significant and popular archaeological attractions in the National Monument, and can only be reached by foot or horseback. The Stone Lions Shrine features a pair of mountain lions, which were carved from blocks of volcanic tuff, creating a shrine that was apparently an important center for prehistoric Indians from all over the area. The shrine still has cultural significance for present-day Indians from the nearby pueblos and is regularly visited by them. One-half mile east of Stone Lions are the remains of Yapashi, one of the largest ruins in the monument and reputed to belong to the ancestors of Cochiti Tribe. Painted Cave, the other primary archaeological attraction of the hike, is a large shelter cave 30 feet up the north side of Capulin Canyon. The walls of the cave are covered with vivid pictographs left by prehistoric Indian inhabitants of nearby dwellings and by early Spanish shepherds. The route chosen for this hike is somewhat arbitrary in that several other trail combinations would also work, but it makes a good introductory Bandelier backpack, traversing the heart of the wilderness backcountry.

Begin at the Visitor Center and drive south across the creek to a parking area for hikers toward the west end of the picnic area. Find the trailhead for Stone Lions and follow the trail west for 0.25 miles until the trail starts gaining elevation and climbs steeply up and out of Frijoles Canyon. On the way up you will have excellent views of the ruins on the north side of the canyon. Once on the canyon rim, the trail intersects a trail coming in from Frijolito Ruin to the east, and continues west to another trail junction a short distance farther on. The trail to the south goes directly to the Stone Lions Shrine and is the one on which you will eventually return, but instead of turning south here, continue on the trail that leads west above the canyon rim for another 3.5 miles to the "Y." This is a junction that will take you back across Upper Frijoles Crossing and on to Ponderosa Campground if you go north, but we will take the south fork instead. The trail follows a side canyon that feeds Alamo Canyon, crosses Alamo Canyon, and diagonals southeast up the steep south side of Alamo. About 0.25 miles south of the canyon rim is another trail junction. The east fork leads to Stone Lions, but we will take the south trail fork, which descends via a long series of switchbacks down into the lush bottom of Upper Capulin Canyon. There is water here and good places to camp, but be watchful for poison ivy, as there are scattered patches in this part of the canyon. You can also camp farther down the canyon to the east, but in the vicinity of the Administrative Cabin (a government facility a couple miles down the canyon), camping is limited to designated sites due to heavy use. From Upper Capulin Canyon it is a 3.5-mile walk east down the canyon, past the Administrative Cabin and the Stone Lions Trail junction, to Painted Cave on the canyon wall to your left. The cave is marked by a sign and can be seen well from below. Once-useable handholds carved into the rock by the Indians lead up to the cave, but these have badly eroded with time and trying to climb into the cave now is both dangerous and prohibited by the monument administration. From Painted Cave, turn back and retrace the trail 2.7 miles back up-canyon to the Stone Lions Trail junction and ascend the trail up the north side of the canyon and continue on to the Stone Lions Shrine about 1 mile farther. The shrine is unmistakable. The eroded stone lions are set in a ring of tilted slabs, and the space between the lions is heaped with deer antlers and various trinkets and offerings left by pilgrims and admirers.

From Stone Lions, follow the trail southeast for 0.5 miles to Yapashi Ruins, a large pueblo ruin which is largely unexcavated. The broken-down walls are still intact enough to indicate the floor plan, and you may be surprised at how small many of the rooms were. The prehistoric pueblo dwellers were small in stature and had limited time, energy, and resources to devote to architectural construction. The rooms tended to be utilitarian—only large enough to accomplish their intended function. Also of interest are some cave ruins across the small canyon to the northwest. The trail from Yapashi back to the Visitor Center (7 miles) continues east, then north, crossing several canyons, the most significant of which is Alamo Canyon. The hike down and out of Alamo Canyon is strenuous with a heavy backpack, and you may be able to camp in the canyon, but since water may not be available in this part of the canyon you should be prepared to continue on to Frijoles Canyon. Once on the south rim of Frijoles Canyon you can return to your car by way of the same trail you ascended. An alternative is to take the trail that heads back southeast along the canyon rim to Frijolito Ruins and continue east for another 0.25 miles, where the trail descends steeply down the side of the canyon to your original starting point. After a short walk to your car, you can rest your aching feet, pop a cold one from the ice chest you left in your car, and remark on the magnificent scenery you have observed.

Hike #5. Tyuonyi Overlook Trail

The Tyuonyi Overlook Trail is a short loop hike that begins at Juniper Campground and makes a loop toward the north rim of Frijoles Canyon, with an overlook of Tyuonyi Ruin in the canyon below. This trail is a convenient way for

Stone Lions Shrine

campers to get a feel for the Bandelier environment on a trail with interpretive information posted at intervals. The total loop distance is 2 to 2.5 miles, with negligible elevation differential.

Begin at the amphitheater at the south end of Juniper Campground and walk south on the trail. After a short distance the trail splits, forming a loop, with each branch of the loop joining again less than 1 mile farther at a small excavated prehistoric Indian ruin. The short side trail that continues south goes to the rim of the canyon and overlooks Tyuonyi Ruins just west of the Visitor Center area. With a nice view down the canyon, it is interesting to imagine the cataclysmic events that built up the area and the processes of erosion which, over hundreds of thousands of years, have shaped the area as it is today. The slightly milky tint of the water in the stream beyond the ruins below is an indication that tiny bits of rock matter are being transported down to the Rio Grande, and that the entire plateau is slowly, inexorably being carried off only to end up as clay deposits in some far-off location. Perhaps many

millions of years from now the clay deposits will be folded back into the earth's crust to reappear as igneous rock in some future volcanic event, thus beginning the cycle anew. You can get carried away thinking about these kinds of things, but mental extrapolations are part of the enjoyment of an area like this. After you have finished postulating your natural history theories, hike back up the trail and complete the loop back to the campground.

Hike #6. Picacho Trail

This trail traverses the U.S. Forest Service Dome Wilderness, located at the western edge of the main Bandelier Wilderness. The north trailhead for the Picacho Trail (shown as the St. Peter's Dome Trail on the topo map) is located near the St. Peter's Dome lookout, and the trail descends northeast of Cerro Picacho, for which the trail is named, crosses Sanchez Canyon, and ends at the south trailhead located at the Eagle Canyon Pumice Mines about 5.5 miles distant. The trail drops from 8,320 feet at the north trailhead to 6,520 feet at the south trail head, for a net differential of 1,800 feet, with an additional 300 feet lost and gained crossing Sanchez Canyon. The trail is often done as a one-way hike using a car shuttle. If the entire trail is hiked beginning and ending at the same trailhead, the total round trip distance is 11 miles, making for a fairly strenuous day hike. If done as a backpack, the most logical camping spots are in Sanchez Canyon, which has a reliable flow of water, and at Turkey Spring, about 2 miles along the trail that heads north from the trail junction at the north rim of Sanchez Canyon. An alternative loop hike is to hike from the St. Peter's Dome trailhead down to the above-mentioned trail junction, north past Turkey Spring to the Boundary Peak Trail junction above Capulin Canyon, and back on the boundary peak trail to the starting point at St. Peter's Dome. This makes an 8-mile loop hike. The Picacho Trail is diabolically located at the junction of four topo maps, requiring all four to cover the area: the USGS 7.5-minute scale Frijoles, Bland, Cañada, and Cochiti Dam maps.

Although you can just as well start from the Eagle Canyon trailhead, I will describe the trail as starting from the St. Peter's Dome trailhead, since the trail goes downhill from this point. From a parking area below the observation point at the top of the dome, hike southwest about 1 mile down a long ridge that leads to a saddle below Cerro Picacho, which is the wedge-shaped summit on the ridge up from the saddle. From the saddle, the trail traverses below the east face of Picacho and works on down past some interesting rock formations to a trail junction 2 miles farther on, above the north rim of Sanchez Canyon. The north fork of the trail contours along below the San Miguel Mountains, of which St. Peter's Dome and Cerro Picacho are part, passes by Turkey Spring, and drops into Capulin Canyon.

The Picacho Trail continues south at the trail junction and drops on down into Sanchez Canyon. If you are inclined to browse, you may want to walk about on the flat slopes of the mesa to the east of the trail junction. These flat slopes were probably utilized by the prehistoric Indians who lived nearby for growing crops, and there are numerous small, crude ruins located about. Perhaps these were shelters used during the growing season when crops required maintenance. Also scattered about are pieces of obsidian, the black volcanic glass that was the material of choice in the area for making skinning tools and projectile points. Obsidian from the area around Bandelier was evidently a trade item in prehistoric times, and it can be found over a wide area of the Southwest. Continuing on the trail into Sanchez Canyon, the trail contours to the west, passing a nice waterfall near the bottom of the canyon. The trail crosses the stream at the bottom of the canyon and contours back up to the east out of Sanchez Canyon and continues to the south trailhead at the abandoned pumice mines less than a mile farther south.

Hike #7. Tsankawi Ruins Trail

Tsankawi is a large pueblo ruin located on a mesa in a small detached section of Bandelier Park about 12 miles from the main section. The primary ruins located atop the mesa were built in about 1400 A.D. Also to be seen on the trail are rock art, cave dwellings, and trails worn into the tuff by thousands of ancient footsteps. The trail is 1.5 miles round trip, with a 200-foot elevation gain to the top of the mesa. The trailhead is reached by driving about 1 mile south on Highway 4 from the intersection with Highway 520 (see the access directions for reaching the Juniper Campground). Just before the intersection with the alternate-route into

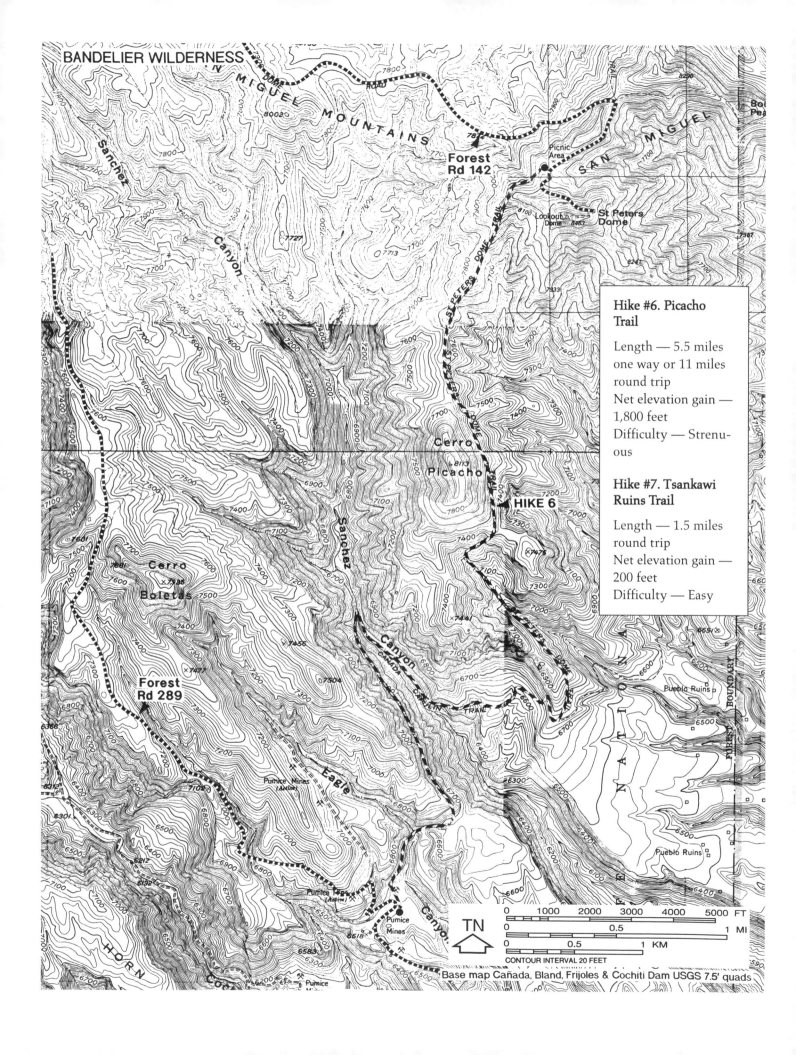

BANDELIER WILDERNESS

Forest Rd 142

SAN MIGUEL

MIGUEL MOUNTAINS

Sanchez Canyon

Picnic Area

St Peters Dome

Lookout Dome

Cerro Picacho

HIKE 6

Sanchez Canyon

Cerro Boletas

Forest Rd 289

CAÑADA CAILIN TRAIL

Canyon

Pueblo Ruins

FOREST BOUNDARY

Eagle

Pumice Mines (Active)

Pueblo Ruins

Pumice Mines (Active)

Pumice Mines

HORN Canyon

Pumice

Hike #6. Picacho Trail

Length — 5.5 miles one way or 11 miles round trip

Net elevation gain — 1,800 feet

Difficulty — Strenuous

Hike #7. Tsankawi Ruins Trail

Length — 1.5 miles round trip

Net elevation gain — 200 feet

Difficulty — Easy

TN

| 0 | 1000 | 2000 | 3000 | 4000 | 5000 FT |

| 0 | | 0.5 | | | 1 MI |

| 0 | | 0.5 | | 1 KM | |

CONTOUR INTERVAL 20 FEET

Base map Cañada, Bland, Frijoles & Cochiti Dam USGS 7.5' quads

Sanchez Canyon,
Bandelier

**For Further
Information:**

*A Guide to Bandelier
   National Monument* by
   Dorothy Hoard, Los
   Alamos Historical
   Society, Los Alamos,
   NM, 1989.

The Trail to Frijoles Ruins,
   a self guiding trail
   booklet, published by
   Southwest Parks and
   Monuments Associa-
   tion, Box 1562, Globe,
   AZ.

The Trail to Tsankawi, a
   self guiding trail booklet
   published by Southwest
   Parks and Monuments
   Association, Box 1562,
   Globe, AZ.

*Bandelier Backcountry
   Trail Map,* a map/
   brochure distributed by
   phpBandelier National
   Monument and
   available at the Visitor
   Center.

*Exploring the Jemez
   Country,* by Roland A.
   Pettitt, revisions by
   Dorothy Hoard,
   published by Los
   Alamos Historical
   Society, Los Alamos,
   NM, 1990.

The Superintendent
   Bandelier National
   Monument
   Los Alamos, NM 87544
   (505) 672-3861

Los Alamos, look for a parking area and Visitor Information Center on the east side of the road where the trail begins. Map coverage for this area is shown on the USGS 7.5-minute White Rock quad. A trail map is included in the guide booklet, which should be available at the trailhead and at the main Bandelier Visitor Center.

The trail leads toward the mesa and splits, with the usual route up being on the left fork of the loop. Shortly beyond are original Indian trails worn deeply into the tuff caused by 400 years of travel up and down the mesa, which was inhabited before Tsankawi was constructed. Also on the way up are the mysterious petro-glyphs that always seem to accompany a major prehistoric dwelling site. At the top of the mesa is the Tsankawi ruin, along with a nice view of the Sangre de Cristo and Sandia Mountains to the east and southeast, and the Jemez Mountains and Pajarito Plateau to the east and south. One of the interesting puzzles of the ancient pueblo dwellers is why they so often located their dwellings on mesa tops, when the water sources and farming plots were sometimes hundreds of feet below. Continuing down the other side of the mesa with the help of a fixed ladder leads past cave dwellings and completes the loop by returning to the original trail fork. Finish by walking back to the trailhead.

When hiking this trail you will see numerous artifacts, mainly in the form of potsherds that you may be tempted to take with you. Once again, it is illegal to remove prehistoric artifacts from Bandelier National Park or from any other public lands. You are also asked not to climb on ruin walls. Help leave this ancient site as intact as possible for others to enjoy.

Cabezon from the South

Cabezon Peak

GENERAL DESCRIPTION

The valley of the Rio Puerco north and east of Mount Taylor is the setting for what I believe is one of the most scenic areas in the state—a semiarid expanse of sweeping vistas accented by sandstone buttes and volcanic mesas and spires. The most striking of the landforms are the numerous volcanic necks or plugs, which can be seen up and down the valley. These are the remnants of extinct lava vents and volcanos that once poured extensive

layers of igneous rock across the landscape. The best-known and the largest of these volcanic necks is Cabezon Peak, a distinctive tower of basalt located about 15 miles west of the town of San Ysidro. Cabezon can be clearly recognized some 45 miles to the northwest from Sandia Peak as a dark, plug-shaped form which rises nearly 2,000 feet above the valley floor. The peak is currently included in a BLM Wilderness Study Area (WSA), an 8,038-acre parcel of land surrounding the peak and bordered on three sides by gravel roads. To the north of the WSA is the ghost town of Cabezon, located on private land and closed to the public. The primary attraction of the WSA is Cabezon Peak, which is regularly climbed by way of a steep path on the southeast side. Cabezon is one of the sacred peaks of the Navajo culture and was climbed by people who preceded the Navajos. The remains of a prehistoric shrine are still in place on the summit. The WSA is remote and wild and, except for Cabezon Peak, receives practically no hiking pressure; there are no formal hiking trails established. The access roads can become impassible to passenger cars during wet weather, but the area is otherwise accessible year round. Hot summer temperatures and cold winter weather make spring and fall the most comfortable seasons to visit. No drinking water is to be found in the area, but if you are observant, there is abundant wildlife to be seen, including deer, coyote, and pronghorn antelope. This is an area that is ideal for the hiker adventurous enough to want to make the steep climb up Cabezon Peak and enjoy the wonderful view from the top. Alternatively, the sparsely vegetated area surrounding the peak provides an opportunity to get away from other hikers in an austere setting of rocky slopes cut by frequent arroyos. Travel time to Cabezon Peak from Albuquerque is 1.5 hours in each direction.

Map Coverage

The best map to get for the area is the USGS 7.5-minute scale, Cabezon Peak map.

Access

Drive 19 miles north on Highway 44 from the village of San Ysidro to a left turn onto a gravel road marked by a road sign indicating the way to San Luís and Cabezon. As you drive the last few miles on Highway 44 on the way to this turnoff, you will see Cabezon Peak in the distance off to the west. After turning west on the gravel road, drive 3.8 miles to a fork in the road. The left fork is a rim road, which leads south along the east boundary of the WSA. However, if your objective is Cabezon Peak, take the right fork, which continues past the mostly deserted community of San Luís and on

to another fork in the road 12 miles from the Highway 44 turnoff. At this point you will be due north of Cabezon Peak, and you should take the road fork that branches off to the south. This road is marked only by a yield sign for traffic in the opposite direction. Continue south, crossing a bridge 1 mile past the last road fork and past a dirt road on the east, 1 mile past the bridge. This dirt road leads southeast toward Cabezon, but 0.7 miles farther south along the main gravel road there is a better-traveled dirt road that leads directly east about 1 mile to the base of the peak. Unless the area is upgraded from the status of Wilderness Study Area, the side roads are open to motor vehicle traffic. This provides the most direct access to Cabezon Peak, but if you want access to the south part of the WSA, continue south on the main gravel road for about 2 miles past the main Cabezon turnoff to another road fork and go left. Go left once again at the next road fork, which leads east to a cattle guard a short distance west of a large set of power lines, and where another gravel road branches off to the north along the east boundary. This is the extreme southeast corner of the WSA, and the last 4 miles of the road on which you have been traveling forms the south boundary of the WSA. You can access the area from this road, or from the road that continues up the east boundary. The easiest way to return is back along the same approach route.

Hiking Trails

This is primarily an undeveloped area, with no hiking trails in place, except for a crude trail that has been worn in by people making their way to the top of Cabezon Peak. The trail is short but gains 1,300 feet to the top, providing a bit of climbing thrill. Steep scrambling is required to negotiate the final section of the peak, which may look totally inacces-

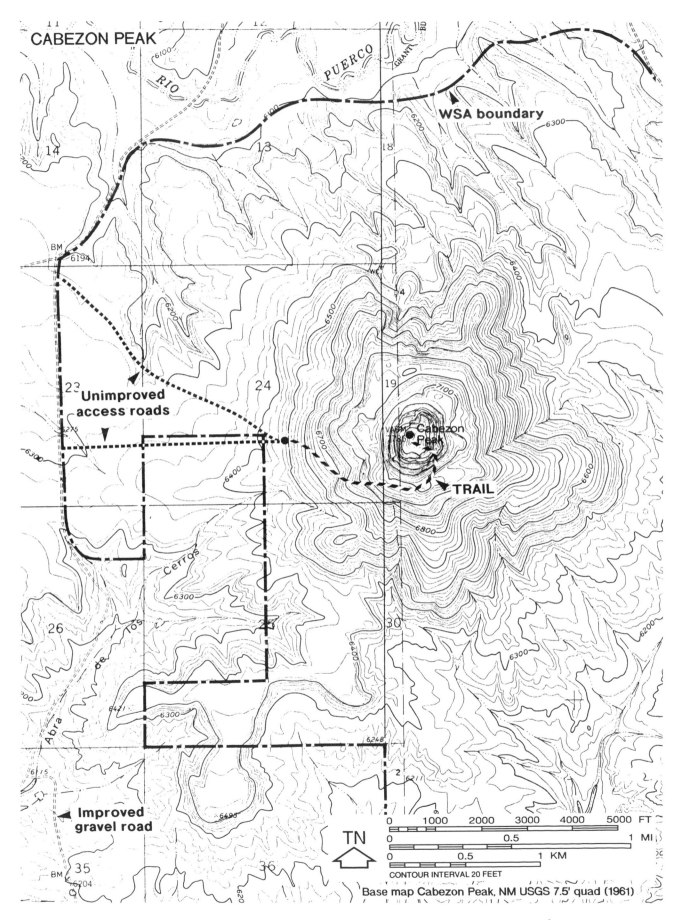

CABEZON PEAK

WSA boundary

Unimproved
access roads

TRAIL

Improved
gravel road

TN

CONTOUR INTERVAL 20 FEET

Base map Cabezon Peak, NM USGS 7.5' quad (1961)

136

sible from below, but is regularly climbed by people of no particular ability or experience at technical rock climbing. No ropes or hardware are needed, and it is a reasonable undertaking for all but the decrepit, acrophobic, or inebriated, but at the same time, the climb should not be taken too lightly. There are steep sections that require careful and deliberate moves, handholds and footholds will need to be tested, and some route-finding will be required. You will need to take care not to wander off-route on to technical rock where you don't belong, and to avoid the climb altogether if thunderstorms are imminent or if there is ice on the rock. Be especially careful not to knock loose rock down on to your friends below, and if you are waiting below, try not to stand in the line of fire. Total round trip hiking time for the hike is about 3 to 5 hours, plus whatever time you spend on top.

TRAIL DESCRIPTION

Cabezon Peak Trail

Begin the hike by parking your vehicle at the east end of the approach road (see access description above) where it begins to get steep and rough. Walk up the remaining stretch of road, which continues no more than a few hundred feet, curving south until it begins to fade out. At this point, you should look for a faint trail that takes off to the east across broad slopes below the peak. Follow the trail until it becomes too faint to detect, except for the small rock cairns which lead up a broad but steep ridge toward the south side of the peak. Near the top of the ridge, where it begins to level off a bit, begin to contour once more to the east and north, cross a fence, and make your way up to the base of the peak. Having arrived below the south face of Cabezon, walk east along the base until you see a cleft that splits the wall above. This is at the southeast side of the peak, and there is a steep trail leading up the scree slopes into the notch. Once you have gained the notch, there are a number of short, steep sections followed by a traverse to the right and a final steep push to the top. The top of the final ascent route, of which there are at least two variations, is marked by a rock cairn to help you locate the start of the route back down. A scramble up loose rock leads to the spacious summit and a wonderful view in all directions. The New Mexico Mountain Club maintains a summit register in which you can record your ascent for posterity and read the impressions recorded by earlier parties, such as that for a wedding ceremony that was performed on the summit.

One final lecture on caution: the steep part of the hike has been climbed frequently enough that there is a detectable path from below the large cleft all the way to the top. If you are unable to detect the worn path, you may be off-route and should not hesitate to retrace your steps until you regain the route. Don't climb up anything that you do not feel you can safely downclimb, and don't be afraid to turn back if the exposure is too uncomfortable for you. Remember to bring along drinking water and, if appropriate, rain gear and extra clothing.

For Further Information:

Bureau of Land Management
Albuquerque District Office
Rio Puerco Resource Area
435 Montaño Road NE
Albuquerque, NM 87107
(505) 761-8700

New Mexico Wilderness Study Report, published by U.S. Department Of the Interior, Bureau of Land Management, Santa Fe Office, September, 1991.

Cabezon, a descriptive pamphlet that is available at the Albuquerque BLM District Office.

Cabezon Peak Trail

Distance about 2.4 miles round Trip
Net elevation gain - 700 feet to the base of the peak; 600 feet the rest of the way to the top
Difficulty - Moderate to strenuous

Boca del Oso

GENERAL DESCRIPTION

Several million years ago an enormous, rugged volcanic lava flow began to form in the Mount Taylor area. This large upland plateau eventually extended some 35 miles to the northwest, spreading across the present-day Rio Puerco Valley in the vicinity of Cabezon Peak. The erosional forces of the ancestral Rio Puerco gradually separated Mesa Prieta to the east from the Great Plateau, and helped define Mesa Chivato, the northernmost tip of the plateau. It is in this

area, about 50 air miles northwest of Albuquerque and on the west slopes of the Rio Puerco drainage to the west of Cabezon, that four contiguous BLM Wilderness Study Areas (WSAs) have been established. Ignacio Chavez WSA and Chamisa WSA lie on the northern tip of Mesa Chivato and its eroded transition slopes, while Empedrado WSA and La Lena WSA occupy the sandstone mesas, valleys, and small canyons to the northeast. This block of land, tortuously gerrymandered around state and private land parcels, totals some 66,000 acres and has been collectively named Boca del Oso ("bear's mouth") after a locally prominent spire in the Ignacio Chavez WSA. Additional public lands surrounding the unit significantly increase the effective total acreage. The individual Wilderness Study Areas in Boca del Oso are separated and defined by several minor dirt roads, but the area is otherwise undeveloped and remote. Particularly distinctive because of

Chico Wash on the East
End of Boca del Oso

the numerous volcanic cones and plugs that exist in the area, it is a land of striking variation in color, topography, and landform, making it one of the most interesting and scenic in the state.

The Boca del Oso area contains a rich diversity of topography, including sandstone and shale outcrops, sandstone mesas, rock terraces, escarpments, volcanic plugs, canyons, and arroyos. The southern part of the area is additionally characterized by volcanic landforms, including basalt plains, cinder cones, exhumed plugs, and extensive talus slopes. Elevation relief varies from 6,000 feet at the Arroyo Chico and Torreon Wash drainages to over 8,200 feet on Mesa Chivato. The higher elevations have significant tree coverage, including ponderosa pine, gambel oak, piñon pine, and one-seed juniper. The middle and lower elevations include isolated junipers but are primarily open grasslands populated by various species of brush and grass. Some of the more prominent vegetation species are broom snakeweed, alkali sacaton, four wing saltbush, sage, galleta grass, Indian rice grass, and grama grass. The major watercourses are additionally populated by narrowleaf and Rio Grande cottonwood, Russian olive, and tamarisk.

No hiking trails are established in the area, making it ideal for the hiker who enjoys primitive off-trail hiking with a high degree of solitude and outstanding scenery. Varied surface geology and occasional prehistoric Indian rock art and isolated artifacts also add interest. Backpacking is generally limited, primarily due to the relative lack of water. The major access roads are gravel but are well maintained. The less-traveled roads sometimes require high vehicle clearance and occasionally four wheel drive. Because of high clay content, even the best roads can be trouble during wet weather, making it advisable to avoid the entire

Ancient Rock Art in Boca del Oso (Empedrado Wilderness Study Area)

area until it dries out. Temperatures can be hot, though not unbearably so, in summer and uncomfortably cold during the coldest part of winter. Plan to bring along all the water you will require, and see that your motor vehicle is gassed up and in good running condition, as you will be a long way from help. Driving time is 1.5 hours one-way from Albuquerque and 2 hours from Santa Fe.

Map Coverage

The best map to get is the U.S. Geologic Survey 1:100,000-scale Chaco Mesa map. If you plan to hike extensively in the area, the BLM version, showing the surface management status, is handy because of the numerous privately owned parcels in the vicinity. USGS 7.5-minute coverage is provided by the Mesa Cortada, Cerro Parido, Guadalupe, Arroyo Empedrado, and Cañada Calladita quads. Another useful map is on the back of a brochure for the Ignacio Chavez and

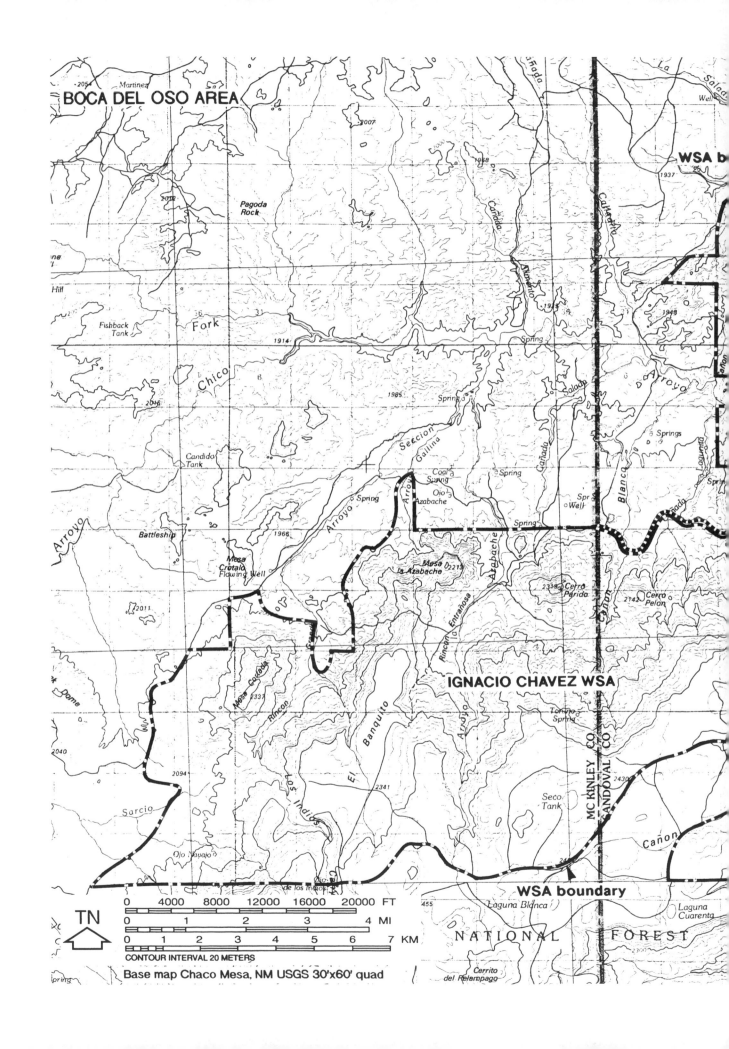

BOCA DEL OSO AREA

WSA b

IGNACIO CHAVEZ WSA

WSA boundary

MC KINLEY CO
SANDOVAL CO

NATIONAL   FOREST

TN

| 0 | 4000 | 8000 | 12000 | 16000 | 20000 | FT |

| 0 | 1 | 2 | 3 | 4 MI |

| 0 | 1 | 2 | 3 | 4 | 5 | 6 | 7 KM |

CONTOUR INTERVAL 20 METERS

Base map Chaco Mesa, NM USGS 30'x60' quad

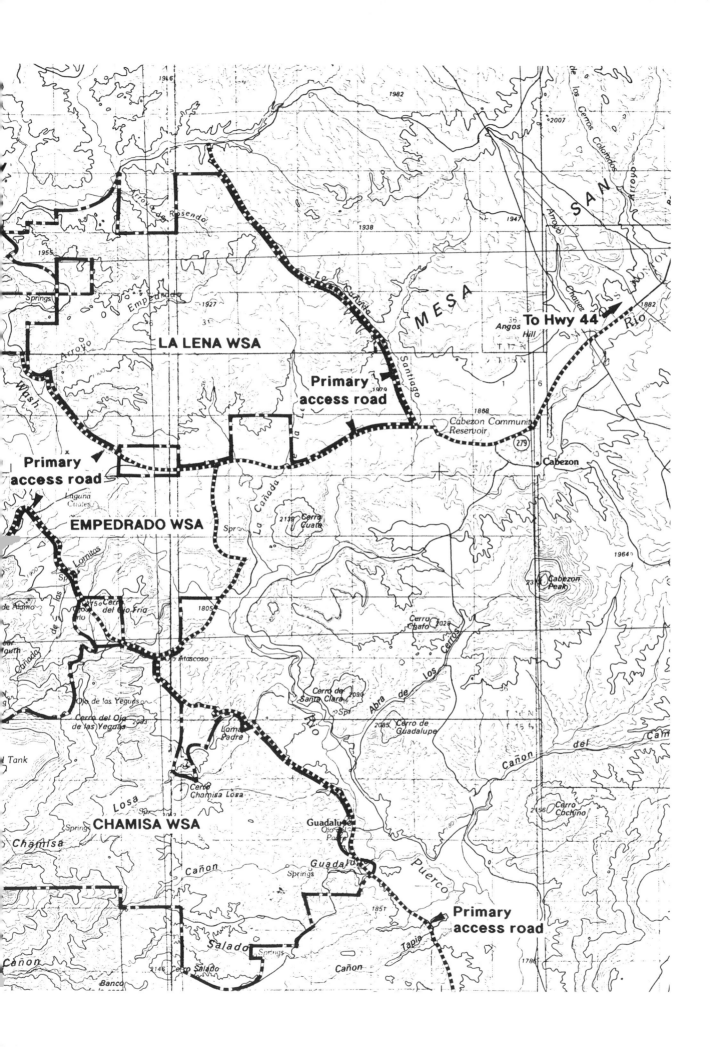

Chamisa WSAs, which can be obtained from the BLM District Office in Albuquerque.

Access

From the town of Bernalillo drive west on Highway 44 through the village of San Ysidro (watch for the speed trap) and continue 17 miles past San Ysidro to an intersecting gravel road on the west side of the highway with a sign pointing the way to Cabezon. Turn left on to this road. Keep right at the first fork, 3.7 miles past the turnoff, continuing past the small community of San Luís, and again keep to the right at the road fork 12.2 miles past the highway turnoff. The left fork of this intersection leads toward Cabazon Peak, the most prominent of the local volcanic plugs and the large shape looming to the south. Back to the right fork, drive another 1.5 miles, passing a water reservoir on the right, to a bridge over an arroyo. A short distance past the bridge is an intersection with the Piedra Lumbre Road, which turns north. This marks the eastern tip of the La Lena WSA at the north end of the Boca del Oso. At this point, I won't attempt to catalog the various roads that travel through the area but will refer you to the map instead. I will repeat some caveats, however: while all roads in the area are public thoroughfares unless otherwise posted, some will become progressively rough enough to require an off-road vehicle, and mud may prohibit travel on some roads, particularly during the winter months, early spring, and after rains.

Hiking Trails

As previously mentioned, no established hiking trails exist in the Boca del Oso, but if you are looking for solitary backcountry hiking over large undeveloped tracts of land with beautiful austere scenery and inspirational vistas, this area

is hard to beat. Keep in mind that lack of potable water is the norm and that you may need some navigational skills in places. Also, this area is really remote. A more manageable problem somewhere else could be a real emergency out here. Hiking alone means taking a chance.

There is pleasant hiking over reasonably moderate terrain off both sides of the Piedra Lumbre Road in the La Lena WSA and the San Luís Mesa and also in the Empedrado WSA. The largest undisturbed areas of land and the more rugged terrain occur in and around the Ignacio Chavez and Chamisa WSAs. To reach the latter areas, start at the Piedra Lumbre Road intersection and take the main gravel road 3.4 miles west to a fork in the road. Take the left fork and travel another 2.9 miles to a bridge over Chico Wash and another 1.4 miles to another road fork. Take the right fork 1 mile to another road fork. At this point, if my directions have been accurate and you have followed them correctly, you should see a sign indicating a camping area for hunters. The road fork to the left continues on and forms the boundary between Ignacio Chavez and Chamisa, while the right fork forms the north boundary of Ignacio Chavez WSA. While in this area, you will be able to see the distinctive Bear's Mouth Pinnacle at the north edge of the Great Lava Plateau to the west. Take either road fork until you find the spot where you want to start hiking. Both roads may have some difficult sections to negotiate, so be prepared to turn back if necessary.

For Further Information:

Bureau of Land Management
Albuquerque District Office
435 Montaño Road NE
Albuquerque, Nm 87107
(505) 761-4504

New Mexico Wilderness Study Report, published by U.S. Department of the Interior, Bureau of Land Management, September 1991.

Ojito Wilderness Study Area

GENERAL DESCRIPTION

Ojito is a BLM-administered Wilderness Study Area (WSA) about 5 miles southwest of the town of San Ysidro and 25 miles northwest of Albuquerque. It is an area of 10,903 acres, bounded by various dirt roads and property lines, which is in a setting of eroded sandstone mesas and outcrops, shallow canyons, and arroyo-etched slopes with intermittent piñon and juniper cover, and grasses and plants typical of the high desert plateau country. The annual precipitation of approximately 10 inches falls mostly from July through September and supports a moderate population of animal life. The WSA is accessible year round, except when the dirt access roads are impaired by fresh snow or heavy rains. Temperatures are often uncomfortably cold in December and January, although generally pleasant during the rest of the year; summer temperatures can become elevated, with July typically being the hottest month. A few water seeps are present in the WSA, but drinking water is something you need to take with you. The total elevation relief in the WSA is only about 600 feet, making it easy to get around, but the sometimes rugged landscape is varied and scenic, and there is a feel of isolation about the area. No established hiking trails are present, but there are several old roads that can be walked and plenty of area to hike cross country. The WSA is

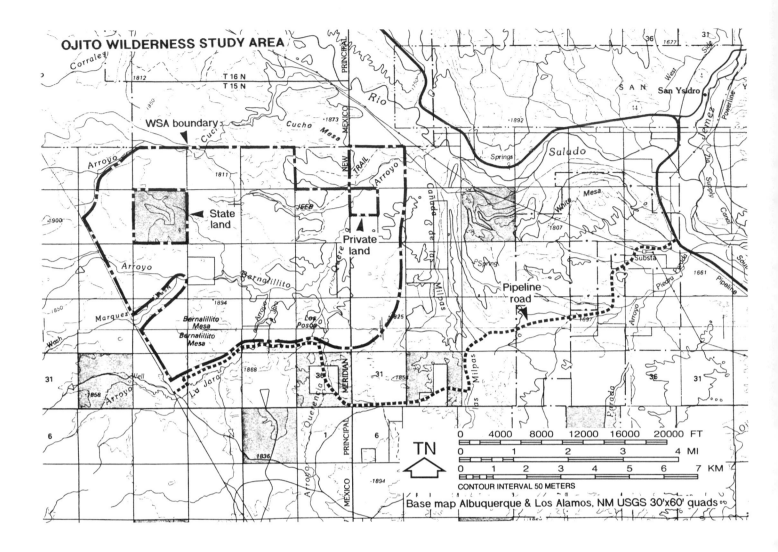

not large, but large enough to support a short overnight backpack, if you are willing to pack in your water. There are charming, secluded spots in which it could be very pleasant to just spend some time, reflect, watch the sun go down, and sleep under the stars. There are no established campgrounds in the immediate area, the closest being at Coronado State Park in Bernalillo and several National Forest campgrounds north of Jemez Springs.

Primitive car camping is allowed on the BLM lands in the vicinity of the WSA.

Ojito and vicinity contains a variety of prehistoric sites, ranging from paleocultures to late Puebloan and Navajo, and nearby Zia Pueblo to the east has been continuously inhabited since before Coronado came to the area. A number of historic old Hispanic homesites are also in the area. Ojito also contains a number of significant fossil sites. Perhaps the most unusual and significant site in the WSA is an ongoing excavation of a large dinosaur fossil at one of the several dinosaur sites in the area. This latest site, which was discovered by a pair of hikers, has yielded the remains of a sauropod, perhaps the massive seismosaurus, which may have weighed 90 tons and approached 90 feet in length. It was estimated to have lived 140 to 195 million years ago. As with prehistoric artifacts, excavating and collecting of fossils in the WSA is forbidden. They do, however, add interest to an already interesting area—an area that is scenic and wild, and a place where you can come to make your own trail and get away from other people. Travel time from Albuquerque is about 1 hour.

Map Coverage

The USGS 7.5-minute topo maps that provide coverage are the Ojito Spring, San Ysidro, Sky Village NW, and Sky Village NE maps. Also, there is a pamphlet available from the Albuquerque BLM Office for the Ojito WSA which includes a map of the area.

Access

Drive west from Bernalillo on Highway 44 until you are within 2 miles of San Ysidro. Just before the highway makes a sweeping turn to the north below White Mesa (the large white-colored mesa to the west), turn south on a well-used dirt road. The road immediately forks, and you should take the left fork past a large sign erected by Zia Pueblo warning of trespassing, etc. This is a county road and you are not trespassing by using it, so continue south on the washboard road marked by reflector posts that indicate a buried pipeline. I shall refer to this road as the Pipeline Road. At 3.9 miles past the Highway 44 turnoff,

you will come to the public lands boundary, and after another 0.6 miles you will come to a fork, where a short spur road gives access to the east side of the WSA and the main road continues left. Take a right turn at the next fork about a mile farther, and continue on the Pipeline Road to the 9-mile point (past Highway 44), where the road turns west at the southeast corner of the WSA. The Pipeline Road continues 2.7 miles west from this point, following along the south boundary of the WSA until it ends at a natural gas facility. There are several rough dirt roads, now blocked to automobile traffic, that travel north into the WSA from this last stretch of road. At the natural gas facility, the road turns north and runs parallel to a set of power lines that determine the west boundary of the WSA for the next 4.5 miles.

Hiking Trails

No trails have been established in Ojito WSA. The best entry points are from the spur road leading to the east side, and at entry points along the roads that follow the south and west boundaries. This is an area for people who like solitary hiking conditions in undeveloped surroundings.

For Further Information:

Bureau of Land Management
Albuquerque District Office
435 Montaño NE
Albuquerque, NM 87107
(505) 761-8700

Mount Taylor

GENERAL DESCRIPTION

Fifty miles to the west of Albuquerque, a once-great volcano dominates the distant horizon. At 11,301 feet in elevation, the grassy, gently contoured summit of Mount Taylor is the legacy of a violent series of eruptions that concluded over two million years ago. The mountain began forming about four million years ago, and for the next two million years, poured forth vast quantities of volcanic materials that have significantly contrib-uted to the geologic and topographic makeup of the area, which includes the broad basaltic plateau on which the mountain is located and the associated volcanic necks around its borders. Mount Taylor is the principal peak on this volcanic plateau, which is known as the San Mateo Mountains on the south end and the Cebolleta Mountains on the north end. The dominating presence of Mount Taylor along with its forests, springs, and wildlife, has long attracted visitors since far back into prehistoric times and still retains a significant spiritual significance to the Navajo as well as nearby Pueblo cultures. The Navajo names for the mountain translate as "big, tall moun-tain" and "turquoise mountain", and the area north of Mount Taylor is one of the first areas to be settled by the Navajos when they initially appeared in the Southwest. The old Spanish name for the mountain was Cebolleta ("little onion"), and this placename is still attached to a number of other locations in the area. The name for the mountain that finally ended up on the maps was given in the 1800s by a local U.S. Army officer in honor of General, and later, President Zachary Taylor. Whether Taylor ever even saw the mountain, I don't know.

Being less than two hours travel time from Albuquerque, Mount Taylor inexplicably receives only moderate attention at best from the hikers in the local area. This may be partly due to the glaring lack of priority placed on the activity of hiking by the administrators of the Mount Taylor District of the Cibola National Forest, relative to the other components of the multiple use doctrine. There is only one officially maintained trail in the entire District, a 3-mile path to the top of the mountain (shown incorrectly on the current version of the Cibola National Forest map) that requires pinpoint directions for locating the trailhead. All this aside, the upper part of Mount Taylor and vicinity is one of the most beautiful areas in the state, with sweeping grassy slopes broken by rock outcrops and groves of aspen and Douglas fir. The views are expansive, and despite a gravel road to the top of nearby La Mosca Lookout, human traffic in the area is generally light. Farther down the mountain, occasional meadows and open ponderosa forests offer enjoyable off-trail hikes for those in possession of topo maps and good navigational skills. In addition to hiking, the mountain offers good mountain biking and cross-country skiing. This is the site of one of the major winter events in the state, the Grants Quadrathalon—a grueling race involving running, cycling, snowshoeing, and cross-country skiing.

The best time of year to hike Mount Taylor is anytime after the snowmelt permits—usually from May through mid- to late October, when winter re-

turns. In addition to dayhiking, there are opportunities for overnight backpacking as well. Car camping is available in two Forest Service campgrounds off the Lobo Canyon approach road. If you do visit Mount Taylor and have the time to spare, the lava beds of the El Malpais National Monument and the nearby Cebolla Wilderness, both located not far to the south, are other interesting areas in the vicinity which provide additional hiking opportunities.

Map Coverage

The best topographic map coverage of the Mount Taylor area is provided by the USGS 7.5-minute scale Lobo Springs and Mount Taylor quads, but the road and trail information is outdated. The Cibola National Forest map is so inaccurate in its current form that you may be better off without it; an updated version is reportedly in the works.

Access

To reach Mount Taylor, drive on Interstate 40 to the east side of the town of Grants and take Exit 85 heading north, then west, 2.6 miles to the first stoplight at First Street. Turn north and go 0.9 miles to the second stop sign, then east on Highway 547 to the next stop light. At the light, Highway 547, also known as the Lobo Canyon Road, turns north and heads out of town, following Lobo Canyon to the east, and passing the Forest Service Ranger Station on the north side of the road at the outskirts of town. You will pass the Lobo Canyon and Coal Mine Canyon Campgrounds after entering the National Forest, and at a little more than 12 miles past the last traffic light the pavement ends just beyond a cattle guard. If you are driving to the trailhead for Trail #77, turn right at the end of the pavement on Forest Road 193 and drive 5.1 miles to

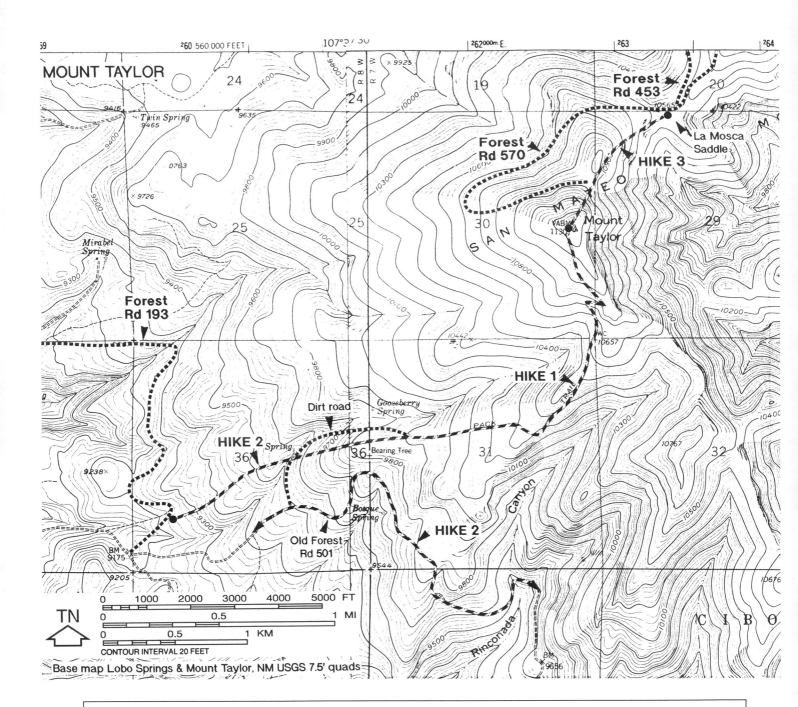

Hike #1. Gooseberry Springs Trail (#77)

Distance — 6.5 miles round trip
Net elevation gain — 2,199 feet
Difficulty — Moderate

Hike #2. Old Forest Road 501 to Rinconada Canyon

Distance — 5.4 miles round trip
Net elevation gain — 640 feet
Difficulty — Easy

Hike #3. La Mosca Trail (#77)

Distance — 1.8 mile round trip
Net elevation gain — 730 feet
Difficulty — Easy

a small, unsigned pullout on the right-hand side of the road. On the opposite side of the road, set back at treeline, is a small trail sign with an arrow marking the entrance to Trail #77. The trail sign is easy to miss from the road, and if you overshoot and end up at the junction of Forest Roads 193 and 501, go 0.15 miles back down Road 193 and locate the trailhead. Trail #77 is the trail that leads to the summit of Mount Taylor, but you may also want to view the summit by driving to the La Mosca Lookout a little over a mile to the north of Mount Taylor. This gives you a good look at the summit area of the mountain, and there is a short trail that runs from the saddle below La Mosca to the top of Mount Taylor. To reach the lookout, proceed up the Lobo Canyon Road to where the pavement ends just beyond the cattle guard, and instead of turning right on Forest Road 193, continue straight and follow the signs to the lookout.

Hiking Trails

The only designated trail on the mountain is Trail #77, also known as the Gooseberry Springs Trail, although the present trail has been rerouted and no longer goes near Gooseberry Springs. The most heavily used trail is the short path leading to the summit of Mount Taylor from the saddle between it and La Mosca Lookout. Water Canyon also has an old trail that comes out near the same saddle, and there is water in the canyon, but it's a steep drop down the canyon with no public access at the lower end. Some of the most enjoyable hiking I have done on the mountain is along old Forest Road 501, which goes east above Bosque Springs—lots of nice meadows and aspen groves to explore, along with occasional running water. I found an obsidian arrowhead on this part of the mountain—I guess the prehistoric Indians liked it, too.

TRAIL DESCRIPTIONS

Trail #1. Gooseberry Springs Trail (#77)

This is probably the major trail of interest on the mountain, and the one to take for reaching the summit of Mount Taylor if you have a half-day or more to spend. The trail from La Mosca Saddle is shorter, but you miss some of the nice forest scenery that the Gooseberry Springs Trail traverses. The round-trip hiking distance is 6.5 miles, with a net elevation gain of 2,100 feet. It should take from 3.5 to 6 hours to complete the hike, which has lots of nice forest and meadow scenery and some great views from the upper part of the mountain.

Locate the trailhead as described in the "Access" section above. The first 0.6 miles is a new section of trail that has been rerouted from the now-closed, old Forest Road 501. The trail runs east from the trailhead on a route that is still fairly faint in places, but with a few rock cairns to help out, it is not difficult to follow. At the 0.6-mile point, the trail passes a trail sign as it drops down out of the forest and crosses a grassy drainage to an old forest road at the east side of the grassy opening. The confusion produced by this intersection provides you with your first major opportunity for losing the trail. This old forest road was formerly a segment of the Gooseberry Springs Trail. The part that continues uphill to the north, past the large informational sign, follows the small canyon around past Gooseberry Springs (near an old stock tank), and intersects the present trail again farther up the ridge to the east. The downhill segment of the road, which runs south, intersects old Forest Road 501, which continues for miles on a number of branches all over the southeast side of the mountain. Neither of these leads to the summit. As the present trail approaches the old road across the grassy clearing, the trail actually turns south before reaching the road and runs parallel to it for a short distance before climbing up to join the road. At this point, directly across the road, a rather inconspicuous trail sign indicates that the trail crosses the road and continues up the hill to the east. I thought that the way this whole intersection was laid out and signed, or not signed, was unnecessarily confusing, but if you pay close attention, you won't have any trouble. After crossing the road, the trail climbs up through the trees along the side of the canyon, passes through a gate, and breaks into a clearing just before joining the upper end of the road that continues up past Gooseberry Springs. The trail continues up the broad open slopes to the east. There are a number of old ruts and trail segments that run in the same general vicinity, but at the east end of the grassy slopes, you come to a ridge with wonderful views on either side, and these various paths coalesce back into a single trail that drops down just to the east side of the ridgeline and heads north uphill toward the summit. A final series of steep switchbacks completes the final push to the top, and as usual, the view from the top is great. A short segment of trail continues on over the summit and drops down to the road from La Mosca Saddle.

Hike #2. Old Forest Road 501 to Rinconada Canyon

This hike begins the same as Hike #1, but instead of continuing to the summit of the mountain, it follows old Forest Road 501 east through the scenic area near treeline, where the fir and aspen forests meet the expansive grassy slopes that cover the upper part of the mountain. The hike arbitrarily ends at Rinconada Canyon, but there are miles of road that continue farther. On the way up to and including Rinconada Canyon, the road is easy to hike, there are several sources of water, and the big open slopes that lead up toward the summit make it hard not to do some side hikes up through the aspen groves and grassy openings. Several side trails leading off of the main road are also interesting to explore, but you need to keep track of your position, as there are essentially no trail signs. This is a pleasant walk, with pretty scenery and a good chance to spot wildlife.

Begin the hike by taking the Gooseberry Springs Trail 0.6 miles to the intersection with the old forest road on the east side of the grassy drainage. Instead of continuing across the road and east on the trail, follow the road south. After you have walked perhaps 0.25 miles, the old road on which you are walking will intersect another dirt road. This is the old Forest Road 501, which is now bermed at the lower end(s) and is closed to motor vehicle traffic. Take the uphill fork of this road, which leads to the east. The road passes just above Bosque Springs, which is far more populated by gooseberry bushes than is Gooseberry Springs, and continues over the top of a gently sloping ridge with open meadows before dropping down across Rinconada Canyon. Rinconada Canyon leads up to just below the summit ridge south of Mount Taylor and has flowing water and camping spots both near the road crossing and higher up the canyon. This is a hike you will enjoy; the scenery is nice, the hiking is easy, and you won't run into many other people, if any at all.

Hike #3. La Mosca Trail (#77)

This small segment at the north end of Trail #77 provides a short round-trip climb to the summit of Mount Taylor from the saddle below La Mosca Lookout on the north side of Mount Taylor. The grade is steep and you have your choice of two starting points, depending upon how much driving you want to do and whether you want a hike that is merely short or very short. In either case, it is an easy hike with some great views from the top of the mountain. This would be a logical trail to combine with the Gooseberry Springs Trail, and do a car shuttle between the end points.

See the "Access" section to reach the Forest Road 193 intersection with the Lobo Canyon Road, just beyond the cattle guard. Go straight at this intersection on Forest Road 239 for 3.5 miles and turn east on Forest Road 453, heading for La Mosca Lookout. Take a right at the road fork a couple of miles up the road, and continue to the La Mosca Saddle 4.5 miles after the Road 239 turnoff. At the saddle, locate a trail that contours up across the open slopes at the head of Water Canyon on a fairly straight line southwest toward the summit of Mount Taylor. This is the standard ascent of the summit from the La Mosca side, running 1.8 miles round trip and gaining 730 feet on a steep but easy climb. The alternative hike to the summit involves driving another 1.9 miles of road, the last part of which is very steep and rocky near the end. If you choose this option, continue on the road to La Mosca Saddle, a little past the turnoff to La Mosca Lookout to the north, to a road fork. The branch that goes east from the fork leads down into Water Canyon, while the branch that cuts uphill to the right, or south, becomes Forest Road 570. Forest Road 570 loops around to the west and circles back to another small saddle on the ridge below the top of the mountain. The trail entrance near the end of the road is obscure, but a segment

of trail climbs on a 0.6-mile round trip path up the final steep grade to the top, gaining 430 feet. This is one you can hike in less than an hour, but you may not want to subject your vehicle to the final steep part of the road.

For Further Information:

Cibola National Forest
  Mount Taylor
  Ranger District
  1800 Lobo Canyon
  Road
  Grants, NM 87020
  (505) 287-8833

Sandia Mountain Wilderness

Hikers on the La Luz Trail (Photo by Alan Kennish.)

GENERAL DESCRIPTION

The Sandia Mountains are part of a localized uplift on the east side of the Rio Grande Valley, running approximately north to south and about 30 miles in length. Encompassing four climatic zones, the Sandias rise from about 6,000 feet to a maximum elevation of 10,678 feet at Sandia Crest. The word *sandia* means "watermelon" in Spanish, but why the name was applied to these mountains is apparently known only to the ghosts of the early Spanish who settled this area hundreds of years ago. Because the Sandia Mountains are situated immediately to the east of Albuquerque, which is the largest population center in the state, they provide one of the most popular hiking areas and one of the most extensive systems of hiking trails in the state. Some 37,000 acres of the mountain have been designated as a Wilderness Area within the Cibola National Forest, and the area is heavily used not only for hiking, but cross-country skiing and rock climbing as well. While some of the hiking trails will see droves of people on the weekends, other trails receive little traffic, and parts of the mountain are truly rugged and solitary. A few of the trails (for example, Piedra Lisa Spring and Osha Loop) provide potential campsites, with nearby water sources that would facilitate overnight backpacking, but most of the hiking done in these mountains is dayhiking. With virtually all the trailheads within a 20 to 30 minute drive from Albuquerque, you can cover a lot of ground in a day. All the major drainages have occasional springs in them, but water is generally not plentiful and you should factor that into your plans. The main hiking season in the Sandias extends from April through most of November. The temperatures at the top of Sandia Crest average about 15 degrees cooler than in the city, and the forested trails offer a nice escape. Heavy snows preclude winter hiking on most of the trails and turn the east side of the range into a ski destination, but some of the lower west side trails are hiked nearly year round. If your time, or endurance, is limited and you want to browse around the high part of the mountain, there is a paved road that leads up the east side to Sandia Crest (see east side access) or a tram that goes to the top from the west side, with a trail that runs along the crest (see Crest Trail description). No campgrounds are located within the Sandia Mountains; the nearest Forest Service campgrounds are located in the Manzano Mountains to the South.

Map Coverage

The best maps to get are the Sandia Mountain Wilderness map produced by the Forest Service and available at the Tijeras Ranger Station and at various commercial outlets around town, and the map included with *Hikers and Climbers Guide to the Sandias*, a guidebook (see "For Further Information" at the end of this section). They are both complete and up to date as of this writing. The USGS maps that cover the area are, from north to south, the Placitas, Sandia Crest, and Tijeras 7.5-minute quads. These give more detailed topographical coverage, but many of the trails either aren't shown or aren't shown correctly.

Access

Access directions for reaching the various trailheads will be included with the individual trail descriptions but will tend to involve some of the same general approach routes. To avoid redundancy, the following general approach descriptions are provided for reaching the different parts of the mountain.

West Side Access. From Albuquerque, drive east on Interstate 40 and take the Tramway Boulevard exit, the last exit before entering Tijeras Canyon, and head north on Tramway Boulevard. This is a city street, which continues north, skirting the eastern edge of the city and running along the base of the foothills and canyons on the west side of the mountains. At the intersection with the road leading east to the tram (8 miles north of the Interstate), Tramway Boulevard bends to the west and continues until it intersects Interstate 25.

South Side Access. From Albuquerque, drive east on Interstate 40, continuing past the Tramway exit and entering Tijeras Canyon. Tijeras Canyon defines the south side of the Sandia Mountain area, which has trails that are accessed from both the Carnuel and Tijeras/Cedar Crest exits off Interstate 40.

East Side Access. From the Tramway Boulevard exit on Interstate 40 at the east end of Albuquerque, drive 6.4 miles east on the Interstate and take the Cedar Crest exit (Exit 175) heading north on Highway 14. Highway 14 travels north along the east side of the mountains, and after 5.9 miles you will come to the intersection with Highway 536, with road signs pointing west to Sandia Peak Ski Area, Sandia Crest, and the Turquoise Trail. Follow Highway 536 for 9 miles, or 0.6 miles past the ski area, where the paved road turns left and follows an uphill route with a sign pointing to Sandia Crest, while a gravel road continues north. The Sandia Crest road switchbacks its way about 5 miles to the top, while the gravel road, or Las Huertas Canyon road, runs north through Las Huertas Canyon and becomes Highway 165, which goes through the community of Placitas, then turns west and continues to an intersection with Interstate 25. In winter, snow cover closes the Las Huertas Canyon road, but the paved Sandia Crest road is kept open, although fresh snows and icy conditions often require four wheel drive or chains.

North Side Access. From Albuquerque, drive north on Interstate 25 to the exit for Bernalillo and Placitas (this is the second of two Bernalillo exits). Take the exit and drive east on the paved Highway 165 toward Placitas. Placitas is an old village of Spanish origin but now primarily an expanding bedroom community, and I'm not sure where it officially starts. But after driving about 6 miles on Highway 165 you will begin to pass through the village, after which the road bends to the south and travels up Las Huertas Canyon, reversing the route described in "East Side Access" above.

Hiking Trails

As previously mentioned, the Sandia Mountain Wilderness has an extensive system of trails, and the nine trails described below are only about a third of those available. They are among the more popular trails and include a variety of ecosystems and trail lengths. With a few exceptions, Sandia trails tend to be well worn and easy to follow, with trailheads and trail intersections usually well marked. The Sandia Mountains were created by an uplift phenomenon that tilted up a large block of the earth's crust to the east of a fault line running parallel to the west face of the mountain. The west face, visible from the city, represents the edge of this block and is steeper and more abrupt than the more gently sloping east side. Trails on the west side tend to be steeper, more craggy, and catch more sun than the more forested trails on the east side. The mountain terrain has much more depth and is more complex than it appears when viewed from a distance. Off trail shortcuts usually turn out to be more of a thrash than was originally realized, and result in a number of lost hikers each season. If you are hiking with children, don't let them get too far up the trail ahead of you, and don't let them throw rocks off the top as there may be hikers on the trails below.

TRAIL DESCRIPTIONS

Hike #1. Piedra Lisa Spring Trail (#135)

This trail is about 5 miles one way in length, with a trailhead at either end, making a car switch feasible if you don't want to rehike back to the same trailhead. It travels across the ridges and canyons of the northwest corner of the mountain range, below the vertical mass of the west face. Water is often available along the route in Del Agua Canyon. The trail gains 1,200 feet from the south trailhead heading north to the high elevation point at the Rincon, then drops 2,000 feet the rest of the way to the north trailhead. The area traversed by the trail north of the Rincon includes some of the most remote parts of the lower mountain, which are fun to explore if you have the time.

To reach the south trailhead, travel north on Tramway Boulevard (see "West Side Access") past the turnoff to the tram, and as the road begins to curve to the west, turn north on the paved Forest Road

333, which leads to the Juan Tabo Picnic Area. Follow the road about 2 miles, where the pavement ends at the turnoff to Juan Tabo Picnic Area, and continue north on the dirt road past the turnoff to a locked gate with a parking area off to the side. A trail sign at the parking area marks the start of the trail, which leads north, climbing up a slope and dropping down into Juan Tabo Canyon. At this point, there are other trails that branch off to the east, but the Piedra Lisa Trail continues to the north across the arroyo bottom and climbs up out of the canyon and takes a steep path up to the Rincon, the rocky ridge that runs east to west and connects a string of small peaks and buttresses. After cresting the Rincon, the high elevation point of the hike, the trail drops down through ponderosa forests, 0.7 miles to the south fork of Del Agua Canyon, where water is sometimes flowing, and continues to lose elevation as it keeps winding to the north, eventually terminating at the north trailhead. The trail is well maintained and easy to walk in its entirety, and except in the vicinity of the Rincon, the elevation gradient is quite comfortable. Hiking time is 2.5 to 4 hours in each direction.

To reach the north trailhead, travel east on Highway 165 toward Placitas (see "North Side Access") about 3 miles from Interstate 25, past the west entrance to Forest Loop Road 445 and 0.25 miles farther to the east entrance. Turn south on the gravel road at the east entrance and drive about 2 miles to a short spur road, which leads east to the Piedra Lisa Spring Trailhead. The spring after which the trail is named is in the canyon nearby and takes its Spanish name ("smooth rock") from the water-polished granite near the spring.

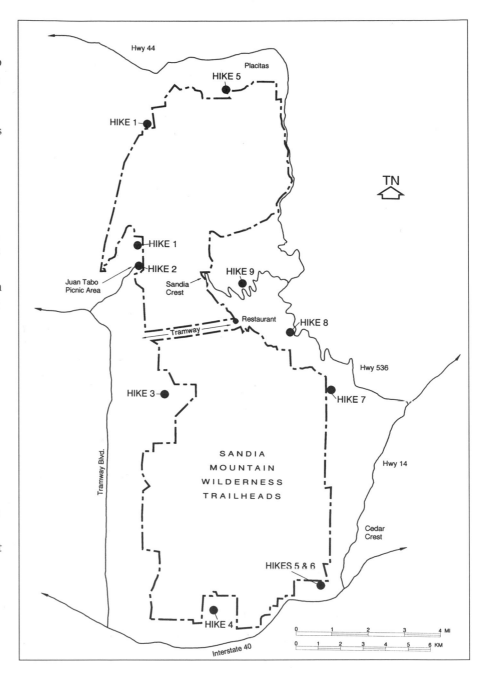

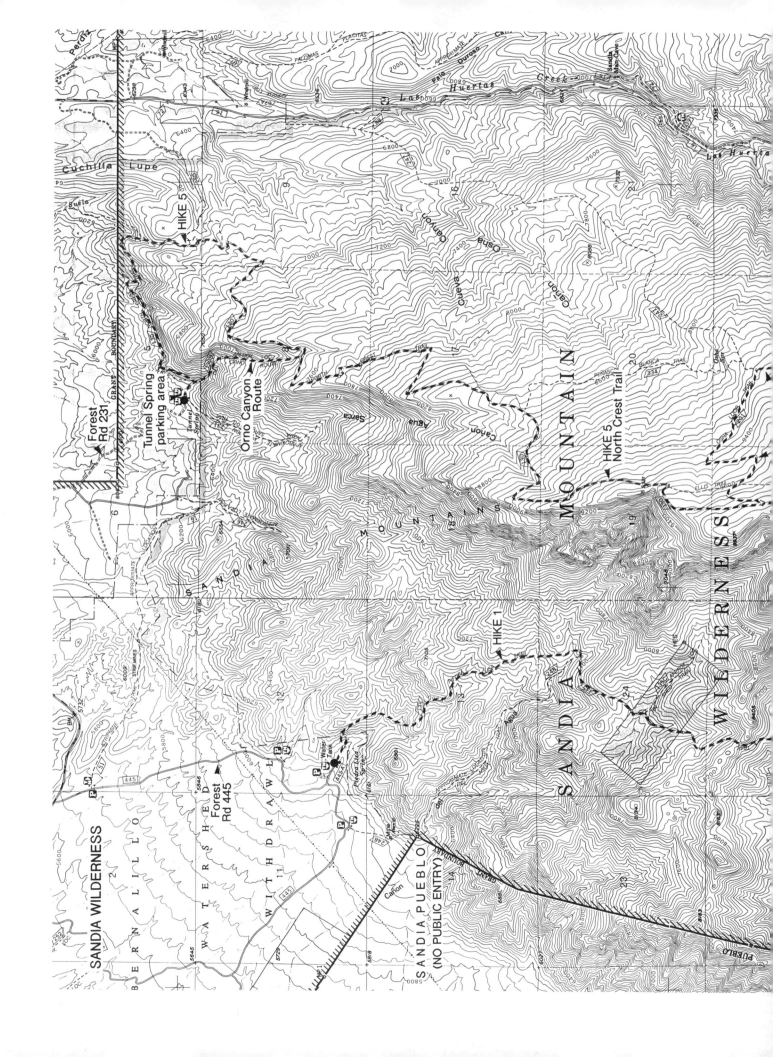

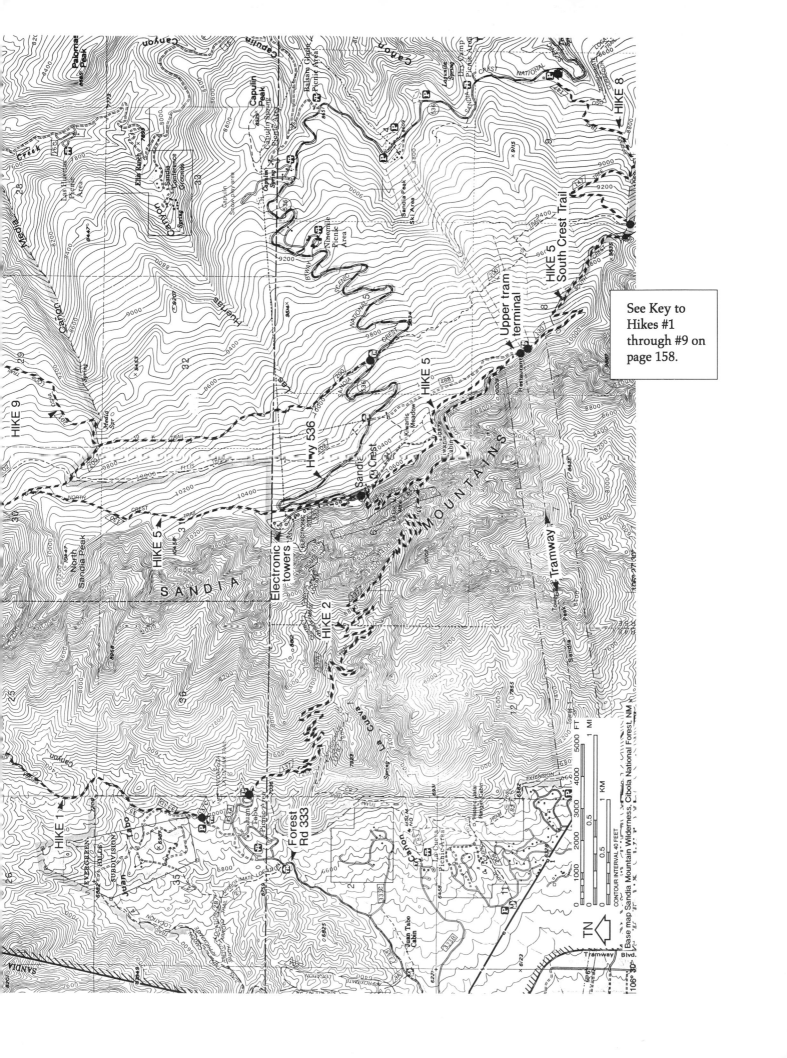

See Key to
Hikes #1
through #9 on
page 158.

Hikes #1 through #5 are shown on preceding pages.

Hike #1. Piedra Lisa Spring Trail (#135)

Distance — 5 miles one way or 10 miles round trip
Net elevation gain — From the south end, gains 1,200 feet to the high point, then drops 2,000 feet to the north end
Difficulty — Moderate to strenuous

Hike #2. La Luz Trail (#137)

Distance — 7 (7.8) miles one way or 14 (15.6) miles round trip
Net elevation gain — 3,600 (3,210) feet
Difficulty — Strenuous

Hike #3. Pino Canyon Trail (#140)

Distance — 9 miles round trip
Net elevation gain — 2,680 feet
Difficulty — Moderate to strenuous

Hike #4. Three Gun Spring Trail (#194)

Distance — 9.6 miles round trip to Deer Pass
Net elevation gain — 3,160 feet
Difficulty — Strenuous

Hike #5. Crest Trail (#130)

Distance — 16 miles one way for south segment, 12.2 miles one way for north segment; 28.2 miles total
Net elevation gain — 4,000 feet for south segment, 4,300 feet for north segment
Difficulty — Strenuous

Hikes #6 and #7 are shown on pages 160–161.

Hike #6. Faulty Trail (#195)

Distance — 9 miles one way, 18 miles round trip
Net elevation gain — 1,240 feet from Canyon Estates trailhead
Difficulty — Moderate

Hike #7. Cienega Trail (#148)

Distance — 4.6 miles round trip
Net elevation gain — 1,700 feet
Difficulty — Moderate

Hike #8. Tree Spring Trail (#147)

Distance — 3.6 miles round trip
Net elevation gain — 880 feet
Difficulty — Easy

Hike #9. Osha Loop Trail

Distance — 7 miles round trip from the Crest Highway
Net elevation gain — 800 feet
Difficulty — Easy to moderate

Hike #2. La Luz Trail (#137)

The La Luz Trail was for many years the most heavily hiked trail on the west side of the mountain, and continues to share that distinction with the recently completed Pino Canyon Trail. It is the standard hiking route to the top of Sandia Crest, the high point of the range at 10,678 feet. La Luz means "the light" in Spanish, and the name apparently derives from the old La Luz mine high up on the west face. The lower trailhead begins in the piñon pine/juniper belt, and the route ends in the subalpine forests at the top, which include aspen, corkbark fir, Douglas fir, and Engelmann spruce. There is lots of beautiful canyon scenery along the way. The trail splits about 200 feet below the summit ridge, with one branch going up to Sandia Crest and the other branch up to the upper tram terminal a little over a mile farther to the south. The view from the top is fantastic, as you look out to the west across the Rio Grande Valley, and you will be sharing it with perhaps several dozen tourists—those who drove up the back side to Sandia Crest, or those who rode the tram up. There is a restaurant at the upper tram terminal, which is also at the top of the ski area on the east side, and there is a gift shop at Sandia Crest. A short segment of the Crest Trail connects the two locations. If you are only going to do one hike in the Sandias, the La Luz Trail would probably get my vote. It is, however, a fairly strenuous hike, with a one-way distance of 7 miles to Sandia Crest or 7.8 miles to the upper tram terminal, and elevation gains of 3,600 feet and 3,210 feet respectively. There are lots of ways to do this hike. You can hike it up and back down, in which case you should have lots of water and moleskin in your pack, or you can have someone meet you at the top (Sandia Crest) or have a car shuttle in place. Or

you can hike up to the tram terminal and buy a tram ticket back down (with a car shuttle), or you can do any of the above in reverse order. Anyway you do it, this is one of the classic hikes in the Sandias or in the state. Hiking time from bottom to top is typically 3.5 to 5.5 hours.

To reach the lower trailhead, drive north on Tramway Boulevard past the tram turnoff (see "West Side Access") and, as the road begins to curve west, turn north on Forest Road 333 toward Juan Tabo Picnic Area. The road is paved the 2-mile drive to the picnic area, where a sign directs you to a turnoff to the east between a set of stone pillars. Drive the side road past the picnic area to an upper-level parking lot, where the road ends. The trailhead is at the east side of the parking area. The lower part of the trail involves a lengthy set of broad switchbacks that gain altitude and eventually bring you out on the north side of upper La Cueva Canyon. From here on, the scenery is exceptional all the way up. Something over a mile farther on, the trail crosses over to the south side of the canyon and the elevation gain picks up as the trail begins to switchback up a long series of talus slopes. The scenery keeps getting better, and you may see or hear climbers on the steep rock faces in this part of the canyon. As the trail reaches a ridge below the top, there is a fork, with one branch leading north up to Sandia Crest and the other south to the upper tram terminal. These final trail branches lead up through the band of Pennsylvanian limestone that caps the mountain and that contrasts nicely with the precambrian granite over which it lies. Should you decide to start your hike from the top at Sandia Crest, drive to the top by the route described under "East Side Access."

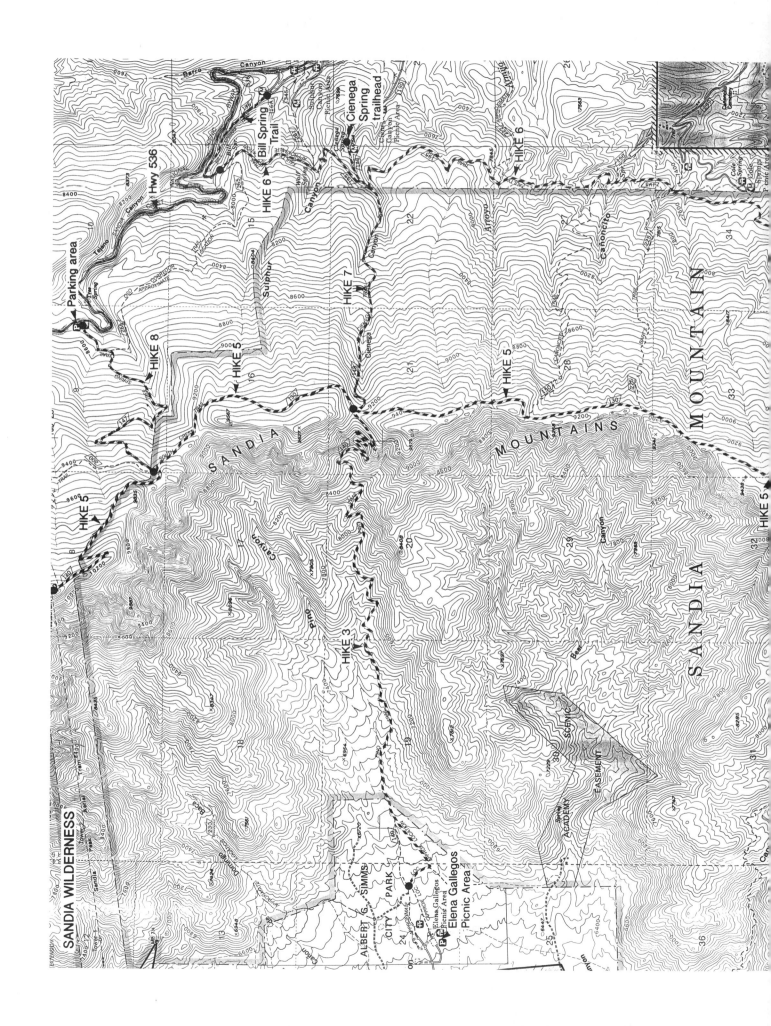

WILDERNESS

South Sandia
Peak
9782

Oso Pass

Deer Pass

HIKE 6

HIKE 6
Alternate
"Y" route

HIKES 5 & 6

South Sandia
Spring

HIKE 5
South Crest Trail

Three Gun
Spring

HIKE 4

Lorenzo

Casa Loma

Hwy 14

Canyon Estates
trailhead

Interstate 40

TN

CONTOUR INTERVAL 40 FEET

1 MI

1 KM

Base map Sandia Mountain Wilderness, Cibola National Forest, NM.

Hike #3. Pino Canyon Trail (#140)

This is another trail that ascends the steep western slope of the mountain. It is a fairly new trail that climbs up Pino Canyon and ends at a saddle on the crest ridge, with Pino Canyon to the west and Cienega Canyon to the east. The round-trip trail distance to the top is 9 miles, with a 2,680-foot elevation gain. The trail is well laid out, easy to follow, and fun to hike. There is usually water available about halfway up below a spring at the 8,120-foot elevation level (purify it). The trail starts below the foothills and travels through scattered piñon and juniper groves before ascending through forests of ponderosa, aspen, spruce, and fir. There are occasional vistas on the way up and very nice scenery at the crest ridge where the trail ends. The standard hike is to climb to the top and return back down the same route, but my favorite way to do this hike is to go up the Pino Canyon Trail and descend the Cienega Trail, which joins at the top and drops 2.3 miles down the east side (see Hike #7), or the reverse route. This variation requires leaving a car at the ending trailhead. The Crest Trail also runs along the top of the ridge where the Pino Canyon and Cienega trails join, which provides the alternative to continue your hike either north or south along the crest ridge.

To reach the lower trailhead, drive north on Tramway Boulevard (see "West Side Access") about 2 miles north of Montgomery Boulevard, where you will see a road sign directing you to the Elena Gallegos Picnic Area via a right turn on to a paved road to the east. Drive east up this access road to the picnic area, where you will be charged a nominal fee to enter, and continue to a parking area at the east end of the picnic area, where a trail sign locates the trailhead. Because of the many paths crisscrossing the vicinity to the east of the picnic area, there may be a little confusion at first, but the trail heads up toward the south end of the canyon entrance, where it enters the Wilderness Area. The lower part of this trail has gotten very popular and is very well worn, so finding it shouldn't be a problem. The trail is easy to follow all the way up, as it stays on the south side of the canyon most of the way before crossing over to the north side and beginning a set of fairly steep switchbacks that traverse back and forth across the head of the canyon and cover the final distance to the saddle at the top of the ridge. A trail sign will mark the obvious intersection with the Crest Trail, and a short scramble up the limestone ledges to the south will provide a great view back down the canyon. This saddle has been used since prehistoric times as a crossing point to get from one side of the range to the other. Cienega Canyon is the canyon to the east of this saddle, and you will also notice the trail sign marking the upper end of that trail. Should you decide to supplement your hike by taking in some of the Crest Trail, a hike along the trail to the south toward South Sandia Peak takes you through some nice terrain. The round-trip distance to South Peak is 8 miles, but you don't have to do the whole thing. Allow 2 to 4 hours to hike the trail in each direction.

Hike #4. Three Gun Spring Trail (#194)

This picturesque-sounding trail begins in Tijeras Canyon at the south end of the Sandias and climbs to Deer Pass on the crest ridge just south of South Sandia Peak (the final climb to Deer Pass uses the top end of the Embudito Trail). It is a trail you may want to avoid during hot weather because of its southern exposure, but it is pleasant during the rest of the year, with the exception that the top part will be snowbound in winter. The trail gets its name from three pistols that were carved on an old watering trough near Three Gun Spring, below which the trail passes just before the steep switchbacks at the head of the canyon. The round-trip distance for this hike is 9.6 miles, or a little more if you intend to scramble on up to South Peak, and the net elevation gain to Deer Pass is 3,160 feet, making it fairly strenuous if you intend to go all the way to the top. The trail is well worn and easy to follow, with many nice vistas on the way up. Three Gun Spring Trail is also used as a starting point to access the start of the Hawk Watch Trail, a short trail leading up to a vantage point where volunteers take a raptor count each spring. Water is available along the Three Gun Spring Trail at Three Gun Spring, and sometimes at a spring above Embudo Canyon.

To reach the trailhead, drive east from Albuquerque on Interstate 40 and take the Carnuel exit (this is the first exit east of the Tramway Boulevard exit), and head east on Old Highway 66 for 1.5 miles to the Monticello subdivision. Turn north into the subdivision and go 0.5 miles to a west turn on to Allegre Street, and then a north turn on to Siempre Verde, which you follow north until the road ends at the mouth of the arroyo that runs out of the canyon. There is currently neither trail sign nor parking facility at this point; however, park your car off to the side and walk up the arroyo a short distance until you can start up a broad path that exits the arroyo to the left. This trail (jeep road) continues north up the broad ridge to the west of the arroyo and leads to the Wilderness boundary, where a trail sign marks the official start of the trail. Just past the Wilderness boundary is another trail sign, which marks the trailhead for the Hawk Watch Trail that travels off to the east. The Three Gun Spring Trail continues north up the center of the canyon through the Sonoran vegetation

typical of this elevation until you pass below the spring, which is located to the east, and begin a series of steep switchbacks that bring you to the ponderosa stands above the head of the canyon. From here, the trail swings to the west to gain the ridge that helps form the east side of Embudo Canyon, turns north along this ridge, passes the intersection with the Embudo Canyon Trail (of which there are two), and continues north to Oso Pass. Oso Pass is a saddle on the ridge separating Embudo Canyon to the south and Embudito Canyon to the north. Three Gun Spring Trail joins the Embudito Trail (#192), which comes up the other side at Oso Pass, and the final segment of trail turns to the east and climbs 880 vertical feet to an intersection with the Crest Trail at Deer Pass on the crest ridge. A trail sign marks this intersection. If you have the energy to make this final push to the top, you should do so, because this is one of the loveliest parts of the mountain. If you have a little extra time and energy to spare, go ahead and scramble to the top of South Peak, about 0.5 miles north of the Deer Park trail intersection. The view from the top will make this last excursion worthwhile. Round trip hiking time is 5 to 9 hours.

Hike #5. Crest Trail (#130)

The Crest Trail, which is mentioned in most of the other trail descriptions, is the longest trail in the Sandia Mountains, and essentially traverses the entire length of the ridge line. The total length of the trail is 28.2 miles, and because the trail is conveniently (or inconveniently, according to your point of view) interrupted by the facilities at Sandia Crest, at the high point of the hike, the trail is often thought of as two separate trails: the South Crest Trail, 16 miles long from the south trailhead at Canyon Estates in Tijeras Canyon to Sandia Crest, with a

4,000-foot net elevation gain; and the North Crest Trail, 12.2 miles long from the north trailhead at Tunnel Springs near Placitas to Sandia Crest, with a 4,300-foot net elevation gain. A third natural subset would be the short segment between Sandia Crest and the upper tram terminal to the south. The Crest Trail serves as a connector for most of the trails that climb up the east and west sides of the range and terminate at the crest ridge line, making possible numerous loop hikes using various side trails. For endurance hikers with tough feet and good lungs, the entire Crest Trail can be hiked in a long day; it has even been run both ways in a day. But most hikers will consider it a more reasonable undertaking to select a portion of the trail as a dayhiking objective, and the possibilities are numerous. The minimum elevation gain possibilities are to start the trail at either Sandia Crest, which can be driven to up the east side, or the upper tram terminal, which can be accessed by tram car from the west side. From these departure points, you can walk either north or south along the Crest Trail and return. You can do a more strenuous hike by walking up the trail from one of the end points to Sandia Crest and a prepositioned automobile. One of the many loop hikes you can do would be to start up the Crest Trail at the south trailhead and hike to the Bart trail, which would be hiked down to the Faulty Trail, and the Faulty Trail would be taken back to the original starting point. Since most of the side trails that intersect the Crest Trail aren't described in this book, you would need a map for the creative loop/car shuttle options; whatever your plans, you should carry a map anyway. Water is unavailable along the length of the Crest Trail, except at South Sandia Spring, about 2 miles south of South Peak, and at Tunnel Spring at the north trailhead. Also, you can purchase soft drinks at Sandia Crest or the tram terminal if you arrive during business hours. Because it would require packing significant quantities of water over steep terrain, backpacking the Crest Trail is not particularly feasible. Hiking times vary with the section of trail hiked, but as a general guide, the average hiker should allow the better part of a day to hike either the North or South Crest Trail.

Directions for reaching the most common access points are as follows:

Sandia Crest. Drive up the east side on the route described under "East Side Access." The North Crest Trail begins just to the north of the parking area below the complex of communication towers. The South Crest Trail begins immediately south of the gift shop.

Upper Tram Terminal. Drive to the turnoff for the tram road, mentioned under "West Side Access," and follow it east to the Sandia Peak Tram Company at the end of the road. You can purchase a tram ticket at the lower tram terminal and enjoy a spectacular ride up the west face of the mountain. The Crest Trail picks up at either end of the upper tram complex.

South Trailhead. Drive east from Albuquerque on Interstate 40 ("South Side Access"), and take the Tijeras/Cedar Crest exit, bearing right toward Tijeras. At the stop sign, turn north under the overpass then turn to the right up the dead-end road that goes through the Canyon Estates residential area. A parking area at the trailhead is located at the end of the road.

North Trailhead. Take the route described under "North Side Access" and drive about 5 miles east from Interstate 25 on Highway 165 to the Forest Road 231 turnoff at a large cluster of mailboxes.

Sandia Mountain
Wilderness

Turn south on the graveled forest road, and follow the main route 1.9 miles to the trailhead at Tunnel Spring, where there is always a nice flow of water coming from the spring. The trail takes off to the east before making a broad loop back around across the head of Orno Canyon. You may notice a fairly well-used trail cutting south up the canyon shortly after the start of the regular trail. This is a shortcut that rejoins the main trail as it cuts across the head of the canyon.

The Crest Trail is well worn and needs no narrative to describe its route. Its many trail intersections are generally well marked, and there is little potential for confusion. It is a popular trail but not at all crowded, except perhaps in the vicinity of Sandia Crest and the upper tram terminal. You will almost certainly end up hiking at least part of the trail if you do any amount of hiking in the Sandias.

Hike #6. Faulty Trail (#195

Located on the wooded slopes of the lower east side of the mountain, the Faulty Trail branches off the Crest Trail beyond the Canyon Estates trailhead and runs north for 9 miles, intersecting a number of other trails along the way. The trail maintains a fairly level contour but has localized ups and downs as it cuts across numerous side canyons on its way north, where it ends at an intersection with the Bill Spring and Oso Corredor trails. The net elevation gain to this point is 1,240 feet. The trail was constructed surreptitiously and later adopted by the Forest Service into its trail system. It was constructed partly along a fault line, which accounts for its name, and is notable for the unusual diamond-shaped tree blazes that mark its route; it has also been known as the Diamond Trail and the Mystery Trail. The trail is easy to follow and fairly popular with hikers. The side trails that are encountered make this an obvious choice for a one-way hike to a different trailhead using a car shuttle; good destinations to accomplish this would be the Cole Springs Picnic Area and the trailheads for the Cañoncito, Cienega, and Bill Springs Trails. The Faulty Trail can also be accessed by one of these side trails. Water is available nearby at several points along the trail, including Cole Springs, Cañoncito Spring, Cienega Spring, and, sometimes, Wolf Spring. Because the Faulty Trail is within forest cover for its duration, it provides a shady alternative in summer, as do the other east side trails, to the more sunlit west side trails.

This hike begins at the south end, at the Canyon Estates trailhead for the Crest Trail. Reach this trailhead by driving east from Albuquerque (see "South Side Access") on Interstate 40 to the Tijeras/Cedar Crest exit. Take the exit, bearing right toward Tijeras, turn north at the stop sign, drive under the overpass, then right on to the dead-end road. The road goes through the Canyon Estates subdivision and ends at a parking area at the trailhead. Hike up the Crest Trail for a little over 0.5 miles, where the Faulty Trail begins at a trail sign and slants north up a rocky slope. Follow the diamond blazes as the trail continues to contour north along the lower slopes of the mountain. At the north end of the trail, you can hike down the Bill Spring Trail to Doc Long Picnic Area, or you can continue up the new Oso Corredor Trail, which is essentially a northern extension to Faulty, 3 more miles to an intersection with the Tree Spring Trail, just above the trailhead.

Hike #7. Cienega Trail (#148)

This is a pleasant little trail that climbs up through the forests on the east side of the mountain to a saddle on the crest ridge, where it intersects the Crest and Pino Canyon trails with a spectacular lookout over Bear, Pino, and Domingo Baca canyons. It is 2.3 miles long (4.6 miles round trip) and gains 1,700 feet. It is steep but doesn't seem excessively so, and it is an enjoyable hike with nice forest scenery. It can be combined with the Pino Canyon Trail for a one-way hike, or with the Crest and/or Faulty trails for a longer loop.

The Cienega Trail begins at the northwest end of the Cienega Picnic Area, where a parking area and trail sign mark the start of the trail. To locate the picnic area, refer first to the "East Side Access" directions. After turning west on to Highway 536 off Highway 14, drive 2 miles to a sign on the west side of the road for the Cienega Picnic Area, and follow the paved access road to the picnic area, and on to the end of the road where the trail begins. A short 0.2-mile walk leads past a flowing stream to the intersection with the Faulty Trail and the only point on the trail that might be mildly confusing. Take care not to turn onto one of the branches of the Faulty Trail, but continue straight on the middle trail branch that takes a steep path up the side of the canyon. This is a nice trail to do in the summer when the weather turns hot; start early in the morning when it is especially pleasant and you are not likely to encounter other hikers. Round-trip hiking time is 2.5 to 5 hours.

Hike #8. Tree Spring Trail (#147)

The Tree Spring Trail is another of the trails that ascend the east side of the mountain, and it is probably the most popular of the east side trails. It is a short trail of 1.8 miles (3.6 miles round trip), with a relatively modest 880 feet of elevation gain. It intersects the Crest and 10K trails at the top end, and a short walk up to the crest ridge provides a spectacular view across Pino and Domingo Baca Canyons to the west. This is another good hot-weather hike up through the forests and is easy to fit into your schedule, with a typical round-trip hiking time of only 1.5 to 3 hours. The spring after which the trail is named is located some distance down the slope from the trailhead on the other side of Highway 536. An interesting side feature of Tree Spring is the nearby discovery, made in 1956, of the fossil remains of a mastodon. At an elevation of 8,470 feet, this is one of the highest sites in the state known to have produced mastodon remains, and they may be from an individual only a few thousand years old.

To reach the trailhead, follow the directions under "East Side Access" to the turnoff for Highway 536 off of Highway 14. Drive west 5.7 miles on Highway 536, where you will see a parking area constructed along the west side of the road, with a trail sign marking the start of the trail just inside the tree line. There was an earlier trail that probably followed an old wagon road that goes up through the same vicinity and occasionally crosses the present trail. However, the main trail is very well worn, and you won't have any trouble following it. If you should care to extend the length of the hike, you can hike down the Oso Corredor Trail, which is crossed shortly above the trailhead, hike north on the 10K Trail, or follow the Crest Trail up to the upper tram terminal.

Hike #9. Osha Loop Trail (#201)

This hike includes not only the Osha Loop Trail but sections of the Crest Trail and 10K Trail. The route described here is 7 miles round trip and has a net elevation gain of 800 feet. The loop part of the trail passes above two reliable springs: Media Spring is immediately below the trail, and Osha Spring is 290 vertical feet below the trail, requiring substantially more effort to reach. The trail gets its name from a wild medicinal herb called osha that grows in the marshy area around Osha Spring. The plant tastes and smells like celery but is in the same family as the poisonous hemlock plant, with a similar leaf structure, so it is risky to experiment with it unless you know what you are doing. This is one of my favorite trails, with lots of varied flora and geology to observe along the way. There are some fine old stands of timber, including some large specimens of aspen, corkbark fir, Engelmann spruce, and Douglas fir. Along the lower parts of the trail are some nice oak groves and stands of ponderosa pine. The trail is well worn and easy to follow, although the stretch of trail north of Media Spring does have some relatively faint spots that are marked with cairns (a rarity in the Sandias) to help locate the route.

To locate the starting point for the hike, refer to the "East Side Access" directions and drive up the road toward Sandia Crest, where the paved road continues past the turnoff for the graveled Las Huertas Road leading to Placitas. After you have passed Nine Mile Picnic Area, begin counting the switchbacks in the road where the road switches from a north heading to a south heading. On the stretch of road between the third and fourth north switchback, you will see a broad road cut through the forest heading north, at the entrance to which is a crude parking area on the north side of the road. Park here and walk up from the parking area into the timber at the west edge of the road cut, where you will pick up the 10K Trail, which heads northwest through the forest. Actually, this is a continuation of the 10K Trail, which begins about 2 miles to the south on the other side of the Crest Road. After you have hiked north on the 10K Trail for 2 miles, you will come to the trail sign marking the start of the Osha Loop Trail. The 10K Trail continues up to the left (you will return back down this branch), and the Osha Loop Trail heads downhill to the east. Follow the Osha Loop Trail down a short distance to a point just above Media Spring, where the trail turns north and continues to an intersection with the Osha Spring Trail (if you want to visit Osha Spring, walk down the Osha Spring Trail to the Peñasco Blanco Trail intersection and follow the latter trail down into Osha Canyon). At the Osha Spring Trail intersection, the Osha Loop Trail turns west and heads uphill, crosses another road cut higher up (the Forest Service is now calling the trail that heads along its length the Ellis Trail), and joins the Crest Trail as it tops out near the ridge line. The road cuts that are referred to were originally intended to be the right-of-way for a more grandiose and "improved" version of the present Crest Road, but the plan was abandoned in the face of popular protest that developed when it became evident how much of the forest would be impacted by the giant new switchbacks that would run the road all over the side of the mountain. The cleared road cuts remain but are slowly being reclaimed by locust and small aspens. At the Crest Trail intersection (not presently marked with a trail sign), the Osha Loop Trail officially ends, but to complete the hike turn and walk south about 0.25 miles along the Crest Trail to a set of stone benches at an overlook above Del Agua Canyon. Just past the overlook, the 10K Trail branches off to the left and leads downhill to the 10K/Osha Loop intersection mentioned earlier. Complete the hike by returning on the 10K Trail back south to the original starting point.

For Further Information:

U.S. Forest Service
Sandia Ranger District
Box 11776
Tijeras, NM 87059
(505) 281-3304

Hikers and Climbers Guide to the Sandias, by Mike Hill, published by University of New Mexico Press, 1983.

Water Fowl Congregate in
the Rio Grande Nature
Center

GENERAL DESCRIPTION

The Rio Grande Nature Center is a
New Mexico state park located within the
city of Albuquerque on the east bank of
the Rio Grande. The park is a 270-acre
preserve situated along the river bosque
—a riparian habitat typical of the densely
wooded belts that form along the moist
river valley bordering the river. The
bosque is an ancient ecosystem that has
assumed its own distinctive blend of life
forms, and presently includes introduced
species and other modifications wrought
by the hand of man. It is a thriving
community of plants and animals that
exists adjacent to a large metropolitan
area, but in most ways it reflects the
nature values as you would expect to find
them in a similar habitat in a more
remote setting. River bosques of varying
depth and complexity have formed along
all the major rivers of the state, and these
thin green strips of vegetation form one

Rio Grande
Nature
Center

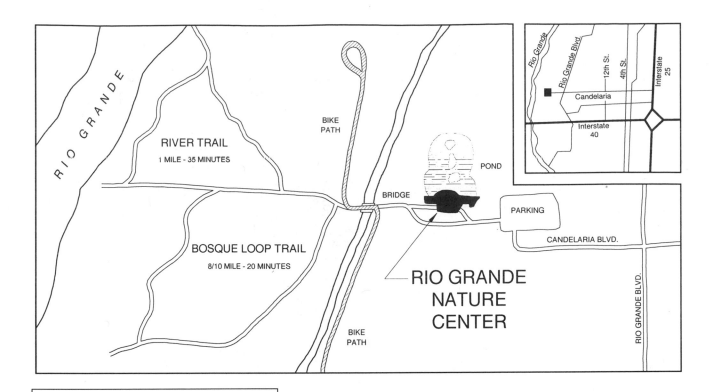

Hike #1. River Trail

Distance — 1.0 mile
Net elevation gain — Negligible
Difficulty — Easy

Hike #2. Bosque Trail

Distance — 0.8 miles
Net elevation gain — Negligible
Difficulty — Easy

of the identifiable types of wilderness ecosystems that the state has to offer. The Nature Center provides an opportunity for the visitor to stroll through and observe this natural resource.

The centerpiece of the Rio Grande Nature Center is a Visitor Center that includes self-guided exhibits dealing with natural and historical information concerning the Rio Grande, and the social implications of a population long tied to its resources and affected by its flows. Also included are a small library and a nearby waterfowl impoundment with viewing area. Leading out from the Visitor Center are nature trails, providing 2 miles of easy walking through the bosque and along the river. A bike path also runs through the area and continues south along the drainage canal. This is a popular area for bird watching, plant identification, and nature photography, and the center conducts special weekend programs for both children and adults. The nature center is open year round every day from 10:00 a.m. to 5:00 p.m., with an admission fee of $1.00 for adults and $.50 for children.

Map Coverage

No topographic map coverage is needed.

Access

From Interstate 40, take the Rio Grande Boulevard exit and travel north for 1.4 miles to Candelaria Boulevard. Turn west on Candelaria and drive to the gate at the end of the road (where the bike trail can be accessed). The parking area is immediately north of the gate, and a short walk to the west leads to the Visitor Center. The walking trails begin to the west of the Visitor Center.

Hiking Trails

The trails begin as a single path that leads west from the Visitor Center and crosses the bridge over the drainage canal. This canal drains what would ordinarily be swampy lands bordering the river and channels the water back into the river south of the city. On the west side of the bridge is the start of the two trails that traverse the bosque. The trails are connected and can be hiked separately or combined into one loop. The River Trail is 1 mile in length, combines a walk through the bosque with a section along the river bank, and is marked with red numbered posts. The Bosque Trail makes a 0.8-mile loop through the bosque, with blue-numbered marker posts along its length. The red and blue marker posts are numbered to correlate to trail guides for each trail, which are available at the Visitor Center. You will get much more out of the hike if you bring along these guides, including quite a bit of information about the river environment and some of the modifications brought by man. Each trail can be easily walked in 30 to 45 minutes. The trails are easy to follow but can be muddy in spots. No pets or firearms are allowed in the area.

For Further Information:

Rio Grande Nature Center
  2901 Candelaria
  Boulevard NW
  Albuquerque, NM
  87107
  (505) 344-7240

Rio Grande Nature Center, a small brochure funded by Friends of RGNC, same address as above.

Riverwalk Trail and *Bosque Trail*, trail guide booklets available at the Visitor Center.

Macaw Petroglyph in Petroglyph Park

Petroglyph National Monument

GENERAL DESCRIPTION

Petroglyph National Monument is an area established along a 17-mile stretch of basalt escarpment capping the west rim of the Rio Grande Valley, immediately adjacent to the city of Albuquerque, and encompassing a string of small extinct volcanos farther to the west. The main attraction of the monument is the prehistoric Native American rock art that abounds in profusion on the dark-colored rocks and walls of the escarpment, and

also the volcanos that stand as sentinels along the skyline west of Albuquerque. To better appreciate the area, it is interesting to understand something of the natural history that produced the setting in which the monument is situated.

There is a great fault system that cuts through the earth's crust and runs from central Colorado, south through New Mexico, and well into the state of Chihuahua in Mexico. Named the Rio Grande Fault after the river that flows along its path, the fault had its beginning some 30 million years ago as the earth's crust was pulled apart along parallel fault lines, with parts of the center section between the fault lines sinking as much as 26,000 feet below the surface on either side, only to be gradually filled in with massive amounts of sand, gravel, and volcanic debris. Eventually, the low spots along the rift filled with water, until these bodies of water were connected by the river that continues to flow down this natural pathway. As part of the subsequent volcanic activity that accompanied the forces being generated below the surface of the earth, a string of five small volcanos along the fault line west of Albuquerque erupted about 190,000 years ago, pouring forth a blanket of basaltic rock from within the earth's mantle across the mesas above the west side of the valley, and creating the basalt escarpment that is clearly visible from the city today.

Petroglyphs are designs that have been scratched or pecked onto the dark veneer on the surface of the rock, and by close examination, it is obvious that the basalt escarpment described above is prime petroglyph material; the surfaces are flat and smooth and the rock has a dark-brown surface coloration. Evidently, the prehistoric Indians were similarly impressed with it, because beginning approximately 1000 A.D. through historic times (but predominantly between about

1300 A.D. to 1500 A.D.), innumerable petroglyphs were placed on the rocks all along the stretch currently encompassed by the national monument, providing one of the finest accumulations of prehistoric rock art in the Southwest. These rock designs continue to speak out through the ages, but what they are saying and why they were placed remains one of the intriguing mysteries of archaeology. Currently, the only developed part of the national monument is the Indian Petroglyph State Park, now incorporated into the monument, located at the north end of Unser Boulevard, and encompassing a particularly rich concentration of petroglyphs. Further park development is planned, once the remaining privately owned land within the park boundaries is acquired.

Albuquerque weather (nice) and paved roads leading to the monument make for year-round hiking conditions, although the only formal trails currently in place are in the existing state park facility, which has a $1.00 per car entry fee. Elevation differential within the monument varies from 5,250 feet at the state park facility below the escarpment on the east side, to 5,830 feet at the summit of Vulcan, the largest of the west-side volcanos. No camping is allowed in the monument, and no water is available. There are several commercial campgrounds in the Albuquerque area but no public camping facilities in the immediate vicinity. The primary vegetation in the monument are four wing saltbush, sand and purple sage, grama and muhly grasses, a few types of cacti, and some nonindigenous species that come from several hundred years of domestic livestock grazing. There are some open spaces within the area that are remarkably remote in character for a national monument this close to Albuquerque, and you can enjoy some off-trail hiking, which is pretty much free of other hikers. But if you are looking for true solitude and don't mind driving some more to find it, there are better places to go.

As a final bit of background information, I will point out that the whole area surrounding the Petroglyph Park is currently in a state of flux: proponents of various development projects, local homeowners, preservationists, landowners, various government officials, and just about everyone else is actively squabbling over how the area around the park should be developed, how much area the park should encompass, and how it should be administered and by whom (it currently falls within the jurisdictions of the National Park Service, the City of Albuquerque, and the New Mexico State Park Division). As a result of all of this, such things as park boundaries, road access, and trail development are bound to change, possibly rendering obsolete some of the material presented in the balance of the section.

Map Coverage

The Petroglyph National Monument is covered by the USGS 7.5-minute scale Los Griegos, Volcano Ranch, and La Mesita Negra SE maps. Because the Albuquerque West Side is growing rapidly, the roads shown on all the maps are well out of date. See access directions below to locate the monument.

Access

The two main points of entry to the monument are the state park facility (currently its status as of this writing) on the east side and the volcanos on the west side. To reach the state park facility, which is the primary visitor entrance, drive west from Albuquerque on Interstate 40 and take the Unser Boulevard exit (Exit 154, the next exit west of Coors Boulevard),

Looking South from the Summit of Vulcan

PETROGLYPH NATIONAL MONUMENT

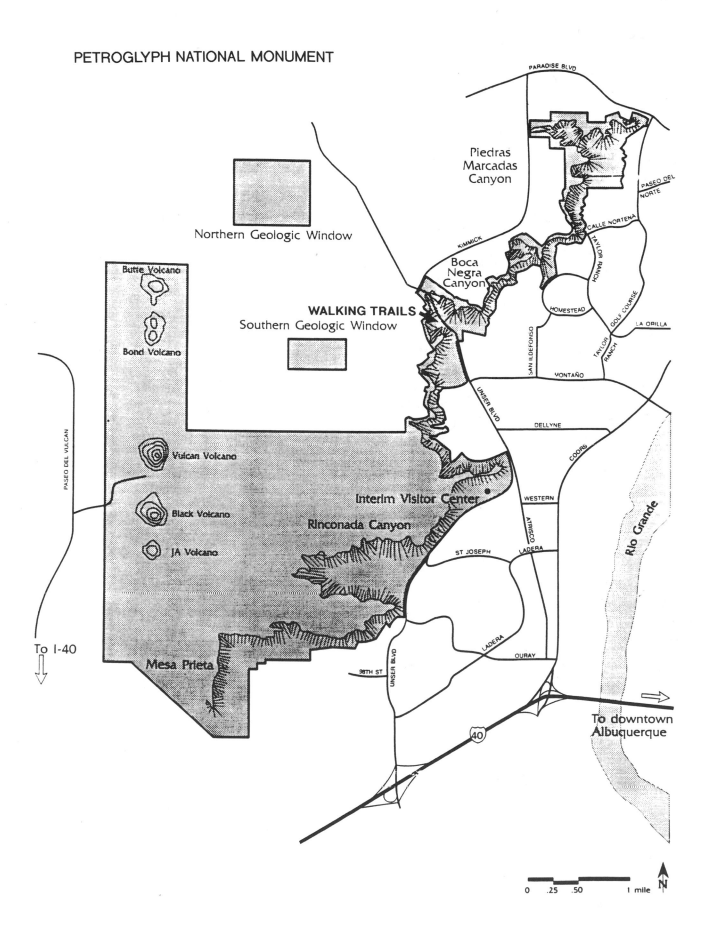

Northern Geologic Window

WALKING TRAILS
Southern Geologic Window

Butte Volcano

Bond Volcano

Vulcan Volcano

Black Volcano

JA Volcano

PASEO DEL VULCAN

To I-40

Mesa Prieta

Piedras Marcadas Canyon

PARADISE BLVD

PASEO DEL NORTE

KIMMICK

CALLE NORTENA

TAYLOR RANCH

GOLF COURSE

LA ORILLA

Boca Negra Canyon

HOMESTEAD

SAN ILDEFONSO

TAYLOR RANCH

MONTAÑO

UNSER BLVD

DELLYNE

COORS

WESTERN

Interim Visitor Center

Rinconada Canyon

ATRISCO

St JOSEPH

LADERA

Rio Grande

LADERA

OURAY

98TH ST

UNSER BLVD

40

To downtown Albuquerque

0   .25   .50   1 mile   N

and drive north on Unser Boulevard. This road will eventually go all the way to the monument, but since it is not yet completed all the way, take a right at the first stop sign north of Interstate 40 at Ladera (no street sign at present). Continue 2.5 miles on Ladera, east then north, to a stop light at Atrisco Boulevard. Turn left on Atrisco and follow it west (the street name eventually becomes Unser) all the way to the Petroglyph Park facility at the base of the basalt escarpment. An alternative route is to travel north on Coors Boulevard, turn left on Sequoia, then west on Atrisco.

To reach the volcanos, drive west on Interstate 40 past the Unser Boulevard exit, and exit going north at the Airport/Central Avenue exit (Exit 149) and continue north on the paved road for 4.8 miles to the intersection with a dirt road that turns right (east) past an "Open Space and Volcano Park" sign. Follow this dirt road for just over 1 mile to an undeveloped parking area to the west of the two prominent volcanos.

Hiking Trails

There are three short, self-guided trails at the Petroglyph Park facility, which lead past many of the more impressive rock art panels. These trails are easy to walk and present a good representation of the rock art typical of this area. Numbered stations along the trails correspond to short written descriptions in the guide pamphlet available at the trailheads. The pamphlet provides interpretations of some of the individual petroglyphs and information on archaeological features, geology, and plant life. It also provides a short discussion of the prehistory and early history of the area. There are also some rough trails that have been worn in above and below the basalt escarpment, which begin west of Unser Boulevard just north of the Ladera turnoff and follow the escarpment north. The ownership situation for parts of the monument is currently in a state of flux, and the most pragmatic approach to off-trail hiking is to hike where you want unless blocked by no trespassing notices. Take care not to touch the petroglyphs that you find or disturb the rocks on which they were placed, as this hastens the process of deterioration.

There is also a short trail that makes a steep but easy ascent of Vulcan and a side trail that leads around to Boca Negra ("black mouth"), a lava vent on the east side of Vulcan. From the parking area at the end of the volcano access route described above, walk east through the fence and follow the broad trail to Vulcan, which is the volcano northeast of the parking area. The main trail leads up to the top, and the Boca Negra trail skirts around the base to the east. There is also plenty of off-trail hiking that can be done to the other volcanos and through the grasslands in the vicinity of the volcanos.

For Further Information:

Petroglyph National
 Monument
 Administrative Office
 123 4th Street, SW
 #101
 Albuquerque, NM
 87102
 (505) 766-8375

Petroglyph National
 Monument
 Visitor Center
 4735 Atrisco Boulevard
 Albuquerque, NM
 87120
 (505) 839-4429

City of Albuquerque
 Open Space Division
 P.O. Box 1293
 Albuquerque, NM
 87103
 (505) 873-6620

Indian Petroglyph State Park Walking Tour, a pamphlet produced by the Office of Open Space, City of Albuquerque, P.O. box 1293, Albuquerque, NM 87103.

Petroglyph National Monument, a pamphlet produced by the National Park Service, U.S. Department of the Interior.

Manzano Mountain Wilderness

Looking South along the Manzano Crest Trail

GENERAL DESCRIPTION

The Manzano Mountain Wilderness is established on 36,970 acres, an area approximately 18 miles long north to south, and 3 to 4 miles wide, which runs down the spine of the Manzano Mountain range about 20 miles southeast of Albuquerque. The Manzano Mountains are a southern extension of the Sandia Mountains and were formed by the same regional uplift process to the east of a north-south fault line, which has produced a relatively steep topography along the west side of the range, and canyons and ridges of gentler elevation gradient along the east side. Along the crest of the range, the limestone surface tends to support numerous grassy meadows with expansive views, broken by thickets of various species of scrub oak, New Mexican locust, mountain mahogany, and other types of scrubby vegetation. The slopes below the crest ridge are covered with forests dominated primarily by Douglas fir, ponderosa pine, and aspen at the higher elevations, and by ponderosa, gambel oak, one-seed and alligator juniper, piñon pine, and big tooth maple at the lower elevations. There are numerous springs in the canyons and populations of deer, mountain lions, and black bears, the latter having a fondness for munching on trail signs. The elevation ranges from about 6,000 feet to 10,098 feet at the summit of Manzano Peak.

Although you are unlikely to find any apple trees growing wild in the Manzanos, the name for the range comes from the Spanish word for apple and apparently derives from the nearby village of Manzano, an old community of Spanish origin that must have once supported numerous apple orchards. Located to the east of the towns of Los Lunas and Belen, the mountains are within a 1.5 hour drive of Albuquerque and contain an extensive system of well-maintained trails. The Manzano Mountains offer a convenient hiking alternative to the higher but smaller Sandia Mountains, the range with which the Manzanos are often associated due to geographical proximity. While there are areas within the Sandia Mountains that offer excellent solitude, the Manzano Wilderness offers an additional set of trails for hikers in the greater Albuquerque area, with similar terrain and environment, and a much lower overall population of human visitors. As in the Sandias, the Manzano Mountains are better suited to dayhiking than overnight backpacking, although there is plenty of area within which to backpack if the general lack of water at the higher elevations is included as a factor in your plans. For car campers, there are a number of Forest Service campgrounds located around the perimeter of the Manzanos, a feature not present in the Sandias. These mountains see an approximate annual precipitation of from 8 to 30 inches, depending upon the elevation level, and in winter much of the area is blanketed in snow from December through March, making the forest roads on the east side impassable for automobile traffic. July and August bring frequent thundershowers, but hiking conditions are generally good any time after the snow has melted away and the access roads are not impeded by heavy rains, although the trails on the west side of the range can be somewhat uncomfortable during hot spells in June and July. You can check current conditions by calling the Forest Service Ranger Station in Mountainair (see "For Further Information" at end of section). Hiking permits are not presently required.

Map Coverage

The best single map to get for the Wilderness is the Manzano Mountain Wilderness map produced by the Forest Service and available at the Ranger Station in Mountainair, the regional Forest Service office in Albuquerque, or at several hiking equipment stores in Albuquerque. The map shows up-to-date trail routes, topography, and brief individual trail descriptions, along with a listing of the individual USGS topo maps. Altogether, the Wilderness map is quite complete and the only one you need obtain.

Access

A detailed description of the forest road access required to reach the trailheads is included with the individual trail descriptions. These forest roads branch off of more general approach routes on either the east or west sides of the range. These are described as follows:

East Side Access. To reach the entry points for the east side of the Wilderness, drive on Interstate 40 east from Albuquerque and take the Tijeras exit, 6.3 miles east from the Tramway Boulevard exit, and head south on Highway 337. You will pass the Tijeras Ranger Station on the east side of the road 0.5 miles after the turnoff, and after another 28 miles you arrive at the intersection with Highway 55. Turn west on Highway 55, which makes a 20-mile loop through the towns of Tajique, Torreon, Manzano, and Punta de Agua, with several forest access routes along the way turning west toward the mountains. After Highway 55 intersects Highway 542, turn south and drive another 5 miles to the town of Mountainair and the Highway 60 junction. Heading west on Highway 60 takes you across below the south edge of the Wilderness and on to Interstate 25.

West Side Access. The only entry point on the west side of the range is the John F. Kennedy Campground, the access route for which is included in the description for the Trigo Canyon Trail. The other entry points on the south and east sides of the range can be approached from the west via Interstate 25 and Highway 60. Exit Interstate 25 at the Bernardo exit, if approaching on Interstate 25 from the south, and drive east on Highway 60. If approaching from the north (Albuquerque), exit Interstate 25 at Belen and travel southeast on Highway 47. Highway 47 joins Highway 60 after a 20-mile drive from Belen. From this intersection you can continue east on Highway 60 to Mountainair, and can reach the east side of the range by reversing the east side access described above.

Hiking Trails

On the north and west sides of the Manzano Wilderness, a land grant along with Indian and military reservations combine to limit access to the mountain range, with the lone entry point being the JFK Campground on the west side. The remaining entry points are all on the east side. The trail system is characterized by a long trail running down the north-south crest of the range, with numerous connecting trails coming up the canyons and ridges on each side, primarily the east side. The Manzano Crest Trail runs 22 miles in length from the north end of the Wilderness as far south as Manzano Peak, with an additional 5.5 miles provided by the Pine Shadow Trail, needed to reach the trailhead at the south end of the Wilderness. The Manzano Crest Trail is not usually hiked in its entirety but is more often used in sections to reach various high points along the range or to provide a link between connecting side trails, providing the opportunity for several loop hikes. The Forest Service lists 15 maintained trails in the Wilderness. Of these, six, plus segments of the Manzano Crest Trail, are used to put together the three hikes described in this section. The hikes described here cover various parts of the Wilderness, and can all be done as day hikes. After having done them all, you will be well acquainted with the Manzanos and will have no further need for a guidebook in doing some of the other trails. To repeat often-stated admonishments, don't fail to take along drinking water and be wary of hiking along the ridgeline when thunderstorms are in the area.

TRAIL DESCRIPTIONS

Hike #1. Fourth of July Trail (#173) to Bosque Trail (#174) Loop Hike

This trail begins at the Fourth of July Campground on the east side of the range. The popular Fourth of July Trail leading up from the campground joins the upper part of the Cerro Blanco Trail, which is hiked the rest of the way up to the Manzano Crest Trail. The Crest Trail is then followed south to the upper end of the Bosque Trail, which is followed back down to the east to the forest access road, where the hike ends if you have done a car shuttle. If not, a final 2.1-mile walk back north along the road returns you to your original starting point. The round trip distance is 7.4 miles with a car shuttle, or 9.4 miles if your hike begins and ends at the campground. Net elevation gain is 1,830 feet from the trailhead to the high point of the hike on the crest ridge near the top of the Bosque Trail. This is a nice, moderate hike along comfortable trail surfaces, with nice views from along the Crest Trail. The trail is mostly well marked but is faint in meadows along the crest, where you must look for rock cairns, and at the top of the Bosque Trail, which has several tricky spots. This area of the mountain is well known for its maple trees, which proliferate along its lower slopes, and which attract droves of sightseers in the fall when the leaves turn a brilliant red. The drive from Albuquerque to Fourth of July Campground takes about 1 hour.

To reach the trailhead take the "East Side Access" route south from Tijeras to the town of Tajique. At Tajique, turn west on Forest Road 55 at the sign for Fourth of July Campground, and take the improved gravel road 6.9 miles to the campground turnoff, where a short spur road leads to the campground. If you are

Hike #1. Fourth of July Trail (#173) to Bosque Trail (#174) Loop Hike

Distance — 7.4 miles round trip with a car shuttle, or 9.5 miles without
Net elevation gain — 1,830 feet
Difficulty — Moderate

MANZANO MOUNTAIN WILDERNESS

HIKE 1

CONTOUR INTERVAL 40 FEET
Base map Manzano Mountain Wilderness, Cibola National Forest, NM

doing a car shuttle to the lower Bosque trailhead, continue on Forest Road 55 another 2.1 miles south past the Fourth of July turnoff to a parking area marked with a sign on the west side of the road, and leave your shuttle vehicle. The section of road south of the campground turnoff could be a problem for a standard passenger car if road conditions are bad.

Return to the Fourth of July Campground and locate the trail sign marking the trailhead for Trail #173 at the west end of the campground, and follow the trail west up the canyon. At about the 0.5-mile point, you will pass a spring that is the last source for water until you have dropped back down on the Bosque Trail near the end of the hike. A short distance up the trail from the spring is the Wilderness boundary and a fork in the trail. Take the right fork and proceed to the Cerro Blanco Trail (#79) intersection. If you are interested in a shorter loop hike, you can follow the Cerro Blanco Trail back down about 1.2 miles to Forest Road 55, and follow the road another 1.7 miles back north to Fourth of July Campground. But since you don't want to miss the view from the top, proceed west on the Cerro Blanco Trail 0.6 miles up to the Manzano Crest Trail (#170) junction and head south. After an initial short, steep section, the 3.2-mile section of the Crest Trail south to the Bosque Trail intersection is easy hiking, with frequent vistas and meadows. Meadow crossings will require that you pay attention to the rock cairns marking the route in places where the trail becomes faint. As you begin to approach the Bosque Trail (#174) intersection, you will come out of the scrubby vegetation on to the east side of a large, flat, open area. The trail continues south along the border of the large meadow and skirts the head of the next major canyon to the east. Shortly after passing the ruins

of an old cabin, look for a trail sign for the Bosque Trail, and follow a path that leads down into the canyon; don't take the old road that contours around to the south. The trail is a little obscure at this point but is marked by an occasional cairn or sign post. Once the trail has dropped down to the center of the canyon, it continues for a distance, then splits, with one branch following the stream bed and the other branch taking a contour up on the north side of the canyon to the left. Take the higher branch to the left, as it takes a steep descent down a ridgeline and comes out at Forest Road 55. The parking area at the Bosque Trail is a short distance down the road to the north. The Fourth of July Campground is another 2.1 miles farther north along the forest road. Allow from 4.5 to 8 hours to do the hike. If you are not in possession of the Manzano Mountain Wilderness Map, the USGS 7.5-minute scale topo map you will need is the Bosque Peak quad.

Hike #2. Red Canyon Trail (#89) to Spruce Spring Trail (#189) Loop Hike

This is a popular loop hike involving the Red Canyon and Spruce Spring trails, two trails that both begin at the Red Canyon Campground and ascend the east side of the Manzanos, terminating at the Manzano Crest Trail. A short segment of the Crest Trail completes the loop. The Red Canyon Trail is 2.2 miles in length and gains 1,680 feet, while the Spruce Spring Trail is 3.4 miles in length, with a 1,120-foot elevation differential. With a 1.2-mile segment of the Crest Trail as a connector, and the high point of the hike at just under 10,000 feet near Gallo Peak on the Crest Trail, the total length of the loop hike is 6.8 miles, with a net elevation gain of 1,960 feet. This makes a nice moderate day hike through pleasant forest terrain, with good views on top.

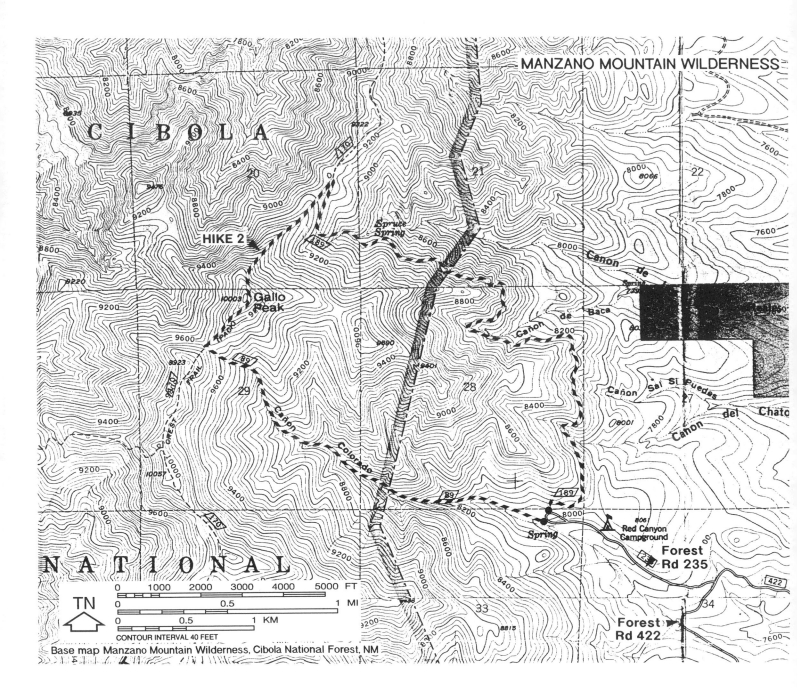

Base map Manzano Mountain Wilderness, Cibola National Forest, NM

CONTOUR INTERVAL 40 FEET

Hike #2. Red Canyon Trail (#89) to Spruce Spring Trail (#189) Loop Hike

Distance — 6.8 miles
Net elevation gain — 1,960 feet
Difficulty — Moderate

Water is present in Red Canyon and at Spruce Spring. I have described the hike as ascending the steeper Red Canyon Trail and descending the more gentle Spruce Spring Trail, but you can do it either way. Total hiking time for the loop is 3.5 to 6 hours.

To find the trailhead, drive to the town of Manzano and turn west immediately

south of town on to Forest Road 253. This is a good road that is suitable for passenger cars unless snowpacked. A 6-mile drive leads to Red Canyon Campground, where both the Red Canyon and Spruce Spring trailheads are well marked. The hike begins at the west end of the campground on the Red Canyon Trail, which follows a stream up the canyon bottom, crossing back and forth numerous times and passing a couple of small waterfalls along the way. At a little more than 1.5 miles the trail climbs out of the canyon bottom, and steep hiking through forest cover leads to the junction with the Manzano Crest Trail (#170). Turn north on the Crest Trail as it continues to climb toward the high point of the hike just below the summit of Gallo Peak, about 10 minutes north of the Red Canyon Trail intersection. A faint trail leads up to the summit of Gallo Peak, if you wish to make the climb. Past Gallo Peak, the trail

enters the downhill portion of the loop and travels along the crest through scattered open areas with nice vistas until you come to the trail sign marking the top end of the Spruce Spring Trail. Turn east down this trail, passing a short side path about 0.3 miles after the turnoff leading down to Spruce Spring, and continue down on a comfortable gradient to the original starting point at Red Canyon Campground. This loop hike is done fairly frequently by Manzano Mountain standards, which means that you still stand a reasonable chance of not encountering other hikers. It is easy to follow and makes a nice day hike. For a different and somewhat longer loop route requiring a car shuttle, try including the Ox Canyon Trail to the south, or hike up to Capilla Peak to the north. Another option would be to hike across the range from Red Canyon Campground on the east side and down the Trigo Canyon Trail

Looking North from Mosca Peak along the Manzano Crest

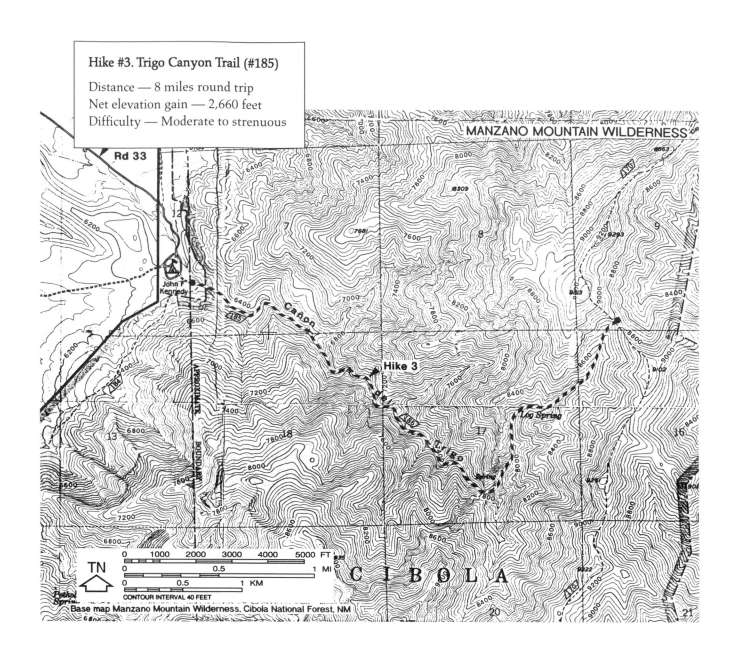

Hike #3. Trigo Canyon Trail (#185)

Distance — 8 miles round trip
Net elevation gain — 2,660 feet
Difficulty — Moderate to strenuous

to the John F. Kennedy Campground on the west side.

Hike #3. Trigo Canyon Trail (#185)

The trails on the west side of the mountain range, which include the Comanche Canyon, Osha Peak, Salas, and Trigo Canyon trails, all start at or near the John F. Kennedy Campground. The west-side trails all tend to be steeper and more rugged, and have more elevation gain than the trails on the east side. They are also longer and hotter in the summer, but more accessible in the winter. The shortest and most popular of these trails is the Trigo Canyon Trail. It is 8 miles round trip in length up to the Crest Trail intersection and back, and has an elevation gain of 2,660 feet. The trail is normally done as a day hike, but with running water along much of its length, it is also suitable for overnight backpacking. A loop hike using one of the other west-side trails is also something to consider, but it would make a long and strenuous day hike. The trail is scenic and not hard to follow on the lower part of the trail, but becomes more faint on the upper part, proving once again that the density of hikers on a trail diminishes according to an inverse function of the square of the distance and the cube of the elevation gain.

To reach the trailhead, take Exit 195 (Belen) off Interstate 25, 27 miles south of Albuquerque, and follow the road south and east toward Belen for 3.9 miles until you come to Highway 309. Turn east on Highway 309 and drive 2.4 miles to a four-way stop. Turn south at this intersection (you are now on Highway 47), and continue south for 2.1 miles to a set of graffiti-covered stucco portals marking the entrance to a dirt road heading east. Turn east on this road, which is rough in places but okay for passenger cars unless road conditions are muddy. This road runs east for 8.3 miles and ends at another dirt road on which you should turn north. Drive 3 miles north of this intersection, where another dirt road turns back to the east and continues another 6.6 miles to the JFK Campground. By this time you may be having doubts as to whether you are at the correct mountain, since there are no road signs after turning off the paved highway, nor is there a sign identifying the campground, nor a sign identifying the trailhead. However, if you make your way to the far east end of the campground at the mouth of the obvious canyon, you will find a parking area with an iron fence at the east end and a Wilderness sign just beyond the entrance, which marks the start of the Trigo Canyon Trail. The trail follows the canyon all the way to the top, and for the first 3 miles there is running water along the canyon bottom, which the trail crosses numerous times. On the way up are some nice meadows and some striking formations of quartzite walls. After passing a well-used shelter cave just over 2 miles up are the first of a series of small waterfalls, as the trail ascends the hard band of rock, with a 25-foot waterfall near the top and a nice view back down the canyon farther on. The final stretch of trail continues on up the canyon passing a final spring with some decent camp sites nearby and ends with a steep ascent up ponderosa-covered slopes to the top of the trail, where it joins the Crest Trail at a small saddle. A trail sign marks this junction.

The trail sign at the upper end is the only one along the entire length of the trail and there are practically no tree blazes, so you will have to rely on the trail surface and a few rock cairns to guide you. The trail follows the canyon bottom, so getting lost is really not a problem, but the upper part of the trail is very faint in places, and you may have to occasionally wander around a bit to locate it. If you find yourself off trail, retrace your steps until you are back on route. Total hiking time is 2 to 4 hours up and 1.5 to 3 hours back down.

For Further Information:

U.S. Forest Service
    Mountainair Ranger
    District
    P.O. Box E
    Mountainair, NM
    87036
    (505) 847-2990

El Morro National Monument

GENERAL DESCRIPTION

Occasionally, in the midst of a thirsty land, there exists a source of precious water. And occasionally there is a prominent landmark to guide the wandering traveler, with smooth rock that is pleasing to the eye, and high walls to block the winds, shade the ground, and provide a perch from which to scout the surrounding plains. Such a place is El Morro, also known as Inscription Rock, which is located in west-central New Mexico about 30 air miles southwest of the town of Grants. El Morro ("bluff," in Spanish) is an impressive prow of sandstone that juts up from the surrounding terrain to form a landmark that has been used by wayfarers for many hundreds, and probably for thousands, of years. In addition to the impressive features of the rock formation, the ancillary attraction that has long made this a favorite stopping place is a constant, never-failing pool of water at the base of the cliffs, fed by rains and snowmelt. Prehistoric Anasazis, probably ancestors of the present-day Zuni Indians, used the pool and lived in stone dwellings on top of the bluffs. These people also placed the first rock carvings on the base of the cliffs—the first of a long series of carvings and inscriptions for which the rock is now famous. Later, the early Spanish, traveling between the pueblos of Zuni and Acoma and the Hopi pueblos in what is now Arizona, camped by the pool and added their inscriptions. Of the many Spanish inscriptions, the earliest and best known was placed by the first governor of New Mexico, Don Juan de Oñate, in 1605—fifteen years prior to the Pilgrim landing at Plymouth Rock. Beginning in 1849, a steady stream of American soldiers, adventurers, and other travelers, passed by the rock and added their names along the base of the cliffs until 1906, when El Morro became a national monument and further rock carving was prohibited. Once protected, the rock cliffs and the hundreds of inscriptions thereon became a tourist attraction and a multicultural record of the history of the state, with many of the inscribed names representing identifiable historical figures. The descriptions are interesting, not only for the content of their text, but because many are also beautifully rendered, contrasting markedly with the standard neo-graffiti usually seen.

El Morro is located on the piñon- and juniper-studded plains to the southwest of the Zuni Mountains at an elevation of 7,200 feet. The national monument is open year round, with hours of 8 a.m. to 7 p.m. in summer and 8 a.m. to 5 p.m. the rest of the year. The most comfortable time of year to visit is from spring through early winter. The Visitor Center at the monument provides introductory information to El Morro in the form of displays and exhibits, and a short film. Two short walking trails provide the opportunity for self guided tours of the inscriptions along the cliff base and the pueblo ruins on top of the rock. These are discussed in more detail below. No overnight backpacking is allowed in the park, but for car campers, there is a campground and picnic area inside the monument, and undeveloped campsites in the National Forest lands of the nearby Zuni Mountains.

Map Coverage

This is an area that does not require a map. The size of the monument is small, and any hiking you do is supposed to be limited to the established trails, which are short and well marked. If you want topographic map coverage of the general area surrounding El Morro, get the USGS 1:100,000-scale Zuni map.

Access

Drive on Interstate 40 to the exit for Highway 53, just west of Grants. Follow Highway 53 south and west for 43 miles until you come to the highway sign for El Morro National Monument. The monument is located immediately south of the highway. It is interesting to note that beginning with the lava flow south of Grants, Highway 53, as it continues to the west, is said to approximately follow the prehistoric trade route that existed between the pueblos of Zuni and Acoma, making it one of the oldest roads in America. This route was also the one taken by the early Spanish when traveling through this part of the country. El Morro was one of the primary stopping points along the old route.

Hiking Trails

Two short trails provide a self-guided tour of El Morro, with points of interest keyed to an interpretive booklet available at the Visitor Center. A paved loop trail runs along the base of the cliffs past the rock inscriptions and the pool of water, and a longer trail incorporates this trail with a climb up to the top of El Morro past several pueblo ruins. The trails close a half hour before the general park closing time. Visitors are asked to stay on the trails and not to touch the inscriptions, climb on the ruins, or throw anything into the pool. The trail that goes on top of the rock leads past some sheer dropoffs that present a potential hazard for unrestrained children, and park personnel may occasionally close the trails when lightning threatens.

TRAIL DESCRIPTIONS

Hike #1. Inscription Rock Loop Trail

This is the trail that leads past the rock inscriptions that are the reason this is a National Monument and not just another interesting rock formation. Somehow, there is something intriguing about the long ago and something commonplace about the present day. Historical timing distinguishes between inscription and graffiti, or artist and vandal. Are these old inscriptions a case of the interesting adventurer recording history or the insensitive narcissist defacing natural beauty? Probably some of both, but with passing time, the accent is definitely on the former. And undeniably, the names and accounts etched into the rock are more interesting when the etchings were placed by the hands of men who were long dead before our grandparents, or even the founding fathers of our country, were born. Although they may have been insensitive and ego-driven, these were not the idle couch potatoes of bygone eras, but people of substance, vitality, and adventure, who actively took part in the evolution of their respective societies.

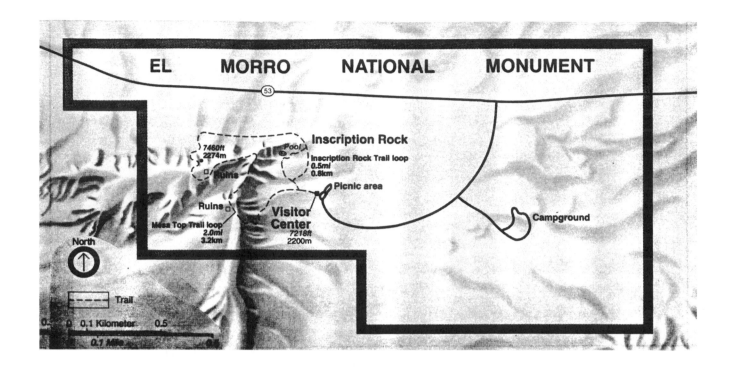

EL MORRO NATIONAL MONUMENT

53

North

↑

Trail

0   0.1 Kilometer   0.5

0.1 Mile   0.5

7460ft
2274m

Pool

Inscription Rock

Inscription Rock Trail loop
0.5mi
0.8km

Ruins

Ruins

Mesa Top Trail loop
2.0mi
3.2km

Picnic area

Visitor
Center
7218ft
2200m

Campground

Hike #1. Inscription Rock Loop Trail

Distance — 0.5 miles round trip
Net elevation gain — Negligible
Difficulty — Easy

Hike #2. Mesa Top Loop Trail

Distance — 2.0 miles round trip
Net elevation gain — 200 feet
Difficulty — Easy

Perhaps the age and style of these inscriptions make the difference, but one gets the feeling that those who created them were of a different cut than the modern immortality-seeking rock scratchers.

The trail is a 0.5-mile loop on an asphalt-surfaced path that is negotiable even for wheelchair traffic. The trailhead is at the rear entrance to the Visitor Center, in which you can first bone up on the history of the area. You will get much more out of the experience if you take the trail guide along with you on your hike. The trail guide is available at the Visitor Center, and it provides a wealth of information on some of the more prominent inscriptions, and on some of the natural and man-made features of El Morro. You can either loop back on the trail to the starting point or continue on the trail that ascends the top of the rock.

Hike #2. Mesa Top Loop Trail

This trail includes the segment of the previous hike that leads past the rock inscriptions and pool, and continues to the top of El Morro, where it loops past several prehistoric ruins and provides a series of views across the surrounding countryside. The trailhead is the same as for the Inscription Trail. The total trail length is 2 miles, with a net elevation gain of 200 feet over a well-constructed path that is easy to hike for all but the woefully out-of-condition. The same trail guide mentioned for the first hike also serves for this segment of trail, and helps interpret the geology of El Morro and the surrounding area, as well as what is known of the partially restored ruins. The ruins date from about 1275 A.D. and may have sheltered as many as 1,000 to 1,500 inhabitants before being abandoned by the early 1400s. The people who lived here drank from rainwater collected in cisterns on top of El Morro and from the pool at the base of the cliffs. They grew crops on the plains below and probably traded actively with other cultures near and far. Some of these people must have walked the old trail to Acoma Pueblo and crossed the broad lava flows on the Zuni-Acoma Trail (see El Malpais National Monument). They left the first of the rock inscriptions on the cliffs and in time moved on for reasons known only to those who are no longer here to tell the story.

The ruins left behind by the nameless ones are fragile and not in need of further deterioration brought about by climbing around on the walls. See and appreciate, but stay on the trail and help preserve the beauty for others.

For Further Information:

Superintendent, El Morro National Monument Route 2, Box 43 Ramah, NM 87321 (505) 783-4226

El Morro Trails, trail guide to El Morro National Monument, published in cooperation with the National Park Service by Southwest Parks and Monuments Association, Box 1562, Globe, AZ 85501.

El Morro National Monument Official Map and Guide, a pamphlet published by the National Park Service, U.S. Department of the Interior.

"La Vieja," A Sandstone
Spire in El Malpais

El Malpais

GENERAL INFORMATION

If you have ever wanted a close-up
encounter with a vast landscape of lava
flows, you could head for Hawaii or some
other far-off locale, or you could save a lot
of time and money and head for the
Malpais, a spectacular lava-filled valley of
115,000 acres that also includes cinder
cones, ice caves, sandstone bluffs, and the
second largest natural arch in the state. *El
malpais* means "the badlands" in Spanish,
and it is an apt description for the miles of

desolation produced over the past 3 millon years, when continued volcanic explosions covered the area with rivers of molten rock and other volcanic debris. The youngest of the lava flows is only 700-1,000 years old and was probably observed, presumably from a safe distance, by nearby prehistoric inhabitants. The area is jointly administered by the National Park Service and the Bureau of Land Management, and includes the El Malpais National Monument, the El Malpais National Conservation Area, the West Malpais Wilderness Area, and the Chain of Craters Wilderness Study Area, all jointly referred to here as El Malpais. The north edge of the lava flow can be observed from a rest stop on Interstate 40 a few miles east of Grants, and from a perimeter system of roads that surround much of the area. For a closer look, there are several hiking trails available, or you can walk out pretty much anywhere you want onto the terrain that varies from fresh-looking lava nearly devoid of vegetation to forests of ponderosa pine. El Malpais is accessible year round, particularly the lower-elevation west side, but can be cold in winter and hot in summer. Mosquitos can sometimes be a problem after a wet spring. Primitive camping is available on BLM-administered lands in the area and in the Cibola National Forest in the Zuni Mountains to the southwest. Nearby established campsites are located at Bluewater Lake State Park to the west and in the National Forest below Mt. Taylor to the north. Hiking in El Malpais requires sturdy footwear, an ability to spot rock cairns that mark the trails, and a propensity not to trip over the rough lava; falling on it doesn't look like much fun. If you plan to hike in very far, topo map and compass are a good idea, and you will need to bring along your drinking water. A good first stop before visiting any of the hiking areas is the El Malpais Visitor

Center, located 8.9 miles south of Interstate 40 on the east side of Highway 117 (see "Access" directions below), or the El Malpais Information Center located at 620 East Santa Fe Street in Grants, where there are a number of handouts available, as well as free advice.

Map Coverage

The USGS 7.5-minute scale maps to get for the various hiking areas are as follows: Hole-in-the-Wall-area—Ice Caves, Ice Caves SE, and North Pasture maps; Big Tubes Trail—Ice Caves and Cerro Hueco maps; Zuni-Acoma Trail—Arrosa Ranch and Los Pilares maps. There are also several trail pamphlets, which include maps, available at the Visitor Center and Information Center mentioned above.

Access

East Side Access. This access provides the most scenic drive to view the Malpais area and also gives access to the east end of the Zuni-Acoma Trail, as well as several other attractions. Begin by taking the Quemado exit (Highway 117 exit) off Interstate 40, 3.9 miles east of Grants, and driving south on Highway 117. The El Malpais National Monument begins on the west side of the highway 6.8 miles south of the interstate, and the El Malpais Visitor Center is another 2.1 miles on down the highway. Another mile south of the Visitor Center is a turnoff to the west, where a 1.5-mile side road leads to a lookout atop sandstone bluffs, with a scenic overlook across the Malpais lava flows. Continuing south 4.8 miles past the Sandstone Bluffs Overlook, you will come to a set of steps over the fence on the west side of the road, which marks the start of the Zuni-Acoma trail, and another 0.5 miles south of the trailhead off to the west is the sandstone formation that is

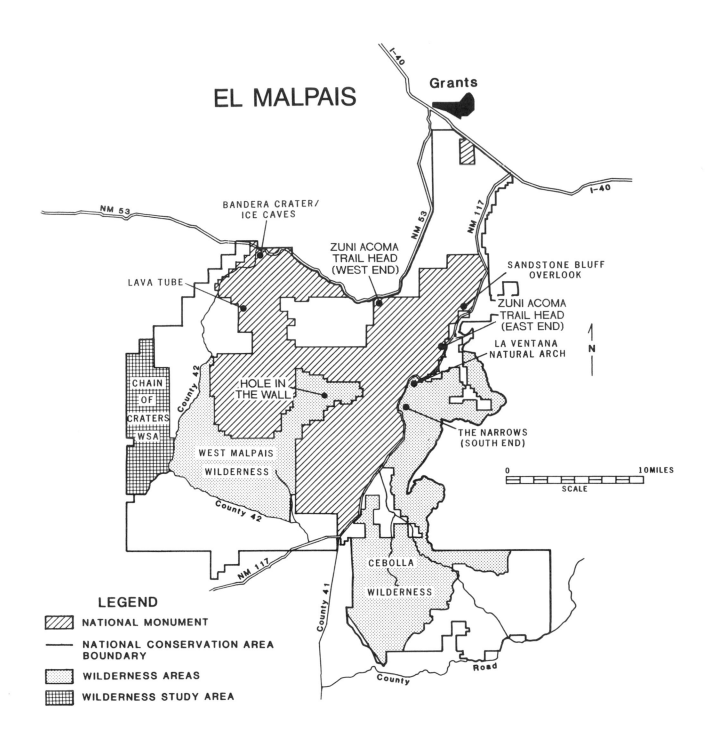

EL MALPAIS

Grants

I-40

NM 53

NM 53

NM 117

I-40

BANDERA CRATER/
ICE CAVES

ZUNI ACOMA
TRAIL HEAD
(WEST END)

SANDSTONE BLUFF
OVERLOOK

LAVA TUBE

ZUNI ACOMA
TRAIL HEAD
(EAST END)

LA VENTANA
NATURAL ARCH

N

CHAIN
OF
CRATERS
WSA

County 42

HOLE IN
THE WALL

THE NARROWS
(SOUTH END)

0   10 MILES

SCALE

WEST MALPAIS

WILDERNESS

County 42

NM 117

County 41

CEBOLLA

WILDERNESS

Road

County

LEGEND

NATIONAL MONUMENT

NATIONAL CONSERVATION AREA
BOUNDARY

WILDERNESS AREAS

WILDERNESS STUDY AREA

called La Vieja. *La vieja* means "old woman" in Spanish and is descriptive of the profile of the formation when viewed from a certain angle, although I have not yet figured out for sure which angle that would be. Continuing south another 2.2 miles from La Vieja brings you to a parking area on the east side of the road with a view of La Ventana ("the window"), a large natural sandstone arch at the head of the canyon to the east. A short trail leads up to the arch. As you proceed south on Highway 117, you will come to a road fork 31.5 miles south of Interstate 40, where a road branches off to the left toward Pietown. Continue on Highway 117 toward Quemado, 2.4 miles past this intersection, where you come to the junction with County Road 42, a dirt road that leads to the west, skirting the south side of the lava flows and connecting on the west end to Highway 53. See more about County Road 42 below.

West Side Access. Take Interstate 40 to the town of Grants, where you take the Highway 53 exit and head south. After you have traveled 15.5 miles south on Highway 53, you will see the west trailhead for the Zuni-Acoma Trail on the east side of the road, and another 4.5 miles brings you to the El Calderon area turnoff, which has several attractions to view, along with a short hiking trail. Another 5.7 miles farther along Highway 53 is the County Road 42 junction, which leads south, then east, across the lava flows, joining Highway 117 on the east end. Just north of the Highway 53/ County Road 42 junction are the Ice Caves and Bandera Crater, two attractions that are privately owned but are destined to become part of the National Monument. For a fee, you can view a pristine 5,000-year-old volcanic crater and the most spectacular of the ice caves that form in some of the underground lava vents.

South of Highway 53 on County Road 42 are the entrances for the Big Tubes area, and near the east end of County Road 42 is the turnoff to the north for Hole-in-the-Wall, a spacious area of ponderosa forest that escaped the lava flows. County Road 42 is 33 miles long, gaining elevation from the east end to the west end. In dry weather conditions it is suitable for passenger car traffic, but in wet weather it can be barely negotiable even with four wheel drive. When the snows are melting in spring or after fresh snowfall, the east end of the road can be dry while the west end is impassible. If you are traveling from east to west and start running into bad road conditions, it will only get worse.

Hiking Trails

Hiking on the lava involves some variable terrain and describing it involves some Polynesian lingo. Hole-in-the-Wall is a giant *kipuka*, a land area within a lava flow where no lava flowed. The ponderosa forest has some old roads through it but no established trails. The Big Tubes and Zuni-Acoma trails are on the lava flow surface and are marked with cairns and upright logs. Of course, lava isn't just lava, and Polynesians have different terms to describe the different types, just as Eskimos are reputed to have many different words to describe snow. Geologists have adopted the Polynesian terms for two types of lava that you will see when hiking the flows. *Pahoehoe* (pa-hoy-hoy) is the ropey-looking lava that looks like a thick batter poured from a bowl, and *aa* (ah-ah) is the chunky, jagged looking lava. One thing that all these areas have in common is a relative lack of topographical relief. This increases the difficulty of navigation, and it behooves you to pay close attention to whatever trail markers are present. Don't forget to bring plenty of drinking water.

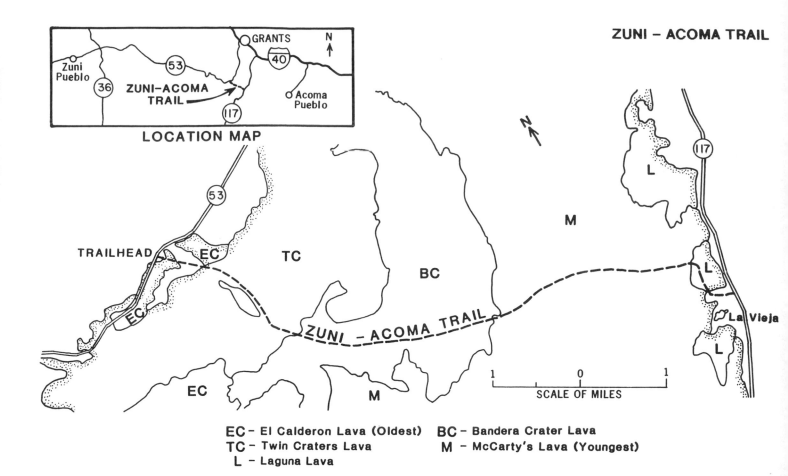

LOCATION MAP

EC – El Calderon Lava (Oldest)   BC – Bandera Crater Lava
TC – Twin Craters Lava   M – McCarty's Lava (Youngest)
L – Laguna Lava

SCALE OF MILES

Hike #1. Zuni-Acoma Trail

Distance — 7 miles one way
Net elevation gain — Insignificant
Difficulty — Moderate (moderate to strenuous if hiked round trip)

Hike #2. Big Tubes Trail

Distance — 1.0 to 1.5 miles round trip
Net elevation gain — Insignificant
Difficulty — Easy

Hike #3. Hole-in-the-Wall

Distance — Variable; about 1 to 8 miles round trip
Net elevation gain — Insignificant
Difficulty — Easy

TRAIL DESCRIPTIONS

Hike #1. Zuni-Acoma Trail

In prehistoric times a well-used trail ran along the path now taken by Highway 53 from Zuni Pueblo to the lava flows, crossed the lava, and continued on east to Acoma Pueblo. This has been called Coronado's route because Coronado also used it, but the trail was already ancient when Europeans first arrived and may be as old as a thousand years. The section of trail that crosses the lava has been adopted as a designated trail in El Malpais and named the Zuni-Acoma Trail. It is 7 miles across one-way and may be started from a trailhead at either end. The net elevation gain is insignificant, but there is lots of up and down along the way, with some difficult footing and not much straight-line hiking. It is a difficult trail to make good time on (count on 5 to 7 hours each direction or a long day round trip), but the lava flows are quite interesting and you won't want to rush along anyway. In fact, you may only want to walk in a few miles and return.

This trail is not a trail in the sense of having a well worn trail surface to follow; it is marked primarily by cairns, or rock piles, constructed from chunks of lava, some of which were placed by the prehistoric Zuni and Acoma Indians and have not been altered since that time. It is interesting that this common and seemingly obvious method of trail marking was arrived at independently by different peoples around the world. From all I have read about the tracking abilities of people belonging to most Stone Age cultures, their ability to follow a trail was likely on a level far surpassing ours, and additional cairns have been added to accommodate our relatively undeveloped skills. You will quickly discover that as soil and vegetation become more scarce, you will have to search intently for these cairns to maintain the trail. It is also interesting to note how the prehistoric trail users occasionally dumped loose lava into a small void to produce a crude but effective bridge and make the path somewhat less circuitous. You can get a trail guide for this trail at one of the information centers.

Both trailheads are easily reached by paved road, and it makes little difference which end you start from. Following the access directions above, reach the east trailhead by driving south of Interstate 40 on Highway 117 for 14.7 miles, or travel 15.5 miles south of Interstate 40 on Highway 53 to reach the west trailhead. One of the interesting geological aspects of the hike is that the path covers several distinctly different lava flows, which are noticeably different in age and texture. Starting from the east side, the trail begins on the valley floor and soon traverses a small patch of Laguna lava, which is relatively old and came from a volcano 14 miles to the west. Shortly thereafter, the trail climbs onto an overlying flow called McCarty lava, which originated about 8 miles to the southwest, and at 700 to 1,000 years old, is the youngest lava in the valley. This is the most textured as well as the most difficult to hike of the lava flows you will cross. After about 2.5 miles, the trail begins to traverse the Bandera Crater lava, which came from the previously mentioned Bandera Crater to the north, and after about another 2 miles you arrive at the Twin Craters lava flow, which originated 7 miles to the northwest at Twin Craters. Complete the hike to the west trailhead by following the trail to the north of a limestone outcrop and finishing over a small section of the El Calderon lava field, which originated some 4 miles to the west and is the oldest lava in the valley. The best way to hike this trail is to do a car shuttle and have a car waiting at the far trailhead. By the time you have hiked once across this lava field, you will have had your fill of lava for the time being and probably won't want to view it all again by returning back across the same trail. Once again, take along plenty of water, expect hot weather in the summer, take along some insect repellent just in case, and pay close attention to the cairns. If you lose the trail, carefully back track until you locate it again. If you can't find it, you can get out by heading either east or west but you may be in for a long afternoon.

Hike #2. Big Tubes Trail

The Bandera Lava Flow is known for its extensive lava tubes, which are the tunnels left by rivers of molten lava that once ran beneath the surface of the lava mass and in some cases can be traced for miles. Where these tubes have collapsed, there are deep pits that provide a striking cross section of the structure. The Big Tubes Trail is a short path of perhaps 1.5 miles round trip which leads to two notable examples of the lava-tube phenomenon, with several others in the immediate vicinity. The trail is rough and not easy to follow if you don't pay close attention to the rock cairns that mark the route. There is just enough forest cover to make it difficult to key on landmarks, and you stand an excellent chance of getting turned around if you lose the trail. Bring your camera along on this hike, and be very careful scrambling around on the loose lava. If you are interested in doing some caving into some of the intact tubes, the Park Service suggests that your equipment include hard hats, boots, protective clothing, gloves, water, and three sources of light. It is worth obtaining the Big Tubes Trail guide at one of the El Malpais information centers.

The trailhead for the Big Tubes Trail is located along a rough dirt road that loops around Cerro Rendija and has both a north and south entrance, separated by the distance of a mile, off of County Road 42. The north end of the loop is a bit shorter and a little less rugged and is the best end to start from. Locate the turnoff by driving 25.7 miles south from Interstate 40 on Highway 53 and turning south on County Road 42, which is followed for 5.5 miles, where a dirt road turns off to the east. This turnoff is west and a little north of the forested basalt cone that is called Cerro Rendija. The dirt road is quite rough, requiring a high road clearance vehicle, and shouldn't be attempted at all in wet conditions or in snow. Drive east on the double track dirt road through a gate, and continue for 2.8 miles to an undeveloped parking area with a sign for the Big Lava Tubes trailhead. From the sign the trail takes off to the east following a series of cairns, which you will occasionally have to stop and search for when the trail changes direction. When hiking in a group, it is actually rather engaging to see who can spot the next cairn first. And in this kind of terrain, it is especially important to keep the group together. The trail comes first to the Big Skylight Cave, a 600-foot-long lava tube with a large collapsed section providing the entrance. The trail splits around the large collapse and rejoins at the far side, with the final section of trail ending at Four Window Cave, which is a 1,200-foot-long cave that gets its name from several smaller roof openings called windows. Both caves can be walked into if you have light sources with you. There are several other collapsed caves and lava formations in the vicinity, which can be explored so long as you keep your bearings and don't lose track of the trail. Complete the hike by returning back over the same path on which you approached. Because of the rough drive in, you may be tempted to

return to County Road 42 by continuing south on the approach road, but it only gets rougher and you will be doing your vehicle a favor to drive back the way you came.

Hike #3. Hole-in-the-Wall.

Hole-in-the-Wall is an area of about 12 square miles that lies atop earlier lava flows but escaped entirely the more recent lava flows, being surrounded by them on almost all sides. The result is a pleasant area of ponderosa forests, aspen groves, and open areas with piñon, juniper, and grasses. Around the periphery of the area you can walk up to the edge of the bordering lava fields and observe where the flows stopped. Hole-

in-the-Wall was almost certainly an attractive area for the prehistoric Indian population, and artifacts can occasionally be found, although as you are by now undoubtedly aware, you are not permitted to remove any that you may find. This would be a good area for backpacking, with lots of good camping spots, but there are no dependable sources of water that I am aware of, so dayhiking or horseback is the standard way to go. Hole-in-the-Wall mostly lies within the West Malpais Wilderness, so no vehicles or mountain bikes are allowed. There are one or more old roads that wander through the area but no established hiking trails. Whether on an old road surface or going cross country, the terrain

The Zuni-Acoma Trail in the Malpais National Monument. Note the cairn.

is gentle to walk over and is easy to negotiate, with open forests and no elevation gain to speak of. On the other hand, navigation can be a problem because the land is flat and forested, with no prominent landmarks with which to orient. This is one of those hikes where you should have a map and compass and keep pretty close tabs on your location. There is plenty of wildlife in the area, and you have a good chance of spotting some if you are observant.

To find the area, travel 34 miles south on Highway 117 from Interstate 40 (see "East Side Access") and turn west on County Road 42. After you have gone 2.1 miles on County Road 42, an unmarked side road will fork off to the north. This is called a cherry stem road (ranger talk for the visual effect on the map when the wilderness boundaries have been drawn to allow a road to intrude into the wilderness), and it continues a little more than 4 miles to a fork and then to the right, passing a deserted farmhouse along the way, for another 0.5 miles to the Wilderness boundary, where the road is blocked. This access road can be driven with care by passenger car under good conditions, but is rough enough to suggest the need for a high clearance vehicle. When the snows are melting in the spring or after wet weather, add four wheel drive to the list. If you can't drive all the way up the road, park and walk the rest of the way. Once in the Hole-in-the-Wall you can spend anywhere from a few hours to all dayhiking around the area with little likelihood of seeing other folks. It is a nice area and doesn't draw that many hikers.

For Further Information:

El Malpais Information Center
620 East Santa Fe Street
Grants, NM 87020
(505) 285-5406

El Malpais Visitor Center
8.9 miles south of Interstate 40 on Highway 117
No telephone

Trail guides for the Zuni-Acoma Trail and the Big Tubes and El Calderone areas are available from the above administrative centers.

La Ventana, Cibola
Wilderness Area

Cebolla
Wilderness

GENERAL DESCRIPTION

To the east and southeast of the El
Malpais National Monument, about 15
miles south of the town of Grants, is the
62,000-acre Cebolla Wilderness. It is an
area of sandstone cliffs, mesas, and
canyons, with grassy fields and meadows,
and scattered forests of piñon, juniper,
and ponderosa. It is also an area of
striking scenic beauty and rich in archaeological significance, with an estimated
several thousand prehistoric sites scattered about the area dating as far back as
11,000 years. The Wilderness Area is
bounded along the west side by Highway
117, and except for a few attractions along
the highway, most notably La Ventana
Arch, the bulk of the area gets very low
visitation in spite of its easy accessibility
and close proximity to Grants and Albuquerque. Although there are no established hiking trails, there are a number of
old roads leading up the canyons, which

are now blocked to motor vehicle traffic, and the mesas that dominate the area tend to be covered with open woodlands that are easy and pleasant to walk through. Scrambling up and down the mesa terraces produces short stretches of strenuous hiking, but the exertion is offset by the sandstone landforms and scenic views, and the danger of negotiating the vertical terrain, which you may choose to avoid if you wish, is minimal, as long as reasonable judgement is used in choosing your route. Dayhiking will most likely be your activity here, but the area is large enough to accommodate some overnight backpacking as well, particularly in the south end, although a scarcity of water is the limiting factor. You will undoubtedly encounter pottery fragments and lithic flakes from the prehistoric Anasazi culture that inhabited the region. These artifacts are fascinating to hold and to speculate upon, but you are obliged by law to leave them where you find them.

The hiking season is virtually year round for the lower and more accessible parts of the Cebolla Wilderness, but the best times of the year to visit are from April through early winter. Winter brings snow and uncomfortably cold temperatures to the area, while summer produces temperatures that can be hot but are generally pleasant. Watch for thunderstorms and lightning danger during the months of July and August. If you are observant while hiking the interior of the area, you may see some of the wildlife population, which includes mule deer, coyote, black bear, and mountain lion. The nearest public campground is probably the Lobo Springs Campground in the Cibola National Forest northeast of Grants (see the "Access" description for Mount Taylor). Numerous primitive camping spots can be found in the nearby public lands, including the entry point for

the Narrows Overlook and the access road to the Hole-in-the-Wall in the West Malpais Wilderness. And as long as you are in the area, you may also want to investigate the nearby West Malpais Wilderness and El Malpais National Monument just to the west of Highway 117 for a somewhat different style of hiking terrain.

Map Coverage

The best single map to get for the Cebolla Wilderness is the El Malpais Recreation Guide Map. This map is jointly produced by the Bureau of Land Management and the National Park Service and shows the entire El Malpais National Conservation Area, of which the Cebolla Wilderness is a part, and the surrounding area, with up-to-date boundaries and access roads. The map is available at the El Malpais Information Center in Grants or the El Malpais Visitor Center on north Highway 117 (see "For Further Information" at end of this section). For more detailed topographic coverage of the Cebolla Wilderness, the appropriate USGS 7.5-minute scale maps are North Pasture, Laguna Honda, Sand Canyon, Cebollita Peak, and Bonine Canyon.

Access

The Cebolla Wilderness is situated lengthwise in a north/south orientation, with Highway 117 running down the west boundary. All of the entry points are reached via Highway 117, which is most commonly accessed by driving Interstate 40 to the Quemado/Highway 117 exit 3.9 miles east of Grants. Continue south on Highway 117 for 8.9 miles past the exit to the El Malpais Visitor Center, where you can ask questions and view interpretive displays. About 11 miles south of the Visitor Center is the parking area, on the

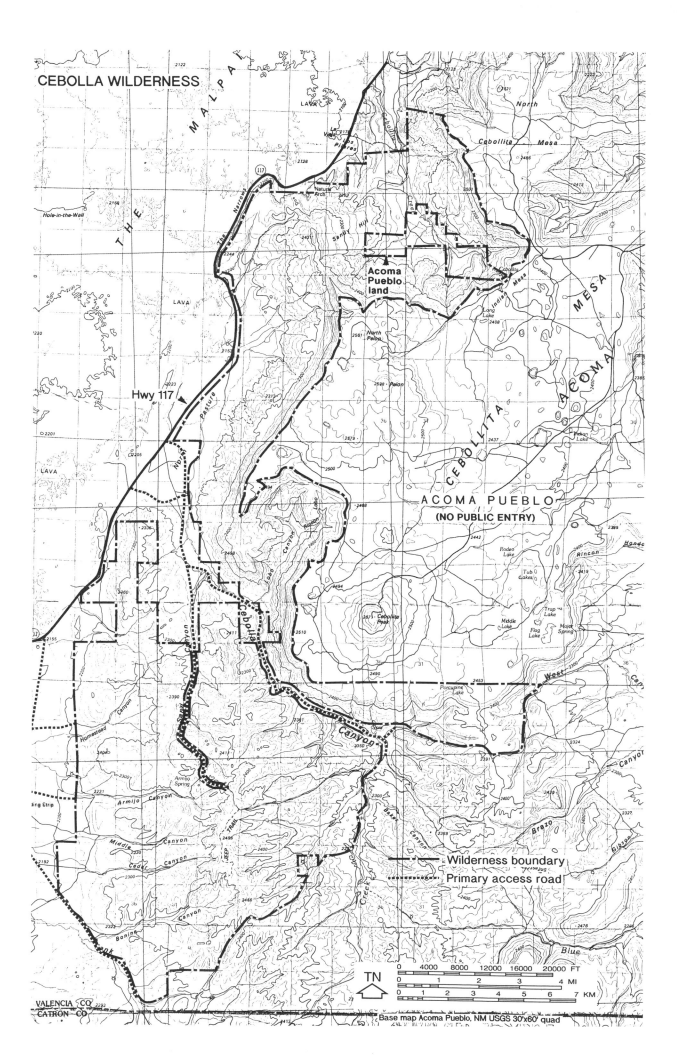

CEBOLLA WILDERNESS

Hwy 117

Acoma Pueblo land

ACOMA PUEBLO
(NO PUBLIC ENTRY)

——— Wilderness boundary
········· Primary access road

TN

0   4000 8000 12000 16000 20000 FT
0   1   2   3   4 MI
0   1   2   3   4   5   6   7 KM

VALENCIA CO
CATRON CO

Base map Acoma Pueblo, NM USGS 30'x60' quad

east side of the road, for La Ventana Arch, which marks the northwest corner of the Wilderness Area. A number of additional entry points, which are described in more detail below, are situated along the highway farther to the south. If you are approaching from the southwest quadrant of the state, you can drive north from the town of Quemado to access the south end of Highway 117. The drive along the highway between the Cebolla Wilderness to the east and the Malpais to the west is one of the more scenic drives the state has to offer.

Hiking Areas

The Cebolla Wilderness is ideal for hikers who enjoy solitary off-trail hiking through interesting terrain that is remote but not so remote as some of the other undeveloped areas of the state. Other than the short path to La Ventana Arch, there is presently no established trail system in the Cebolla Wilderness. There are, however, a number of areas or attractions in the Wilderness that naturally invite hiking interest. These areas are described individually below in a departure from the normal trail description format used elsewhere in the book. Trails may eventually be put into some of these areas, but for now it is a matter of following whatever old roads or paths that may be present or taking your map and heading off cross country. If you hike very far to the east, keep in mind that the Acoma Indian Reservation borders the Wilderness area on the east side, and the Reservation is closed to trespassing without prior permission from the tribal government. Take along drinking water, as there are few sources of water, and some of these are not very dependable or inviting.

HIKING AREA DESCRIPTIONS

La Ventana Natural Arch

This is more of a scenic attraction than a hiking area, but it is easy to get to and worth the short hike to investigate. La Ventana, "the window" in Spanish, is the largest natural arch in the state and was sculpted by the natural erosion forces of water, wind driven sand, and freezing moisture. The sandstone cliffs in which the arch is formed are of a formation called Zuni sandstone, which originated as deep layers of wind-deposited sand dunes, laid down 170 to 140 million years ago when the region was part of a vast inland desert. To reach the arch, drive 8.5 miles south of the El Malpais Visitor Center on Highway 117 to a parking area on the east side of the highway as the road bends toward the west. The arch is visible from the highway, but a short trail leads from the parking area to the arch for a closer look. Don't try to scramble up over the top of the arch; it is possible, but difficult and dangerous.

Narrows Overlook

As the highway continues south from La Ventana Arch, the route passes along a 2-mile stretch, with massive sandstone cliffs as much as 500 feet high on the east side and the broad lava flow on the west side. The narrow corridor between, where the highway runs, is called the Narrows, and this natural passageway has almost certainly been used as a route of travel as long as man has existed in the area. Raptors can often be seen soaring above the cliffs, which can be hiked up to, and which provide a spectacular view west across the Malpais. To access the cliffs, drive south on Highway 117, 3.6 miles south of La Ventana or 12.1 miles south of the Visitor Center to a dirt road that turns off the highway to the east. The turnoff is past the narrows and at a bend in the highway where it turns from west to south. The dirt access road is blocked to further travel by motor vehicles at the Wilderness boundary, and a primitive camping area is situated nearby. The road can be hiked for about 2 miles to the north, and near the top of the road a 0.5-mile walk to the west brings you to the Narrows Overlook. The elevation gain of several hundred feet is gradual and not unpleasant.

Cebolla Canyon

Cebolla Canyon splits the Wilderness, effectively dividing it in half, and provides an access to some of the broad mesas on the east side. A dirt road travels the length of the canyon, which has been cherry-stemmed into the Wilderness (meaning that the Wilderness boundaries have been gerrymandered to exclude the road from the Wilderness, so that it may be driven) and is accessible by passenger car when conditions are dry. Reach the turnoff by driving south on Highway 117, 16.6 miles south of the Visitor Center to a dirt road on the east side of the highway, with a closed gate and a pipe frame above the gate. Turn east on the road, closing the gate behind you, and drive east then south toward the windmill as the road follows the canyon. At about 3 miles past the turnoff, an alternative route branches off to the right and follows Sand Canyon, while the Cebolla Canyon road continues left. Another 2.5 miles brings you to the Wilderness boundary, as the road enters a well-defined canyon. This stretch of road develops mud holes when the weather has been wet and, in this case, is not for passenger car traffic. The Wilderness boundary continues on both sides of the road for the next 4 miles, and there are numerous opportunities to park your

vehicle and walk up across the mesa country to the west. Note your landmarks so that your outing will not develop into a search operation to locate your car on the return leg of your hike.

Homestead Canyon

Homestead Canyon is a small canyon that penetrates the Wilderness on the west side and contains an old dirt road that is blocked to motor vehicle traffic, and as is the case with the other limited access roads, mountain bikes as well. The old road runs northeast for about 3.5 miles, skirting the edges of the piñon/juniper mesa landscape, and ends at the Sand Canyon road. There are interesting short side hikes off the old road in both directions. To locate the Homestead Canyon road, drive south on Highway 117 for 22.5 miles past the Visitor Center, where the road to Pietown branches off to the left from Highway 117, which continues on to Quemado. Take the Pietown road and continue south for 2.2 miles, where the dirt road leading to Homestead Canyon turns off to the east and continues for a little over a mile to the Wilderness boundary.

Dittert Archaeological Site

The Dittert Site was named after archaeologist Alfred Dittert, who did work on approximately 300 prehistoric sites in the Cebollita Mesa region between 1947 and 1952. This is one of the more significant sites in the area and has cultural ties to the Chacoan system some 100 miles to the north, but it also has unique regional characteristics that indicate cultural influences from farther south and west. The Dittert Site was built and occupied from the 11th to the 13th century and was built atop a mound from an even earlier occupation. Roof beams, which were dated using the tree-ring

Old Ruins in Armijo
Canyon

method, were determined to have been cut between 1226 and 1267 a.d.. The occupants abandoned the dwellings when they were in good shape, with roofs intact and room furniture still in place; they apparently intended to return but never did. The site was acquired by the BLM in 1958 and stabilized in 1976. This is only one of hundreds of sites within a radius of a few miles, and one can only marvel at the lengthy period of occupation by the sturdy members of this culture in an environment that seems marginal but must have been to their liking. And one can only ponder their eventual fate. To reach the site, travel 22.5 miles south of the Visitor Center on Highway 117 and take the Pietown turnoff as described above for the Homestead Canyon access. Continue 1.6 miles south of the Homestead Canyon turnoff, or 3.6 miles south of Highway 117, to a dirt road leading east opposite a sign for the King Brothers' Ranch (the ranch has recently been acquired by the BLM in a land swap, so the ranch sign may be history by the time you visit). Drive east on the dirt road, which looks marginally passible by passenger car unless the road is muddy, for a little over a mile where the road is blocked at the Wilderness boundary. This is the road that continues on up into Armijo Canyon. Walk up the road for 0.3 miles, where it turns north and crosses the arroyo. At the north side of the arroyo, one branch of the road continues east along the arroyo while the other continues north across the grassy slopes. Follow the faint latter road for almost 0.5 miles to a series of ruins near the treeline. You can return to your vehicle on a more direct line by hiking southwest, crossing the arroyo, and proceeding straight to the boundary sign.

Armijo Canyon

Armijo Canyon is another west-side canyon with an old road, now blocked to cars and bikes, following the canyon up well into the heart of the Wilderness Area. Lots of off-trail hiking through the wooded mesas and hills is available on both sides of the road. The road extends about 3 miles into the Wilderness boundary, but it is 7 miles to the east boundary, with 4 miles of Wilderness to the south and north, providing plenty of space for solitary dayhiking. There is an interesting old historic cabin 2.5 miles east into the Wilderness along the Armijo Canyon road, and another interesting structure at Armijo Spring, a short distance up the side canyon to the north. Both have been stabilized by the BLM. Numerous prehistoric sites are also in the area. A good all-day outing is to combine a hike into the Armijo Canyon vicinity with a visit to the Dittert Site, which sits just to the north of the entrance into Armijo Canyon. The access to Armijo Canyon is the same as previously described for the Dittert Site. At the Wilderness boundary sign at the end of the access road, continue east on foot down the road that continues east past the sign. When the road turns north and crosses the arroyo, continue east on the road branch that continues to follow the arroyo up the canyon. You can follow the road to its end, or beyond, or make your own path in whatever direction you wish.

For Further Information:

El Malpais Information
    Center
620 East Santa Fe
    Avenue
Grants, NM 87020
(505) 285-5406

El Malpais National
    Monument (Visitor
    Center)
P.O. Box 939
Grants, NM 87020
(505) 285-4641

El Malpais National
    Conservation Area
201 East Roosevelt
    Avenue
Grants, NM 87020
(505) 287-7911

Bureau of Land Management
    Albuquerque District
    Office
435 Montaño NE
Albuquerque, NM
    87107
(505) 761-8700

Petaca Pinta Wilderness Study Area

GENERAL DESCRIPTION

The Petaca Pinta Wilderness Study Area (WSA) is an 11,668-acre block of BLM land located about 50 air miles southwest of Albuquerque in a setting that features a wide variety of scenic landforms. The high elevation point of the area at 7,300 feet is Petaca Pinta Mesa, a sheer, isolated sandstone mesa approximately in the center of the WSA, and the low point is at Blue Water Canyon, a steep and narrow box canyon located at

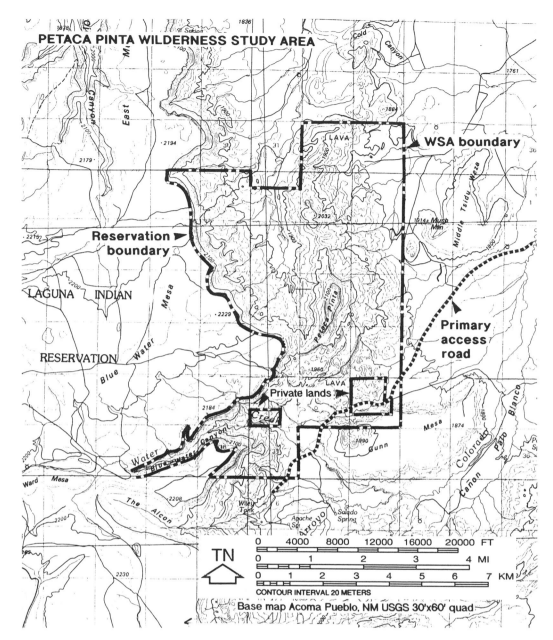

the southwest corner. In between the elevation extremes are outcrops of sandstone and lava, weathered sandstone and basaltic erratics, smooth, grassy benches, rolling mesas and grasslands, wide drainages, and isolated canyons and boulder fields, all remote and untracked. The vegetation consists primarily of scattered stands of juniper along with cacti, yucca, and various types of shrubs and grasses. The best time of year to visit this area is from early spring through early winter, although mid-summer can prove to be uncomfortably hot. The semiarid climate tends to be dry and generally pleasant. No reliable sources of surface water appear to exist within the area, except for a few seeps in Blue Water Canyon, but the area seems to support a viable population of deer, coyote, and probably mountain lion. The Petaca Pinta WSA is within easy driving distance from

Albuquerque (1.5 hours) and is an appealing alternative for the dayhiker who prefers the solitude of a remote and undeveloped wilderness setting with dramatic and varied scenery. The opportunities for photography, reflection, and solitary off-trail wandering are excellent.

Map Coverage

The USGS 7.5-minute topo maps covering the Petaca Pinta WSA are the Broom Mountain, Cerro del Oro, East Mesa, and Marmon Ranch quads. The area is also shown on the USGS Acoma Pueblo 1:100,000-scale map.

Access

Drive 27 miles west of Albuquerque on Interstate 40 and take the Highway 6 exit (Exit 126) heading south. Just under 2 miles south of the exit, where Highway 6 bends back to the east, turn south on an improved gravel road across the highway from some buildings. After driving 1.6 miles on the gravel road, you will come to a road fork. Bear left at the fork on to New Mexico 55, another improved gravel road that continues south. Follow the main road for another 6.9 miles, until you come to a cattleguard, at which point you should turn right just before reaching the cattleguard on to a dirt road that heads west across an area with basaltic outcrops, keeping just north of the fence line. After driving 3.5 miles west from this last turnoff, you will come to another road junction, where you turn south and cross a cattleguard a short distance farther, with a BLM sign notifying you to remain on existing roads and close all gates. From the cattleguard, another 13 miles of following the main road brings you to a small cattleguard, which may have a barrier you will have to open and close. At this point, you will have reached the east boundary of the WSA, which begins at the fence line to the west of the road. The high, rugged-looking ridge off to the west is Petaca Pinta Mesa, and a good place to begin your introductory hike into the area is anywhere along the road from the large stock reservoir just beyond the cattleguard to the next dirt road intersection 0.5 miles south. The best place to park is at the reservoir, and you should be careful not to damage the fence as you cross it. Also, be sure to reclose any gates that you need to open along the access road on the way in.

Hiking Trails

There are no hiking trails established in Petaca Pinta WSA. The primary hiking objectives are probably Petaca Pinta Mesa and Blue Water Canyon, but anywhere you go will be scenic and interesting. Loose rock abounds on the steeper slopes, and some of the sandstone slopes have friable, exfoliated patches, so hike with care and remember that this area is remote. Bring along all the drinking water you will need.

For further Information:

New Mexico Statewide Wilderness Study, Volume 2: Appendices Wilderness Analysis Reports, published by the U.S. Department Of the Interior, Bureau of Land Management, New Mexico State Office, Santa Fe, NM, September, 1986.

Albuquerque District Office
Bureau of Land Management
435 Montaño NE
Albuquerque, NM 87107
(505) 761-4504

Looking Northwest from
Ladron Summit

Ladron Peak

GENERAL DESCRIPTION

Ladron Peak and its surrounding cluster of peaks forms a rocky granite upthrust, located about 15 miles northwest of Socorro, that rises over 3,000 feet above the surrounding plains on the western margin of the Rio Grande rift. This small but distinct mountain range can be clearly seen through the haze from the Sandia Mountains, 60 miles to the northeast, jutting sharply up into the distant skyline. The Ladron ("thief") Mountains, and the rugged and relatively inaccessible land surrounding the range, provided a base of operations for early livestock rustlers, and before that, for fierce bands of Navajo and Apache raiders, who preyed upon nearby Spanish, Mexican, and American settlements located along the Rio Grande as far north as Albuquerque. Dating from the 17th century, the area has seen various military engagements through the years, the last recorded being the ambush in 1881 of a U.S. Cavalry force in the Rio Salado Box south of Ladron Peak by a band of Apaches led by the famous chief Nana. The area is steeped in legend, and stories persist, some true—some probably not— of conquistadors, buried Civil War cannons, lost treasure, lost bandit gold, lost mines, and desperado hideouts. There is also evidence that prehistoric man had inhabited this region beginning at least 10,000 years ago.

An area 14 miles long north to south and about 8 miles wide east to west, including the Ladron Peak massif at the north end and extending to the Rio Salado at the south end, has been designated by the BLM as the Sierra Ladrones Wilderness Study Area (WSA). This is a landscape that ranges from 5,200 feet to 9,176 feet in elevation and incorporates a varied terrain, including rolling grasslands, arroyos, rocky ridges, and rugged canyons. The conifer forests of the higher elevations are sprinkled with gamble oak, alligator juniper, and various broadleaf species near water sources. Piñon pine and one seed juniper are common over the entire area, as are yucca and different species of cacti. The climate is typical of Southwestern desert mountain areas, with maximum summer daytime temperatures in the 90 to 100+ degree F range, and temperatures in the higher elevations 10 to 15 degrees cooler. Winter daytime temperatures in the lower elevations tend to range from mild to cold, depending on the weather, while the higher elevations will become snowbound. Generally, any time but the coldest part of winter or the hottest days of summer, produces temperatures that are pleasant for hiking. Wet weather results in poor conditions on the access roads, particularly from the south approach, and lightning can pose a special hazard during thunderstorm season in late summer. Under normal conditions, water tends to be limited in availability, consisting primarily of a muddy trickle in the Rio Salado and a few springs in the major canyons surrounding the Ladron Peak area. The WSA currently contains 45,308 acres with some private inholdings, and at least the majority of this is probably destined to be upgraded to Wilderness status. The primary attraction of the WSA is Ladron Peak, which attracts a small but steady flow of trekkers to attempt the strenuous scramble to the summit. This is a nontechnical climb, but it is over difficult terrain without the benefit of a trail. The balance of the WSA appears to receive very little outside visitation at all.

Map Coverage

For supplementary topographic map coverage of the area, the USGS 15-minute scale Riley quad is the best overall map to get, if it is still available. Equivalent coverage in the 7.5-minute scale is provided by the Ladron Peak, Riley, Carbon Springs, and Silver Creek quad maps.

Access

The Sierra Ladrones WSA can be approached by driving north from Magdalena or by driving west from Interstate 25, with the latter being the most direct route to Ladron Peak and the north end of the WSA. For the Interstate 25 access, drive 50 miles south from Albuquerque on Interstate 25 and take the Bernardo/Mountainair exit. As the exit ramp loops west, take the paved road leading west, over the cattle guard and the steel bridge across the Rio Puerco. The following milages are measured from the Interstate exit. At the 1.5-mile point, veer right at the locked gate on to County Road 12 (good quality gravel road), and continue right at the next fork at 8.6

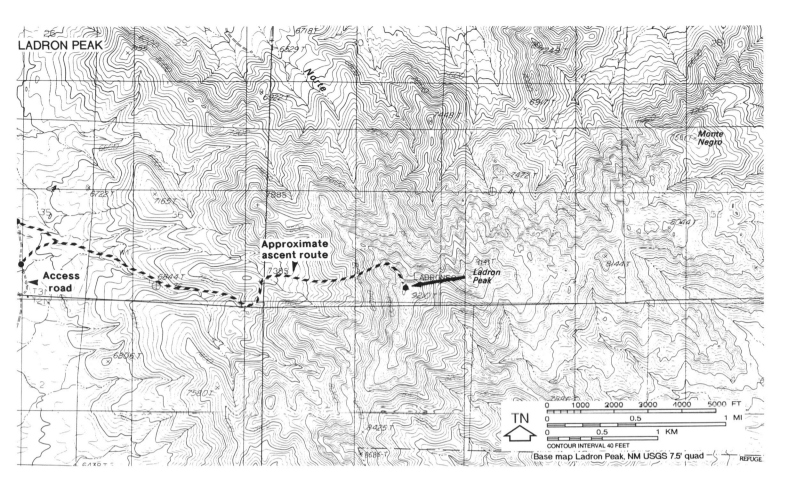

LADRON PEAK

Approximate
ascent route

Access
road

Monte
Negro

Ladron
Peak

TN

| 0 | 1000 | 2000 | 3000 | 4000 | 5000 FT |

| 0 | | 0.5 | | 1 MI |

| 0 | | 0.5 | | 1 KM |

CONTOUR INTERVAL 40 FEET

Base map Ladron Peak, NM USGS 7.5' quad

REFUGE

miles (by the small roadside shrine, if it's still there). Stay on the main road, passing County Road 72 at mile 11.8, and continue on to the road junction at mile 21.9. At this point, the north end of the WSA is to the east. The right, or west, branch of the road fork skirts the west WSA boundary and continues on to the ghost town of Riley. The left road fork leads southeast toward Ladron Peak. If this is your objective, begin by taking the left fork 0.6 miles to another fork in the road. Both branches of this fork lead to the same endpoint, although the more traveled road to the right is in better condition. Drive on this road a little over 4 miles farther, past a ranch house, and a few hundred yards beyond to where the road begins to deteriorate. Park your car here, being careful not to block the access to the rough section of road, which continues for a distance. You are on private land here, so respect the fact that you are being allowed access. After parking, follow the old road east as it leads up a canyon and turns into a footpath that follows a length of black plastic pipe, which continues to a spring at the head of the canyon. A steep bush-whack up the northeast side of the canyon from the spring leads to a saddle on the ridge above the canyon. At this point, the west face of Ladron Peak is directly before you, and you will have to drop down off the ridge and continue east up the peak by dead reckoning to complete the climb. I have been to Ladron Peak several times using the route described above, and have been told by an agent of the landowner over whose land the final stretch of road covers, that access is permissible, so long as road access is not blocked. However, if any of the final road access ends up being blocked, due either to a change in attitude by the land owner or a change in the status of the public land (Wilderness designation), then the walking part of the approach may increase in distance. In this case, the west face of Ladron Peak is clearly visible, and you won't have any trouble figuring out which direction to hike.

To approach from the south via Magdalena, turn north off Highway 60, just east of the United New Mexico Bank building in Magdalena, and then, just past the old Magdalena train station a short distance farther, turn right on to Forest Road 354. This road leads north about 28 miles to a crossing of the Rio Salado at the ghost town of Riley. If the weather has been wet, the river may be too deep to cross, but normally it is little more than a sandy riverbed. After you have crossed the Rio Salado, go right at the intersection just to the north, where the west boundary of the WSA is reached shortly beyond, and continue on the primary dirt road for 8.6 miles to a fork in the road.

This is the junction that was reached at the 21.9-mile point on the north access route. The southeast branch leads toward Ladron Peak.

Hiking Trails

There are a number of old ranch roads that wander about on the lower elevation parts of the WSA but no designated trails. These roads may or may not be open to vehicle traffic, depending upon the future wilderness status of the area, but can be hiked in any case. There are many square miles of empty country here in which to explore, but drinking water is a limiting factor. The primary route up Ladron Peak is as described above, with the final ascent a cross-country scramble up loose scree slopes, brush thickets, and granite slabs, with a number of different routes possible. The summit is the high point of the range at approximately 9,200 feet elevation, depending on which map you look at, while the actual summit of Ladron Peak is shown on the maps as a shorter peak about 0.5 miles to the east. The area to the north of Ladron Peak and Monte Negro offers a longer approach to the top, with some remote wooded hiking terrain and water in the deep canyons. Either way, climbing Ladron Peak is a rugged undertaking not appropriate for especially frail hikers.

For Further Information:

Bureau of Land Management
Socorro Resource Area
198 Neel Avenue
Socorro, NM 87801
(505) 835-0412

New Mexico Statewide Wilderness Study, Volume 3: Appendices, Wilderness Analysis Reports, U.S. Department of the Interior, Bureau of Land Management, New Mexico State Office, Santa Fe, NM, September 1986.

Zuni Salt Lake Area

Eagle Peak and Mesita Blanca
Wilderness Study Areas

GENERAL DESCRIPTION

The hiking area described in this section involves two adjacent BLM Wilderness Study Areas (WSAs) totaling 49,177 acres: Eagle Peak WSA and Mesita Blanca WSA. This combined area of land is located several miles south of Zuni Salt Lake in west-central New Mexico approximately 20 miles west of the town of Quemado. Although located on private land and not itself an area of hiking potential, Zuni Salt Lake is a local feature of considerable interest. The lake was formed in a collapsed volcanic caldera and has been sustained over thousands of years by water draining into the depression, which has no outlet. Through constant evaporation, the water in the lake has achieved salt densities significant enough to cause a large surface area of the lake to crystallize over. The lake was an important source of pure salt for Indian cultures extending far into prehistory and undoubtedly contributed to the high number of prehistoric sites in the area. Zuni Salt Lake is integrated into the religious beliefs of the Zuni, Navajo, Apache, Acoma, and Laguna tribes, and members of these tribes continue to journey to the lake to worship and to gather salt, which some consider to be superior in taste to that commercially available. With the arrival of the Spanish in 1540, the lake became known historically when they praised the quality of the salt in their writings. Among the early Indian tribes, the significance of the salt lake was such that the area was considered neutral ground, regardless of current hostilities. The lake is currently owned by the Zuni Tribe, is fenced, and may or may not be posted against trespassing. In any case, a good view of the lake can be had from the county road above the west rim of the basin.

Eagle Peak and Mesita Blanca are adjacent areas set aside by the BLM to study the potential for their inclusion into the Wilderness system. They are 32,748 and 16,429 acres, respectively, with an elevation gradient of between 6,400 feet and 7,679 feet, with the high point being the Red Hill cinder cone on the Mesita Blanca WSA. Although the areas are large enough for limited backpacking, the lack of water makes dayhiking more practical. The best time of year to visit would be anytime but the hottest part of summer or the coldest winter months. In this semiarid climate the annual precipitation is 11 inches, with half the total tending to fall during the brief thundershowers that occur from July through September. Summer temperatures average in the 80s during the day but can top 100 degrees F. Winter temperatures are typically 40 to 50 degrees F during the day but can go much lower. Typical plant life includes piñon and juniper, sage, Apache plume, saltbush, rabbit brush, mountain mahogany, and gamma grasses. Wildlife species include mule deer, pronghorn antelope, coyotes, bobcats, kit foxes, porcupines, red tailed hawks, and golden eagles. Wintering bald eagles are also known to exist.

This region of the state lies within the southern portion of the Colorado Plateau and shows the effects of volcanism, which is typical of many areas bordering the great plateau where the earth's crust thins out from the center area. Cinder cones, basalt formations, and scatters of igneous rock exist alongside the older sandstone mesas, broad rolling grasslands in the lower elevations, and colorful assortments of cobbles and gravels brought in from distant eroding highlands and deposited by meandering rivers many eons ago. These deposits of heterogeneous multicolored rock add a nice visual contrast. In addition to the diverse geology, one of the interesting aspects of hiking in this area is the high density of prehistoric Indian sites dating from about 6,000 B.C., which are well represented in both WSAs. These sites include rock art panels, scatters of artifacts, and dwelling ruins. Alongside the prehistoric stuff, both WSAs are occasionally visually impacted by the hand of modern man, usually by something having to do with cows, but on balance the areas are very scenic, with varied terrain, and they are large enough to provide considerable hiking space and offer a high degree of solitude. Other than a few ranch roads, there are no trails in the area, and it is doubtful that any more than a few hikers ever visit. The interior areas away from the main access roads are remote, and the cinder cones and lava flows, sandstone mesas, and interconnecting canyons and grasslands provide a true wilderness setting.

Map Coverage

An overall perspective of this area is provided by the USGS 1:100,000-scale Quemado map. More detailed coverage is shown by various USGS 7.5-minute scale maps as follows: for the Eagle Peak WSA—Armstrong Canyon, Blains Lake, Lake Armijo, Tenaja Mesa, Tenaja Mesa SW, and Zuni Salt Lake; for the Mesita Blanca WSA—Blaines Lake, Goat Springs, Salazar Canyon, and Zuni Salt Lake.

Access

The Zuni Salt Lake area is accessed via Quemado, which can be reached by driving west on Highway 60 from Socorro, taking Highway 117 south from the Quemado exit off Interstate 40 a few miles east of Grants, or by driving north on Highway 32 from the southwest corner of the state. From Albuquerque and points north, the Highway 117 route is marginally shorter (137 miles from Albuquerque) and requires 3 to 4 hours to reach the hiking areas.

Upon reaching Quemado, continue west a short distance past town, drive 1 mile past the Highway 32 intersection, and turn north on a paved road with a "No Thoroughfare" sign. At 1.5 miles past the turnoff, the road turns to gravel, and at the 6.5-mile point the northeast corner of the Eagle Peak WSA is reached about halfway along the small mesa to your left. At 0.2 miles past this point, just before the bridge over the arroyo, is the first of a number of dirt roads that turn south into the WSA. You are currently allowed to drive on any of these existing roads, unless otherwise posted; however, they tend to be rather primitive and require at least a vehicle with high clearance. Immediately before mile marker 18 on the primary gravel road, there is a fork in the road, and you want to take the left branch to another road fork a short distance beyond. The left branch of this second intersection leads south through a closed gate to Zuni Salt Lake, and the right branch continues west and south around the basin of the lake. This is a county road, which continues south for 20.5 miles to Highway 60 and runs between the Eagle Peak and Mesita Blanca WSAs. Continue on this road and drive 0.4 miles past the last intersection to another fork in the road, taking the left fork, at which point you should be able to look down to the east and view the lake. Another 2.6 miles past this intersection is your first opportunity to turn east onto the Eagle Peak WSA at a rough dirt road just before a cattle guard. Another 2.4 miles south of this intersection is the northeast corner of the Mesita Blanca WSA. For approximately the next 12 miles, there are occasional roads, which turn east into the Eagle Peak WSA or west into the Mesita Blanca WSA, until you pass the southern boundaries of the areas. The last several miles of the county road lead south to an intersection with Highway 60. This intersection is about 21 miles west of Quemado, between mile markers 14 and 15, and opposite the road that goes south to Luna.

An alternative route to access the west side of Mesita Blanca WSA, and in particular the Red Hill cinder cone and lava flow, is to travel west on Highway 60 from Quemado, 0.2 miles past mile marker 11, and turn north on a wide gravel road just before a small cluster of buildings that are shown as "Red Hill" on some road maps. At 4.8 miles north of the turnoff, you will come to a dirt road leading east directly to Red Hill, which is the large cinder cone just to the northeast. The main gravel road continues north and west, skirting the edge of the Red Hill lava flow.

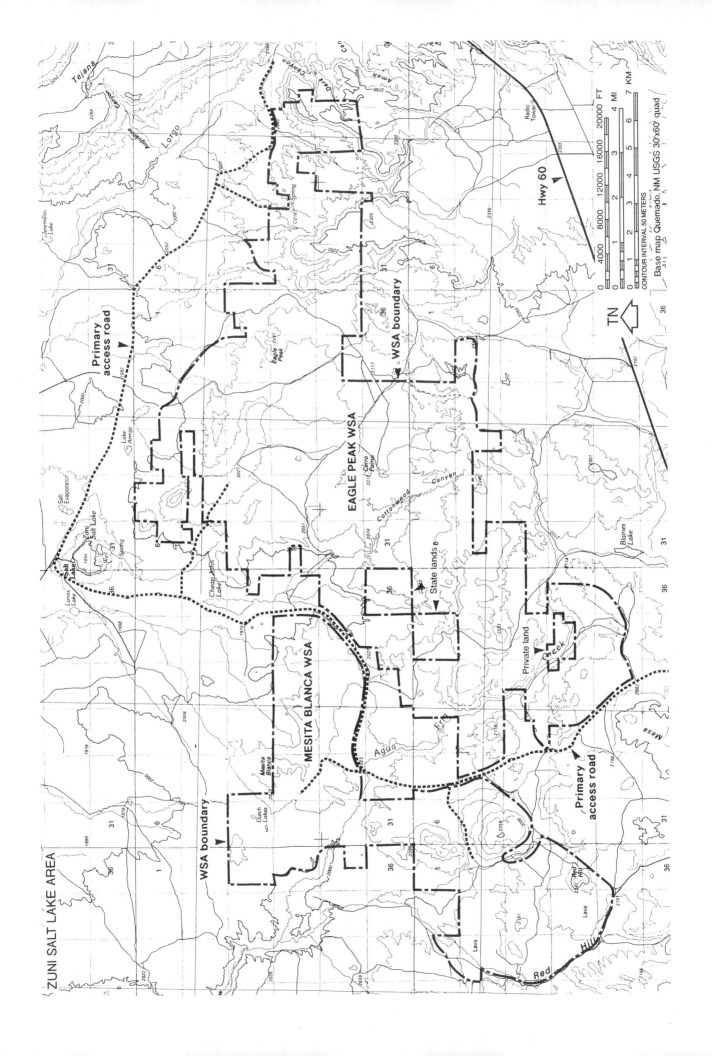

ZUNI SALT LAKE AREA

Primary access road

WSA boundary

EAGLE PEAK WSA

MESITA BLANCA WSA

WSA boundary

WSA boundary

State lands

Private land

Primary access road

Hwy 60

TN

CONTOUR INTERVAL 50 METERS
Base map Quemado, NM USGS 30'x60' quad

For Further Information:

Bureau of Land
    Management
    Socorro Resource Area
    198 Neel Avenue NW
    Socorro, NM 87801
    (505) 835-0412.

*New Mexico Statewide
Wilderness Study,
Wilderness Analysis
Reports,* U.S. Depart-
ment of the Interior,
Bureau of Land
Management, New
Mexico State Office,
Santa Fe, NM, May
1985.

Eagle Peak Wilderness
Study Area

Hiking Trails

No trails are established in either of the WSAs, although a number of old ranch roads wind through the areas; some can be driven, or hiked when they get too rough to drive. Good hiking destinations are the Red Hill lava flow via the alternate access described above, and the rough mesa country in the interior of both WSAs via the county road that splits the two areas. The ranch roads tend to be limited to the grasslands. All the available terrain is well suited to cross-country hiking, being open and spacious and with plenty of landmarks to help with navigation. If you are spending several days in the vicinity, there are numerous possibilities for rustic campsites back away from the primary access roads along one of the side roads that enter the WSAs. You will need to bring all of your water with you.

Rugged Terrain of the
Sierra de Las Canas and
Presilla Wilderness Study
Areas

Sierra de Las Canas and Presilla Wilderness Study Areas

GENERAL DESCRIPTION

Sierra de Las Canas and Presilla are two adjacent BLM Wilderness Study Areas (WSAs) of 12,838 and 8,680 acres, respectively, located about 7 miles east of the city of Socorro. The two areas are divided by a north/south portion of the Quebradas Road, a BLM-designated back-country byway. It is a remote area with few visitors that is easy to access and suited to people who prefer solitary off-trail hiking in an undeveloped setting.

The area is located in an arid setting, with maximum summer temperatures in the 90-degree F to over 100-degree F range and mild winter daylight temperatures. The most comfortable time of year to visit is before June or after August. Precipitation averages 10 inches per year, with most of the rainfall occurring during the months of July through September. The eastern end of the area contains a small but rugged desert mountain range with sheer rock escarpments, deep narrow canyons, and mesa tops. The rest of the area is characterized by rugged limestone and sandstone hills and broken desert badlands cut by large arroyos. The elevation varies from 4,700 feet to 6,200 feet, and the vegetation is typical of the Upper Chihuahuan Desert at the northern extreme of its range. The predominant vegetation types include desert shrub, piñon pine and juniper, creosote bush, salt bush, and cacti. Of particular interest are the frequent stands of the picturesque, cane-like ocotillo cactus. The English translation for Sierra de Las Canas means "mountain of the canes," and the term presumably refers to the ocotillo cactus that abounds in the area. When hiking this area, you will need to take along your drinking water, as there are no springs or other sources of water in the vicinity. The driving time required to reach Sierra de Las Canas/Presilla from Albuquerque is within 2 hours.

Access

The best access to reach this hiking area is via the Quebradas backcountry byway road. Begin by driving on Interstate 25 to the Escondida exit a few miles north of Socorro, where you leave the Interstate and proceed back under the highway headed east. Continue a short distance to the small village of Escondida, where the main road turns north and continues a little over a mile to a turnoff on the east side of the road to Escondida Lake. Take the turnoff, and proceed across a bridge over the greatly diminished Rio Grande. You will presently pass the community of Pueblito and come to a road fork where the road turns to gravel and heads south, paralleling the low hills to the east. About 0.6 miles after turning south, another gravel road turns off to the east, which is marked with a sign identifying it as a backcountry byway. This is the Quebradas Road and it continues for another 24 miles until it intersects County Road 129. This road can be adequately negotiated by passenger car, although a high clearance vehicle might be required after heavy rains. After turning on to the Quebradas Road, keep to the main road, avoiding the numerous side roads. After the road has curved toward the south, about 7 miles from its start, you will come to the north boundaries of the Sierra de Las Canas and Presilla WSAs, which are presently not marked. About another 2.5 miles farther south is a sign identifying the Presilla area to the west. This is a good spot to park your vehicle and hike either east or west. The Presilla WSA ends with the next road heading west off the Quebradas Road (this forms the southern boundary), while the Sierra de Las Canas WSA continues to be defined on its west and south sides by the Quebradas Road. The road eventually terminates at County Road 129. If you decide to return from the south end, take County Road 129 south for 3 miles to Highway 380, and continue west for 11 miles on Highway 380, where it joins Interstate 25.

Hiking Trails

There are no established trails within the areas described, only a lot of rugged, open terrain with some nice scenery and interesting plant life. Perhaps the most logical direction to head is east to the

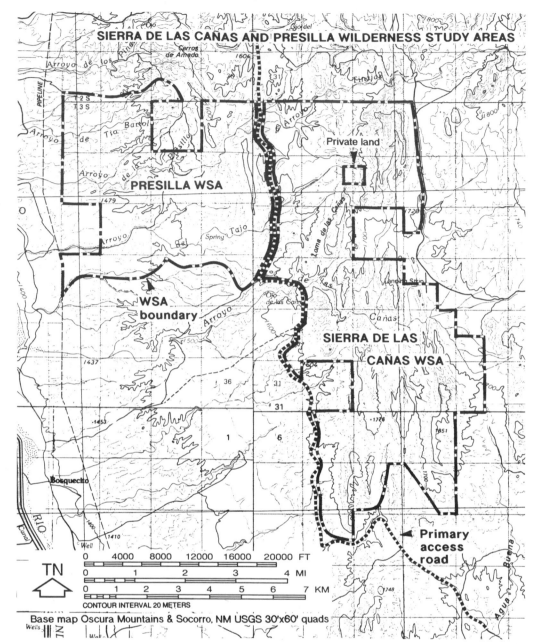

SIERRA DE LAS CAÑAS AND PRESILLA WILDERNESS STUDY AREAS

PRESILLA WSA

Private land

WSA boundary

SIERRA DE LAS CAÑAS WSA

Primary access road

0   4000   8000   12000   16000   20000 FT
0   1   2   3   4 MI
0   1   2   3   4   5   6   7 KM
CONTOUR INTERVAL 20 METERS
Base map Oscura Mountains & Socorro, NM USGS 30'x60' quads

TN

For Further Information:

New Mexico Statewide Wilderness Summary, Volume 2, published by the U.S. Department of the Interior, Bureau of Land Management, New Mexico State Office, Santa Fe, NM, May 1985.

Bureau of Land Management
Las Cruces District Office
1800 Marques Street
Las Cruces, NM 88005
(505) 525-8228

small Sierra de Las Canas Mountain Range, which can be ascended without too much difficulty. From the top, you get a nice overview of the entire area. This area is a good alternative if you are looking for a day hike in a new area. As mentioned before, the landscape is rugged, but the scenery is pleasant and there is plenty of solitude.

Map Coverage

Map coverage of the entire area is provided by the USGS 1:100,000-scale Socorro map. The appropriate USGS 7.5-minute scale maps are the Oscura Mountains, Bustos Well, and Loma de Las Canas maps.

Jornada del Muerto Wilderness Study Area

GENERAL DESCRIPTION

Jornada del Muerto ("journey of death") is the name given by the 16th-century Spanish to a large and empty wilderness of grasslands, sand barrens, and lava flows located east of the Rio Grande between Las Cruces and Socorro. The area lies between the San Andres Mountains on the east and the Fra Cristobal and Caballo Ranges on the west, and is one of the most remote regions in the state. The early Spanish caravan route between Chihuahua and Santa Fe generally followed the path of the Rio Grande, but a frequent variation of the route was to cut north through the Jornada del Muerto where the river swings to the west, and rejoin the Rio Grande below Socorro. This desolate and waterless shortcut of almost 90 miles shortened the trip by a day and cut out some swampy and difficult stretches along the river, but a cost was paid by the hundreds who perished through Indian attacks and the unforgiving nature of the Jornada Del Muerto, and its very name indicates that it must have been approached with an ominous dread by the early travelers who passed through. This is quite a large area, which includes land in and to the west of the White Sands Missile Range, and much of the area is difficult to access. Despite its forbidding name, however, the Jornada del Muerto is in a scenic and expansive setting, with interesting landforms and pockets of green vegetation.

The Jornada del Muerto Wilderness Study Area (WSA) is a 31,147-acre unit located almost entirely within a 760,000-year-old lava flow on BLM land about 45 miles southeast of Socorro, and bordered on the east side by the White Sands Missile Range. The WSA is located within the Chihuahuan Desert zone, with numerous outcrops of lava and basalt mixed with rolling hills and ridges, and interspersed with frequent sandy depressions supporting grasses and shrubbery.

Yuccas along the Jornada del Muerto

Trees are few and far between, and the most notable forms of plant life in the area are the tall and picturesque soaptree yuccas that grow in profusion on the lands surrounding the lava flow. The source of the lava is a cinder cone immediately to the west of the WSA. Large game in the area includes deer, antelope, and coyotes, with a population of smaller animals that have evolved an uncharacteristically dark coloration to adapt to the dark rock. The weather permits year-round hiking, but temperatures can get uncomfortably hot in mid-summer. Sources for drinking water are not present, but even with an annual precipitation rate of approximately 8 inches, there is enough moisture around in scattered locations for mosquitos to breed, particularly in the spring or when rain has been plentiful. Travel time to Jornada del Muerto WSA is about 3 hours from Albuquerque and the access is not difficult if conditions are dry. Other than a few weirdly out-of-place Army trucks that have been junked on the White Sands Range side of the fence, the only vehicles you are apt to see after you leave the pavement, if any, are an occasional ranch truck. The WSA is truly remote, and if you need help there isn't likely to be much around, but if you like solitude, this place fits the description.

Map Coverage

If you can still find the USGS 15-minute scale Val Verde and Malpais Well maps, these provide the most detailed coverage for the fewest number of maps. Otherwise, the USGS 7.5-minute scale coverage requires the Pope, Harriet Ranch, Tucson Spring, and Fuller Ranch maps. The USGS 1:100,000-scale Oscura Mountains map covers all but the southern tip of the area but is really not very useful overall. A good map to get for the approach roads in the area is *The Roads of New Mexico*, a state atlas published by the Shearer Publishing Company.

Access

From Interstate 25 south of Socorro, take the San Antonio exit heading east on Highway 380. After you have driven 7 miles east of Interstate 25 on Highway 380, turn south on the Fite Ranch Road (County Road A153), and check your odometer as the milages referred to in the balance of this description will be from the Highway 380 turnoff. At the 1.6-mile point, take the right-hand fork in the road, and at 3.7 miles keep to the branch that continues straight. At mile 12.2 the road forks again, and you should take the left fork, marked with the BLM sign, toward Harriet Ranch, and at mile 18.7, again take the left fork. As you reach the 21.5-mile point, you will come to another road fork near a corral with a BLM sign pointing west toward Harriet Ranch. Instead, take the left fork that continues south along the fence line, and a little over 2 miles farther you will draw even with the lava flow to the west of the road. This marks the northeast corner of the WSA, which continues along the west side of the road for about the next 10 miles. A good point to pull off the road and access the lava flow is at the 27.8-mile point, where the road makes a jog to the west and a double-track ranch road leads in that direction toward the fence line. Park your vehicle and cross the fence, being careful not to damage it, and head west for the lava.

When the road conditions are dry, the access roads, which are gravel or dirt once you leave Highway 380, should present no problem for standard passenger cars, although there will be a few rough spots. But if there have been recent rains, numerous small lakelets form at various points along the road, and some of these may require four wheel drive. These roads

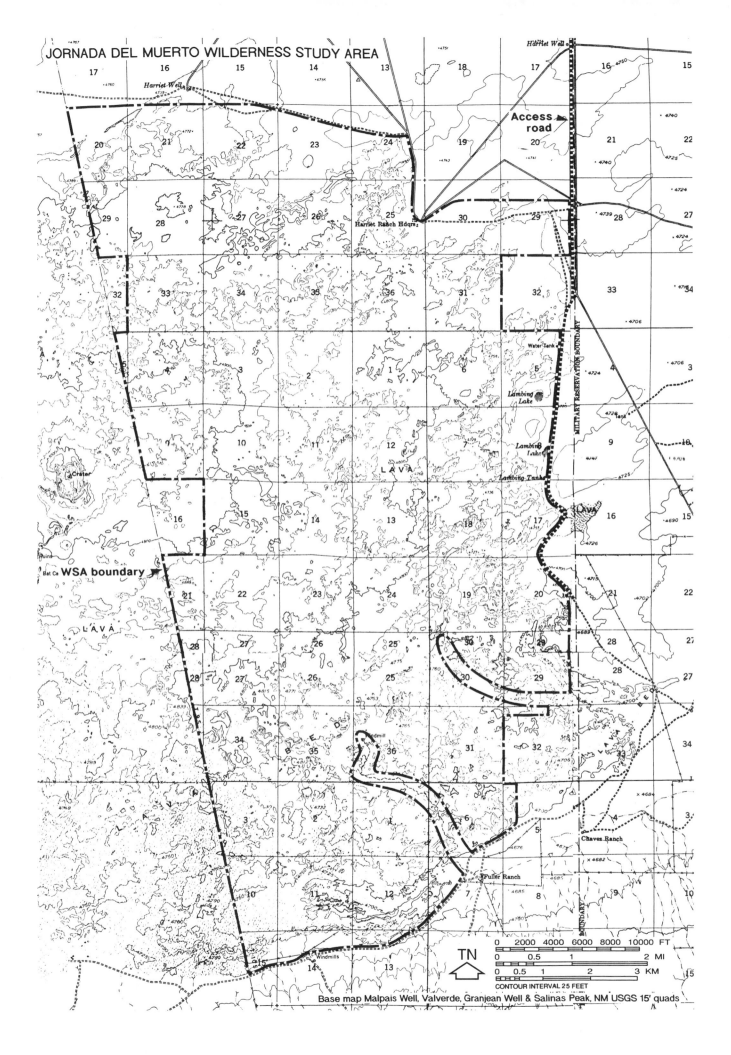

JORNADA DEL MUERTO WILDERNESS STUDY AREA

TN

| 0 | 2000 | 4000 | 6000 | 8000 | 10000 FT |

| 0 | 0.5 | 1 | 2 MI |

| 0 | 0.5 | 1 | 2 | 3 KM |

CONTOUR INTERVAL 25 FEET

Base map Malpais Well, Valverde, Granjean Well & Salinas Peak, NM USGS 15' quads

are remote, and it is a long walk out if you get stuck or run out of gas.

Hiking Trails

There are no hiking trails established within the WSA nor are you likely to encounter anyone else while hiking there. The terrain is open and easy to walk through, with interesting lava formations and grassy basins where lava tubes have collapsed and filled in with sand. This is a relatively old lava flow, and it contrasts with the more rugged terrain of more recent flows. There are a limited number of nearby landmarks and if you plan to hike very far into the lava field, you will need to take note of those that are available in order to return as near as possible to your starting location. Not to belabor the point, but this is a very remote area, and you should be aware of the possible consequences of hiking alone. Take along drinking water and sun protection, and enjoy an area that is wild and undeveloped.

For Further Information:

Bureau of Land
    Management
    Socorro Resource Area
    198 Neel Avenue NW
    Socorro, NM 87801
    (505) 835-0412

Bureau of Land
    Management
    Las Cruces District
    Office
    1800 Marquess Street
    Las Cruces, NM 88005
    (505) 525-8228

New Mexico Statewide Wilderness Study: Volume 3, Wilderness Analysis Reports, U.S. Department of the Interior, Bureau of Land Management, New Mexico State Office, Santa Fe, NM, September 1986.

Bosque del Apache National Wildlife Refuge

GENERAL INFORMATION

The Bosque del Apache Wildlife Refuge is a 57,190-acre facility located on the Rio Grande floodplain about 90 miles south of Albuquerque, or 13 miles south of Socorro. It is sandwiched between three small, undeveloped Wilderness Areas totaling an additional 30,287 acres—the Little San Pascual Wilderness on the east side, and the Indian Well and Chupadera Wilderness Areas on the west side. As you might expect, the primary attraction for

which Bosque del Apache is famous is wildlife, but most specifically the great flocks of migratory birds that winter in the refuge. The wildlife refuge was established in 1939, with the primary idea to develop a protected habitat for the then-endangered great sandhill crane. The improvements began with the construction, by the Civilian Conservation Corps, of water impoundments consisting of individual tracts separated by low dikes, which are flooded with water from the Rio Grande in the fall to provide nesting and breeding grounds, and then drained in the spring. Today, the sandhill crane is out of trouble, and thousands of the birds, along with a few of the endangered whooping cranes, visit annually. Altogether, nearly 300 bird species can be seen at the Refuge, but it is the impressive flocks of ducks, geese, and cranes, along with numerous species of raptors, which are most responsible for drawing a steady

Bosque del Apache in February

stream of birdwatchers each winter. A 15-mile paved loop road winds through the refuge to assist the public in viewing the birds, and interpretive displays and printed information are available at the Visitor Center across the highway to the west of the viewing area.

Bosque del Apache provides a fairly diverse plant environment, including the water impoundment basins with typically aquatic plantlife, open fields used for growing supplemental wildlife food crops, and bosques, or densely wooded riparian tracts with cottonwood and tamarisk predominating. On both sides of the Refuge, rising up out of the river bottom-land, are the upland environments, beginning with brush-covered sand dunes and phasing into a more complex land-scape of gently rolling terrain heavily cut by arroyos, small ridges and mesas, and low mountain peaks. This upland environ-ment is primarily contained within the previously mentioned Wilderness Areas and has the aridity and sparse, scrubby plantlife typical of a desert upland.

A Native culture known to the Spanish as the Piro inhabited the area in early times; then came the Spanish, and the Apaches for whom the Refuge is named, and from whose fearsome raids no other group was safe. And, finally, came the Anglos. Today, the invasion routes are from the north and south along Interstate 25, bringing the tourist armed with binoculars and the long lens.

The best time for visiting the Refuge, if you want to see the large bird flocks, is from the months of November through February, with weather that can be either mild and pleasant or very cold. Otherwise, the best months are in the spring and fall when the days are warm and the nights cool. In the summer the impoundment reservoirs are drained and the daytime temperatures can get uncomfortably hot. No camping is allowed within the Refuge,

and the best alternatives are probably at Elephant Butte Reservoir south of the Refuge or in the National Forest areas west of Socorro. No permits are neces-sary for dayhiking, but overnight use of the Wilderness Areas requires a permit obtainable at the Refuge Headquarters.

Map Coverage

The U.S. Geologic Survey 1:100,000-scale Oscura Mountains map shows Bosque del Apache plus the surrounding area. A Bosque del Apache National Wildlife Refuge map is available at the Refuge Headquarters/Visitor Center.

Access

Drive on Interstate 25 to Exit 139, located 8 miles south of Socorro, and take the exit east toward San Antonio. At the blinking traffic light just under a mile east of the Interstate, turn south on State Highway 1 and continue south for 8 miles to the Refuge Headquarters (Visi-tor Center). The loop tour road and the only hiking trail currently established are directly across the road from the Head-quarters. A $2.00 entry fee is in effect.

The Indian Well Wilderness is best accessed off Highway 1, south of the Visitor Center, and the Little San Pascual Wilderness is reached by driving about 7 miles east of San Antonio on Highway 380 and turning south on the Fite Ranch Road. I have not hiked the Wilderness Areas, so you will need to get more detailed access directions at the Visitor Center. All primary roads are paved, but dirt roads such as the Fite Ranch Road may be trouble if conditions have been wet.

Hiking Trails

At this time only one hiking trail has been established in the Refuge or adja-cent Wilderness Areas, a short loop hike

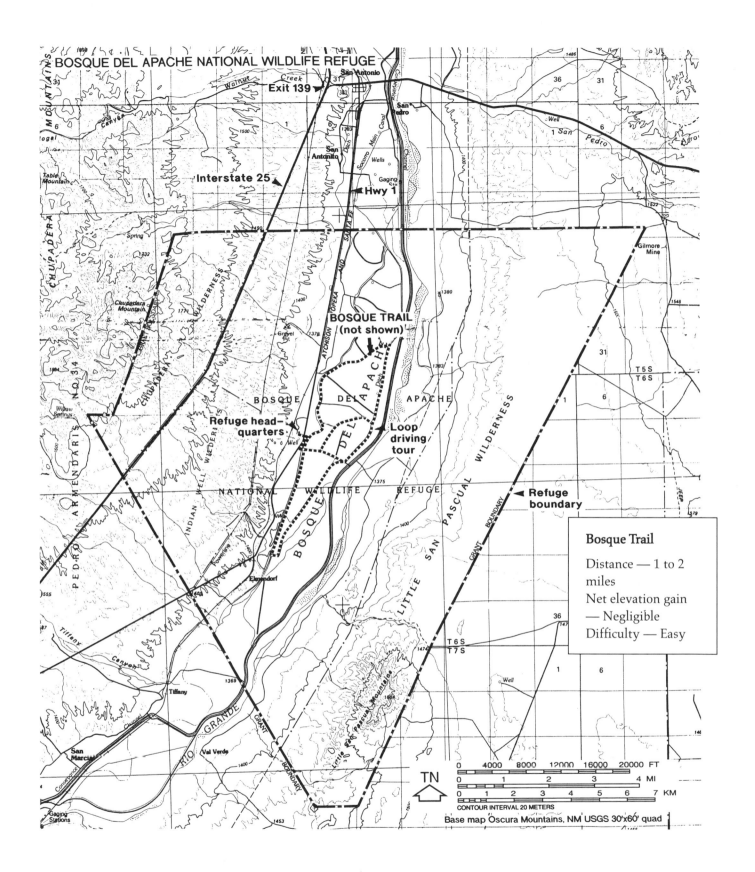

BOSQUE DEL APACHE NATIONAL WILDLIFE REFUGE

Exit 139

Interstate 25

Hwy 1

BOSQUE TRAIL
(not shown)

Refuge head-
quarters

Loop
driving
tour

Refuge
boundary

TN

0   4000   8000   12000   16000   20000 FT
0   1   2   3   4 MI
0   1   2   3   4   5   6   7 KM
CONTOUR INTERVAL 20 METERS
Base map Oscura Mountains, NM USGS 30'x60' quad

Bosque Trail

Distance — 1 to 2
miles

Net elevation gain
— Negligible

Difficulty — Easy

through the Bosque off the loop tour road, but there are plans for several more trails to be constructed in the near future, including a loop hike through the Indian Well Wilderness.

Backcountry hiking in the wilderness areas is allowed, but permission must be obtained for overnight use. No water is available, so bring along what you will need.

TRAIL DESCRIPTION

Bosque Trail

The Bosque Trail is a short loop hike of between 1 and 2 miles, depending upon the particular version hiked, which winds through the cottonwood and tamarisk woodlands in the heart of the Refuge. It is an easy hike, with negligible elevation gain, which affords the opportunity to get out and stretch your legs in a tranquil setting away from the observation and access roads. Raptors can occasionally be seen perched on the high branches and possibly some of the mammalian wildlife as well.

Locate the trailhead by driving 8.7 miles along the one-way main tour loop road to an observation tower, where a trail segment cuts south into the bosque. An alternative start is provided at a parking area another 0.5 miles farther along the loop road. After leading into the bosque, the trail forks into two alternative loops, which travel through essentially the same type of terrain and end up interconnecting. The entire trail system is easy to follow and can be hiked in about a half hour.

Geese Flying over the Bosque del Apache

For Further Information

Bosque del Apache
   National Wildlife
   Refuge
P.O. Box 1246
Socorro, NM 87801
(505) 835-1828

Withington Wilderness

GENERAL INFORMATION

The San Mateo Mountains are a north-south oriented range of mountains that sit to the west of the Rio Grande rift and at the east end of the vast Datil-Mogollon volcanic field that extends westward to Arizona. The volcanoes in this area, including those that formed the San Mateos, began to erupt about 25 million years ago and deposited vast quantities of light-colored ash and tuff, which you will find much in evidence as you explore the mountains and valleys of the San Mateo and Magdalena ranges. Because of the relatively greater age of the mountains, when compared to some of the more recent volcanic areas of the state, nature has somewhat muted the evidence of their volcanism but has left them as a sharply upthrusted set of peaks and ridges with some rugged terrain and formidable elevation gain. Withington Wilderness is a Forest Service-administered wilderness located in the Cibola National Forest at the north end of the San Mateo Mountains, about 15 miles southwest of the town of Magdalena. The Wilderness Area contains 18,889 acres and is named for Mt. Withington, a 10,115-foot peak located at the west boundary of the area. Four trails are located in or adjacent to the wilderness, and with a 3,400-foot elevation differential within the area, they are all steep; I suspect that overnight backpacking is the exception and dayhiking

Looking Southwest toward the Withington Wilderness

the rule. Water availability varies from an overabundance during spring runoff to scarcity during the dry part of summer, when some intermittent flows can still be found in the major canyon drainages. The climate is pleasant in the spring as soon as the weather begins to turn warm, although access can be a problem until things dry out in mid- to late May, and remains so through the summer until the snows start. Summer temperatures can be a bit toasty in the lower elevations, and the most enjoyable time to visit is probably in the fall. Two Forest Service campgrounds are situated just west of the Wilderness (no water) and provide some nice campsites in the forests of ponderosa, aspen and Douglas fir that cover this part of the area. The two main attractions in the area seem to be Beartrap Campground and the summit of Mt. Withington, which is accessible by road and has a fire lookout on top. I say this because, in several visits to the area, these are the only places where I have ever seen any other people, and I have never seen any other hikers on the trails. In fact, the grand total of all individuals I have ever seen anywhere in the area would probably fit comfortably into a small school bus. In other words, this Wilderness is the place to come to get away from people. The camping is good, the trails are fair, and, although readily accessible, it seems remote. Your vehicle should have high clearance, and in wet weather should have four wheel drive as well. The access roads can get pretty rough at the far ends, and for the west-side access, large trailers and RVs are probably not a good idea. Travel time from Albuquerque is a little under 3 hours.

Map Coverage

The Withington Wilderness is shown on a special Withington Wilderness map produced by the Forest Service. This map is in an interim form at present. For a good overall perspective of the trails and roads in the area, get the Cibola National Forest map for the Magdalena Ranger District. The USGS 7.5-minute scale maps of the area are the Monica Saddle, Mt. Withington, Bay Buck Peaks, and Grassy Lookout maps.

Access

West Side Access. Drive 11.8 miles west from the town of Magdalena on Highway 60 to an intersectionon with a road sign that points the way south to Mt. Withington and Beartrap Campground. Turn south on the gravel road, which crosses the Plains of San Agustin, once the bed of a huge Pleistocene lake, and on to the junction with Forest Road 549 at the 8.5-mile point south of Highway 60. Continue straight on Road 549 as it climbs 5.8 steep miles to the Forest Road 138 turnoff toward Mt. Withington, another 3.2 miles distant. The west fork continues 1.4 miles to Beartrap Campground, or 3.9 miles to Hughes Mill Campground. As stated before, you should at least have a vehicle with high road clearance, unless you have been given information to the contrary. You can also approach these points from the south, but I don't know what the road conditions are like.

East Side Access. At the west end of the town of Magdalena, turn south on to Highway 107. This highway is paved for the first 2.6 miles before metamorphosing into a broad gravel road that continues south for another 14.3 miles to a junction with Forest Road 52. This intersection can also be reached by taking the Highway 107 exit off Interstate 25, about 26 miles south of Socorro, and driving northwest on Highway 107. Drive west on Forest

Road 52 for 3.3 miles, where Forest Road 56 branches off to the east (primitive road) and follow Forest Road 56 as it drops down into Big Rosa Canyon. At 2.7 miles past the last intersection, you will come to a sign pointing out the Potato Trail. The road is washed out and closed a short distance farther south.

Hiking Trails

The trails in this area have an upper trailhead along the main crest of the range, with the lower trailheads located in the canyons that drop off to each side. The trailheads are well marked, and the trails are identified along their length by frequent tree blazes. The trails don't receive much traffic from either hikers or horses, and the trail surfaces vary from moderately worn near some of the trailheads to very obscure at points farther along the trails. It will be necessary to pay attention to the blazes to help stay on route. All the trails have some water along the way, but this is variable and you should bring your water with you for day hikes. The elevation gradients tend to be steep, particularly near the top end.

The trails described here include the Potato Trail, which cuts across the Wilderness Area, and the Chimney Canyon/Hughes Trail, which lies outside the Wilderness to the west but joins at the top. The two remaining trails available are the Monica Trail, which is a short, 1.7-mile trail northwest of Mt. Withington and is, frankly, not very interesting, and the Water Canyon Trail, which provides a similar hiking experience to the Potato Trail. Water Canyon also cuts across the Wilderness Area, roughly paralleling Potato Canyon, but the lower trailhead is currently not accessible by motor vehicle, as it lies about 3 miles beyond the washout in Big Rosa Canyon.

TRAIL DESCRIPTIONS

Hike #1. Potato Trail (#38)

Find the lower trailhead for this trail by following the "East Side Access" description and driving west up the double track dirt road at the Potato Trail sign. A short drive leads to a large berm just before the Wilderness boundary. The trail is 6 miles up to the top of the crest below Mt. Withington, with 3,000 vertical feet to gain. An additional 0.8-mile (and 315 vertical feet) walk up Forest Road 138 gains the summit of Mt. Withington and is a worthwhile extension to the hike if you plan to go all the way up. The upper trailhead can be reached by driving 0.6 miles south of the Mt. Withington turnoff on Forest Road 138 (see "West Side Access"), where a sign indicates the Potato Trail on the east side of the road and the Chimney Canyon Trail on the west side. Because of the steepness of the top part of the trail, the lower trailhead is the more reasonable departure point if you plan to do a round-trip hike from the same trailhead, so the hike is arbitrarily described as starting from the lower trailhead in Big Rosa Canyon. Begin by walking west from the road berm up the bottom of the canyon. One of the first things you will notice are the effects of the flash floods that occasionally roar down the canyon bottom. This is not the place to be with big rain happening up-canyon. You will begin to pick up tree blazes to help you keep on the slightly worn trail as it generally keeps to the bottom of the canyon. The predominant vegetation types at the bottom of the trail include piñon pine, ponderosa pine, one-seed juniper, Apache plume, narrow leaf cottonwood, and some large old alligator junipers; on a hot day, there is a detectable difference in temperature between

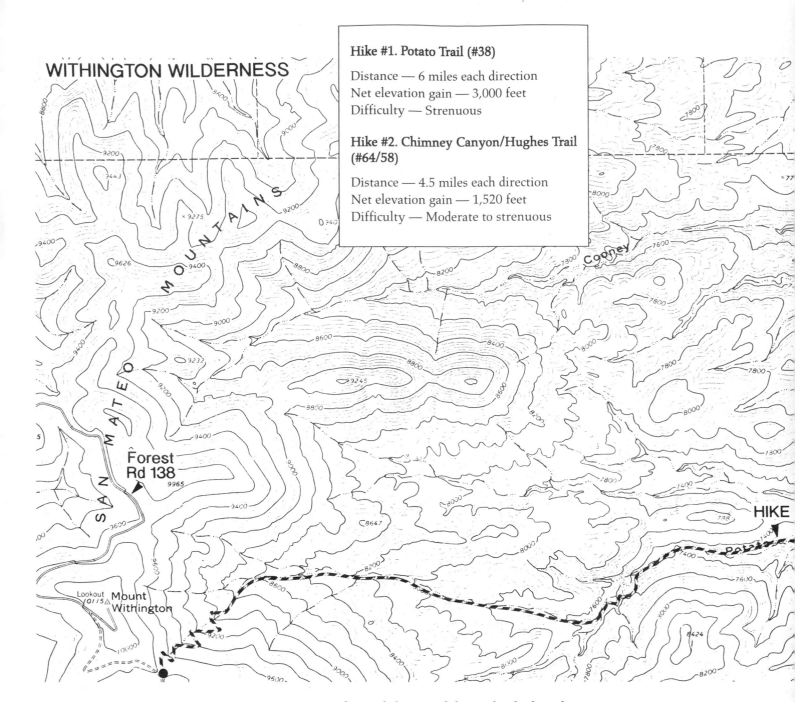

WITHINGTON WILDERNESS

Hike #1. Potato Trail (#38)

Distance — 6 miles each direction
Net elevation gain — 3,000 feet
Difficulty — Strenuous

Hike #2. Chimney Canyon/Hughes Trail (#64/58)

Distance — 4.5 miles each direction
Net elevation gain — 1,520 feet
Difficulty — Moderate to strenuous

SAN MATEO MOUNTAINS

Forest
Rd 138

Lookout
10115

Mount
Withington

HIKE

this and the top of the trail, which ends in forests of ponderosa, aspen, and Douglas fir. As you continue up the canyon, you won't have a continuous visible trail surface to follow, but keep to the main canyon and keep looking for tree blazes. At about the 3-mile point, the trail climbs up the south side of the canyon to skirt a steep, narrow section and then drops back down into the canyon bottom. A short

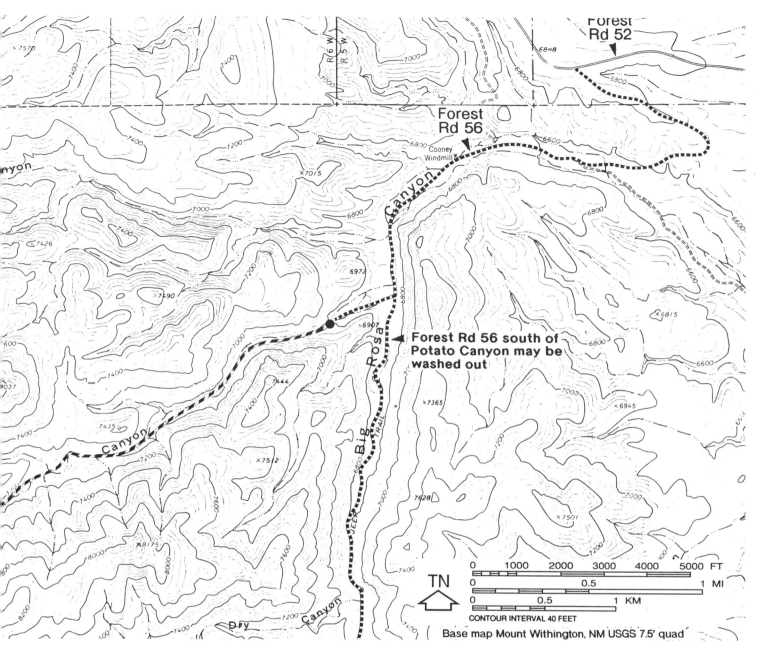

Forest Rd 56 south of
Potato Canyon may be
washed out

TN

0	1000	2000	3000	4000	5000 FT
0		0.5			1 MI
0		0.5		1 KM	

CONTOUR INTERVAL 40 FEET

Base map Mount Withington, NM USGS 7.5' quad

distance farther up, you should take the
right fork of the canyon, which continues
up to the west. When you reach the head
of the canyon, the elevation gradient
begins to increase severely, and the trail
climbs out of the drainage to the left and
begins a series of broad switchbacks as it
climbs up the forested slopes heading for
a saddle on the ridge to the southwest.
Not to belabor the point, but it will be

especially important to watch for the tree
blazes. Once in the forests, you will be
unable to see landmarks to help you
navigate, and the blazes and trail surface
will be all that you will have to go on.
Once at the top, or at whatever point you
decide to turn back, follow the route back
to the trailhead to complete the hike.

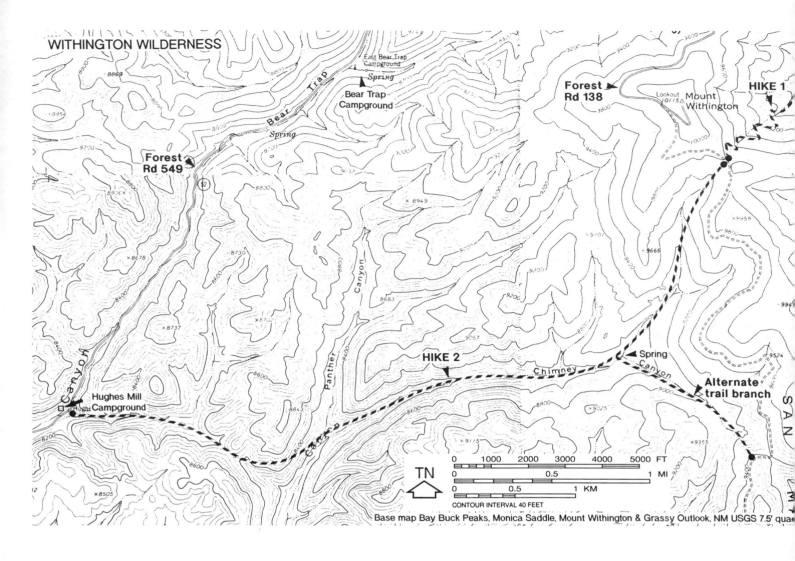

Base map Bay Buck Peaks, Monica Saddle, Mount Withington & Grassy Outlook, NM USGS 7.5' qua

CONTOUR INTERVAL 40 FEET

Hike #2. Chimney Canyon/Hughes Trail (#64/58)

This trail system goes from the lower trailhead at Hughes Mill Campground, a small Forest Service campground in Beartrap Canyon, to the upper trailhead above the north fork of Chimney Canyon, just south of Mt. Withington. An alternative branch also ascends the south fork of Chimney Canyon. The trail is 4.5 miles long (one way) and gains 1,520

feet. It is somewhat better worn than the Potato Trail and somewhat less steep. The upper part of the trail follows Chimney Canyon, which has some striking cliffs of tuff and basalt near the upper end and occasional flows of water along the way. It does not lie within the Wilderness Area, but that is a moot point, as the forest terrain through which it travels has essentially the same wilderness character. There seems to be some inconsistency between the Forest Service map and the trail signs as to which part of the trail is the Hughes Trail and which is the Chimney Canyon Trail, but it doesn't really matter. The trail can be started from either the lower or upper trailhead, and because the trailheads are connected by only 6.7 miles of road, it is particularly easy to do a car shuttle and hike the trail in one direction. If you start from the lower trailhead, you can also do a loop hike by returning on the 6.7-mile road segment.

To locate the trailheads, see the "West Side Access" directions. From the intersection of Forest Road 138 and the Beartrap Campground turnoff, drive 2.8 miles up Forest Road 138 to a sign marking the upper trailhead, or drive 3.9 miles up Beartrap Canyon to reach the lower trailhead at Hughes Mill Campground. If beginning at the campground, start by walking east across the road and following the small canyon, looking for blaze marks on the trees to locate the trail. The trail is pretty obscure at first, and it will be necessary to look for the blazes. At about 0.5 miles up the canyon, the trail follows a drainage to the right and climbs over a saddle and then contours down into Chimney Canyon. Walk up the canyon and take the right fork, which is taken on up to a spring below a broad, flat area. The trail forks here and both branches lead to the top. I like the north branch because it is better worn and makes a shorter loop, if you decide to return on the road segment, down to the Beartrap Campground turnoff, then past Beartrap Campground to the starting point at Hughes Mill Campground. If you do this hike from the top end, it will be important not to miss the turnoff where the trail climbs up out of Chimney Canyon and over to Hughes Mill Campground.

For Further Information:

Cibola National Forest
  Magdalena Ranger
  District
  Box 45
  Magdalena, NM 87825
  (505) 854-2281

Apache Kid Wilderness

GENERAL INFORMATION

The Apache Kid Wilderness consists of 44,650 acres located in the Cibola National Forest about 28 miles southwest of the town of Magdalena in the southern part of the San Mateo Mountains. The Wilderness was named for a renegade Apache Indian, who is now thought not to have been the Apache Kid, but a former subchief in the Warm Springs Tribe headed by Cochise. He had stolen a prized horse from a local rancher and was trailed by a group of vigilantes to a site near Blue Mountain, where he was killed in ambush and buried in about 1906. His gravesite remains as a historical reminder of the fierce bands of Apache warriors who roamed these mountains and exacted a grim toll from the settlers, miners, and travelers in the area. In this saga one of the most notable personalities who roamed these parts was Victorio, the famous Apache war chief who was the namesake for Vicks Peak. In addition to Vicks Peak and Blue Mountain, other significant summits in the wilderness area include San Mateo Peak and West Blue Mountain, the high point at 10,336 feet elevation. The highest elevations support a subalpine environment of spruce, fir, aspen, and limber pine, below which is a broad ponderosa zone, which phases on down into an Upper Sonoran zone at the lowest elevations, with plant life that includes piñon pine, alligator juniper, apache plume, and mountain mahogany.

The geology is primarily volcanic in origin, with numerous steep side canyons, some of which contain pleasant, grassy bottoms with seasonal flowing streams of water (which don't appear to support a population of fish). The total net elevation differential of the area is almost 4,000 feet.

This is an area that clearly does not receive a very significant amount of hiking pressure, despite the ideal conditions that it presents. The Wilderness and surrounding forest area contains numerous hiking trails, with water and good campsites along many of them, and there are several nearby campgrounds for car camping. The mountains receive significant snow cover in winter, and scattered patches may still be present in the high elevations by May, with good hiking conditions continuing thereafter until late October or early November. Mid-summer produces temperatures that will be uncomfortable at lower elevations but tolerable on most of the trails. No permits are needed.

Map Coverage

The best map for the hiking trails is the Apache Kid Wilderness map produced by the Forest Service. It is in an interim form at present and the completed version should be a significant improvement. The Cibola National Forest map (Magdalena Ranger District) is also useful. The

appropriate USGS 7.5-minute scale maps
are the Vicks Peak and Blue Mountain
quads, and the San Juan Peak and Steel
Hill quads for the far east side.

Access

The access points for the trails described in this section are at or near
Springtime Campground on the south
side of the Wilderness, and at Water
Canyon on the north side.

Springtime Campground Trailhead. Drive
on Interstate 25 to Exit 115 (32 miles south
of Socorro) and take the exit for Highway
107. Drive across the overpass to the east
side of the Interstate and turn south on
Highway 1, which parallels the Interstate,
continuing 11.6 miles to a west turn on to
Forest Road 225. Alternatively, you can
take Exit 100 off of Interstate 25 and travel
about 5 miles north on Highway 1 to reach
the Forest Road 225 junction. It is a 13.2
mile drive west on Forest Road 225, an all-
weather gravel road, to reach the campground. Driving time after leaving the
Interstate is about 1 hour. Springtime
Campground can also be reached by
traveling 14 miles north on Forest Road
139 from the small town of Monticello.
This is a longer approach and the road is
rougher, but the scenery is nice. Luna Park
Campground is located 6 miles south of
Springtime Campground along this road.

Water Canyon Trailhead. If approaching
from the north, take the Socorro exit off
Interstate 25 and continue south through
town, turning west on Highway 60
toward Magdalena and Datil. At 45 miles
west of Socorro, past Magdalena and
immediately before reaching the VLA
(Very Large Array) complex of radio
telescopes, turn south on Highway 52
toward Dusty and Beaverhead. The
highway soon turns to gravel and continues south 21 miles to the Highway 163

A Bear-Chewed Sign in
the Apache Kid
Wilderness

junction (stay left on Highway 52 toward
Dusty and Winston) and an additional 16
miles to the junction of Forest Road 478,
where you turn east. Stay on Forest Road
478, which has numerous stream crossings including a short stretch up the
center of the streambed at mile 8, pass the
Forest Road 96 turnoff at mile 9, and
drive to the end of the road at 12.9 miles,
where a washout currently prevents
further vehicular progress. There is a nice

campsite, just off the road, where you can park your vehicle. This spot is 0.2 miles short of Coffee Pot Canyon and 1 mile short of Water Canyon, both of which are marked with road signs, and you will have to make the extra distance to the trailhead on foot, unless the road has been repaired by the time you visit. It won't matter, however, because the walking is easy along the spacious bottom of Red Canyon, which is like a continuous meadow through ponderosa pine forest, with a stream that appears to flow much of the year. Upon reaching Water Canyon, turn south up the canyon in the direction indicated by the sign.

If you are approaching this hiking area from the south, take the Highway 52 exit off of Interstate 25, 8 miles north of the town of Truth or Consequences, and continue on Highway 52 for about 56 miles to reach the Forest Road 478 turnoff. Travel time to reach the trailhead area where you park your vehicle is about 2 hours after leaving the Interstate on the south approach, and 2.5 hours from the north. Because the forest road gets rough near the end, it would be advisable not to do this approach in a passenger car, and because of the stream crossings, you should probably wait until about early May or later.

Hiking Trails

The hiking routes described in this section cover less than one third of the total trail mileage available in the wilderness, but give a good representative selection of what is available. These hikes are long, strenuous dayhikes if done in their entirety, but they can also be done as backpacks of one or more nights, particularly in the case of Hikes #2 and #3. As usual in this kind of area, you can piece together various other trails to design your own backpacking route, but I would offer the following observation:

the trails that go up over the high ridges tend to be quite steep and may not be worth the effort with a heavily loaded pack as there are few good campsites in the high places with dependable water sources. My backpacking preference is to hike up one of the canyons and make camp along a stream below the final steep section of trail. From your camp you can dayhike up to the high part of the range, enjoy the hiking more, and have more time to visit your objectives. Also note that these hikes can be made into less strenuous day hikes by hiking less than the full distance suggested in the route descriptions; the scenery is nice all the way up. The bears in this mountain range have a strange fetish for chewing up trail signs and, although the signs are periodically replaced by the Forest Service, you may have to rely on a trail map to identify trail junctions. Some of the trails are very faint but are usually adequately marked with tree blazes.

TRAIL DESCRIPTIONS

Hike #1. Springtime Campground to San Mateo Peak

This is the most-used trail in an underused hiking area. It is most often done as a day hike to and from San Mateo Peak, on the summit of which is an old fire lookout tower. There are backpacking possibilities here, with the most likely camping spot near San Mateo Spring on the way up, although the spring may not be flowing during summer and fall. The hike can also be modified by including trails that connect from the southwest or by continuing to destinations north along the ridge from San Mateo Peak. The lower part of the trail faces south and can be hot during summer, so bring along adequate water. The round-trip trail length as

---

Hike #1. Springtime Campground to San Mateo Peak

Distance — 8.4 miles round trip
Net elevation gain — 2,739 feet
Difficulty — Strenuous

Hike #3. Indian Creek Trail

Distance — 16.6 miles round trip net elevation gain — 2,382 feet (plus another 680 feet lost on the second mile of the hike) Difficulty — strenuous

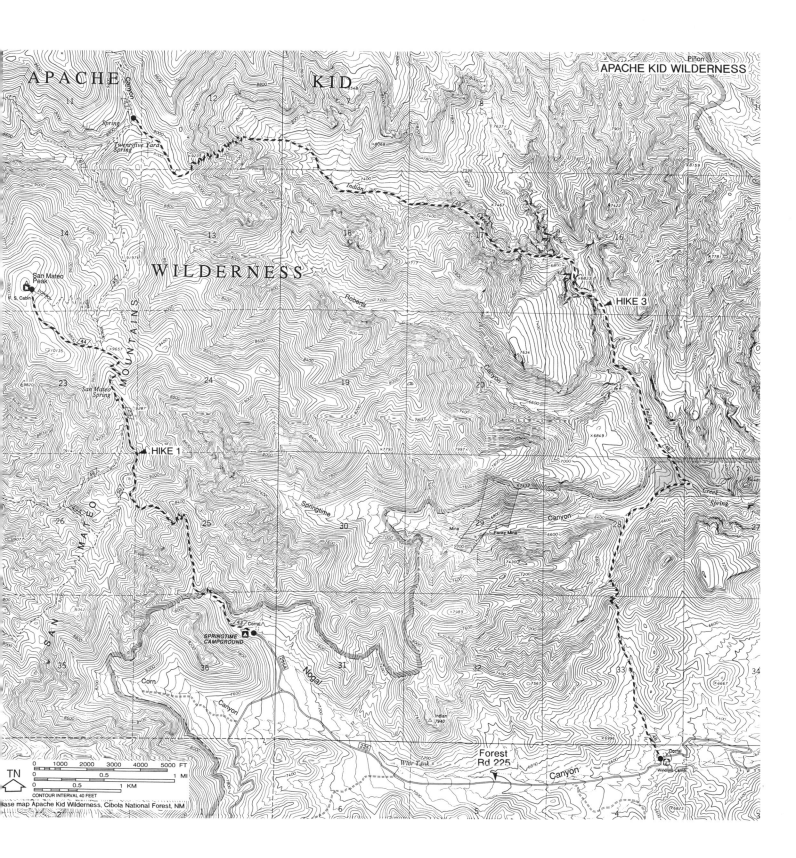

Stream Flowing through
Red Canyon

described here is 8.4 miles, providing the most direct access to the top of the range. The elevation gain of 2,739 feet makes for strenuous hiking.

This hike begins up the south end of the Apache Kid Trail (#43), which has the trailhead located within the Springtime Campground. The trailhead is signed and the trail is easy to follow. The first 2.2 miles of the trail climbs up steep, unrelenting slopes to gain the crest of the summit ridge, with the first trail junction shortly thereafter. Stay on Trail #43 heading north on fairly level terrain past Trail #50 and the junction with Trail #49 a short distance farther on. San Mateo Spring is about 0.3 miles on up the trail, just above a concrete cistern. Above the spring the trail gets steep again as it climbs 0.6 miles to the junction with Trail #44. Turn west on to Trail #44 and complete the final 0.8 miles up to San Mateo Peak. There are some nice views from the summit and if you have the time and energy, you can return to Trail #43 and make your way north toward the "Apache Kid" gravesite. Reaching this objective will nearly double the total hiking distance.

Hike #2. Red Canyon to Blue Mountain Loop Hike

This is probably my favorite hike in the region. The loop route goes from Red Canyon, up Water Canyon and on to Blue Mountain, and returns down Coffee Pot Canyon. It covers a lot of ground, but the scenery is especially pleasant and it tends to be cooler in the hot part of the year. There is good camping all along the lower parts of Water and Coffee Pot canyons when the streams are flowing, including a good spot at the always dependable Pot Hole Spring, 3.1 miles up Water Canyon at the Wilderness boundary. The total round-trip hiking distance starting at the

> **Hike #2. Red Canyon to Blue Mountain Loop Hike**
>
> Distance — 15 miles round trip
> Net elevation gain — 2,970 feet
> Difficulty — Strenuous

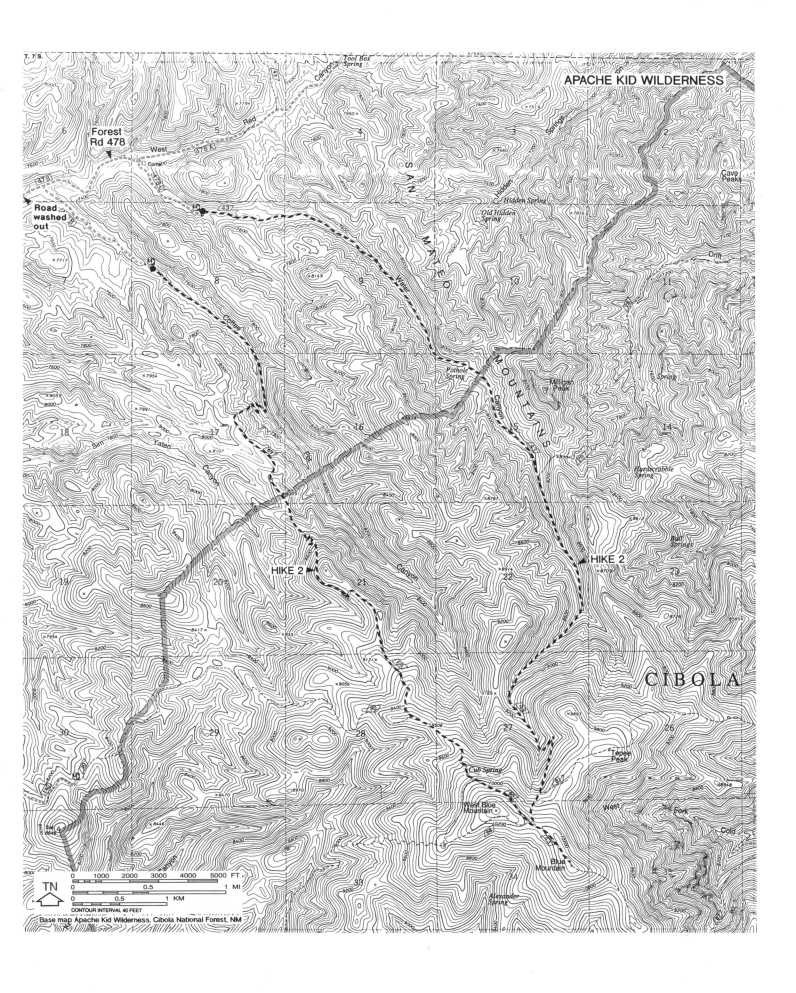

APACHE KID WILDERNESS

CONTOUR INTERVAL 40 FEET
Base map Apache Kid Wilderness, Cibola National Forest, NM

washed-out section of road in Red Canyon is 15 miles, or a little less if you are able to drive as far as Water Canyon. Net elevation gain to Blue Mountain is 2,970 feet. The trails on this route are secluded enough so that you will see few, if any, other people, but there seems to be just enough horse and foot traffic so that the trails won't be hard to follow.

Locate the Red Canyon trailhead as previously described. If the dirt road is still washed out when you visit, you will begin hiking at the road closure sign and follow the road east up the canyon. You will pass a sign indicating Coffee Pot Canyon 0.2 miles up the road and come to the Water Canyon sign about 0.6 miles farther on. You can, as an alternative, continue almost a mile past Water Canyon to the junction with Trail #43 and hike south on Trail #43 to intersect Water Canyon about a mile to the south. This segment of Trail #43 is obscure (look for the blazes on the trees south of the trail sign) and offers no advantages to starting at Water Canyon, unless you like extra gain and loss of elevation. Back to Water Canyon, turn south on the old four wheel drive road that wanders up Water Canyon. Follow the road on a gentle grade, joining Apache Kid Trail (#43) 1.5 miles up the canyon, and continue on the trail, which now follows the canyon another 1.6 miles to the Wilderness boundary. There is a good campsite here at Pot Hole Spring. After the Wilderness boundary the canyon narrows and begins a steep ascent to the top. By the time you reach the junction with Trail #81, 3.6 miles past the Wilderness boundary, you have done most of the work. The final 0.5 miles passes the Trail #90 junction and goes south along the ridge to the summit of Blue Mountain, which sports a derelict Forest Service cabin. There is a water cistern behind the cabin, but once you have seen the water it is unlikely that

you'll be thirsty enough to want any. Trial #43 continues to the south, reentering the forest on the south side of the ridge toward Cyclone Saddle, Apache Kid gravesite, and points beyond, or you can continue on the loop by heading back north on Trail #43 from Blue Mountain. When you get back to the Trail #90 junction, bear left on to Trail #90, passing the Trail #68 junction a short distance beyond, and reach Cub Spring 0.4 smile down the trail, just after another trail junction. Many of these trail signs have been chewed into oblivion by bears, so you may need to have your trail map handy. Cub Springs is a pleasant area and the first reliable supply of water since leaving Water Canyon, but the entire area is on a slope and doesn't appear to offer good campsites. The trail continues into the aspen trees east of Cub Springs and begins a long descent down a series of ridges, turning north on to Trail #69 about 0.5 miles below Cub Spring, and ending with a steep drop into Coffee Pot Canyon, which is followed the remaining 2 miles down to Red Canyon. A short walk takes you back to your vehicle. The canyon trails cross the stream bed frequently, which shouldn't be a problem unless the streams are extraordinarily high, in which case a pair of lightweight wading shoes would be good to have along.

Hike #3. Indian Creek Trail

The Indian Creek Trail travels north into the southeast corner of the Wilderness and then turns west and climbs up to join the Apache Kid Trail (#43) south of Apache Kid Peak and returns along the same route. It makes a long, tiring day hike of 16.6 miles, with a net elevation gain of 2,382 feet, which doesn't count another 680 feet lost along the second mile of the trail. However, the trail goes through some very pretty scenery and spectacular geology, and the last 2 or 3

miles can be omitted from the hike, making it a more moderate undertaking. There are lots of good campsites along Springtime Canyon and Indian Creek within 0.5 miles or so of the junction. There appears to be at least intermittent flows along significant stretches of these streams pretty much year round. The trail runs through the entire gamut of plant life that the area has to offer, from the high desert environment at the bottom, through the riparian and ponderosa cover, which exists for most of the trail, and on up to the spruce, fir, and aspen on top. The lower half of the trail is easy enough to follow, but the upper half obviously gets very little use and is impossible to follow in stretches except for the tree blazes. The deep, narrow canyons on the upper mid-part of the trail are quite rough to hike and not well suited to heavy backpacks. There is also poison ivy and stinging nettles in these canyons, so be alert when wearing shorts. The lower part of the trail catches lots of sun, so you may find it a little warm in mid-summer.

To find the trailhead, follow the access directions to Springtime Campground. When you have reached a point along Forest Road 225 that is 3 miles east of Springtime Campground, you will see a corral on the north side of the road, with a sign for Indian Creek Trail #48. The trail goes up an arroyo northwest of the corral, where you will see a trail sign. The beginning of the trail is a bit obscure, but it heads north along the west side of the fence and then moves out on to the piñon/juniper slopes, continuing north below a string of small peaks up to a saddle. A steep series of switchbacks leads down the other side of the saddle into a canyon bottom that goes north, joining Springtime Canyon about 0.5 miles past the bottom of the switchbacks. This part of

Looking North into the Indian Creek Drainage in the Apache Kid Wilderness the hike is quite lovely, with easy walking and lush vegetation. Indian Creek is joined 0.3 miles on down the trail. The various historic ruins in this area indicate that it must have been regarded as a nice spot in which to live. When you reach a signpost near this stream junction, cut across on the faint trail that crosses Indian Creek and starts northwest along the north bank. The next mile of trail goes up easy terrain, with nice views of the canyon walls, and then turns west into a deep, narrow canyon. The trail is not well marked here, but you should follow the main streambed. The deep canyon is lush with plant life and has towering basaltic walls on either side, making for a very striking scene. The trail is very rough and obscure, constantly recrossing the stream, and you will have trouble locating it in spots, but you can't get too far off track because of the narrowness of the canyon. Once you hike above the narrow part of the canyon, the terrain opens up to broad ponderosa slopes as the trail begins to work up a system of ridges toward the crest ridge below Apache Peak. You will really have to search for tree blazes here to stay on trail. There are also a few rock cairns to help you through the stands of scrub oak. The final mile of trail is very steep, as it climbs up over the final ridge and drops down a short but also steep distance to join Apache Kid Trail (#43). If you make it this far, an easier return would be to make a loop hike back south down Trail #43 to Springtime Campground and walk the road back to your starting point for about the same total hiking distance. If you have done a car shuttle to Springtime Campground, the round-trip distance of this loop is 13.7 miles, and if you decide not to go all the way up Indian Creek Trail and to return the way you came, it won't matter, as you will only have to drive 3 miles to retrieve the other car.

For Further Information:

Cibola National Forest
Magdalena Ranger District
Box 45
Magdalena, NM 87825
(505) 854-2281

Magdalena Mountains

GENERAL DESCRIPTION

The Magdalena Mountains are a smallish but steep range of peaks and ridges with a north-south orientation, the north end of the range being immediately east of the town of Magdalena and the south end less than 20 miles distant. The root name for all of this came from the isolated peak two miles south of the town and just west of the main range, which can be prominently viewed from Highway 60, named Magdalena Peak by the Spanish. The mountains are close cousins to the nearby San Mateo Mountains, being uplifted by the same volcanic forces, with the uplift of the Magdalenas accompanied by a down drop of the plains to the east of the mountains along the Magdalena fault, which lies along the eastern base of the mountains. This has resulted in an accentuated vertical profile for the range, topped by South Baldy Peak at 10,783 feet, which commands a scenic position on the skyline as you are driving west from Socorro. The high part of the range accumulates significant snowfall through the winter, which helps keep year-round water flows going in several of the canyons. The typical hiking season is from late April or early May, or even earlier for the lower-elevation trails, through late fall. Temperatures are generally pleasant throughout this period but may get a little warm for some folks during the hot part of summer.

This entire region is rich in mineral resources, and many old mines, large and small, dot the landscape, with a number of small, privately owned inholdings in the mountainous areas, which are otherwise contained within the Cibola National Forest. A surprisingly well-developed trail system is in place, which seems to get regular use, probably primarily to the proximity of Socorro, but the usage is not, by any reasonable definition, heavy. Even though the Magdalena Mountains are not located within a designated Wilderness Area, motorized vehicles are excluded from the trails, although mountain bikes are allowed, and some of the trails do appear to provide good mountain biking. Because of the relatively small size of the area, the trails are best suited for dayhiking, but there is enough water around to permit overnight backpacking as well. For overnight car camping there is a Forest Service campground in Water Canyon. To use a common point of reference, travel time from Albuquerque to the Magdalenas is about 2 to 2.5 hours depending upon your hiking trail. For a mountain area with an established trail system, this is one of the more obscure hiking areas of the state. Should you decide to try it, I think you will be favorably impressed.

Map Coverage

The USGS 7.5-scale topo maps for Magdalena and South Baldy cover practically the entire range. For trails on the southeast corner of the range, you will also want to get the Molino Peak quad. Note that not all the trails are shown on these maps, so a good supplemental map is the Cibola National Forest Map for the Magdalena Ranger District.

Access

There are a number of entry points for the Magdalena Mountains, both on the east side from Highway 60 and on the west side from roads south of the town of Magdalena. Water Canyon Campground provides a good central starting point for reaching the trails described below, as well as several others. Directions for reaching the campground are as follows:

From Interstate 25, take the Socorro exit and head west out of town on Highway 60. After you have gone about 14 miles from Socorro, just north of mile marker 124, you will come to an intersecting road on the west side of the highway with a highway sign indicating the way to Water Canyon Campground. Turn west on the paved road and continue 4.5 miles to the end of the pavement, where the campground begins.

Hiking Trails

Because the mountain range is steep, the trails also tend to be steep if hiked along their entire length. The notable exception would be the North Baldy Trail. That's the bad news; the good news is that the trailheads are well marked, the trails are easy to follow, and in cases such as the Copper Canyon Trail, you can omit the steepest part of the trail and still have a nice hike. On the trails that I have hiked, the path is generally well enough worn in to make the way obvious, although adequate tree blazes are also provided in the forested areas, and rock cairns in the open areas where the trail gets obscure.

There are 15 designated trails in the Magdalena Mountains, two of which I have chosen to describe in this section. Together, they present an interesting sample of the hiking trails available.

TRAIL DESCRIPTIONS

Hike #1. Copper Canyon Trail (#10)

Copper Canyon begins on the east side of the mountains and runs up the side of the range, ending just below the crest ridge. The trail that follows up the canyon is pleasant and shady over most of its course, running through open forests that begin with oak and ponderosa pine on the lower section and graduate through Douglas fir, aspen, and white pine on the upper part. The first 3 miles of the trail gains elevation on a steady but reasonable elevation gradient, with the final part of the trail splitting into two forks in the last mile with both branches making a steep, rocky climb to join the North Baldy Trail at the crest ridge. A good part of the trail seems to have been put in over an old wagon road, which provides a wide, easy-to-follow route with a trail surface that is comfortable to walk on. Water is more or less continuously available from the nearby stream that runs most of the length of the canyon, and decent campsites are available at several points up the canyon. The trail can be hiked up and back along the same path, or a car shuttle can be worked to make a hike between the Copper Canyon and North Baldy trailheads in either direction. The elevation gain to the top of the spur trail at the south terminus is 3,100 feet, and to the main terminus at the north end is 2,880 feet.

To locate the trailhead for the Copper Canyon Trail, drive the access road to the Water Canyon Campground to the point

Hike #1. Copper Canyon Trail (#10)

Distance—8 miles round trip
Net elevation gain—2,880 feet
Difficulty—Moderate to strenuous

Hike #2. North Baldy Trail (#8)

Distance—10.5 miles round trip
Net elevation gain—1,100 feet
Difficulty —Moderate

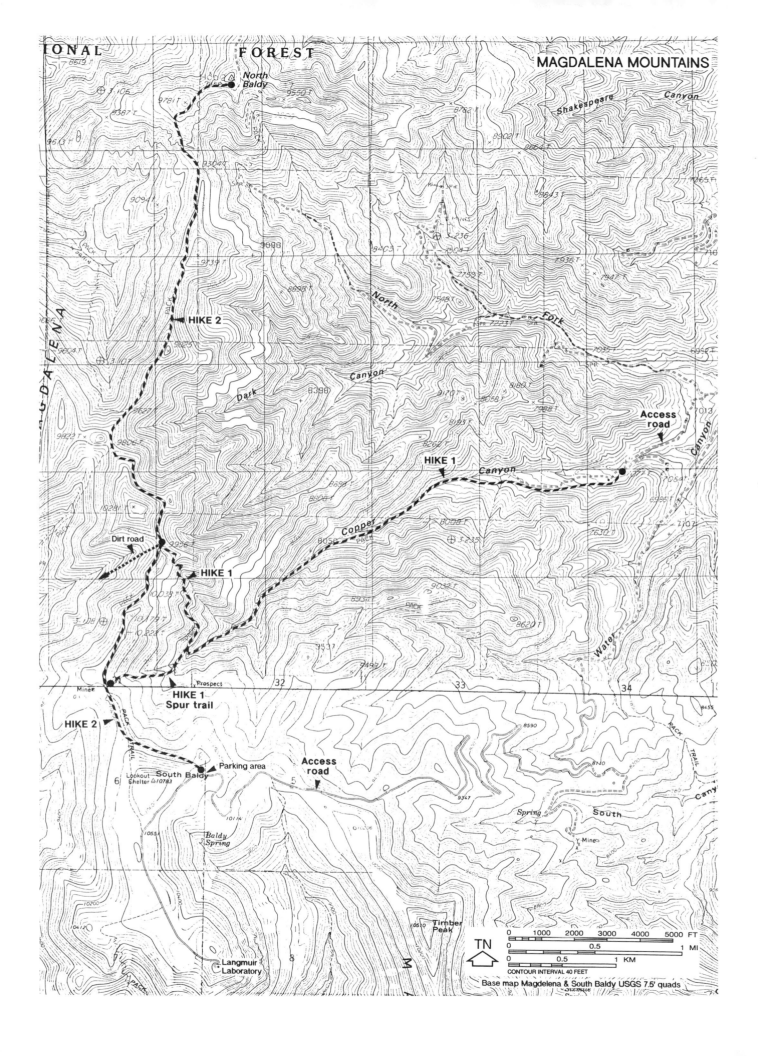

MAGDALENA MOUNTAINS

North Baldy

HIKE 2

HIKE 1

Access road

HIKE 1

Dark Canyon

North Fork

Canyon

Copper Canyon

Dirt road

HIKE 1

HIKE 1
Spur trail

Prospect

Mines

HIKE 2

Water

Access road

Parking area

Lookout
Shelter South Baldy
△10783

Baldy
Spring

Spring South Canyon

Mine

Timber
Peak

TN

0   1000   2000   3000   4000   5000 FT

0   0.5   1 MI

0   0.5   1 KM

CONTOUR INTERVAL 40 FEET

Langmuir
Laboratory

Base map Magdalena & South Baldy USGS 7.5' quads

where the pavement ends just as the campground is reached. At this point, take the dirt road that branches off to the right, and again take the right fork as the road branches a short distance farther and leads over a cattle guard. From the cattle guard, the main road continues for 0.8 miles to a broad parking area, just before an ambitious-looking creek crossing with a sign that identifies the place as Copper Canyon. This last stretch of road has some rough spots, which may compel passenger car occupants to park and walk the final distance. From the Copper Canyon sign, walk across the creek and a short distance up the road, which continues across the creek, to a sign marking the trailhead. The trail cuts up the hillside and contours to the west up the canyon, following a route along the south side of the canyon above the deserted community of old buildings that are strung along the grassy canyon bottom. The trail is easy to follow and pleasant to walk as it parallels the creek, crossing it back and forth at several points. After a little over 3 miles, the main trail cuts back to the right and begins a steep contour up the slopes at the head of the canyon, ending in a series of switchbacks to the top, while a spur trail branches off to the left and makes a similar ascent toward the south end of the canyon. Both trail branches intersect the North Baldy Trail at the top of the crest ridge, with excellent views to both sides of the range. If you are picking up the Copper Canyon Trail from the top end, you will come to the spur trail intersection along the North Baldy Trail about 1 mile north of the trailhead, and the intersection of the main Copper Canyon Trail 1 mile farther north. The spur trail intersection is marked with a trail sign in an open, grassy saddle, while the north intersection coincides with a mine road that is bladed up over the top of the crest.

Looking East from the North Baldy Trail into Copper Canyon

Hike #2. North Baldy Trail (#8)

This is a trail that follows the crest ridge of the mountain range from just below South Baldy Peak at the south end to North Baldy Peak at the north end. The trail is unusual in that it starts high along the crest due to the presence of an access road, without the necessity of having to toil your way to the top. The elevation differential is a reasonable 1,100 feet, although additional elevation is lost and gained along the 5+- mile (10.5-mile round trip) trail length. The trail runs through patches of open forest and grassy meadow areas, with frequent scenic views across the mountain range and the distant terrain beyond. It is easy walking and, except for a couple of tricky spots, easy to follow. There is no water along the trail, so bring along what you will need, and be watchful for thunderstorms, as there is no place to escape except back the way you came or down a side trail. The North Baldy Trail intersects the upper ends of a number of connecting side trails that could be included into the hike with a car in place at the lower trailhead.

To locate the North Baldy trailhead, take the gravel road through the Water Canyon Campground and follow the signs to the Langmuir Laboratory, a research site used to study lightning phenomena, operated by New Mexico Tech in Socorro (New Mexico is said to be second only to the state of Florida in the annual incidence of lightning strikes). The laboratory is situated at the top of the range near South Baldy, and the gravel road winds its way up to the site, passing a number of trailheads along the way. The road is narrow and rough but passable by passenger car, unless rain or snow is a factor. After you have driven 7.8 miles past the campground, you will come to a small parking area on the right-hand side with a sign for North Baldy Trail (#8). Climb up the steep slope to the north, following cairns to a small saddle that represents the high elevation point of the hike. From the saddle, the trail traverses to the west through the trees and comes out at an open grassy area on top of the crest ridge north of South Baldy. This is tricky spot number 1. Instead of turning north and walking along the top of the ridge, follow the cairns down the west side of the ridge into the trees and follow the trail, which now turns north and travels along below the ridge. The trail regains the top of the ridge about 0.3 miles farther north, where the Copper Canyon spur trail joins. One mile north of this intersection, where the north branch of the Copper Canyon Trail joins, is tricky spot number 2. Here you will see an obvious road that has been bladed over the top of the ridge. As soon as you have crossed over to the north side of the road, drop down the east side of the ridge and locate a trail that contours along below the ridge. This detour avoids the large peak to the northwest, which sits atop the ridge and eventually regains the ridge at a saddle where the Mill Canyon Trail joins. The Hop Canyon Trail intersection is a little farther on, with the final stretch of trail continuing north along the ridge to North Baldy Peak, where an old four wheel drive road comes in from the north. Complete the hike by returning on the uphill leg back to the original trailhead.

For Further Information:

Cibola National Forest
 Magdalena Ranger
 District
 Box 45
 Magdalena, NM 87825
 (505) 854-2281

Horse Mountain

GENERAL DESCRIPTION

Horse Mountain is a compact peak of volcanic origin bordering the Plains of San Agustin about 25 miles southwest of Datil, and currently the site of a 5,032-acre BLM Wilderness Study Area (WSA). The mountain is named after Horse Springs, a nearby watering spot along a major trail-drive route for cattle and sheep that was in use as recently as the 1950s, and a small nearby ranching community of the same name. The springs were named after an incident in the 1800s, when some soldiers lost a horse on the way from Socorro to Fort Tularosa and found it at the springs on the return trip. This area also contained the ranches of two interesting 1800s characters, Montague Stevens and Agnes Morley, who each wrote books (Stevens's *Meet Mr. Grizzly* and Morley's *No Life For A Lady*) that recorded their experiences of 19th-century life in the southwestern part of the state. In the case of Stevens, a one-armed hunter of noted skill, his experiences recounted his primary avocation of hunting grizzly bear. Both books provide a fascinating glimpse into frontier life in the area when it was still wild.

The summit of Horse Mountain is at 9,450 feet, rising rather abruptly some 2,500 feet from the rangeland at the foot of the mountain. There are no trails, but there is plenty of off-trail dayhiking to be

Horse Mountain Wilderness Study Area, Looking East

done, although steep elevation gradients are a fact of life on most of the mountain. With little in the way of water sources, overnight backpacking potential is limited. The most common hiking objective would probably be the summit of the peak, where a nice panorama awaits, particularly of the San Agustin Plains, the site of a huge Pleistocene lake.

The climate of the area is semiarid in nature, with warm to hot summer temperatures, making spring and fall the most comfortable times of year to hike. The mountain sees enough snow in winter to limit hiking during those months when it is a factor. Precipitation averages 14 inches annually, primarily concentrated in the thunderstorm season from July through September. The vegetation cover tends to be primarily piñon and juniper, with associated shrubs, grasses, and cacti, and ponderosa pine and some Douglas fir at higher elevations. Some broadleaf species, primarily oak, can be seen on the north-facing slopes. The surface geology features a mixture of basalt and sandstone, which creates many colorful walls and ridges along with a few spires. The volcanic rock is rather loose on some slopes, making for difficult hiking and

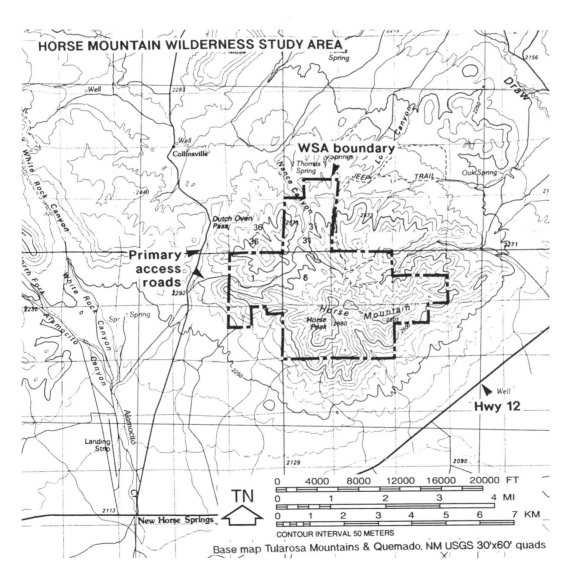

HORSE MOUNTAIN WILDERNESS STUDY AREA

CONTOUR INTERVAL 50 METERS
Base map Tularosa Mountains & Quemado, NM USGS 30'x60' quads

requiring a certain amount of caution. Animal life on the mountain includes mule deer, pronghorn antelope, black bear, and mountain lion.

Map Coverage

The USGS 7.5-minute scale quads covering the Horse Mountain WSA are Wallace Mesa, Log Canyon, Horse Mountain West, and Horse Mountain East. Large-scale coverage is shown on the 1:100,000-scale Tularosa Mountains and Quemado maps.

Access

The only good access I could find for this area was via a good-quality county gravel road that runs north/south along the west edge of the mountain. To locate this road, drive west from Socorro on Highway 60 for 61 miles to Datil, then bear south on Highway 12 and drive about 26 miles to New Horse Springs, a mostly derelict cluster of buildings located between mile markers 48 and 49. Just west of a windmill on the north side of the road, but before the old store, turn north on a wide gravel road that continues north for a little over 4 miles to a rough dirt road that turns off to the right, goes through a gate, and ends a short distance farther on. This is a good spot to begin hiking for a fairly direct route to the top of the mountain. The terrain is straightforward if steep, and you can reach the top by gradually working your way east up the ridge system that begins near the terminus of the side road. Alternatively, continue north past the turnoff, where there are opportunities to park your car, over the next 1.5 miles and hike east across terrain that is somewhat less strenuous. The gravel access road is in good condition, but after heavy rains, be prepared to turn back if mud becomes a factor.

Hiking Trails

No established trails are present, nor will there probably be any. This is a remote spot that probably receives next to no hiking interest, and being surrounded by cow country, probably will be dropped from wilderness consideration. So why include it in this book? Because it is an area that is wild and remote, with lots of solitude, nice forest, and interesting geology. The hiking is rugged and it isn't for everyone, but to put it in a different perspective, if Horse Mountain were located in Kansas it would probably be a state park with a large parking lot at the base, paved roads leading to it, and trails all over the mountain. So I include it as one of those unknown but available hiking areas that you may someday want to try out.

For Further Information

Bureau of Land Management
Socorro Resource Area
198 Neel Avenue NW
Socorro, NM 87801
(505) 835-0412

New Mexico Statewide Wilderness Study, Wilderness Analysis Reports, U.S. Department of the Interior, Bureau of Land Management, New Mexico State Office, Santa Fe, NM, May 1985.

Continental Divide Wilderness Study Area

GENERAL DESCRIPTION

Named for the Continental Divide, which runs east-west through its center, this BLM Wilderness Study Area (WSA) is located about 29 miles south of the town of Datil on the south edge of the Plains of San Agustin. At 68,761 acres this is a sizeable WSA; however, if adjacent BLM lands are considered, the effective size of the area is even greater. The elevation ranges from 6,780 feet on the lower west side to 9,212 feet at the summit of Pelona Mountain near the east boundary. The basaltic ridges and mountains, well-defined canyons, and rolling grasslands and mesas that comprise the area are impressively situated, rising picturesquely above the grassy San Agustin Plains. Although large enough to backpack within, the general nonavailability of water in the area makes dayhiking more manageable. The best time of year to visit is from March through mid-June and from September through mid-December. The summer months are fine, if you don't mind elevated temperatures, and the winter months see cold weather and frequent snowfall.

The widely-located tree cover of piñon and one-seed juniper is typical of the semiarid climate in the region. Also in abundance is the distinctive alligator Juniper, including some very large specimens perhaps 800 years old. Ponderosa pine is plentiful over most of the

area, producing forested slopes very pleasant to walk through. Wax currant, squawbush, and mountain mahogany are also common. The possibilities for viewing wildlife are significant, with mule deer, elk, pronghorn antelope, coyote, black bear, mountain lion, and golden eagle being some of the indigenous species.

One of the features of special interest in the region, although not included in the area likely to be of most interest for hiking, is the San Agustin Plains. The local depression which constitutes the Plains is the bed of an ancient lake. Some 12,000 years ago, when the climate was much wetter, the lake measured about 11 miles by 34 miles and was 150 feet deep. This is known from the terraces on the existing walls of the depression that once marked the shoreline of the lake. Early

Continental Divide
Wilderness Study Area,
Looking down
Cottonwood Canyon

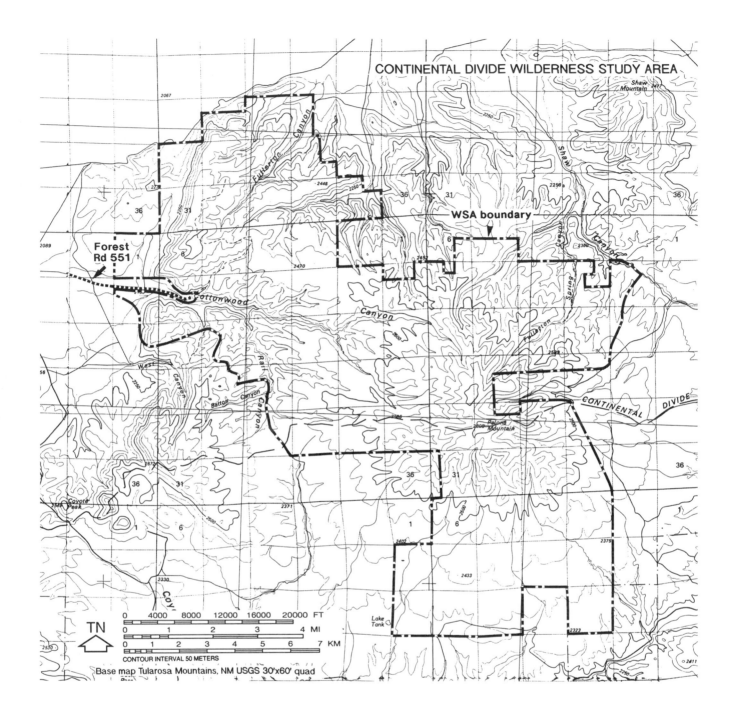

man was drawn to the area as early as 10,000 years ago (and some claim much earlier than that), leaving paleo-culture lance heads of the Folsom period in the vicinity. By 4,000 to 5,000 years ago the lake had dried up, but while it was still in existence the waters at the shoreline created a cave, currently located within the Continental Divide WSA, which was later occupied by a succession of prehistoric cultures and which is now known as Bat Cave. It was named after the beneficial little inhabitants that can always be seen at sundown, flitting about and feeding on the insects that were pestering you earlier in the day (being located far away from Gotham City, Bat Cave was apparently never inhabited by Batman). Anyway, many interesting artifacts have been excavated at the various levels of occupation, but the primary reason that Bat Cave is well known to archaeologists is the discovery of a primitive variety of corn that is among the earliest ever found in North America, and which predated pottery in the region by 2,000 years. This, and the many other artifacts recovered, have given scholars a valuable source of information in helping to decipher the cultural patterns of long-forgotten peoples. This glimpse of prehistory also adds a certain interest and mystery to the area for the present-day hiker. It is an area that is seldom visited, and is without hiking trails, but contains a lot of empty territory for the hiker who enjoys solitude and a primitive wilderness setting.

Map Coverage

Broad-scale map coverage for the area is provided by the USGS 1:100,000-scale Tularosa Mountains map. USGS 7.5-minute map coverage is shown on the following maps: Fullerton, Paddy's Hole, Mojonera Canyon, Rael Canyon, O Bar O Canyon, Indian Peaks West, and Pelona Mountain.

Access

The Continental Divide WSA has its better access routes located on the north, west, and south sides, with probably the primary route, and the one described here, being the road system leading to Cottonwood Canyon on the west side. From Socorro, take Highway 60 west for 61 miles to Datil. Bear south on Highway 12 at Datil and drive another 28 miles to Horse Springs (Old Horse Springs), and then another 6 miles past Horse Springs to Bursom Road, which is also marked as

Forest Road 28. Turn south on Bursom Road, and follow it across the Plains of San Agustin, with scenic views all around. At 9.2 miles past the turnoff the road forks; take the left fork (Road #28), and continue to another fork at the 15.4-mile point. Bear left on Forest Road 551 to an intersection a few hundred feet farther on, with a sign directing you west to Cottonwood Canyon 5 miles distant. Drive this road across private land to the entrance to Cottonwood Canyon. At this point, the road goes from smooth to rough, and a high clearance vehicle will be required to drive the last 2 or so miles up the canyon. There are several flat areas along this road that can be used to make a campsite. With the exception of the final stretch up the canyon, the gravel road system from Bursom Road on is well maintained and suitable for passenger car, except, perhaps, in wet weather.

Hiking Trails

No hiking trails are established in the WSA, although roads leading into the canyons tend to turn into steep jeep roads that climb up to the mesa tops and wander around as faint double-track roads. Since the piñon, juniper, and ponderosa tree cover is open, it is an easy area in which to get around on foot, and a good way to go is simply to go cross country and make your own path; just be sure you can find your way back. If you are camped in Cottonwood Canyon, the upper end of the canyon makes a nice day hike, and the mesa tops above also offer good hiking; I ran into a herd of elk up there and saw other wildlife down in the canyon. You will need to carry water, as you can't count on finding any, and there may be enough gnats to make insect repellent a good idea.

For Further Information:

Bureau of Land Management Socorro Resource Area 198 Neel Avenue NW Socorro, NM 87801 (505) 843-0412

New Mexico Statewide Wilderness Study, Wilderness Analysis Reports, U.S. Department of the Interior, Bureau of Land Management, New Mexico Office, Santa Fe, NM, May 1985.

Gila Wilderness

GENERAL DESCRIPTION

The Gila Wilderness, at approximately 570,000 acres, is the largest designated Wilderness Area in the state, and its size is effectively magnified by the adjacent 202,016-acre Aldo Leopold Wilderness and the surrounding 3.3-million-acre Gila National Forest, of which it is a part. The Gila Wilderness is also the oldest designated Wilderness Area in the entire nation, having been formally established by Congress in 1924. The area is located in the southwest quadrant of the state in a rugged setting of mountains, mesas, and river canyons. The tallest peaks are nearly 11,000 feet high, and the lowest elevations are below 6,000 feet, providing a broad zone of plant life. The animal life is plentiful and includes large populations of elk, deer, black bear, mountain lion, and wild turkey; the once-plentiful grizzly was hunted into extinction by the 1930s. Trout is also plentiful in many of the creeks and rivers of the Gila. Numerous trails are established throughout the Wilderness Area, which tend to follow the water courses, ridges, and large mesas. Some of these are popular for dayhiking, but a multiday backpack trip is needed to penetrate and explore the large interior. The Gila is an ideal backpacking destination with lots of trails, plentiful water sources and good campsites, and relatively few other hikers. The Gila area is basically a mountainous area, with extensive forests overlying rock types that are primarily igneous. Despite its southern latitude, it accumulates significant snow cover in the winter, which melts out in some areas to provide good hiking conditions by March, although the higher elevations, and trails following the larger water courses, are not normally optimal for hiking until early to mid-May or later. By June the temperatures in the lower elevation areas begin to heat up but are pleasant in the higher country. Hiking conditions are good through late October or early November, with July and August bringing the normal rainy season, and late September and October the fall colors of the deciduous leaves and the last window of gentle weather before winter. Late October and November also bring on the hunting season, and if you want more information on the latter, you should check with one of the ranger stations. Because of the large size of the Gila National Forest and its extensive system of trails, roads, and campgrounds, there are nine separate ranger districts administering the area. These are listed at the end of the section.

With the exception of the very earliest arrivals, of which we know very little, the story of human drama in the Gila Wilderness and vicinity begins perhaps with what is called the Mogollon (mo-go-yohn) Indian culture. This prehistoric group developed into a sophisticated pueblo culture and existed in the area before apparently vanishing in about 1300 A.D. The most extensive of their ruins are preserved in Gila Cliff Dwellings National Monument, near the confluence of the Middle and West Forks of the Gila River, and can be accessed by paved highway. After the Mogollon culture came the Apache culture, which hunted and camped in these mountains and valleys, and whose fierce and territorial presence helped to limit further settlement in the region until substantial gold and silver deposits were discovered in 1875. From then through the end of the century, this part of New Mexico read like a script from a wild-west movie. Vast cattle ranches and rowdy mining camps combined with the Apache wars to produce a rich blend of mayhem, complete with shootouts, murders, lynchings, massacres, claim jumping, cattle rustling, and grizzly encounters. Many interesting and famous individuals too numerous to mention operated in the area at one time or the other, including Generals Miles and Crook, Tom Horn, James Cooney, Elfego Baca, Ben Lilley, Billy the Kid, the Ketchum Brothers, Butch Cassidy and the Wild Bunch, virtually all the famous Apache chiefs, and the famed Buffalo Soldiers. Many of the place names on the map relate to these people and their encounters, and when hiking the Gila it is interesting to speculate how many of these other characters may have traveled the same paths in the not too distant past. This is a fascinating area to read and learn about, but aside from that, it is also one of the really premier hiking areas in the state.

Map Coverage

The best single map to get for the Gila Wilderness is the Gila Wilderness Visitors Travel Guide & Map, which is produced by the Forest Service and available at ranger stations and other Forest Service outlets. It shows the topography, trails, access roads, and campgrounds, and is available in the durable, water-resistant version. The only deficiency, other than the 200-foot contour intervals, is an absence of forest overprint. The USGS 7.5-minute scale topo maps covering the area are numerous, but are specified for the individual hiking trails in the trail descriptions.

Access

Detailed access directions, which are included with the individual trail descriptions, begin with several major approach routes that are summarized as follows:

North side access. There are several variations, but perhaps the most straightforward one is to drive west from Socorro on Highway 60 to Quemado and turn south on Highway 32 at the intersection just west of town. Follow Highway 32 on a scenic drive to Apache Creek (you can also arrive at this point by turning south on Highway 12 at Datil), and continue on Highway 12 to Reserve. At Reserve stay on Highway 12, taking a right turn at the intersection in town, and continue about 7 miles west of town, where Highway 12 T's into Highway 180. Turn south on Highway 180, which skirts the west end of the Wilderness Area as it runs through Alma, Glenwood, Cliff, Silver City, and beyond. The entire highway description described thus far is paved, with a travel time from Albuquerque to Reserve of about 3.5 hours.

An alternative route to access points in the vicinity of Snow Lake can be made by turning south on Highway 52 just before reaching the VLA (Very Large Array) site west of Magdalena, and following the route, which turns into Highway 163, toward Beaverhead and then Snow Lake. This is a gravel road, which is dusty but in good condition except for some rough stretches as you approach Snow Lake. It is shorter than the paved route but involves a similar driving time and is not the route to take in wet weather. If you are starting from Las Cruces or El Paso, approach from the south as described below.

South side access. There are two basic approaches to the south side of the Gila Wilderness. If you are starting from Las Cruces or El Paso, start by driving west from Las Cruces on Interstate 10/70. Continue to Deming and take the Highway 180 exit heading north to Silver City. Highway 180 continues to Glenwood, Highway 12, and other points of access on the west and north side. If you are approaching from the north, take the Highway 152 exit off Interstate 25, about 16 miles south of Truth or Consequences and head east through Hillsboro. Highway 152 leads to the intersection with Highway 35 (which leads up toward the Cliff Dwellings National Monument) at the community of San Lorenzo, and continues on west and joins Highway 180 at the town of Central just before reaching Silver City. Highway 180 continues on around the west end of the range. This is a paved route, but leads over some mountain passes, which can get slippery after fresh snows.

Hiking Trails

The Gila Wilderness is a large area with an extensive system of trails in place. Some, particularly in the vicinity of the National Monument on the south side, receive fairly heavy use, but the Gila trails are mostly uncrowded. It is a popular hiking area but spacious enough so that you don't run into that many other hikers and horse riders—just enough so that most of the trails are worn enough to be easy to follow. As you would expect with an area this size, there is some significant variation in types of

terrain and ecosystems, and at the risk of oversimplifying, I will provide some general observations. The west end of the Wilderness is higher in elevation, has the higher peaks, and is the last part to open up in the spring. The forests are denser and tend toward fir, spruce, and aspen. The trails tend to be steeper, and water is relatively plentiful. The middle part of the Wilderness east of Mogollon Baldy Peak includes a lot of high, ponderosa-clad mesa country cut by numerous river drainages. There are lots of nice routes with moderate elevation gain, trout streams with cottonwood trees and broad parks for camping, and some of the more popular trails. The east part of the Wilderness, east of the Cliff Dwellings National Monument, is also characterized by broad mesas cut by numerous drainages, but is lower in elevation, drier and hotter in the summer, and has thinner forests, with extensive piñon and juniper coverage, in addition to ponderosa and riparian. Unfortunately, this part of the Wilderness is one of the foulest examples of the perversion of the so-called National Forest multiple use concept, which in this case translates to a large taxpayer-subsidized cattle operation. In all fairness, the east side of the Gila includes some beautiful, secluded country that you may someday want to hike, and I have included several short hikes from this area in the subsequent route descriptions—but if you are looking for an introduction to the Gila, you may want to start out farther west. I have grown accustomed to and have even developed a certain tolerance for some cattle in wilderness areas, but too many of the east side trails go across overgrazed mesas where the trail, if there was one, has been appropriated as one of their own by the local cow herds, and is indistinguishable among the various sets of cow trails that wander between stock tanks amid the occasional

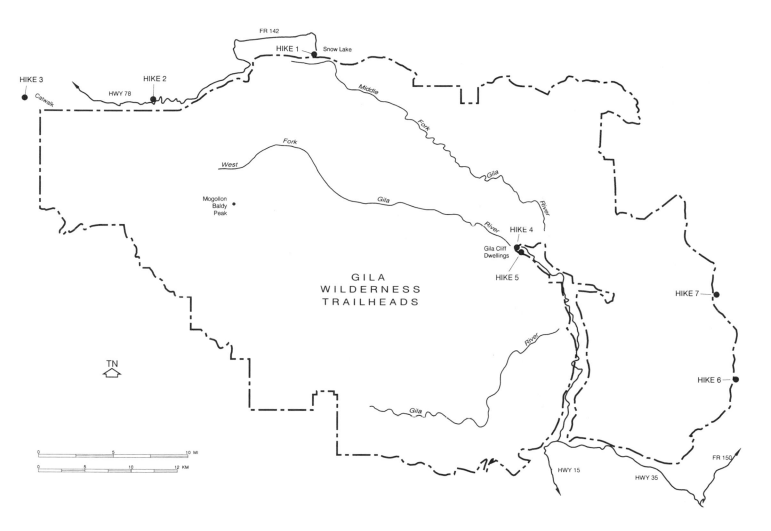

wreckage of feed troughs, derelict corrals, and other ranch debris. The riparian water course areas are often thrashed, the ubiquitous cow chips seem as numerous as the fallen leaves, and the trails, even trail junctions, are often unmarked after you get past the trailhead. In this country, you had better know how to use map and compass. In this part of the wilderness the dominant life form is the cow, and the Forest Service (in all fairness, with considerable pressure from not only stock owners but with blatant interference from local county officials as well) has primarily managed, or mismanaged, this region for the benefit of the rancher—definitely not for the benefit of the land, the native wildlife, the endangered fish populations,

or the hiker. But don't let this last venting of frustration scare you away from the entire Gila. Overall, it's a great area.

The hikes described in this section include a variety of the good routes, long and short, dispersed through different types of terrain across the breadth of the Wilderness. These give a good introduction to the area, but if you prefer to try some of the more secluded areas or want to link together a longer loop trip, there are numerous possibilities. Several of the hikes are loop trips that suggest a multiday backpack, but if you aren't interested in that, do the hike partway and you'll still have fun. The hikes described here are generally not strenuous, but some are long enough to give

Campsite in the Ponderosa Forests below Clayton Mesa

your feet a good pounding, so take that into account. Also, for the trails that follow the river drainages, you will want to bring along a pair of lightweight running shoes for wading, as you will almost surely get your feet wet. The Gila is a good place to observe wildlife, with large populations of deer, elk, black bear, mountain lion, and turkey.

TRAIL DESCRIPTIONS

Hike #1. Snow Lake to Turkeyfeather Pass Loop Hike

This is a backpacking trip of two or more nights that starts down the upper Middle Fork of the Gila River from Snow Lake and makes a loop across Iron Creek Mesa, down a portion of Iron Creek, and back across Clayton Mesa to the Middle Fork. The total loop distance is 24.9 miles,

with a net elevation gain of 1,135 feet, not counting some additional up and down. The USGS topo maps that cover the route are the 7.5-minute scale Loco Mountain, Lilley Mountain, and Mogollon Baldy Peak quads. I have made numerous hiking trips down the Middle Fork from Snow Lake, sometimes taking the loop route described here and sometimes keeping to the river, and I never get tired of it. It is probably my favorite part of the Gila. The scenery, campsites, fishing, and hiking are all top-notch. On the first and final leg of the hike, the Middle Fork Trail switches back and forth across the river a number of times—typical of the river trails in the Gila. This part of the river probably averages about 15 to 20 feet across, with knee-deep water at the crossings unless you go too early in the year, in which case the water will be crotch deep and exciting, if not dangerous—something to keep in mind if you have small people along. In

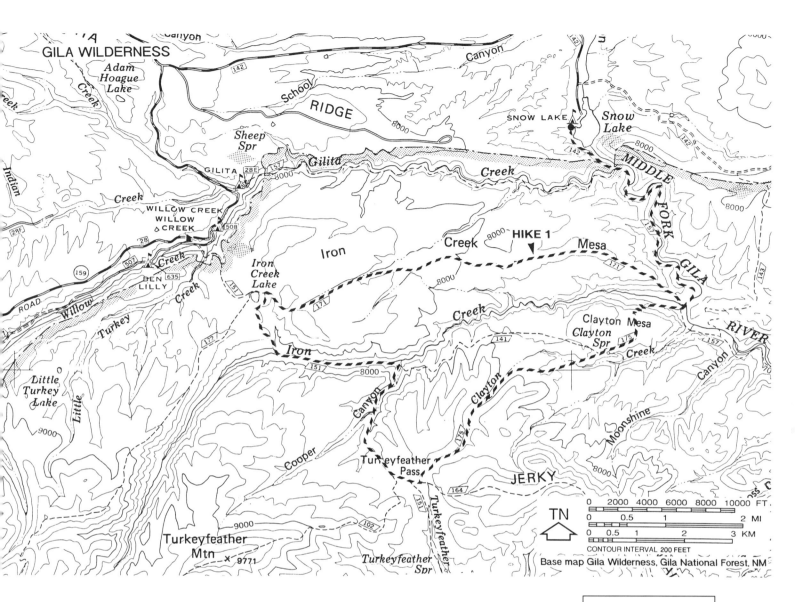

Hike #1. Snow
Lake to
Turkeyfeather Pass
Loop Hike

Distance — 24.9
miles round trip
Net elevation gain
— 1,135 feet
Difficulty —
Moderate

either case, you will be periodically wading through the water, so I like to take along a pair of lightweight running shoes for hiking this stretch of the trail. It is probably best to wait until mid- to late April to do this trip; any earlier and the weather and water levels are a bit chancy. After a heavy winter, it would probably be a good idea to put the trip off until early May.

To access the trailhead at Snow Lake, refer to the general "North Side Access" directions above. The most straightforward approach is to turn east on Highway 159 off highway 180 about 1 mile south of the town of Alma and drive toward Mogollon, a once-colorful mining town of a century ago, which became one of the better-known ghost towns in the state and has more recently metamorphosed into something of a picturesque art colony. On the east side of town, Highway 159 turns to gravel and continues east to an inter-

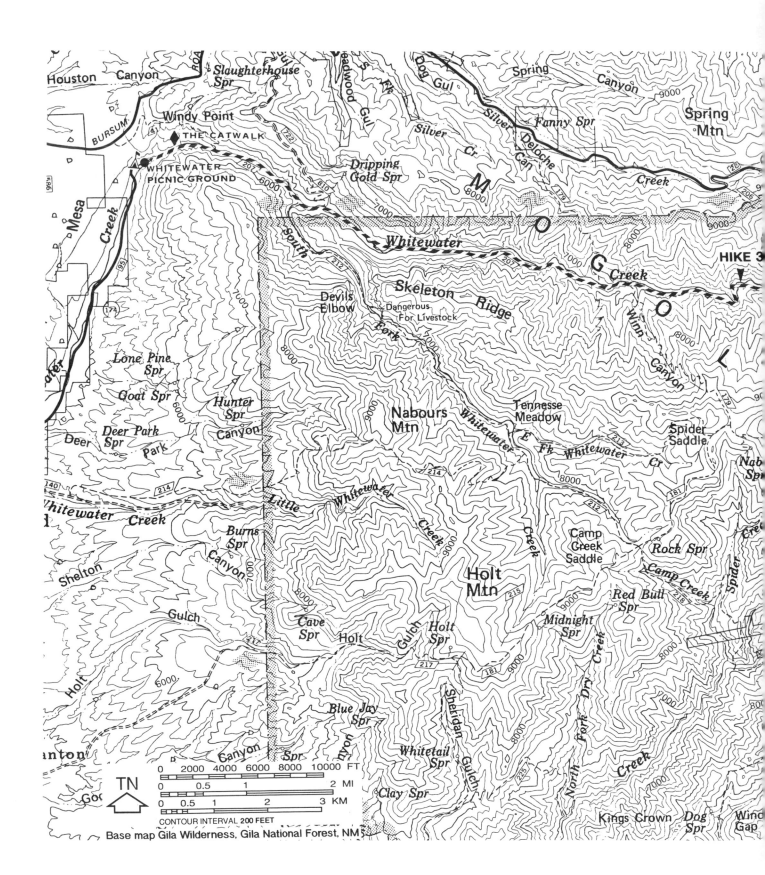

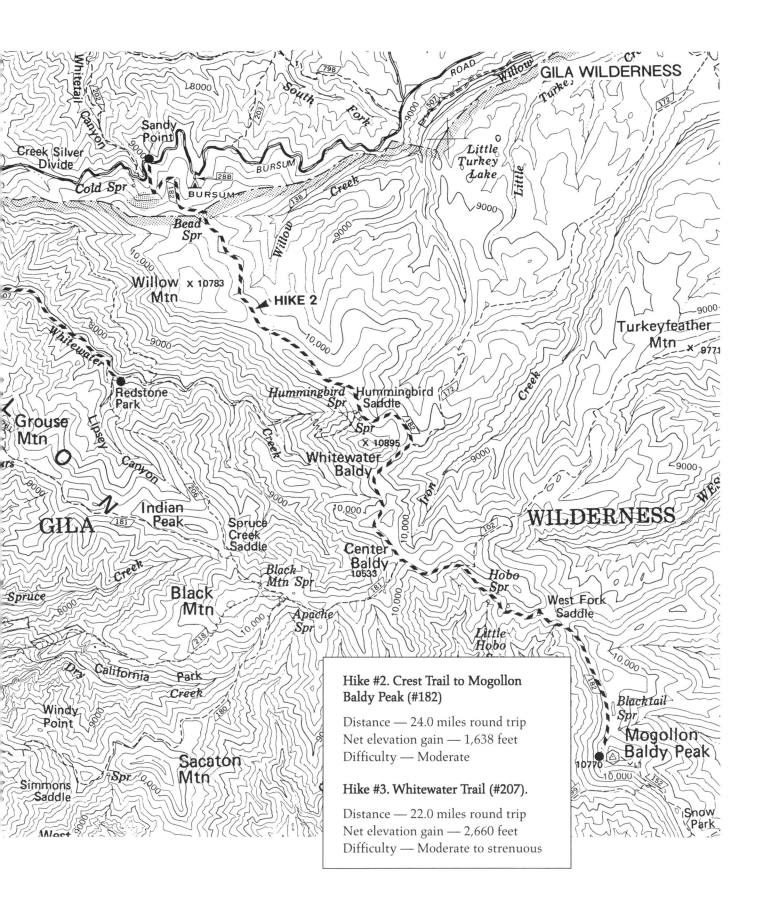

Hike #2. Crest Trail to Mogollon
Baldy Peak (#182)

Distance — 24.0 miles round trip
Net elevation gain — 1,638 feet
Difficulty — Moderate

Hike #3. Whitewater Trail (#207).

Distance — 22.0 miles round trip
Net elevation gain — 2,660 feet
Difficulty — Moderate to strenuous

section about 3 miles beyond the Gilita Campground turnoff, where an east turn on to Forest Road 142 leads the final 6.5 miles to Snow Lake. Early in the spring or after a big snow, the section of Highway 159 between Mogollon and Snow Lake may be closed, and it will be necessary to approach by driving south from the town of Reserve on Highway 435. This turns into an approach from the north on Forest Road 28 to the above-mentioned intersection. On either approach, the roads are good and can be traveled by passenger car. The final approach route is to drive 12 miles west of Magdalena on Highway 60 and turn south on Highway 52 just before the VLA (Very Large Array) radio telescope facility and follow the signs to Beaverhead and then Snow Lake. This is a long drive on gravel roads and takes about the same time as the longer, paved approach. It is a scenic way to go, but don't take it if the weather has been bad.

Begin the hike by driving to a parking area on the west side of Snow Lake and following a path that leads south along the lake shore, east across the earthen dam at the south end of the lake, and on south along the outflow, to the stream junction where Gilita Creek becomes the Middle Fork of the Gila River. Here, you make your first river crossing and follow the trail 3.2 miles downstream past some log cabin ruins to a beautiful stretch of river ending with a popular camping area at a grove of large cottonwoods where Iron Creek joins. Continue the hike by walking west along the treeline on the north side of the Iron Creek drainage, where Trail #171 makes a fairly strenuous ascent up the tip of Iron Creek Mesa and continues west across the mesa through ponderosa pine and alligator juniper on a 6-mile stretch to a trail junction just below Iron Creek Lake. The lake is shallow and marginally worth the additional effort to hike up and view; a

better area to camp is to turn south at the trail junction on Trail #151 and drop down to Iron Creek. The trail continues east along Iron Creek for a little over a mile to a junction with Trail #141. This trail climbs up on to Clayton Mesa and runs east, joins Trail #175, and continues to the east end of the mesa and drops back down to Iron Creek, then follows the south bank of the creek back to the Middle Fork where the loop hike began. Complete the hike by returning back up the Middle Fork to Snow Lake. The trail is well signed and easy to follow, with the exception of a couple of marshy areas on Clayton Mesa where you may have to search a little. Water availability and fishing are supplied by the Middle Fork and Iron Creek. Carry water with you across the mesas.

Hike #2. Crest Trail to Mogollon Baldy Peak (Trail #182)

This hike goes down the spine of the Mogollon Mountains, the highest part of the Gila National Forest, on a 12-mile route beginning at Sandy Point, on the road east of the town of Mogollon, running south to the summit of Mogollon Baldy Peak (10,770 feet), and returning back to Sandy Point, for a round-trip distance of 24 miles. The trail continues on past Mogollon Baldy Peak, but the trip described here is a three-day backpack, with two nights spent at Hummingbird Saddle on the way down the crest, and the day in between used to do a day hike down to Mogollon Baldy Peak and back. The trail runs over or near the summits of the highest peaks in the range and is above 10,000 feet for most of the way. The net elevation gain of 1,638 feet understates the reality of additional elevation being lost and gained along the way but is still relatively moderate considering the elevation gradient of the area. There are occasional clearings along the route, with spectacular views, but dense forests provide the primary backdrop, with towering specimens of aspen, Engelmann spruce, corkbark fir, Mexican white pine, and largest of all, Douglas fir. This is a good trip to do in summer when things begin to heat up at the lower elevations; I have walked across fairly extensive snow drifts on the trail in mid-June, so this time of year through fall would be a good time frame within which to plan a hike. Although far from being crowded, the trail is reasonably popular by Gila standards and is well enough worn to be easy to follow the entire way. The trail is also well marked with trail signs. Hummingbird Saddle has lots of good campsites with a dependable spring nearby, and as the name suggests, there is a local population of hummingbirds. Hobo and Blacktail springs also provide camping possibilities that are more marginal, both in terms of space and water. The USGS 7.5-minute scale topo maps of the area are the Mogollon Baldy Peak and Grouse Mountain quads.

To reach the trailhead, drive on Highway 180 to a turnoff on to Highway 159 about 1 mile south of the town of Alma. Travel east on Highway 159, which is paved as far as the old mining town of Mogollon. This partially restored survivor of the gold and silver mining boom and Apache wars is worth a short side trip to investigate, if you have the time. The pavement ends at the east side of town but continues as a good-quality gravel road, although it has some sharp turns and may be trouble if you are towing a long trailer, and will be snowpacked if you arrive too early in the spring. Sandy Point is reached 8.2 miles east of Mogollon and has a large parking area on the north side of the road, with a trail sign marking the start of the trail across the road to the south.

The trail immediately commences with a climb of almost 800 feet up to the

Wilderness boundary, after which the elevation levels out and contours through the forest along the crest, finishing the first 4.75 miles at Hummingbird Saddle, a low spot on the crest ridge immediately north of Whitewater Baldy, the highest point in the range. As previously mentioned, this is the premier camping area of the hike, with a number of level campsites and a spring located a short walk to the west along the trail leading down toward Redstone Park. From Hummingbird Saddle, a tiring day hike of 14 miles round trip leads south down the crest to Mogollon Baldy Peak and back. There is a fire lookout on Mogollon Baldy, and from the summit of the peak is a series of spectacular vistas in all directions; the final strenuous climb up the peak is well rewarded. There are also several other trails leading both east and west from the Crest Trail, and from trail junctions within several miles of Hummingbird Saddle. If you have several nights to spend, this would make a fine base camp from which to explore a lot of nearby territory. Keep in mind that this is the high part of the range and probably not the best place to be when a lot of lightning storms are happening.

Hike #3. Whitewater Trail (#207)

Whitewater Creek flows out of the northwest corner of the Wilderness, fed at its origins on the upper east end by runoff coming from the Mogollon Mountains. The creek consists of two main branches, the North and South Forks, each of which has a trail that runs along its length. Both forks appear to be of similar size and are known as good fishing streams. The trail described here follows the North Fork as far as Redstone Park, a round-trip distance of 22 miles, with a net elevation gain of 2,660 feet. The trail continues east past Redstone Park to the Crest Trail at Hummingbird Saddle, but this last segment of trail has some serious elevation gain. The majority of the route is situated down in the river canyon, with enough stream crossings to require a pair of lightweight shoes for wading if you want to keep your hiking boots dry. There are lots of camping spots and, of course, plentiful water along almost the entire route. The first several miles of the trail is heavily hiked, with the primary reason being the well-known Catwalk, one of the main tourist attractions in the area, located 0.5 miles up the trail from the trailhead at Whitewater Picnic Ground. The story of the Catwalk begins with the discovery of gold and silver deposits in Whitewater Canyon in the late 1800s, and the construction of a mill to process the ore at the entrance of the canyon. Water was needed for the large electric generators that powered the mill, and for the short-lived town which sprang up nearby, and as the flow of water often dried up this far down the canyon, the idea was conceived to pipe water down from farther up the canyon. This was accomplished by the construction in 1893 of a steel pipeline, encased in sawdust to prevent freezing, which reached about 3 miles up into the canyon, and which was elevated in the narrow part of the canyon and attached to the sheer canyon walls by supports drilled into the rock. This elevated portion of the pipeline, as much as 20 feet above the river level, was known by the workmen who had to service it as the "catwalk." It was eventually torn down after the mill enterprise failed, but was reconstructed in 1935–1936 by the CCC, and later improved by the Forest Service in the form of an elevated walkway for the purpose of a recreational attraction for the Gila National Forest. Today, the Whitewater Trail incorporates this Catwalk section, which was designated in 1978 as a National Recreation Trail. Thousands of

people hike the Catwalk each year, but the crowds thin out fast as you continue up the canyon past the elevated portion of the trail.

To reach the trailhead at Whitewater Picnic Ground, drive on Highway 180 to the town of Glenwood and turn east on Highway 174. The road is not presently identified with a highway sign, but is the obvious paved road heading east with a sign indicating the way to the Catwalk and Whitewater Picnic Ground 5 miles distant. The road is paved all the way to a large parking area located immediately west of the large sycamore trees shading the picnic area.

The trail begins at the parking area and runs past the picnic facility and on to the Catwalk. This is a perennial flash-flood problem area, and there are signs posted warning of this danger; it is something to keep in mind as you proceed up the canyon. Past the steel Catwalk, the trail climbs up on the north side of the canyon for a distance of perhaps 2 miles and runs above the stream to avoid trail maintenance problems from flash flooding, before dropping back down to stream level. This is the only part of the hike where water is not close at hand. As you come to the major fork in the canyon, take the left trail branch up the North Fork. The trail continues up the canyon bottom, passing the Trail #179 junction at Winn Canyon, all the way to Redstone Park. There are plentiful campsites along this stretch, and some stream wading with lots of shady foliage. There are also occasional patches of poison ivy along the stream that you will want to avoid; if you can't identify this plant, better take along a plant handbook. If you want to continue to Hummingbird Saddle, be prepared to climb and take along some water. Otherwise, turn around and retrace the route back to the picnic area. The trail is well worn and easy to follow, but if you want

to bring along topo maps to supplement the Wilderness map, the USGS 7.5-minute scale Holt Mountain and Grouse Mountain maps are the ones to get.

Hike #4. West Fork/Middle Fork Loop Hike

The West Fork and Middle Fork of the Gila River are two of the primary tributaries that run through the Gila Wilderness, beginning in the high western end of the Wilderness, and joining near the Cliff Dwellings National Monument Visitor Center. There are trails of 35 and 41 miles, respectively, that follow the length of each of these two river branches and provide the opportunity for a long, one-way backpack trip, with good camping and fishing in scenic and peaceful river environments. As an alternative to the one-way hike up one of the river branches, the hike described here takes a 23.8-mile round-trip loop that includes segments of both rivers, with a total

elevation gain of 1,520 feet. This makes a moderate trip of two or more nights, covers some nice country, and makes a good introductory backpack into the Gila. This is a fairly popular loop hike, and the initial sections of both the West Fork and Middle Fork Trails which begin in the cliff dwellings area are among the most heavily hiked in the entire Wilderness, but as is often the case, I have not encountered many other people beyond a few miles of the trailhead. The trails are well marked and easy to follow. Because of the numerous river crossings (if you come from a part of the country with more plentiful water, you will think of these as creeks rather than rivers), this is not an ideal cold-weather hike, nor should it be done too early in the year when the water is flowing high with spring runoff; mid- to late April through October is about right. There are a number of Forest Service campgrounds in the general

West Fork of the Gila River

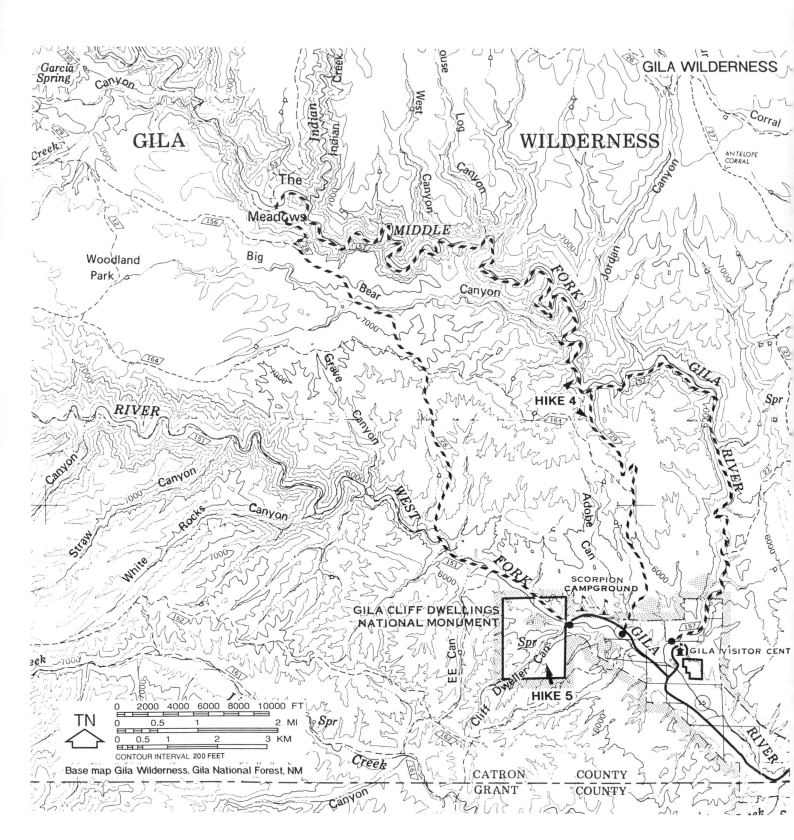

vicinity, the nearest located in the National Monument west of the Visitor Center. For supplementary topo map coverage, you will need the Gila Hot Springs, Little Turkey Park, and Woodland Park 7.5-minute scale quad maps.

To locate the trailhead at the Cliff Dwellings National Monument, take Highway 152 by one of the routes described under "South Side Access," and turn north on to Highway 35 at the community of San Lorenzo. Stay on Highway 35, which is paved, the remaining 45-mile drive to the Monument; the Visitor Center is located at the end of the highway, and there is a staff member present during daylight hours to answer questions. After you have finished at the Visitor Center, drive a short distance back across the bridge and take the road that goes west to the cliff dwellings. Park in the farthest parking area and find the trailhead for the West Fork Trail (#151) at the west end of the lot. Driving time from Albuquerque is about 5 to 5.5 hours.

I have somewhat arbitrarily described the hike as starting on the West Fork Trail and finishing on the Middle Fork Trail. Begin by hiking west on the West Fork Trail for 2.2 miles to the intersection with Trail #28, which heads northwest up and over the mesa to the Middle Fork. The Middle Fork can be gained on the first day of the trip if you get started early enough, but I like to camp on the West Fork the first night and fish the stream or explore farther up the river. The hike across the mesa (no water) is a 6.8-mile route that ends with a steep descent into the canyon of the Middle Fork at a spot known as the Meadows. This is a popular camping spot, and when you see it you know why—a very lovely spot with grassy meadows and big ponderosas and broadleafs. The remaining distance back down the Middle Fork Trail (#157) includes an interminable number of stream crossings, and you should have some lightweight shoes with which you can wade and hike, as this is something you may not want to subject your hiking boots to. The return leg back down the Middle Fork is normally broken into two days; it's a long hike (14 to 16 miles, depending upon how you finish), and doing it in one day is something of a forced march. Several miles from the end of the Middle Fork Trail is the junction with Trail #729, which cuts across the mesa to the corrals by the campground near the start of the hike. You can continue to follow the Middle Fork Trail the rest of the way and end up at the same place, but by this time you will probably be ready to stop walking through the river and take the shortcut back. One drawback to the Trail #729 shortcut, however, is that you will miss a popular hot spring located 2 miles up the Middle Fork from the Visitor Center. The choice is yours. A short hike back to the parking area at the cliff dwellings from the end of Trail #729 (or the Visitor Center) completes the hike.

Hike #5. Cliff Dwellings Trail

This is the tourist route that runs up and through the main set of cliff dwellings that are the centerpiece of the National Monument. The trail is an easy 1-mile loop that gains 175 feet of elevation and has numbered points of interest that are keyed to an interpretive booklet that is available either at the Visitor Center or the trailhead. The ruins are over 700 years old and belonged to a prehistoric group that is referred to as the Mogollon culture. The original inhabitants mysteriously abandoned the site in the early 1300s, but the clues left behind in the partially restored ruins provide significant insight as to the Stone Age lifestyle of the ancient inhabitants and how they coped with their natural environment. This is a small part of our national heritage and well worth the short hike to see and enjoy.

The road access is the same as that described for Hike #4. You will want to go by the Visitor Center for the National Monument, where informational displays provide a background for the prehistoric culture of the area. Drive west on the road that turns off just before the bridge south of the Visitor Center to locate the parking area for the cliff dwellings. The trail begins at the foot bridge that crosses the river and proceeds up to the series of naturally formed caves that contain the ruins. You are asked to stay on the trail and not to climb on any walls or structures.

Hike #6. Caves Trail (#803) and Brannon Park Trail (#700)

Forest Road 150 runs between Highway 35 at the south end to Wall Lake and

Log Cabin Ruin along the Middle Fork

Beaverhead at the north end, essentially defining the east boundary of the Gila Wilderness, and acting as a corridor separating the Gila Wilderness from the adjacent Aldo Leopold Wilderness immediately to the east. Several campgrounds are located along Forest Road 150s and a number of trails run west into the Gila Wilderness from this road. Despite the cow problem discussed earlier, there is some attractive country in this part of the Gila, and both the campgrounds, which are nice, and the trails, tend to be more secluded. Although I haven't hiked all of them, I feel that the longer hikes I have done in this part of the Wilderness had significant segments that were either too impacted by ranching activity or too difficult to follow (or both) to recommend in this book, but I did find several short hikes that were quite pleasant, including the two described here, and the one that follows this description. They all start from Forest Service campgrounds, which makes it handy for an early morning or late afternoon outing from your campsite. The Caves Trail and Brannon Park Trail are both described together here in the same section because they are both short hikes that start from the same trailhead and can both be easily done in the same day, or you can take your pick. The segment of the Brannon Park Trail described here is only the top 3 miles of the trail. The entire trail is 11.5 miles one way, and would require a car shuttle to the south trailhead at Highway 35 if you wanted to do the entire trail and not have to retrace the route. The USGS 7.5-minute topo map that covers the area for these hikes is the North Star Mesa quad.

Caves Trail is an easy walk of 1.5 to 2.0 miles round trip with perhaps 100 feet of elevation differential, that runs down Rocky Canyon out of Rocky Canyon Campground, a small facility with only two or three units. The trail is not especially spectacular, but just an enjoyable walk along a stream bed with intermittent water and grassy banks, flanked by open groves of oak and ponderosa pine, leading to a series of natural shelter caves in the shallow canyon walls. It is an easy hike that would be good for kids, or anyone else not fond of steep hiking, and you will probably have the whole trail to yourself. Brannon Park Trail coincides with Caves Trail for several hundred yards, before branching away and climbing up to a gently sloping mesa above the north side of Rocky Canyon where Brannon Park is located. Brannon Park is a lovely meadow surrounded by timber, and it is the site of an old homestead. Except for the initial climb up to the mesa, the elevation gradient is minimal; the scenery is pleasant, and you can easily do the hike in 3 to 4 hours.

To reach the trailhead, see the discus-

Fishing in Iron Creek during Spring

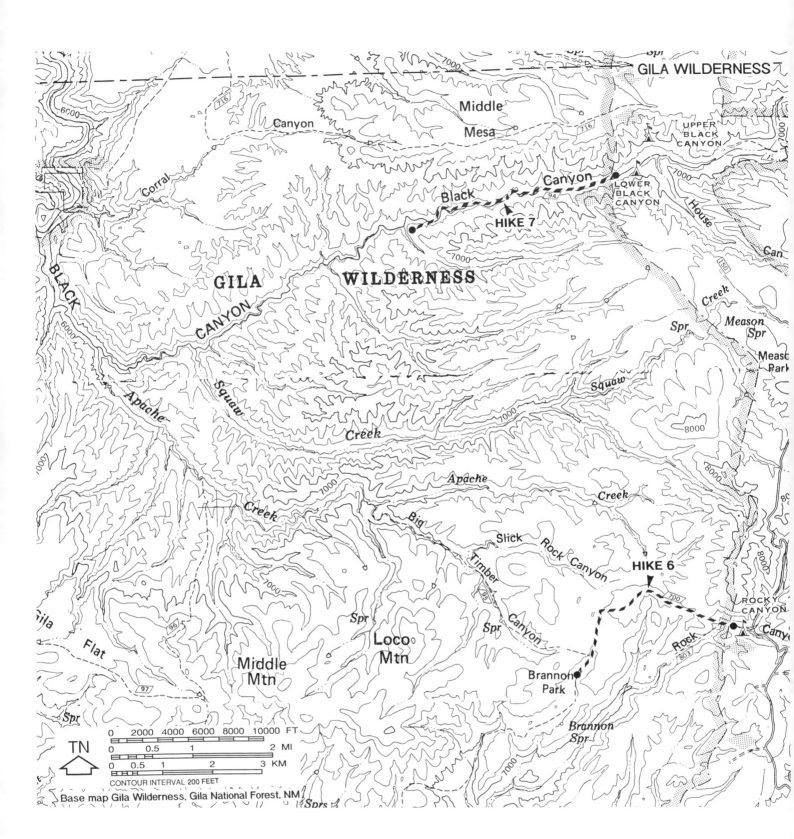

sion under "South Side Access" in the first part of the section to locate Highway 152, and drive to the community of San Lorenzo. Turn north on Highway 35 at San Lorenzo, and follow the paved highway 15.2 miles to a gravel road that turns off to the north with a sign indicating the way to Wall Lake; this is Forest Road 150. Before you reach this intersection is the Mimbres Ranger Station, 11 miles on Highway 35 north of the Highway 180 turnoff, where you can stop and ask questions if you wish. As you start up Forest Road 150, you will pass a sign advising that the road is rough and requires a high axle vehicle. This applies to the section of road north of Rocky Canyon (Rocky Canyon Campground), particularly if there have been recent rains, but you should have no trouble reaching the campground by passenger car. After you have driven 12.4 miles on Forest Road 150, there will be a sign on the west side of the road for Rocky

Canyon Campground and Trails #803 and #700, and a short road leading to the campsites. The trailhead at the campground is unmarked, but begins at the west end of the campground and follows the creek drainage for several hundred yards to a trail sign where Trails #803 and #700 split. Trail #700 goes right to Brannon Park, and Trail #803 takes the left, or south, branch and continues on down Rocky Canyon. The Caves Trail (#803) is generally faint and, in fact, often consists of a trail on both sides of the creek bed, but just stick to the drainage and you can't get lost. The shallow caves begin to appear on the north side of the canyon less than a mile from the trail sign. After the path dissolves into the creek bed below the caves, hike back to return. If you are hiking the Brannon Park Trail, take the Trail #700 option at the trail junction, and continue on the trail as it follows the north bank of the drainage for a short distance before making a short, steep climb up the side of the canyon, before gradually looping back to the south. The cows have found this area, too, and you may have to contend with a few stray trails, but stick to the most-traveled route and you shouldn't have any real trouble keeping to the trail. A gradual descent along the mesa to the south leads to Brannon Park. Within 0.5 miles past the park, the trail begins a steep descent to the west as it continues toward the south trailhead. Turn back and return to the campground to complete the hike.

Hike #7. Lower Black Canyon Trail (#94)

Black Canyon is a major feeder tributary of the Gila River, joining just below Gila Hot Springs. The canyon runs across both the Gila and Aldo Leopold Wilderness Areas and is bisected by Forest Road 150, at which point the trail down the canyon begins at the Black Canyon

Campground. The trail is an easy hike of 6 miles round trip, with a 320-foot elevation differential. It is a pleasant path that follows the stream, which flows year round, through open meadows and the broadleaf and ponderosa foliage of the canyon bottom. Read the narrative for the Caves and Brannon Park hikes in the previous section for background and access information concerning the area.

To reach Black Canyon Campground, drive north from Highway 35 on Forest Road 150 for 22 miles to a bridge across the stream at the bottom of the canyon. The campground is on the west side of the road just before the bridge, and if you have your choice, continue on the side road west above the first campsite and drive across the stream to the campsites on the north side of the stream. The last 10 miles of Forest Road 150 leading to the canyon are rough and may require a high

clearance vehicle. A standard passenger car may suffice, depending upon road conditions, but you better check with the Mimbres Ranger Station first. From the west end of the Black Canyon Campground, the trailhead is obscure, but you should have no trouble locating the trail, which heads west along the open slopes above the north bank of the stream. There are a number of stream crossings, but when I did the trail the water was low and I was able to keep my boots dry; with higher water this may not be the case. The route down the river continues on an easy grade for 3 miles until the canyon narrows at an old corral. The topo map shows the trail continuing on down the canyon all the way to the Gila River, but the official trail ends here, and I suspect that the rest of the way below this point gets pretty rough. Unless you care to try it, hike back up the canyon to complete the hike. The USGS topo map for this hike is the 7.5-minute scale Middle Mesa quad.

For Further Information:

Forest Supervisor
Gila National Forest
2610 North Silver Street
Silver City, NM 88061
(505) 388-8201

Luna Ranger District
Box 91
Luna, NM 87824
(505) 547-2611

Glenwood Ranger District
Box 8
Glenwood, NM 88039
(505) 539-2481

Mimbres Ranger District
Box 79
Mimbres, NM 88049
(505) 536-2250

Reserve Ranger District
Box 117
Reserve, NM 87830
(505) 533-6231

Silver City Ranger District
2915 Highway 180 East
Silver City, NM 88061
(505) 538-2771

Wilderness Ranger District
Route 11, Box 100
Silver City, NM 88061

Quemado Ranger District
Box 158
Quemado, NM 87829
(505) 773-4678

Cliff Dwellings National Monument
(505) 536-9488

The Gila Wilderness: A Hiking Guide, by John A. Murray, published by the University of New Mexico Press, Albuquerque, NM, 1988.

Gila River Canyon, Looking North

The Densely Wooded
Slopes of the Black Range

Aldo Leopold Wilderness
(Black Range)

GENERAL DESCRIPTION

The Aldo Leopold Wilderness is a
202,016-acre tract located on the eastern
side of the Gila National Forest in the area
known as the Black Range. In order to avoid
being redundant, I would ask you to read
the information under the general description for the Gila Wilderness. The Gila and
Aldo Leopold Wilderness Areas lie side by
side, separated on the map only by a
narrow corridor bordering Forest Road 150,
and as you would expect, they share many

of the same features, in terms of such
things as flora, fauna, and natural history.
The Aldo Leopold is characterized by a
range of high peaks running north to south
down the center of the area, with a trail
running down the crest line of the range,
part of which defines a segment of the
Continental Divide, and trail systems
running up to the crest line from both
sides. Though still sizeable, the area is
smaller and has a less-diverse terrain than

the Gila Wilderness, but it is also noticeably wilder and less visited. Parts of it are also more difficult to access by automobile, particularly the north and east sides. An early description of the region by James O. Pattie, a Kentucky trapper who ascended the headwaters of the Gila River in 1825 while in search for beaver, is interesting to recount. He described his trip as being impeded by tall grasses, heavy timber, tangled grapevines, and brushy thickets. No doubt the situation with the tall grasses and heavy timber has been subsequently altered considerably by cows and lumbermen, but it is still one of the wilder sections of forest that you will find in this part of the country. The Wilderness was named in honor of Aldo Leopold, the great naturalist whose efforts were instrumental in getting the nation's first Wilderness Area established in the Gila National Forest in the year 1924. Before the Wilderness designation, the area was part of what was called the Black Range Primitive Area. Several Forest Service campgrounds are located along Highway 152 on the south side of the Wilderness west of Emory Pass, and along Forest Road 150 on the west side. For most of the Wilderness, a good time to plan a trip would be from about mid-April through late October, although the highest parts of the range may not be free of snow until mid-May.

Map Coverage

The best single map to get is the Visitors Travel Guide and Map for the Aldo Leopold Wilderness. This map is available from most of the local ranger stations or from other Forest Service map distribution centers in the state. Some of these facilities are listed at the end of the section. The map shows topography as well as trails; if you want finer detail, the USGS topo maps that cover the area are listed with the individual trail descriptions.

Access

Detailed directions for locating the trailheads are included with the trail descriptions; however, the following general access directions will help you find the Wilderness Area.

If you are traveling from El Paso or Las Cruces, the most direct access is to take Interstate 10/70 to Deming, then Highway 180 to the Highway 61 turnoff, which goes north to San Lorenzo. From San Lorenzo, take Highway 152 northeast to reach the south part of the Wilderness, or to reach the west side of the Wilderness, take Highway 35 northwest 15.2 miles from San Lorenzo to a gravel road that turns off to the north toward Wall Lake. This is Forest Road 150, which travels north along the west boundary of the Wilderness.

If you are coming from Albuquerque or other points north, drive south on Interstate 25 to the Highway 152 exit, 16 miles south of Truth or Consequences. Drive west on Highway 152 through Hillsboro and Kingston and over Emory Pass, which is located on the south side of the Wilderness at the crest of the Black Range. If you are headed for the west side of the Wilderness, continue on Highway 152 to San Lorenzo, where Highways 61 and 35 join, and turn northwest on Highway 35 and drive 15.2 miles to the Forest Road 150 intersection. The Mimbres Ranger Station is located 11 miles up Highway 35 from the Highway 152 turnoff, should you want to stop and ask directions or questions.

A good bit of the east and far north sides of the Wilderness involve dirt access roads that are either hard to locate, really out of the way, virtually impassable—or sometimes a combination of these. Should you want to explore this part of the Wilderness, I leave it to you to find your own way.

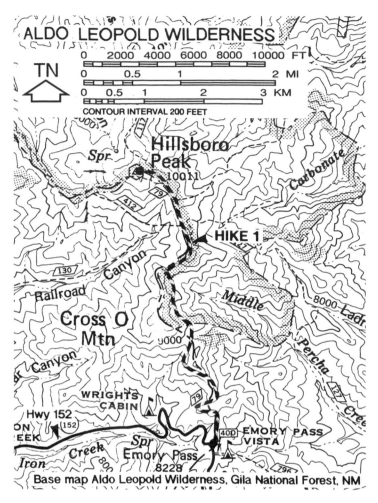

ALDO LEOPOLD WILDERNESS

CONTOUR INTERVAL 200 FEET

Base map Aldo Leopold Wilderness, Gila National Forest, NM

Hike #1. Hillsboro Peak Trail (#79)
Distance — 9.4 miles round trip
Net elevation gain — 1,817 feet
Difficulty — Moderate

Hiking Trails

I made my first backpacking trip into the Aldo Leopold Wilderness in 1981 and have made several hiking trips into the area since, and the total number of people I encountered were two small parties—one on the Hillsboro Peak Trail and one on the Mimbres River Trail—and no one on any of the other trails. This gives an indication of the hiker density in this Wilderness and points out that for secluded hiking in a nice forest environment, even for trails with water, the Aldo Leopold Wilderness is hard to beat. The trails mostly follow ridges or drainages and are worn enough on the more popular trails so that navigation generally isn't a problem, but on the more obscure trails, be prepared to do some searching. On the latter trails, you'd better tighten up your map and compass skills, and it wouldn't be a bad idea to have some standard USGS topo maps to supplement the Wilderness Map. Trail signage is sometimes minimal, but usually adequate. There is plenty of rugged country in this Wilderness, which has probably changed very little in many areas since the late 1800s, when the mining towns surrounding the range were booming. But tucked within the rugged terrain are many surprisingly gentle places that are quite lovely and inspirational. As can be seen by looking at the map, there are quite a few trails to choose from. I have described three of them in this section, but if you want more, there are plenty of possibilities.

TRAIL DESCRIPTIONS

Hike #1. Hillsboro Peak Trail (#79)

This trail begins at Emory Pass, a saddle on the crest line of the Black Range, now traversed by Highway 152. Ignoring the fact that the pass had regularly been used since prehistory by a succession of cultures as a crossing point over the mountain range, it was named for a U.S. Army Lieutenant, W. H. Emory, who was guided over the pass by Kit Carson in 1846. The trail takes a 9.4-mile round trip path, with a net elevation gain of 1,817 feet to Hillsboro Peak (10,011 feet), a major summit located along the top of the range, basically following a route along or near the crest line all the way to the peak. Forest cover of oak and ponderosa pine is common on the lower part of the trail, and grades into Douglas fir, white pine, and aspen higher up. Locust is common all along the path. There are frequent vistas along the way, and at the summit of Hillsboro Peak is a fire lookout tower, which you are permitted to ascend when it is not in use. From the cabin atop the tower there is a spectacular 360-degree view of the entire range. The trail is well worn all the way, although one or two tricky trail junctions could use signs. There are no water sources on the way up, making this trip more appropriate for dayhiking than overnight backpacking. There is apparently a spring on the north side of the peak down from the summit, but its location isn't obvious. The area is shown on the USGS 7.5-minute Hillsboro Peak quad map.

To reach the trailhead, take Highway 152 to Emory Pass, west of the old mining town of Kingston, and take the short, paved spur road that goes north from the summit of the pass up to a parking area at an overlook. The trail is marked by a trail sign at the west end of the lot, and proceeds up the ridge, merging with a dirt road after about 0.25 miles, which continues past a Forest Service heliport facility. After you pass through a gate beyond the heliport, the trail forks; take the branch that climbs up. The trail is straightforward from here to the final ridge southeast of Hillsboro Peak, where you will come to two trail junction signs in quick

The Interior of a Cabin atop Hillsboro Peak Fire Lookout Tower

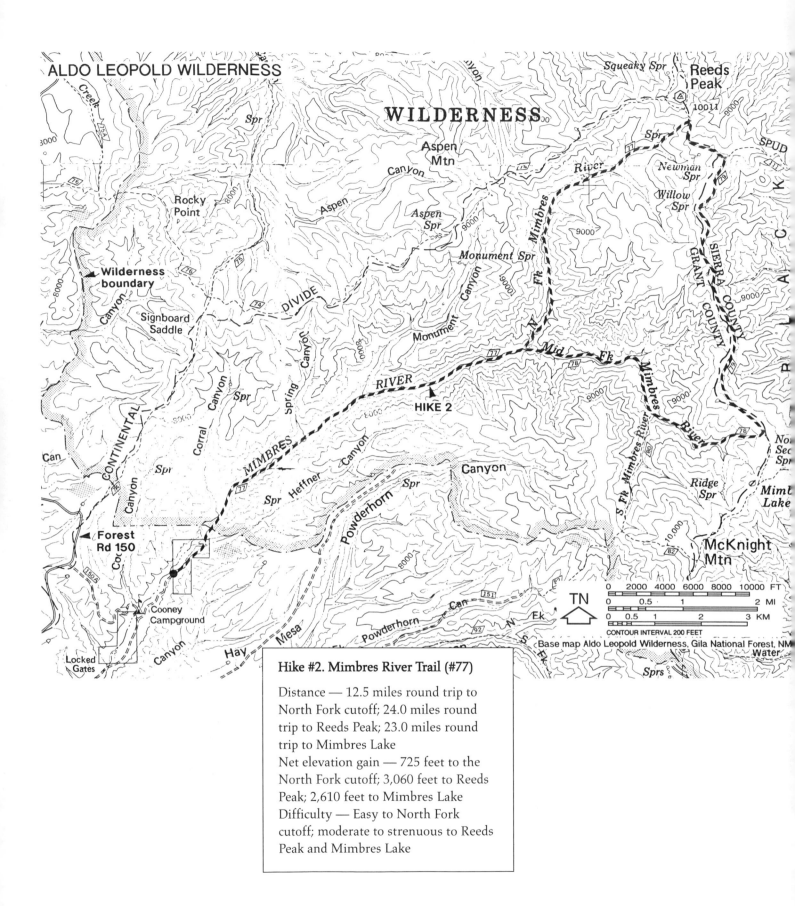

ALDO LEOPOLD WILDERNESS

WILDERNESS

Reeds
Peak

Squeaky Spr

Aspen
Mtn

Newman
Spr

Willow
Spr

Rocky
Point

Monument Spr

SIERRA COUNTY

GRANT COUNTY

Wilderness
boundary

DIVIDE

Signboard
Saddle

Mid

Fk

RIVER

HIKE 2

Canyon

Canyon

Ridge
Spr

Mimt
Lake

Spr

Heffner

Spr

Forest
Rd 150

Cooney
Campground

McKnight
Mtn

Locked
Gates

Powderhorn

Hay

Mesa

Canyon

Powderhorn

TN

CONTOUR INTERVAL 200 FEET

Base map Aldo Leopold Wilderness, Gila National Forest, NM

Hike #2. Mimbres River Trail (#77)

Distance — 12.5 miles round trip to
North Fork cutoff; 24.0 miles round
trip to Reeds Peak; 23.0 miles round
trip to Mimbres Lake
Net elevation gain — 725 feet to the
North Fork cutoff; 3,060 feet to Reeds
Peak; 2,610 feet to Mimbres Lake
Difficulty — Easy to North Fork
cutoff; moderate to strenuous to Reeds
Peak and Mimbres Lake

ALDO LEOPOLD WILDERNESS (BLACK RANGE)   280

succession. The second of these is where the Hillsboro Peak Bypass Trail branches off to the left. This is the standard crest trail that follows the ridge line and eliminates the climb up over Hillsboro Peak, but for our hike take the other branch, which climbs up to the north. This last segment of trail is steep as it gains the final 750 feet to the summit. Shortly below the summit is another trail junction sign for the Animas Divide Trail (#117). If you actually try and locate this trail, you will have some idea of the route-finding efforts you will be put to in hiking some of the more lightly used trails in the Wilderness. To continue to the summit of the peak, walk past the trail sign and turn uphill on the spur trail that goes left a short distance beyond. The summit is a flat, open area with lots of wildflowers along with the lookout tower and living quarters. If permitted, climb up into the tower and have a look around before starting back down. This is one of those hikes that shouldn't be planned too early in the spring. After a heavy winter there will probably be snow drifts across the upper part of the trail until well into the month of May. Also, when doing the hike during the rainy season, get started early in the day to avoid the afternoon thunderstorms, although one benefit of this hike during wet weather is that you have paved access roads all the way to the trailhead. The total time to complete the hike will probably take between 4.5 to 6 hours for most people.

Hike #2. Mimbres River Trail (#77)

The Mimbres River is the largest of the water streams in the Aldo Leopold Wilderness, draining a portion of the west slope of the Black Range. There is a trail system that runs from near the Cooney Campground all the way up the river and its major branches. The river is large enough to support a population of trout,

but small enough so that four or five steps across the tops of protruding rocks at the crossings are enough to get you across without getting your feet wet— except in springtime or after rains, when the river is swollen. The canyon bottom is graced with wide, grassy clearings and stands of ponderosa pine, narrowleaf cottonwood, and large gambel oaks. In fall, the leaves from the various deciduous species of trees and shrubs turn gold and orange, further enhancing the natural beauty of the setting. In this time of year, when the piñon trees are shedding their edible seeds, you can also collect the gamble oak acorns that drop down on the trail, which are not only edible, but even though it may run contrary to your prior acorn tasting experiments, can be rather tasty as well. Both kind of seeds were important food sources for the Indians, and probably the early settlers who lived in the area. This hike can be done as an easy day hike, or a multiday backpacking trip, with numerous good campsites along the river up to the North Fork/Middle Fork junction, and along the trails that follow these river forks up to the crest ridge, or near Mimbres Lake. The distances and elevation gain for the various trail options are 12.5 miles round trip and 725 feet gained to the North Fork/Middle Fork trail junction, 24 miles round trip and 3,060 feet gained to the summit of Reeds Peak, and 23 miles round trip and 2,610 feet gained to Mimbres Lake. You can also camp near the North Fork/ Middle Fork junction and do a long, strenuous day hike around the loop to Reeds Peak and Mimbres Lake. This is a hike you will probably enjoy more if you do it after the snows have melted out and the river has settled down—probably about mid-May through late October. Early October, before the weather turns cold, is ideal, as it is for most of the other hiking areas around the state. The USGS

7.5-minute topo maps for this hike include the Hay Mesa quad map for the trail up to the North/Middle Fork junction, with the addition of the Reeds Peak quad for Reeds Peak, and the Victoria Park quad for Mimbres Lake.

To locate the trailhead, begin by locating Forest Road 150 from the general access directions provided above. There is a sign at the turnoff from Highway 35 warning that the road is rough and requires a high axle vehicle; this applies to sections of the road beyond the Mimbres River turnoff. Forest Road 150 is a good-quality gravel road over the 7.4 miles to the Mimbres River turnoff, where a road sign points the way to a gravel road heading east and indicates a 1-mile distance to the Mimbres River and Cooney Campground. Another sign indicates that the route is not for wet weather or low clearance vehicles. This is probably good to heed, primarily because the road crosses the river bed at the campground, and if the river is up a bit the crossing could be marginal for passenger cars. After crossing the river, continue on the road that leads northeast up the river about 1 mile to a wide gravel area blocked by private gates, with several private residences just beyond. Park here out of the way of traffic and locate the trail sign at the south end of the parking area.

The trail begins by following the dirt road that heads up the river canyon above the private residences. The trail continues along the same heading after the road ends, until well past the cabins, before dropping down to the river, but there are several spurious side trails to deal with in this area, and if you drop down too soon, just continue to follow the river on up until the main trail is joined. After you have gotten away from the private land, the trail is well defined and easy to follow, occasionally crossing back and forth across the river as it continues on an easy grade 6.25 miles to the junction where the North Fork and Middle Fork divide. The Middle Fork is shown as the South Fork on the USGS map, but I believe Middle Fork is correct. A trail sign marks this junction but is looking a little worse for wear and may not be there by the time you arrive. Here, the canyon forks narrow and steepen, with a trail branch (Trail #77) going left, or north, 5.75 miles up the North Fork to Reeds Peak, and one heading up the Middle Fork (Trail #78) 5.25 miles to Mimbres Lake. The trail branch to Reeds Peak joins the Crest Trail below the peak, then turns north to another trail junction shortly beyond, followed by a final steep ascent to the summit. The grassy summit is the highest point around and has a fire lookout on top with views in every direction. The trail going up to Mimbres Lake also ends up joining the Crest Trail. A hike of 0.5 miles south along the crest on this trail leads just above the small, shallow lake, inexplicably located in a clearing in the forest on a bench near the crest ridge. The trail along the crest ridge connects Reeds Peak with Mimbres Lake, making possible a loop hike. The trail branches that ascend the North and Middle Forks are strenuous but not hard to follow, and there is water along the way and some nice camping spots as well.

Hike #3. Upper Black Canyon Trail (#72)

Upper Black Canyon Trail begins at Black Canyon Campground, a Forest Service facility of several campsites strung along a picturesque stretch of canyon bottom just west of the Wilderness Area, and continues for 13.5 miles (27 miles round trip) east up Black Canyon all the way to the Continental Divide at the crest of the Black Range. The trail is an eastern extension of the shorter trail running west down the

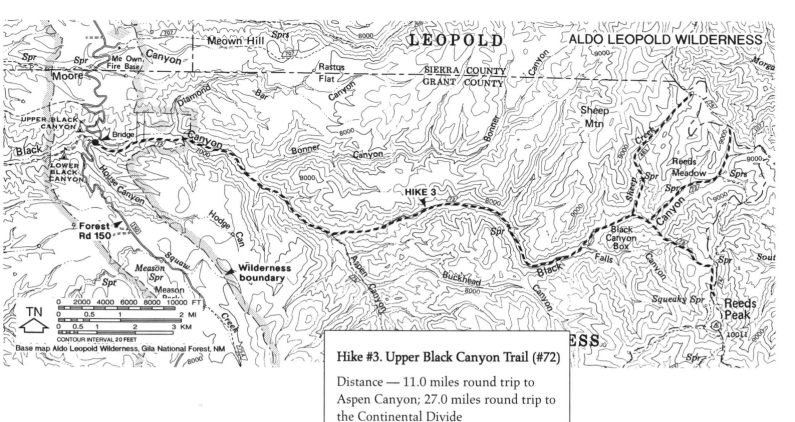

Hike #3. Upper Black Canyon Trail (#72)

Distance — 11.0 miles round trip to Aspen Canyon; 27.0 miles round trip to the Continental Divide

Net elevation gain — 430 feet to Aspen Canyon; 2,200 feet to the Continental Divide

Difficulty — Easy to Aspen Canyon; moderate to the Continental Divide

canyon into the Gila Wilderness. This hike makes a very pleasant day hike, or backpack trip, along a year-round stream that is in some ways similar to the Mimbres River hike. There are broad, open clearings set among groves of pine, fir, oak, and cottonwood, with steep canyon walls rising up on both sides. The elevation gradient is gentle over most of the trail, and even the total elevation gain of 2,200 feet to the Continental Divide is rather moderate for the length of the trail. There are both water and good campsites along the trail, and you are almost certain to have plenty of solitude. I doubt if the trail gets much hiking traffic—it may see more use from horse riders—but in any case, the path is well enough worn for the most part. There are obscure sections and some competition from cow or game trails, but the pathway stays along the river bottom, so there is really no possibility of getting lost. I have

only had time to do a day hike up Black Canyon on a trip where the primary objective was a hike into the Gila Wilderness, and I have not been beyond the Aspen Canyon junction. The milage to that point is 11 miles round trip, with a gentle elevation gain of 430 feet. It makes a very nice day hike, but I am anxious to return and backpack the entire trail; it should be an excellent trip, and there are some interesting-looking side trails as well. The USGS 7.5-minute scale topo maps needed to cover the entire hike are, from west to east, the Middle Mesa, Bonner Canyon, and Reeds Peak quad maps.

The approach to the trailhead begins by turning north on to Forest Road 150 from Highway 35. You may need to refer to the "Access" directions earlier in the section to find this intersection. Drive north on Forest Road 150 for 22 miles until the road drops down into Black Canyon and comes to a bridge over the stream, with Black Canyon Campground on the west side of the road just before the bridge. This is a good place to park your vehicle— it is also a nice place to camp. The last 10 miles of the road leading to the campground are rough, and a high clearance vehicle would be preferable, although a passenger car should do okay, unless road conditions are bad; better check with one of the ranger stations listed at the end of the section if you're making the trip in your Corvette.

From the Black Canyon Campground,

walk east under or around the bridge and follow the stream until you come to the gravel road, which continues along the stream to the Wilderness boundary at the end of the private land. The trail continues past the boundary sign along the broad canyon floor, which narrows somewhat a little over a mile prior to the Aspen Canyon junction at the 5.5-mile point. A side trail branches off to the right up Aspen Canyon, while the main trail continues on the left fork and proceeds up Black Canyon. According to the map, the trail passes another side trail to the north about 6.5 or 7 miles farther up the canyon at Sheep Creek, and then branches at the head of the canyon just below an old homestead, with each branch leading up to the divide. There appear to be lots of potential campsite areas, with water almost all the way up the canyon. Route-finding on the upper part of the canyon shouldn't be a problem, but be sure and take your map(s) along in any case.

For Further Information:

Black Range Ranger
  District
  P.O. Box 431
  2601 South Broadway
  Truth or Consequences,
  NM 87901
  (505) 894-6677

Mimbres Ranger District
  Box 79
  Mimbres, NM 88049
  (505) 536-2250

Forest Supervisor
  Gila National Forest
  2610 North Silver
  Street
  Silver City, NM 88061
  (505) 388-8201

White Mountain Wilderness

GENERAL DESCRIPTION

South-central New Mexico is a land of lonely plains and basins, an arid and beautifully austere landscape cloaked in cholla, yucca, mesquite, creosote, and saltbush, broken by lava flows and rocky outcrops, and populated mainly by rabbits, cows, and coyotes. It is a land steeped in the legends of the shadowy Mogollon Indians of prehistory, the warlike Apache, lost gold mines, and Billy the Kid and the Lincoln County range wars. However, in the midst of all this, isolated peaks and broad mountain ranges rise up like eternal sentinels and break the continuity of the desert landscape, providing islands of green trees and flowing water. The greatest of these mountain uplifts is the White Mountain range, located immediately east of the Tularosa Basin with a high point of 11,973 feet at the summit of Sierra Blanca Peak. This is a wonderful hiking area—the scenery is excellent, and the uncrowded hiking trails are among the best in the state, suitable for day hikes or multiday backpacking trips.

Located just north and west of the town of Ruidoso in the heart of the White Mountain range is the White Mountain Wilderness, a north-south oriented area of about 48,000 acres within the Lincoln National Forest. The Wilderness begins immediately north of Sierra Blanca and the Mescalero Apache Reservation, and continues north for about 12 miles. The elevation ranges from around 6,000 feet to over 11,000 feet at the south boundary. The plant life begins with juniper, piñon pine, and mountain mahogany at the lower elevations and varies with altitude to include oaks, maple, ponderosa pine, aspen, fir, and spruce. Box elders, willows, and cottonwoods grow along the various water courses. Along the crest of the range, particularly to the south, are broad grassy slopes and meadows, which combine with the pockets of forest cover to produce spectacular scenery. The area is home to abundant wildlife including deer, black bear, and coyote. The major canyons all have running water over at least part of their length and isolated springs are scattered about, including a few not shown on the maps. The springs are generally dependable year round, although a few of those that seep up through the ground can occasionally present a challenging water-collection problem, particularly after having been trampled by a herd of cows into a slimy moonscape of mud and excrement. I guess this is my only major objection to the way the area is managed; it would seem to be a simple matter to fence off some of these seeps at the source for the humans and still have water for the animals a short distance downstream, but it must not be that easy.

The climate in the White Mountains is mild and pleasant from spring through fall. Though some of the lower-elevation parts of the mountain are accessible year round, the higher elevations receive significant snowfall in winter that may not fully melt out until June. The thunderstorm season typically arrives during July and August, and perhaps the best time to visit is during the fall before the snow flies, when the weather is usually nice and the foliage begins to change colors. Several Forest Service campgrounds are located outside the Wilderness on the east side of the range, although the South Fork Campground is closed after the summer season. The Three Rivers Campground provides camping facilities on the west side of the range and is open year round. Travel time to these access points from Albuquerque is a little over 3 hours. No permits are needed to hike in the White Mountain Wilderness, but permission must be obtained from the Mescalero Tribe to enter the Indian Reservation on the south side of the range.

Map Coverage

The best overall map to get and the only one you really need obtain is the White Mountain Wilderness Map, a special Lincoln National Forest map produced by the Forest Service. This map shows both trails and topography, and has a durable water-resistant finish. For finer topographic detail, the USGS 7.5-minute scale Nogal Peak, Church Mountain, and Angus quads cover the area that includes the Wilderness.

Access

The primary entry points to the Wilderness are the South Fork Campground and vicinity on the east side, and the Three Rivers Campground on the west side. To reach the South Fork Campground from the north, travel east from the town of Carrizozo on Highway 380, 9 miles to the Highway 37 junction, then 13 miles south on Highway 37 to a road sign indicating a turnoff to Bonito Lake and South Fork Campground. Alternatively, you can reach this turnoff by driving north from Ruidoso, 6 miles on Highway 48, then 1.3 miles west on Highway 37 to the campground turnoff. From this intersection, County Road C9 (labeled as Forest Road 107 on the forest map) runs west 3 miles to Bonito Lake, then another 1.8 miles past the lake to a sign indicating a road fork leading south to the campground. In fall, the campground is closed, and a parking area is provided just below the closed gate. The road is paved all the way to the campground.

The Three Rivers campground on the west side of the range is accessed by driving south from Carrizozo or north from Alamogordo on Highway 54 to the Three Rivers turnoff, which is easy to miss, since the only features to mark the intersection are a derelict white building and a sign for the Three Rivers Petroglyph National Recreation Site. Travel east from this point on County Road B30/Forest Road 579. The Petroglyph site is passed 4.5 miles from the turnoff, and the pavement ends shortly thereafter. The Three Rivers Petroglyph Site is an interesting area with prehistoric rock art and two short trails, and is discussed in a separate section of this book. Drive east past the end of the pavement for about 3 miles to a road fork, and continue straight on Forest Road 579 as County Road B30 branches off to the right. Another 7 miles east brings you to the campground at the end of the road.

Hiking Trails

The Forest Service lists nine separate trails in the White Mountain Wilderness, which are, for the most part, easy to follow and well marked, with trail signs at the intersections. Traffic on the trails is light to moderate. The primary connector trail is the Crest Trail, which follows a 22-mile route along the crest of the range from the northeast part of the Wilderness around to the southeast corner. The other trails generally ascend the slopes of the range from either side to join the Crest Trail. Hiking routes can be put together using various side trails, with the Crest Trail as a connector. The hikes described in this section include a backpack trip requiring one or two nights on the trail, and two day hikes. These are all nice hikes with lots of beautiful scenery, and offer a choice of distance and difficulty. As with any mountain area, remember to treat any drinking water you find along the trail, and be prepared to deal with rain and cooler-than-expected temperatures.

TRAIL DESCRIPTIONS

Hike #1. Crest Trail (#25)/South Fork Trail (#19) Loop Hike

This hike would normally be done as a backpacking trip, although it would be possible as a long day hike by a well-conditioned hiker. It runs through the center of the Wilderness and requires a short car shuttle between the end points to complete the loop. The total round-trip trail distance is 17 miles, with a net elevation gain from the starting trailhead to the high point on White Horse Hill of 1,220 feet, followed by a drop of 2,500 feet to the end of the hike at South Fork Campground.

Begin by following the access directions to South Fork Campground, where the hike ends, and drop off a vehicle. In a second vehicle, drive back to the intersec-

tion with Forest Road 107 (just to the north of the campground) and turn west, following the road, which shortly thereafter turns to gravel, for 2.4 miles, where Forest Road 108 branches off to the north. Drive north on Forest Road 108, climbing up past an old mining operation and several smaller side roads, until 3 miles past the turnoff, where a trail sign at a bend in the road just past a cattle guard indicates the trailhead for Crest Trail #25. The road is rough but should not be a problem unless the weather has been especially wet. There is a small parking area here on the west side of the road, with the trail entrance on the west side.

The trail begins with a short initial climb followed by a long, gradual contour through groves of oak trees across the slopes below Nogal Peak. Since the trail begins at a fairly high elevation, there are nice views almost from the beginning. A little more than an hour along the trail are the Tortolita and Water Canyon Trail junctions, and perhaps 0.5 miles farther is Turkey Spring. There is a good campsite nearby, but obtaining water from the spring during dry seasons of the year may require patience, and is made more difficult because of the cow problem. Ditto for the next spring 0.25 miles farther on, where Trail #42 splits off to the south. Either trail fork can be taken to continue the hike, although Trail #42 is a little more obscure in the open spaces and has some boot-sucking mud bogs on it. The trail branches rejoin near Argentina Spring, which has clear water flowing and good campsites nearby. There is also good camping near Cabin Spring, a short distance along the Doherty Ridge Trail, which branches off to the west a little over a mile south of Argentina Spring. Continuing south from the Doherty Ridge and Little Bonito Trail junction, the Crest Trail climbs up through some open

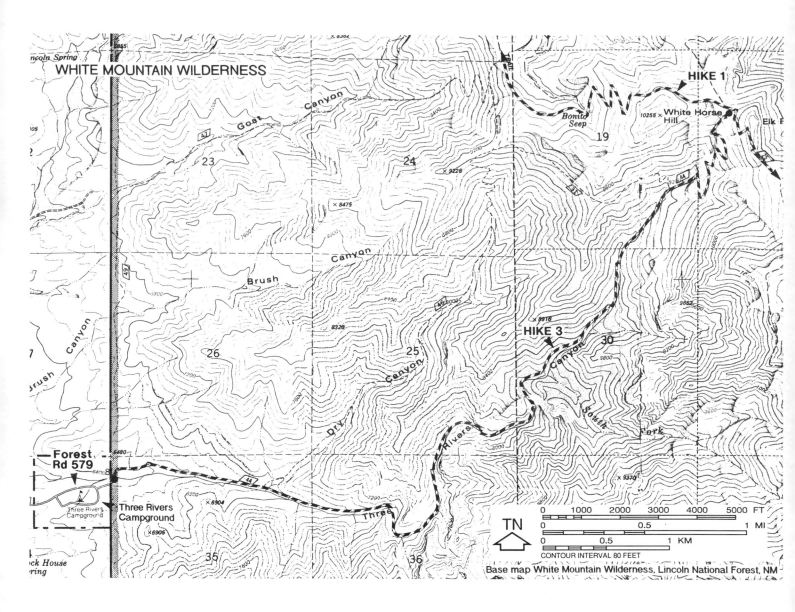

Hike #1. Crest Trail (#25)/South Fork Trail (#19) Loop Hike

Distance — 17 miles round trip with car shuttle
Net elevation gain — 1,220 feet
Difficulty — Moderate

grassy areas, passes the Barber Ridge Trail junction, and leads up out of the forest onto an open ridge. Continuing south on this ridge, the terrain really begins to open up as White Horse Hill comes into view to the east. The Crest Trail keeps to the ridge, passes the Goat Canyon Trail junction, and contours down to Bonito Seep, which provides a reliable flow of water, and the Bonito Trail junction. There is a good campsite at the top of the ridge above the ponderosa grove just to the north. Continue on the Crest Trail by switchbacking up the west slope of White Horse Hill, or climb the ridge above the ponderosa grove until you cut the trail, and continue on a contour below and to the north of the summit to another trail junction at a saddle on the east side. You may find this last stretch of trail a little rough on the legs if you are wearing shorts. At the trail junction, Aspen Trail branches off to the north and Three

Rivers Trail to the southwest. The Crest Trail continues with a climb up through the woods to the southeast to gain a high ridge with spectacular views, and passes by a small spring a short distance before joining the Bluefront and South Fork trails. This intersection is about 11 miles from the start of the hike and is about the midpoint of the Crest Trail, which continues on to the south and east, where it ends at Monjeau Peak. To continue this hike, turn off on to the South Fork Trail (the Bluefront Trail leads to the same destination) and follow it on a 6-mile descent down the South Fork of the Rio Bonito to the South Fork Campground. There is a dependable flow of water down this creek and occasional campsites along the bottom of the canyon. During the spring when the water is running high, stream crossings will probably mean wet feet, and the Bluefront Trail alternative is worth considering. The hike ends at

Open Slopes Surrounding White Horse Hill, Viewed from the West

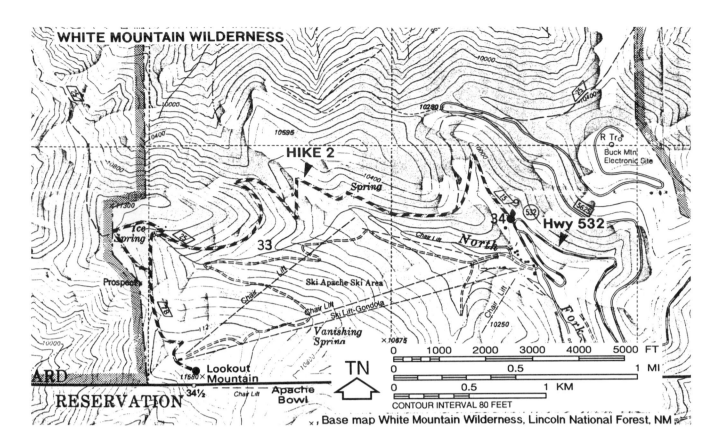

HIKE 2

Spring

Ice
Spring

Prospect

33

Chair Lift

North

34½

Hwy 532

Buck Mtn.
Electronic Site

R Tr

Ski Apache Ski Area

Chair Lift

Ski Lift-Gondola

Vanishing
Spring

Fork

10250

Lookout
Mountain

Chair Lift

Apache
Bowl

RESERVATION

ARD

TN

| 0 | 1000 | 2000 | 3000 | 4000 | 5000 FT |

| 0 | | 0.5 | | 1 MI |

| 0 | | 0.5 | 1 KM | |

CONTOUR INTERVAL 80 FEET

Base map White Mountain Wilderness, Lincoln National Forest, NM

South Fork Campground and a short car shuttle completes the trip.

Hike #2. Lookout Mountain Hike

This is a hike through some very pretty forest scenery, which incorporates the Scenic Trail (#15), part of the Crest Trail (#25), and the Lookout Mountain Trail (#78). The hike begins at the Sierra Blanca/Ski Apache Ski Area and takes a 6.8-mile round-trip route up to Lookout Mountain, which stands above the ski area, a couple of miles northeast of Sierra Blanca Peak. Elevation gain is 1,820 feet, which results in a steep but otherwise easy hike. This hike begins in the high part of the range with spectacular scenery all around, and is normally done as a day hike. Hiking traffic is heavy on the Scenic Trail but is otherwise moderate to light. A good flow of water is available on the way up at Ice Spring.

Locate the trailhead by driving west on Highway 532 from its junction with Highway 48. This intersection is about 2 miles north of Ruidoso and 4 miles south of the Highway 37 junction. After a drive of 12 miles, the highway ends at the ski area, but at the last curve in the road before it heads east into the ski area, look for a trail sign for the Scenic Trail on the right-hand side of the road, with a small parking area just beyond the sign. The Scenic Trail makes a fairly steep 0.6-mile ascent where it joins the Crest Trail. From this junction, head south (left) on the Crest Trail for a gradual 2-mile ascent through forest and meadows until you come to an unmarked intersection, where the Crest Trail cuts sharply up to the right and Trail #78 continues straight (this is the lower variation of Trail #78; you can also turn up on the Crest Trail and join the upper variation of Trail #78 higher up). Walk down Trail #78 to the next

> ### Hike #2. Lookout Mountain Hike
>
> Distance — 6.8 miles round trip
> Net elevation gain — 1,820 feet
> Difficulty — Easy to moderate

bend, where Ice Spring flows from the rock just above the trail. The trail climbs up from the spring for 0.25 miles, where a trail sign for Lookout Mountain Trail (#78) points up the trail branch that cuts back up to the north. This is evidently a rerouting of the lower part of Trail #78, which ends a short distance farther north, where it joins the Crest Trail. Instead of taking this branch, continue on the trail in the direction you have been heading as it skirts above the ski area and makes the final ascent up Lookout Mountain. From the summit you will be treated to a scenic 360-degree view. Complete the hike by returning on the ascent route, or by taking a slight variation by following the above-mentioned upper branch of Trail #78 across to the Crest Trail, instead of the lower branch, which joins just below Ice Spring.

This is a pleasant hike on easy trails with just enough elevation gain for a good workout. If you only have time for one day hike in the White Mountains and you can't spend all day, this hike would be a good choice.

Hike #3. Three Rivers Trail (#44)

The Three Rivers Trail is the primary route up the west side of the range, beginning at Three Rivers Campground and gaining 3,640 feet to the upper end, at a junction with the Crest Trail just east of White Horse Peak. It is a rather strenuous hike of 11.2 miles round trip, which is usually done as a day hike, although there are numerous campsites located along Three Rivers Canyon through which the trail ascends. If you are not interested in climbing all the way to the top, it still makes a nice hike if done part way. The canyon is like an oasis set in the dry, rugged western slopes of the mountains, with a year-round flow of water that supports a population of small brook trout. The plant life changes significantly

from the bottom to the top, providing a nice variety of scenery. If you can arrange a car shuttle at the South Fork Campground, this trail combines with the South Fork Trail and a small segment of the Crest Trail to make an 11.9-mile hike that is somewhat less strenuous if done from east to west.

To find the trailhead, follow the access directions given above to the Three Rivers Campground, and drive to the east end of the Campground to the parking area by the stream. The trail begins east from the parking area and goes a short way before crossing the stream and continuing along the canyon on the north side of the stream through towering forests of ponderosa and fir. The canyon bottom over the first half of the hike is relatively flat, and the forest cover is open and very pleasant to walk through. The year-round stream is picturesque and provides many tempting spots to rest or just hang out. The lower part of the trail near the campground can get fairly crowded during summer weekends or holidays, but you are not likely to see many people, as it steepens in the upper part of the canyon. On this section of the trail, the view begins to open up to the west, and occasional stands of aspen produce a different feel to the landscape. A final steep set of switchbacks leads up to the Crest Trail junction, where the Three Rivers Trail ends. If you have the time and energy, a scramble up to the summit of White Horse Hill, just west of the trail junction, is worth the effort for the view up and down the mountain range, with the Tularosa basin to the west. Complete the hike by returning back down the canyon. The campground is open year round, and its lower elevation on the west side of the range makes the lower part of the Three Rivers Trail accessible all year long

For Further Information:

Lincoln National Forest
    Smokey Bear Ranger
    District
    901 Mechem Drive
    Ruidoso, NM 88345
    (505) 257-4095

Lincoln National Forest
    Supervisor's Office
    Federal Building, 11th
    and New York
    Alamogordo, NM
    88310
    (505) 437-6030

White Mountain Wilderness Map, Lincoln National Forest, prepared by U.S.D.A., Forest Service, Southwestern Region, 1988.

White Mountain Wilderness, a handout with trail and general Wilderness information, available from the Smokey Bear Ranger District Office in Ruidoso, NM.

Lincoln National Forest District Recreational Information, a pamphlet available through the Supervisor's Office in Alamogordo and the District Office in Ruidoso.

Hike #3. Three Rivers Trail (#44)

Distance — 11.2 miles round trip
Net elevation gain — 3,640 feet
Difficulty — Strenuous

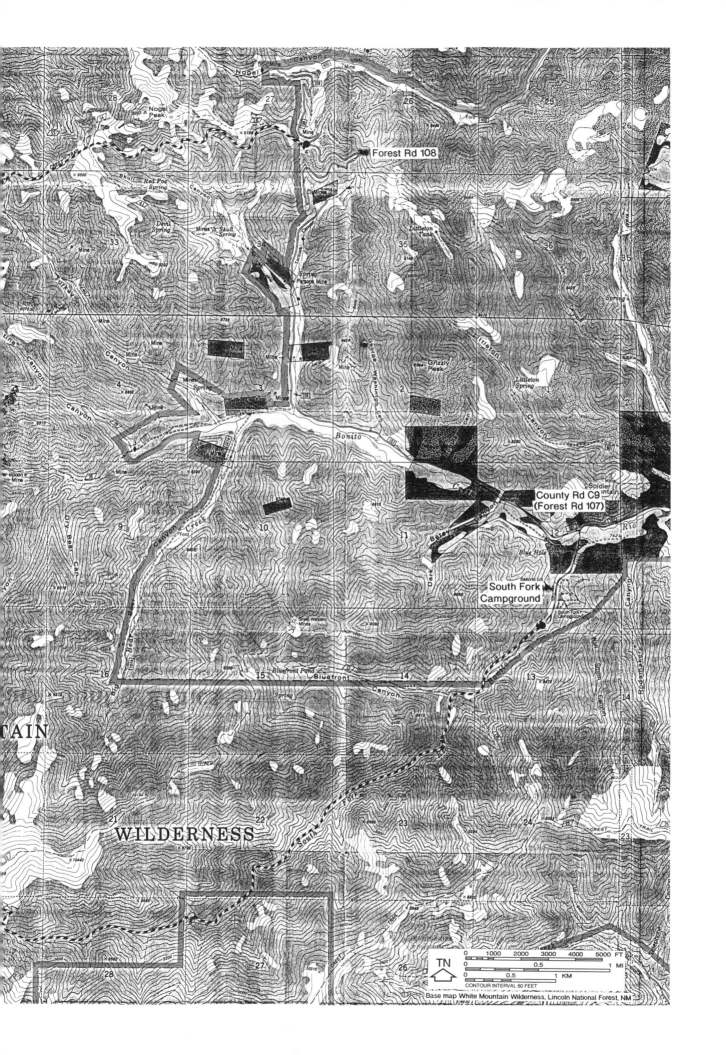

Forest Rd 108

County Rd C9
(Forest Rd 107)

South Fork
Campground

WILDERNESS

TN

| 0 | 1000 | 2000 | 3000 | 4000 | 5000 FT |

0   0.5   1 MI

0   0.5   1 KM

CONTOUR INTERVAL 80 FEET

Base map White Mountain Wilderness, Lincoln National Forest, NM

Capitan Peak Summit. Note the misspelling in the Forest Service place marker.

Capitan Mountains Wilderness

GENERAL DESCRIPTION

The Capitan Mountains are an isolated east-west range in the southeast quadrant of the state. The Wilderness Area is a 35,822-acre parcel located in the high, rugged east end of the range, about 15 miles northeast of the town of Capitan. The summit of the range is at 10,179 feet, and the base is almost 4,000 feet lower, making for a lot of steep elevation gradients and a noticeable divergence between the Upper Sonoran vegetation of the foothills and the old-growth forests of spruce, fir, and aspen (typical of the Canadian Zone) on top. One of the rockier mountain ranges that I can remember, the geological process here involves igneous rock that pushed up between layers of sedimentary rock, with most of the overlying sedimentary rock subsequently eroding away. An interesting sideline to the Capitan Mountains, which are included in the Lincoln National Forest, was the discovery of a small bear cub found here after a major forest fire in 1951. He was nursed back to health and given the name Smokey, and you know the rest of the story—he became the mascot for the great Forest Service fire prevention campaign, provided a nickname for highway patrol officers, and achieved a greater nationwide name recognition (and probably approval rating) than any human the country has produced since.

Water is present here and there in the

range but generally is not abundant, and you will need to carry drinking water on most of the trails. The only water I saw on the trails described in this section was that which I wrung out of my socks after hiking through the wet grassy meadows high on the mountain. The lack of water acts as a limitation to overnight backpacking, but if you are willing to carry along the necessary quantities, there are excellent campsites all along the summit ridge. And because this area seems to get very little hiking pressure, you are apt to have your pick of spots. There are no Forest Service campgrounds in the Capitans; the nearest ones appear to be on the east edge of the White Mountain Wilderness farther to the southwest.

Hiking in these mountains involves pleasant forest surroundings and nice views, with temperatures that are pleasant from spring through fall. Snow accumulations limit access from winter through early spring, and recent heavy rains may limit travel on some of the access roads. Check with the Ranger Station in Ruidoso for road and trail conditions.

Map Coverage

If you can still find any of the USGS 15-minute scale maps to purchase or copy, the Capitan Mountains map will take in almost all of the Wilderness Area, with the Arabela map catching the lower part of the Capitan Peak Trail. Otherwise, the USGS 7.5-minute scale coverage maps required includes the Capitan Pass and Capitan Peak maps for the Summit Trail, and the Capitan Peak, Kyle Harrison Canyon, Arroyo Serrano West, and Arabela maps for the Capitan Peak Trail. Alternatively, the Lincoln National Forest Map (Smokey Bear, Cloudcroft, and Mayhill Ranger Districts), or the Lincoln National Forest Travel Map, shows the trails and access roads but not the topography.

Access

Summit Trail. Drive on Highway 380 to an intersection with Forest Road 56, the Capitan Gap Road, which is located 2 miles east of the town of Capitan. Turn north on Forest Road 56, which continues north as a wide and well-maintained gravel road for 5.4 miles, until you are greeted by a sign warning you that the remainder of the road is primitive, not maintained, and hazardous for public use. If it has been raining recently, you should turn around at the sign and head for the Capitan Peak Trail, the White Mountains, or some other location. However, if road conditions are dry (the first 2 miles of road beyond the sign present the only potential mud problems), you should be able to drive most of the remaining road to the Summit Trail with four wheel drive or even a high clearance, two-wheel-drive vehicle. The next 1.7 miles of Forest Road 56 leads north past the warning sign up the Capitan Gap, at which point the road cuts back to the east and starts a long, rocky climb as it continues on or below the crest of the range. The road eventually alternates between level stretches and steep stretches that are rocky and rough but not particularly bad, unless you try to do it in a Trans Am or something similar. After you have gone 8.5 miles past the warning sign, you will come to a sign for Corral Canyon; this is about 1.3 miles past the Santa Rita Canyon/Ferris Canyon sign. At the Corral Canyon sign is perhaps your last good opportunity to pull your vehicle off the road and hike the remaining 2.3 miles of road up to the communications facility, which lies near the trailhead for the Summit Trail. This remaining stretch of road deteriorates into some horrendous stretches that climb up rocky talus slopes, with little opportunity to turn around and retreat. The road surface is formidable and somewhat three

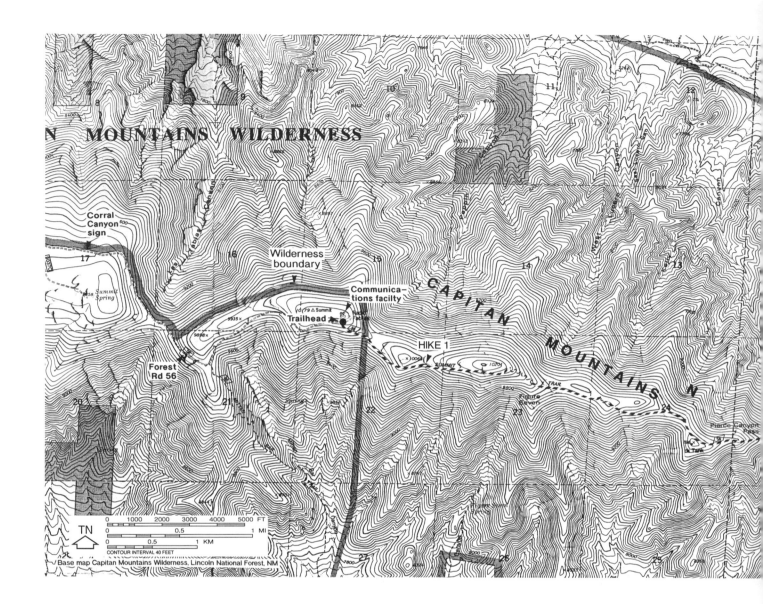

Base map Capitan Mountains Wilderness, Lincoln National Forest, NM

dimensional, but it seems to be driven fairly regularly by four wheel drive vehicles and pickups with compound low gearing. You will pass the trailhead shortly before reaching the communications facility, where you can park your vehicle.

Capitan Peak Trail. From Highway 380 at the east end of the town of Capitan, turn north on Highway 246 and travel 32.5 miles, as the road skirts the west and north sides of the Capitan Mountains, to the intersection with Forest Road 130 (this intersection can also be reached by taking Highway 246 north and west from Roswell). Along the way, you will pass Smokey Bear State Park, which has various exhibits and a short trail to Smokey's gravesite. Turn south on Forest Road 130 and follow it 3.8 miles to the sign marking the trailhead for the Capitan

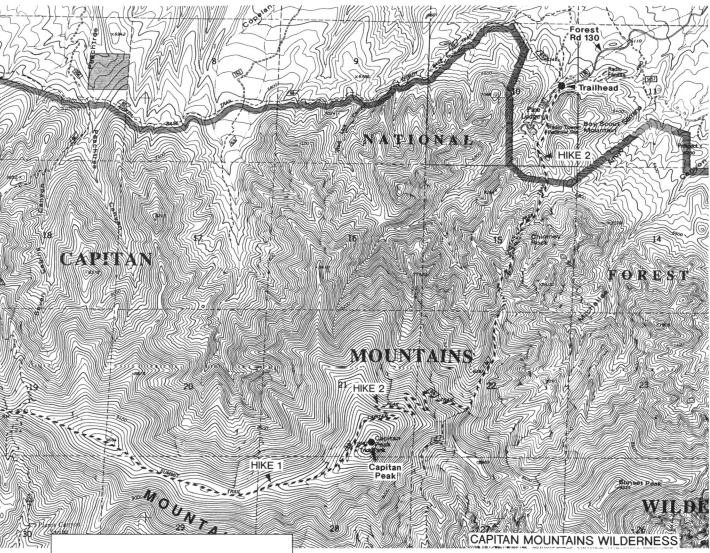

Hike #1. Summit Trail (#58)

Distance — 14 miles round trip to
Capitan Peak
Net elevation gain — Loses 900
feet to Pierce Canyon Pass, then
gains 840 feet to Capitan Peak
Difficulty — Easy to moderate

Hike #2. Capitan Peak Trail (#64)

Distance — 14 miles round trip to
Capitan Peak
Net elevation gain — 3,880 feet
Difficulty — Strenuous

Peak Trail. The forest road is rocky but
looks to be negotiable by passenger cars
with a reasonable amount of road clearance. You can park at the standard
trailhead, or continue up the rough road a
short distance farther where the road ends.

Hiking Trails

The trail layout for the Capitan Mountains Wilderness is similar to that for
several of the other isolated mountain

ranges in the state: there is one trail, which runs along the crest of the summit ridge and connects the other trails, which start near the base of the mountain and travel up the sides to join the crest or summit trail at the top. There is also a trail along the north base of the Wilderness. There are eight designated trails in the Wilderness, and although I haven't hiked them all, none of them apparently receives very much hiking traffic, but they are still well-enough marked so that route finding is generally not a problem. The Summit Trail has a very moderate elevation differential, but the trails that climb to the top are steep enough to be classified as strenuous. The trail intersections are usually well marked with trail signs, although as is the case with numerous other mountain areas in the state, the local black bear population enjoys chewing on the signs, and you will find them in various states of readability. Actually, the particular chewing fetish here seems to involve a preference for the posts on which the signs are mounted. I have long been curious as to this trail-sign chewing phenomenon and have finally arrived at a theory: The government (in a secret conspiracy to provide work for the sign-making industry) requires in its sign procurement process that the signs and mounting posts be pressure-treated with something that tastes good to bears, like maybe a solution of hot bacon grease, prior to installation. Now, black bears may be shy and reclusive, but they like to eat and they have big, strong teeth that could chew the hatch off a Sherman tank if it contained food. So with trail signs, it's a total mismatch; when the bears get through with them, they end up looking like training targets on a hand grenade range. Just remember to bring a trail map with you.

TRAIL DESCRIPTIONS

Hike #1. Summit Trail (#58)

As the name implies, the Summit Trail runs along the summit ridge, covering 7 miles from the communications facility at the true summit of the range on the west end to Capitan Peak on the east end, for a round-trip distance of 14 miles. The trail actually passes below Capitan Peak, with a short spur trail leading up to the peak, and continues about 2 miles farther to the east, but the segment of trail continuing east of the peak is of little interest compared to the summit of Capitan Peak, unless you intend to access trails #62 or #64. Capitan Peak is a lovely grass-covered summit with the finest views in the range, and the Summit Trail provides a scenic approach hike that is also the easiest, with a modest net elevation differential of less than 1,000 feet. The most difficult part may be the drive up to the trailhead (see "Access" directions), but even if you decide to hike the last 2 miles or so of the approach road, the hike is still worthwhile, since the west end of the trail is perhaps the nicest part, as it travels through frequent meadows that are truly beautiful with lots of wildflowers and good views off to the south. The trail runs through numerous stretches of broken talus and a formidable amount of work has been done, in the not-too-recent past, excavating the trail surface down into the rock, which is piled to the side, creating the appearance of low parallel rock walls bordering the trail in places. The trail surface is good and easy to follow, and since it basically follows the top of the crest line, it is an easy matter to find the route again if you do happen to temporarily lose your way.

The trailhead is clearly marked on the east side of the approach road just below the communications facility on the summit. The trail drops down along the ridge to the east and alternates between open meadows and forest cover over a 4-mile stretch that leads to Pierce Canyon Pass, where side trails drop down the sides of the mountain in both directions: Seven Cabins trailhead, 6 miles to the north, and Forest Road 256, 4 miles to the south. From the pass, the trail continues another 3 miles east, where a trail sign indicates a faint spur trail to the south leading to Capitan Peak. Make your way up the ridge to the summit, bypassing some Forest Service structures on the way up. You will want to spend some time on the summit admiring the view all around, including a nice view back west along the summit ridge on which you approached; that is, unless part of the view you are observing includes approaching black clouds and lightening bolts, in which case you should beat a hasty retreat back off the summit. This is a hike you are almost sure to enjoy, and it may even be worth enduring the drive up the approach road. Just make sure you come in a stout vehicle, and get started early, particularly if you expect rain. Total time to do the hike is 6 to 9 hours. If you hike up the final stretch of the approach road add another 2 to 3 hours.

Hike #2. Capitan Peak Trail (#64)

This trail is a strenuous day hike of 14 miles round trip and 3,880 feet of elevation gain, which leads up the northeast side of the range to Capitan Peak. The approach road to the trailhead is the easiest of any of the trails on the mountain, making this a good choice when the weather has been rainy. You could do a backpacking trip using this trail, but there are no water sources along the trail and you probably won't want to pack the necessary quantities on your back. If you

do, however, the best campsites are at numerous locations along the summit ridge. The route primarily climbs through pleasant forest cover with some fine, large specimens of fir and spruce and lots of ponderosa and aspen, and occasional scenic views on the upper part of the trail. The trail surface is good and the trail is easy to follow, although there are a few competing side paths that intersect on the lower part of the trail. The trailhead and trail intersections are marked with trail signs, which currently have not been eaten by bears, although this could change. In any case, it is easy to find your way along the route, which includes a segment of almost 2 miles of the Summit Trail to gain access to Capitan Peak. It is worth pushing all the way up to the summit of Capitan Peak, which is situated in an inviting open area of grass and shrubbery with outstanding views in every direction. The hike provides a good workout and an enjoyable outing.

Read the "Access" directions to locate the trailhead. At the trail sign, the trail contours along the hillside above the Pine Lodge cabins and you will pass a side trail that provides an alternative starting point, if you should want to drive the last part of the access road. After you have ascended past the last of the cabins, the trail begins a fairly steep ascent to gain a ridge system leading up the mountain. There are occasional views to the north and switchbacks on the steepest sections to take the edge off the grade. After the trail tops out on the summit ridge, there is an intersection with the Summit Trail and the Pancho Canyon Trail. Take the Summit Trail to the west and follow it as it keeps climbing 1.5 to 2 miles, past a long open area on the mountain side with a good view west along the summit ridge, to a trail sign shortly beyond, which points south toward Capitan Peak. You may notice a faint trail along the way, which cuts north up the mountain side and which has evidently been worn in by people dropping down off the peak to cut the trail, but you are probably better off following the main trail. From the Capitan Peak trail sign, scramble up the indistinct side trail for several hundred yards to the summit. This is a great lunch spot if the weather is nice. The Summit Trail, which continues west, provides a nice continuation to the hike if you have the time and energy, but otherwise, complete the hike by dropping back down your ascent route.

For Further Information:

Smokey Bear Ranger
  Station
901 Mechem Drive
Ruidoso, NM 88345
(505) 257-4095

Three Rivers
Petroglyph Site

Three Rivers Petroglyph
Site, Looking East toward
the White Mountain
Range

GENERAL DESCRIPTION

Three Rivers Petroglyph Site is located
on the arid floor of the Tularosa Basin, west
of the White Mountain range and between
the towns of Carrizozo and Tularosa. The
central feature of the site is an extraordinary collection of some 20,000 petroglyphs
placed on the boulders of a basaltic ridge by
the prehistoric inhabitants of a nearby
village. Petroglyphs are a form of rock art,
including symbols depicting animal life,
human forms, or geometric patterns that
are carved or pecked into the dark surface
veneer covering the rocks. The people who
created the petroglyphs were of the Jornada
Branch of the Mogollon Indian culture, a
culture that evolved about 900 A.D. into a
society identified by recognizable traits and
artifacts. These people settled in the area in
about 1000 A.D. and vanished some 400
years later, an interval of time representing
many generations of families and indicative
of a society that was well adapted to the
environment and possessed of the mores
and precepts that maintained a cohesive
social order. They subsisted by hunting
game and gathering wild edible plants, and
took advantage of the nearby year-round
stream of water flowing out of the White
Mountains to grow corn, beans, and squash.
And they engaged in commerce by trading
extensively with other tribes throughout
the Southwest. Did this ancient community
resemble something of an early day art
colony that developed from a locally
pervasive tendency toward organized

artistic avocation, encouraged by the
fortuitous presence of a natural canvas in
the form of smooth basaltic slabs? Or were
the petroglyphs a rigidly controlled part of
the religious and social ritual? Or perhaps a
few talented locals simply enjoyed doodling
on the rocks in their spare time. Your guess
is as good as any, for even though there are
plenty of theories to go around, the time
and information gap between the prehistoric cultures and even present-day Indian
societies that may be distantly related to
them, is simply too great to fully understand the why and wherefore of the old
rock art. Too much has been lost in the
interim. And so, while the subject matter of
some of the petroglyphs carries through,
you are left with your own guesswork and
the speculation of other learned individuals
to fill in the missing pieces of the puzzle.
But one thing seems certain: when you

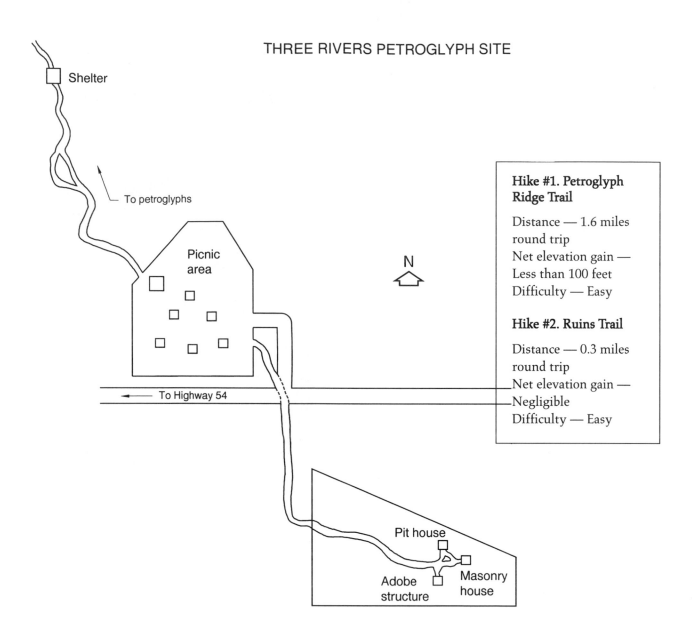

Hike #1. Petroglyph Ridge Trail

Distance — 1.6 miles round trip
Net elevation gain — Less than 100 feet
Difficulty — Easy

Hike #2. Ruins Trail

Distance — 0.3 miles round trip
Net elevation gain — Negligible
Difficulty — Easy

look upon these renderings, you see not only an interesting artistic presentation, but you look into the soul of a human being who was fundamentally much the same as yourself, expressing a definite concept for a definite purpose.

At the center of the Recreation Site is a picnic area with shelters and restrooms. Overnight camping is permitted. Additional camping is available a short drive farther to the east at the Forest Service Three Rivers Campground (see "Access" directions for

the White Mountain Wilderness). Two short trails with interpretive signs are included within the Recreation Site, one leading along the main petroglyph ridge and the other to the nearby, partially excavated village. The site is open year round and weather is usually not that much of a factor, although it can get hot in summer and you should have a good sun hat. Since the area is accessible by paved road, the brief thunderstorms that happen in late summer and early fall should not limit access, although you will want to avoid the high spots when lightning is imminent. When you visit, bring along water to drink, don't forget camera and film, and don't touch any of the petroglyphs.

Map Coverage

This is a small area, and not appropriate for a topo map. There is a small map of the area shown on the guide brochure available at the picnic area or from the Las Cruces BLM office.

Access

Drive on Highway 54, 28 miles south from Carrizozo or 17 miles north from Tularosa, to Three Rivers, an apparently uninhabited wide spot in the road, which is mainly identifiable by a road sign marking the turnoff to the Three Rivers Petroglyph Site. Turn east on County Road B30/Forest Road 579, and continue a little under 5 miles to a BLM sign that directs you to the petroglyph site just north of the road.

Hiking Trails

The trails at the recreation site are short walks with negligible elevation gain, on manicured paths from which it would be almost impossible to get lost. Though you won't get much exercise on these trails, the archaeology is interesting and worth the trip to see if you are in the area. From the top of the Petroglyph Ridge Trail, there is a nice view of the surrounding Tularosa Basin and the White Mountains off to the east.

TRAIL DESCRIPTIONS

Hike #1. Petroglyph Ridge Trail

This is the trail to the main body of petroglyphs, which begins at the northwest corner of the picnic area and leads up along the crest of the prominent ridge to the north. The round-trip distance is 1.6 miles along a well-worn path. This is one of the most extensive collections of Native American rock art in the Southwest, and your progress along the trail will be slow, as there are numerous places to diverge off the main trail and view the many petroglyphs scattered about the ridge. There are many panels of rock art and nice views of the surrounding landscape, so allow adequate time to explore. The rock art is an irreplaceable treasure and should not be touched, chalked, or otherwise impacted. And if you see anyone defacing rock art or adding their own, shoot on sight (my preference) or notify the BLM at (505) 525-8228 or 1-800-NEIGHBOR.

Hike #2. Ruins Trail

The trail to the prehistoric village site begins at the east end of the picnic area and leads south across the access road to an area of subtle mounds and outlines where the ancient village was located. The diverse assortment of potsherds (no collecting allowed) that proliferate throughout the vicinity help attest to the lengthy occupation period. Several dwellings have been excavated, and interpretive signs help explain what is known about the site and the former inhabitants. Here, dreams were dreamed, lives were lived, and small dark-skinned, desert-hardened people began the short walk to the basalt ridge to the northwest to scout for game and draw their mysterious symbols on the blackened rocks.

Although you probably won't encounter any, rattlesnakes inhabit the vicinity, and caution is advised, particularly if you have children along.

For further Information:

Bureau of Land Management
Las Cruces District Office
1800 Marques Street
Las Cruces, NM 88005
(505) 528-8228

Guide to Three Rivers Petroglyph Site and Picnic Area, a brochure available at the picnic area, the Las Cruces BLM office, and several other BLM offices around the state.

Rim Trail in the Sacramento Mountains

Sacramento Mountains

GENERAL INFORMATION

The Sacramento Mountains are the soaring escarpment that you see when driving from Carrizozo down to Alamogordo, which borders the Tularosa Basin on the east side. The range is 90 miles long in a north-south direction and includes several subranges, including the Jicarilla, Capitan, and Sierra Blanca Mountains, but is usually thought of as that part of the range south of Highway 70 at the north end down to the

Guadalupe Mountains at the south end. From the steep west side, where the mountains rise almost 5,000 feet above the floor of the Tularosa Basin, the range slopes gently to the east, with extensive forests in the vicinity of 9,000 feet elevation providing numerous trails and campgrounds. This area is included in the Lincoln National Forest, and the administrators have seen fit to open most of the trails to motorized vehicles up to 40 inches wide (this magic number was evidently intended to include anything smaller than a jeep), but I have had the good fortune of not encountering any of these on the trails and it may not be that much of a problem. The geology of the mountains includes a thick layer of limestone overlying a granite base, and most of the trails have rocky sections of broken limestone or granite. Water is fairly abundant in the range, but its availability depends on the individual trail. The climate and plant life vary widely depending upon the elevation; the lower part of the west side (Dog Canyon) produces year-round hiking in a Chihuahuan Desert environment, with typical vegetation such as agave, sotol, mesquite, and ocotillo cactus, while the higher areas in the vicinity of Cloudcroft and Mayhill primarily include forests of ponderosa pine, aspen, and Douglas fir, with high grassy meadows and a hiking season that begins when the snows melt out in April, until mid- to late November. The desert hiking is most pleasant if avoided during the hottest part of summer, but this time of year is ideal for the higher forest trails. The Sacramento Range was the frequent home and hunting ground of the Apache Indians, and the present-day Mescalero Apache Reservation is located in the range just to the north of Highway 70. The town of Cloudcroft was established when the Southern Pacific Railroad built a rail line to the location to transport logs out of the mountains, and it remains today as a tourist destination with plenty of Forest Service campgrounds in the vicinity to accommodate car campers. While the Sacramento Mountains are relatively overlooked by New Mexico hikers, they are popular with our friends from the state of Texas, and with good reason: they have a lot of nice scenery, some good hikes, and are worth the trip to visit.

Map Coverage

The best maps to get for trail coverage are the Lincoln National Forest Map for the Smokey Bear, Cloudcroft, and Mayhill Ranger Districts (this is all one map), and the Travel Map for the Lincoln National Forest. The latter map is the better of the two, in that it more or less duplicates the information on the standard forest map while showing more trails, and also includes the other ranger districts. It also distinguishes between the trails that permit motor vehicle traffic and those that do not. The travel map can be obtained at the local Forest Service Ranger District offices (see "For Further Information" at the end of the section) or at the Regional Distribution Center in Albuquerque. USGS 7.5-minute scale map coverage is included with the individual hiking trail descriptions.

Access

To reach the Dog Canyon hike, take Highway 70/82 south from Tularosa or east from Las Cruces to the Highway 54 intersection on the south edge of Alamogordo. Drive south on Highway 54, 8.7 miles to the turnoff for Oliver Lee State Park, and continue east 4.2 miles to the Visitor Center for the park.

The other hikes described below use the town of Cloudcroft as a reference point. To reach Cloudcroft, take Highway 70 to about a mile north of Alamogordo, where Highway 82 branches off to the east. Follow Highway 82 east for 16 miles to Cloudcroft. All the hikes described in this section have trailheads that are accessed by paved roads.

Hiking Trails

The Travel Map for the Lincoln National Forest shows quite a few trails in the Sacramento Mountains, from which I have selected three hikes that offer some

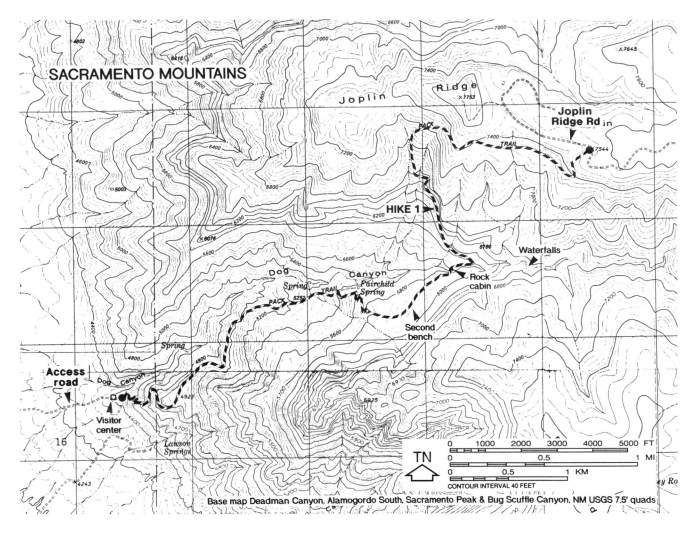

Base map Deadman Canyon, Alamogordo South, Sacramento Peak & Bug Scuffle Canyon, NM USGS 7.5' quads

divergent alternatives in difficulty, trail length, and ecosystems. The trails are easy to get to and are traveled enough that they are well worn and easy to follow, even though tree blazes are scarce and trail signs have often been chewed up by bears. The Cloudcroft Ranger Station is located at the west end of town and is a handy stopping-off point for trails in that vicinity if you have questions. Afternoon rain showers are common in late summer, particularly in the higher elevations, and some rain gear should be included in your day pack. And, of course, don't forget to pack some water.

TRAIL DESCRIPTION

Hike #1. Dog Canyon Trail (#106)

Dog Canyon is one of the major canyons that breach the steep western escarpment of the Sacramento Range and provide a natural route to the high forests to the east. It is complete with a year-round flow of water in parts of the canyon and blessed with some excellent scenery, which includes waterfalls, towering rock walls, grassy benches, and picturesque Chihuahuan vegetation in the lower part of the canyon. This natural pathway has been used by man for over

> **Hike #1. Dog Canyon Trail (#106)**
>
> Distance — 8.4 (or 4.8 to Line Cabin) miles round trip
> Net elevation gain — 3,150 feet (or 1,400 feet to Line Cabin)
> Difficulty — Moderate to strenuous

4,000 years and was a notable refuge of the Apache Indians in their well-known struggle against the U.S. Army. The canyon offered food and water, was easily defended, and provided an escape route to the mountains to the east. A number of skirmishes were fought there, and numerous accounts of these can be found in the old Army reports and in the recollections of white and Apache participants. The local history of the area was also flavored by two other characters who homesteaded near the mouth of the canyon in the late 1880s. Francois-Jean "Frenchy" Rochas was a French immigrant who ran cattle and cultivated an orchard just outside the canyon, and was found murdered in his cabin in 1894. An archaeological excavation of the cabin site produced valuable insight into the lifestyle of the Frenchman in his solitary existence, and his partially reconstructed cabin can be viewed by visitors to the Oliver Lee Memorial State Park. The State Park is established at the mouth of the canyon and was named for Oliver Lee, a cattleman and state legislator who lived about a mile from the canyon and once controlled the largest ranching enterprise in southern New Mexico. He was a colorful and controversial (he was a politician) figure who was indicted for the murder of one man and is thought by some to be responsible for the demise of Frenchy Rochas as well. The State Park includes a campground and a Visitor Center with historical paraphernalia and interpretive information. There is a small fee charged to enter the State Park, and, therefore, to hike the trail.

The Dog Canyon Trail is a steep path that climbs from the park Visitor Center to the forests above the canyon and can be done as a 4.2-mile one-way hike, with a car shuttle in place on the Joplin Ridge forest road about 1 miles southwest of Sacramento Peak. Or it can be hiked to the top and back as a 8.4-mile round-trip

Looking West from the Dog Canyon Trail

hike. The elevation gain to the top is 3,150 feet. The most commonly hiked variation for this trail is to hike up to the Line Cabin, a partially standing rock cabin just beyond the Second Bench, and return back down the trail. This is a 4.8-mile round-trip hike, with 1,400 feet of elevation gain. The Line Cabin is situated along a flowing stream 0.5 miles below a series of scenic waterfalls, and provides a refreshing rest stop before either heading back down the trail or continuing on to the steep upper section. Spring and fall are the best times of year to do this trail; things get toasty hot in June and July. However, an early morning start will make for a pleasant summer hike. Allow a full day to hike all the way up the trail and return, or a half day to do the round trip to the Line Cabin. Take along plenty of drinking water, a brimmed hat, and rain gear. If you want to bring along topo maps (although they aren't really needed), the ones to have are the USGS 7.5-minute scale Sacramento Peak and Alamogordo South quads.

To locate the trailhead at Oliver Lee State Park, refer to the "Access" directions above. The trail begins at the east end of the Visitor Center (there is a short nature trail leading down into the canyon that you may want to explore first) and heads up a series of switchbacks on the south side of the canyon. This lower section of trail goes up rock slabs and is a little faint in places but not hard to follow; by the time the trail has reached the First Bench, a relatively level plain 500 feet above the initial steep section, the trail is well worn and very obvious all the way to the top. The trail levels out for a distance and then completes an ascent to the Second Bench, a broad, grassy field with nice scenery all around, which probably offers the best area for camping. The trail up to the Second Bench goes through vegetation typical of the Chihuahuan Desert, which

most hikers will find unusual as well as beautiful. This section of trail also has two spur trails that branch off to the left, one leading to a spring at a grove of mountain ash down the side of the canyon; the main trail takes the right fork in both instances. From the Second Bench, it is a short descent to a stream crossing at the small clearing where the Line Cabin is located. This clearing is a bit small and crowded with hikers to make a good campsite, but it makes a good rest spot. A 0.5-mile side hike up the creek leads to the waterfalls. Above the Line Cabin, the trail steepens as it ascends the "Eyebrow," a rock band of cliffs. This ancient Indian trail ascends about 1,000 feet in the next mile to gain the upper rim of the canyon before leveling out and completing the final mile to the marked trailhead at the Joplin Ridge Road. Even if you don't intend to go all the way to the top, it is worth hiking up the next 0.5 miles or so above the Line Cabin. The views on this stretch are the best on the entire hike. You have a super view of the canyon below and of the Tularosa Basin beyond, including the south end of the White Sands dune field.

Hike #2. Rim Trail (#T105)

The Rim Trail is a 14-mile-long (one-way) path through oak, aspen, and conifer forests that follows a route near the crest of the range and has been knitted together from a combination of old Indian trails, railroad grades, and logging roads, with a few new connecting stretches thrown in. The elevation gain from the trailhead to the high point of the trail is a modest 1,200 feet, which results in a comfortable hiking gradient through the shade of pleasant forest surroundings with occasional vistas. The trail is popular, although not heavily hiked, and is well worn and easy to follow, despite some of the trail intersections not being marked with trail signs. This is one of the trails that permits

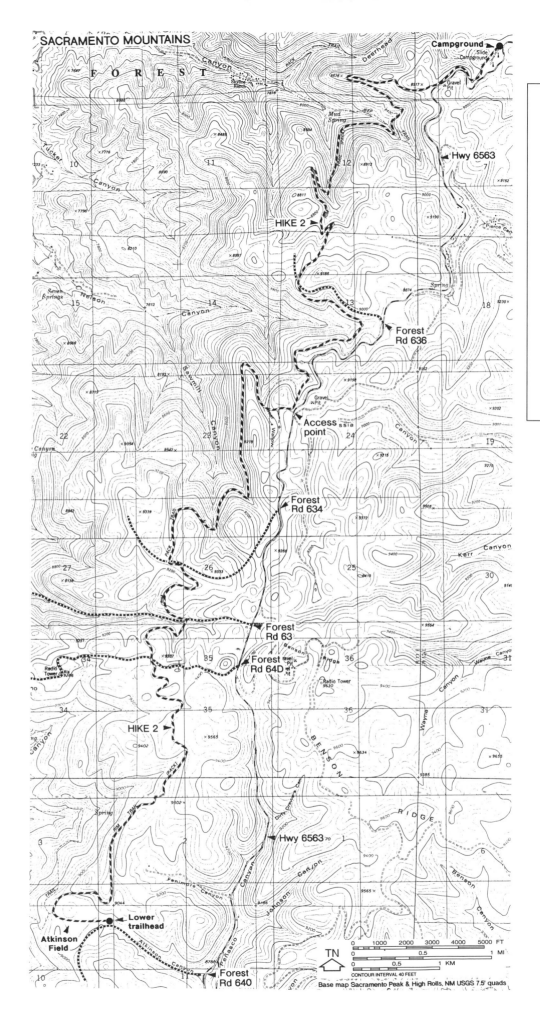

SACRAMENTO MOUNTAINS

F O R E S T

Campground
Slide
Campground

Hwy 6563

HIKE 2

Forest
Rd 636

Access
point

Forest
Rd 634

Forest
Rd 63

Forest
Rd 64D

Radio Tower

HIKE 2

Hwy 6563

Lower
trailhead

Atkinson
Field

Forest
Rd 640

TN

0   1000 2000 3000 4000 5000 FT
0   0.5   1 MI
0   0.5   1 KM
CONTOUR INTERVAL 40 FEET
Base map Sacramento Peak & High Rolls, NM USGS 7.5' quads

Hike #2. Rim Trail (#T105)

Distance — 14.0 miles one way or 28 miles round trip

Net elevation gain — 1,200 feet

Difficulty — Easy to moderate

Hike #3. Osha Trail (#T10)

Distance — 2.6 miles round trip

Net elevation gain — 150 feet

Difficulty — Easy

309

motorcycles, etc., and in fact, a sign at the trailhead informs the visitor that the trail is "Adopted and Maintained" by the Prairie Dawg Motorcycle Club. Even though the Dawgs seem to be more into adoption than trail maintenance, the trail surface is in reasonably good condition, all things considered. Another unusual feature of the trail is the placement of mile markers along the trail, beginning at the north end, which help you keep track of your progress. There is great potential for flexibility in planning a modified variation of the Rim Trail hike, because both end points can be accessed and there are a number of additional access points along the length of the trail. Highway 6563 runs roughly parallel to the trail on the east side, and four different forest roads run west from the highway to cut the trail, and there are two or more points of access where the trail contours to within a short distance of the highway. The use of a car shuttle is especially appropriate for this trail to do a one-way hike, either the full length of the trail or using one of the intermediate access points. Water is not available along the trail and should be carried with you. The weather should be mild and pleasant during most of the hiking season, but the high country can see cold and wet conditions just about any month of the year, and appropriate rain gear and warm clothing should be carried along just in case. Hiking time to do the full trail one way is 6 to 9 hours; occasional campsites are to be found for backpacking, but no water. The USGS 7.5-minute scale topo maps for the area are the Sacramento Peak and High Rolls quads.

To locate the north trailhead, drive to the Highway 130/6563 intersection at the west end of Cloudcroft, and follow Highway 6563 south for 0.2 miles to the entrance to the Slide Group Campground. Park there at the parking area and find

the trailhead, marked by a trail sign, at the fence just across the entrance road. The south trailhead can be reached by driving south on Highway 6563, 8.6 miles south of the Highway 130/6563 intersection to Forest Road 640, a dirt road that travels west up Atkinson Canyon. Drive up Forest Road 640 a little over 1 mile and take a double-track dirt path that branches off to the right from the Forest Road just before a large dirt berm. This spur road leads about 100 feet to the east edge of a large grassy meadow (Atkinson Field) where the route is blocked by logs. There is no trail sign at present, but if you follow the dirt road on across to the west side of the meadow and into the tree line, you will intersect the Rim Trail, which turns north and leads through the forest above the meadow. The trail also continues south for some distance farther, but it is not clear just where it eventually ends and Atkinson Field is generally regarded as the south terminus at present.

As previously mentioned, the trail is straightforward and easy to follow, and no running trail narrative is necessary. Take along a copy of the trail map in this book to help you locate the intermediate access points, or get a trail handout from the Cloudcroft Ranger Station, which includes a map of the trail along with some additional trail info. You may be momentarily confused when the trail crosses some of the forest roads, but the entrances are clearly marked on both sides of the roads and you won't have any trouble. As you are marking your progress with the mile markers, you may notice that some mile intervals seem to be taking twice as long to accomplish as most of the others; you will discover that this is because a few of the markers are missing. If you are the analytical type, the mile markers are also a good way to pin down your typical hiking speed—a good thing to know when estimating trail distances hiked on similar terrain.

Hike #3. Osha Trail (#T10)

This is a short 2.6-mile loop trail with little elevation gain and easy access points. It is an easy hike and just long enough to give you a flavor of the forest environment in the Cloudcroft area, or you can use it as a warmup for one of the longer trails. The trail is well used and easy to follow as it loops through forest cover of spruce, fir, and aspen. You may encounter wet spots along the trail, but no drinking water. The name for the trail comes from the osha plant. A folk medicinal herb uses the root of the plant, and although the plant smells like celery, it resembles the highly poisonous Hemlock plant and should not be sampled unless you are sure of your identification. Sample the trail food you brought with you instead. The hiking season begins for the Osha Trail as soon as the winter snows have melted, usually by early April (but expect a lot of mud until things dry

out) and lasts until the snows begin to accumulate again in late fall. Expect afternoon rains in July and August.

The primary access point for the trail is at a small parking area on the north side of Highway 82, about 1 mile west of Cloudcroft. There is also a short spur trail leading to the hike from the Pine Campground, which can be reached by driving east about 0.5 miles from Cloudcroft on Highway 82 and turning north on Highway 244 for 0.6 miles to the campground entrance on the west side of the road. From the Highway 82 trailhead, there is a sign at the trailhead that tells you that you are in the right place, and a path that leads north up into the woods. This is the steepest part of the hike, as the short initial section climbs uphill to gain the main loop. After you intersect the loop trail, you can turn either east or west and return via the loop back to this intersection. Allow 1 to 2 hours to do the hike.

For Further Information:

Cloudcroft Ranger Station
P.O. Box 288
Cloudcroft, NM 88317
(505) 682-2551

Mayhill Ranger Station
P.O. Box 5
Mayhill, NM 88339
(505) 687-3411

Forest Supervisor, Lincoln
National Forest
Federal Building, 11th
and New York
Alamogordo, NM
88310
(505) 437-6030

Oliver Lee Memorial State
Park
409 Dog Canyon Road
Alamogordo, NM
88310
(505) 437-8284

White Sands National Monument

GENERAL INFORMATION

White Sands National Monument is a 147,200-acre preserve located 15 miles southwest of the city of Alamogordo in south-central New Mexico. It contains the major part of the largest gypsum dune field in the world, a dazzling expanse of fine-grained gypsum sand stretching across miles of consecutive dunes, some of which are 30 or more feet high. The process that caused the dunes to form began long ago when water draining off the mountains and highlands surrounding the Tularosa Basin began dissolving vast gypsum deposits located within the mountains and redepositing the gypsum in shallow lakes at the lowest part of the basin. The prevailing winds periodically dry up the lake beds and carry off the disintegrated gypsum crystals, in the form of fine grains of sand, toward the northeast. Thousands of years of sand storms have resulted in a thick and extensive blanket of brilliant white sand, which forms into dunes and marches inexorably in the direction of the wind. A Visitor Center is located at the entrance to the Monument just off Highway 70/83, which contains the usual Visitor Center stuff, including interpretive displays as well as the only water to be found. A 16-

Early Morning in White Sands National Monument

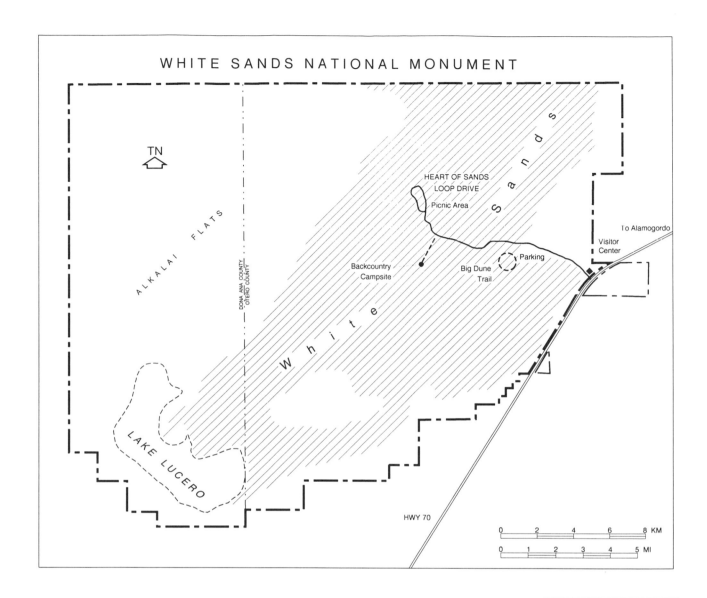

WHITE SANDS NATIONAL MONUMENT

HEART OF SANDS
LOOP DRIVE

Picnic Area

To Alamogordo

Visitor
Center

Parking

Backcountry
Campsite

Big Dune
Trail

TN

ALKALAI FLATS

DONA ANA COUNTY
OTERO COUNTY

White   Sands

LAKE LUCERO

HWY 70

| 0 | 2 | 4 | 6 | 8 KM |
| 0 | 1 | 2 | 3 | 4 | 5 MI |

---

mile round-trip road leads from the
Visitor Center into the heart of the dune
fields and provides access to the only
established hiking trail in the Monument.
The climate in the area tends to be hot
and dry for much of the year, making the
cooler months the best time to visit.
Winter is generally pleasant, unless the
weather is unusually cold. Surprisingly, a
hardy selection of plant life, including
soaptree yucca, rabbitbrush, squawbush,

four-wing saltbush, and Indian rice grass,
is able to adapt and grow on all but the
most active dunes. Because the water table
is often quite near the surface, tamarisk
and cottonwood trees are occasionally
seen. No permits are required for
dayhiking, but a small entrance fee is
collected at the access road. Backcountry
camping is allowed, but a permit must be
obtained at the Visitor Center. No car
camping is allowed within the Monument,

> **Hike #1. The Big
> Dune Trail**
>
> Distance — 1 mile
> loop
> Net elevation gain
> — Negligible
> Difficulty — Easy

and the nearest public campground alternatives are in the Lincoln National Forest 35 miles to the east, the Aguirre Springs Campground in the Organ Mountains 30 miles to the southwest, and the Oliver Lee Memorial State Park 10 miles south of Alamogordo. Walking through these sand dunes is truly a unique experience and well worth the trip. Don't make the mistake of failing to bring along enough drinking water or of forgetting to bring your camera and sunglasses.

Map Coverage

The best map to get for an overall perspective of the area is the U.S. Geological Survey 1:100,000-scale Sands map. The 7.5-minute maps won't do you much good. There is also a small map of the area on the White Sands brochure available at the Visitor Center.

Access

From the town of Alamogordo drive southwest on Highway 70/82. At the 13-mile point, you will see the turnoff to the Park Headquarters just off the road. The dunes road begins just behind the Visitor Center. The Big Dune Trail begins several miles down the road at a parking area to the left.

Hiking Trails

The White Sands dune field is immense, but it is unlikely that you will get too far away from the access road. You just don't have to get very far back in the dunes to get away from people and to enjoy the scenic beauty of the area. If you do plan on hiking very far back in, bring water and a compass. The best way to get started is probably to hike the one established trail in the monument, the Big Dune Trail.

TRAIL DESCRIPTION

Hike #1. The Big Dune Trail

Locate the trailhead at the parking area several miles along the paved access road from the entrance. This is a loop trail about 1 mile in length, which can take up to an hour to hike, or considerably less, depending upon how extensively you scope out the scenery. Trail guides are available at the trailhead or in the Visitor Center, which correlate to numbered posts marking the trail. For each station, the guide provides interpretive insight into the plant life, wildlife, or geology of the area. You can follow the station posts to complete the hike or add a few side hikes to investigate other interesting areas. This is an easy hike with negligible elevation gain which you may find pleasant to do barefoot—but do bring your shoes along with you.

For Further Information:

White Sands National
  Monument
  Box 458
  Alamogordo, NM
  88310
  (505) 479-6124

The Big Dune Trail Guide,
  Published by South-
  west Parks and
  Monuments Associa-
  tion, Box 1562, Globe,
  AZ 85501

Organon Mountains

GENERAL DESCRIPTION

The Organ Mountains are a localized north-south range in the south-central part of the state, standing due east of the city of Las Cruces and extending toward El Paso. From the base of the mountains on the east rim of the Rio Grande trough, they soar abruptly upward, climbing approximately 4,000 feet to a high point of 9,012 feet at the summit of Organ Needle. The central feature of the range is the picturesque ridge of rugged granite spires, vaguely resembling a row of great organ pipes, and forming a significant landmark visible throughout the region. The mountains are spectacularly wild and primitive, especially as one gains eleva-

tion and nears the jagged granite spires and towers. The arid climate permits only about 16 inches of precipitation on the upper elevations of the mountains and about half that lower down, so water is not abundant and the vegetation cover is what you would expect in a high desert environment. Ponderosa pines in the upper reaches give way in the lower elevations to plant life such as piñon, juniper, mountain mahogany, creosote, yucca, cacti, and numerous desert shrubs and grasses. The wonderful diversity of plant life is interesting to study and identify, and in particular, the cactus blooms in spring and summer are not to be missed. The flowers of the barrel cactus are magnificent and have formed the focal point of innumerable color photographs. Also of special interest is the alligator juniper, the bark of which looks to have taken its inspiration from the swamp reptiles of Louisiana. And speaking of

Rugged East Face of the Organ Mountains

reptiles, there are abundant rattlesnakes in the area, mostly encountered off trail and mostly in the spring and fall, when the weather is most comfortable for hiking. Although spring and fall are the logical hiking seasons for the Organs, hiking can be done year-round with some allowance for local weather conditions. Summers can get toasty hot, especially lower down, winters can range from pleasantly mild to uncomfortably cold, and late summer brings the thunderstorm season.

The Organ Mountains are located primarily on lands administered by the Bureau of Land Management, but include some state land and a number of private inholdings, which formerly included the Cox Ranch on the west side, subsequently purchased by the Nature Conservancy and transferred to the BLM. A 7,283-acre piece of the mountain has been set aside as a BLM Wilderness Study Area (WSA), and there is good reason to expect eventual Wilderness designation. Partly because the mountains are near sizable population centers, and because the large, high-quality granite walls offer some of the best rock climbing in the state, the Organs see a fairly significant amount of human visitation for this part of the state. However, the hiking terrain often tends to be steep, rugged, and dry, and lack of solitude is seldom a problem after leaving the trailhead. There are trails that range from easy to difficult, and the granite walls are hard to beat for color and beauty. The brilliant nature portrait produced when the early morning or late afternoon sun lights up a pink granite face with a splash of yellow lichen will be ample reward for your efforts on the trail. Don't forget your camera.

Map Coverage

The best map coverage for the Organ Mountains is provided by the USGS 7.5-minute scale Organ map for the north end of the range, and the Organ Peak map of the same scale for the south end.

Access

The primary entry points for the Organ Mountains and those to note for the trails described below are the Aguirre Spring Campground on the east side of the range, and the west trailhead for the Baylor Pass Trail, and the Cox Ranch, on the west side. Access directions are as follows:

Aguirre Spring Campground. From Interstate 25, take the Highway 70/Main Street exit and drive east on Highway 70, 14.5 miles to San Augustin Pass and then a little farther to a highway sign marking a turnoff to the south toward the campground. The access road leads 5 miles south to the campground and picnic area over a steep, winding course that is suitable for passenger cars but not trailers over 22 feet. The campground contains 55 units, with toilet facilities but no drinking water. A small camping fee is charged, and the campground is limited to overnight campers after 10 p.m. The entrance gate is closed at 8:00 p.m. from April through September, and at 6 p.m. from October through March.

West Trailhead for Baylor Pass Trail. Drive 10.5 miles east of Interstate 25 on Highway 70 to the Baylor Canyon Road. Turn south on this gravel road and continue for 1.9 miles to a sign directing you a short distance east to the Baylor Pass trailhead, where there is a small parking area.

Cox Ranch and La Cueva Picnic Area. Follow the above description to the west trailhead for the Baylor Pass Trail, except instead of turning off the Baylor Canyon Road to the trailhead, continue south on the Baylor Canyon Road another 6.8 miles, past the turnoff where the road runs into the Dripping Springs Road. Here, a road sign will direct you east on the Dripping Springs Road another 2.3 miles to the A. B. Cox Visitor Center, an historic ranch now administered by the BLM. Along the way, to the north of the road, is the La Cueva Picnic Area. A $3.00 fee is required to enter the area, which is for day use only. The entrance gate closes at 8 p.m. from April through September, and at 6 p.m. from October through March. Hikers on the Dripping Springs Trail must be out when the gate closes. An alternative approach from Las Cruces is to drive east on University Drive (Exit 1 off Interstate 25). University Drive eventually becomes Dripping Springs Road.

Hiking Trails

Hiking trails in the Organ Mountains are concentrated in the northern part of the range. These include several established trails maintained by the BLM, as well as numerous others that are unmarked and obviously without official sponsorship. The latter category of trails include some that are easily apparent, but are mostly obscure paths put in by climbers to the many rock formations in this part of the mountain. A word of caution here: technical rock climbing is an activity that requires the proper equipment and training; too many people have paid the ultimate price for crossing the line between rock scrambling and rock climbing. The southern part of the mountain range is mostly located within the Fort Bliss Military Reservation and thus not open to hiking without special permission.

The trails described in this section are some of the more popular Organ hiking routes. Others can be found in *A Hiking Guide to Doña Ana County, New Mexico* by Greg Magee (see "For Further Infor-

mation" at end of this section), or in the only hiking guide to the area, written by Professor Richard Ingraham of New Mexico State University. The trails in the latter source, which may be available locally (my copy is an old, unpublished version), tend toward obscure climbing approaches. Be sure to take drinking water along on the trails; the natural water sources are few, not always enticing, and the water from these sources should always be purified before being consumed in any case.

TRAIL DESCRIPTIONS

Hike #1. Pine Tree National Recreation Trail

This is a popular hiking trail on the east side of the range, starting at Aguirre Spring Campground and making a 4.5-mile loop that goes up through the ponderosa pines on the slopes south of the campground, which provide the namesake for the trail. It is one of the two trails on the mountain designated as National Recreation Trails. The net elevation gain of 1,200 feet makes this a rather steep trail, but it is well marked and easy to follow for an easy to moderate hike. Typical hiking time is 2.5 to 4 hours.

The trailhead is located by following the access directions to Aguirre Spring Campground, and continuing a short distance beyond the campground entrance to a large sign on the south side of the campground, which marks the start of the trail. The trail starts to the south and soon forks, with the two forks completing the loop. You can do the hike in either direction; the branch to the left is somewhat steeper and I somehow prefer to hike the steep leg going up rather than down (although it doesn't make much difference in this case), so I will describe the hike as going in that direction. The trail crosses a small stream as it contours

Rock Scrambling below Organ Needle on the
Ridge above Indian Hollow

around a rocky rib and begins a steep
ascent up the side of a broad ridge. About
an hour into the hike, the trail cuts back
up to the left to gain the crest of a shallow
saddle, from which a short walk north to
the point of the ridge leads to a nice vista
off to the north. Also, there is a faint trail
leading east from the saddle toward
Indian Hollow and the great granite dome
called Sugarloaf. Continuing up on the
main trail, you again cross a stream that
looks to be fairly dependable and complete a fairly level contour across a series
of ridges at the high elevation section of
the trail. Along this stretch is an unimproved campsite on a flat spot near the
trail. The remainder of the trail involves a
short but steep descent, leading to a
longer, more gradual stretch of trail that
takes you back to the trail fork near the
campground.

Hike #2. Indian Hollow Trail

The Indian Hollow Trail is not an
officially maintained trail, but receives
fairly regular use by people hiking to
Indian Hollow and by climbers gaining
access to some of the slabs and walls in
the area, most notably Sugarloaf, the
impressive granite dome that can be seen
prominently from Highway 70, and
which provides the longest and one of the
most classic rock climbs in the Organ
Mountains. Indian Hollow is formed as
the basin below Sugarloaf to the southeast and the Organ Needle ridge to the
southwest. If you are hiking in for an
overnight trip, the basin provides running
water, good campsites, and excellent
scenery. The hike into Indian Hollow is
rough and unimproved but not hard to
follow, over a 4.8-mile round-trip route,
with a net elevation gain of 930 feet. It is
also possible to approach via the Pine Tree
Trail with an unmaintained cut-across to
Indian Hollow, but this involves more

elevation gain and loss. If you want to extend the hike a bit, you can make a steep scramble up from Indian Hollow to the saddle below Sugarloaf or to the ridge below Organ Needle.

To find the trailhead, drive to the Aguirre Spring Campground and locate the Pine Tree Trailhead shortly past the campground entrance. Continue 0.75 miles past the trailhead sign to an unimproved parking area on the right as the road turns back to the left. From the parking area, the trail heads southeast across level terrain, then climbs over a broad saddle to the right of a rocky point. Continue over the saddle, down across an arroyo and poorly defined ridgeline, to the main drainage coming down from the south. The trail then continues up this drainage for a mile or more, gradually gaining elevation until you are at a point a little to the north and west of Sugarloaf. There is a stream running along the base of the dome, and it is a nice area to spend some time exploring. As mentioned before, you can continue by scrambling up to the saddle north of Sugarloaf or up to the ridgeline to the southwest. It has been a long time since I hiked this trail, but I recall that the way was well-enough worn and Sugarloaf a prominent-enough landmark so that the route was reasonably easy to locate.

Hike #3. Baylor Pass National Recreation Trail

This is the other Organ Mountain trail, in addition to the Pine Tree Trail, that has been designated as a National Recreation Trail. As the name implies, the trail crosses the mountain range at Baylor Pass, with a trailhead on the east side of the range at Aguirre Spring Campground and a trailhead on the west side at Baylor Canyon Road. The Trail is 6 miles long one way, with a net elevation gain to the pass of 770 feet from Aguirre Spring Campground and 1,525 feet from Baylor Canyon Road. The hike is most often done from one trailhead or the other to the high point at Baylor Pass, then back to the starting point. The trail distance to the pass from Aguirre Spring Campground is about 2 miles (4 miles round trip) as opposed to 4 miles from Baylor Canyon Road (8 miles round trip), making the leg from Aguirre Spring, with its smaller elevation gain, the more popular alternative. A good way to do this hike would be to use a car shuttle and hike the trail the full 6-mile distance one way. Otherwise, if you want to see the whole trail, you are looking at a 12-mile round-trip hike. This is a popular trail, currently open to hiking, horseback riding, and mountain biking, which is well marked and easy to follow.

See the "Access" directions above to locate the trailheads at Aguirre Spring Campground and Baylor Canyon Road. A well-marked trailhead consisting of trail sign and parking area on the road north of the Aguirre Spring campsites provides the start of the trail on the east side. The trail heads west on a gentle but sustained grade through high desert vegetation, with piñon pine, scrub oak, and one-seed and alligator juniper. There are nice vistas at the pass on the crest of the ridge and on the way up. Also, there is a primitive campsite just west of the ridge. The trail on the west side of the mountains drops down toward Baylor Canyon and finishes with about a mile of relatively level hiking to the west trailhead. The west side of the trail catches more sun, making it a good winter hike but a hot one in the summer.

Hike #4. Rabbit Ears Canyon Trail

This is another unmaintained but fairly popular trail, which follows an old

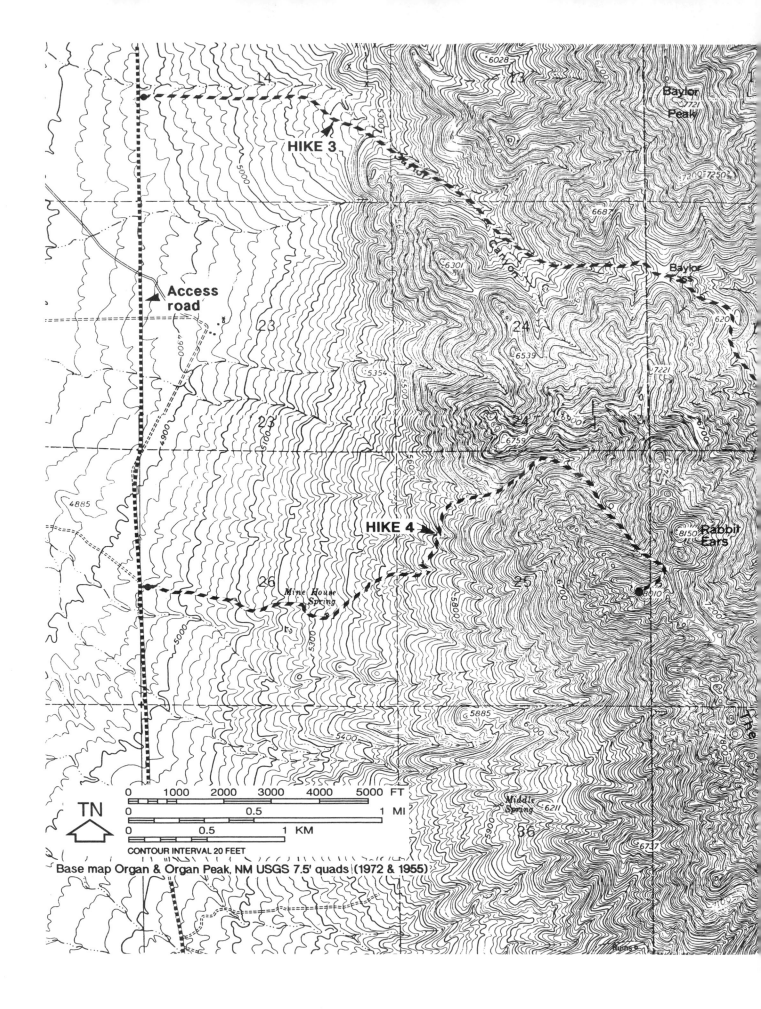

HIKE 3

Access road

HIKE 4

Mine House Spring

Baylor Peak

Baylor

Rabbit Ears

Middle Spring

TN

| 0 | 1000 | 2000 | 3000 | 4000 | 5000 | FT |

0   0.5   1   MI

0   0.5   1   KM

CONTOUR INTERVAL 20 FEET

Base map Organ & Organ Peak, NM USGS 7.5' quads (1972 & 1955)

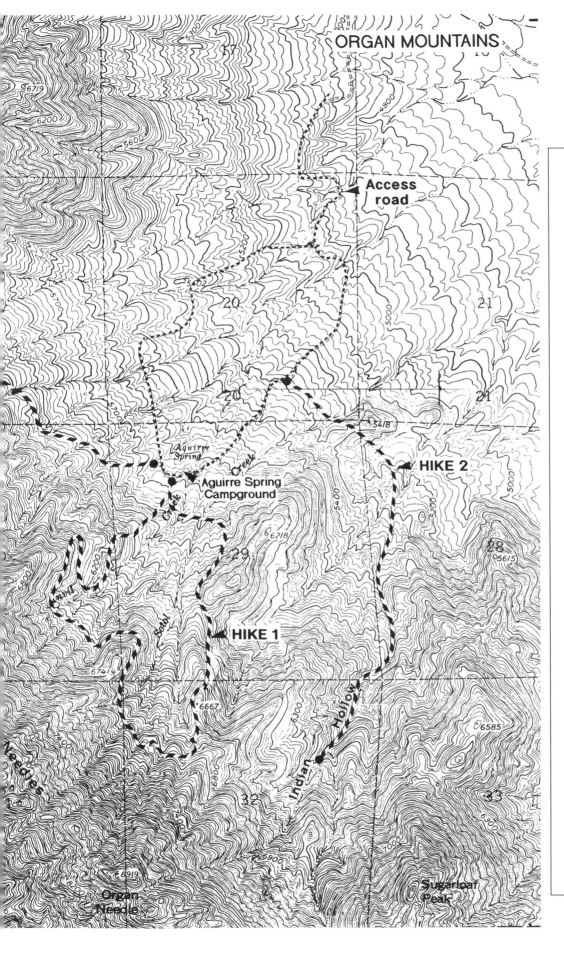

ORGAN MOUNTAINS

Access road

HIKE 2

HIKE 1

Aguirre Spring

Aguirre Spring Campground

Indian Hollow

Organ Needle

Sugarloaf Peak

Hike #1. Pine Tree National Recreation Trail

Distance — 4.5 miles round trip
Net elevation gain — 1,200 feet
Difficulty — Easy to moderate

Hike #2. Indian Hollow Trail

Distance — 4.8 miles round trip
Net elevation gain — 930 feet
Difficulty — Easy to moderate

Hike #3. Baylor Pass National Recreation Trail

Distance — 6 miles one way; 12 miles round trip
Net elevation gain — 770 feet from east side; 1,525 feet from west side
Difficulty — Easy to moderate

Hike #4. Rabbit Ears Canyon Trail

Distance — 7.0 miles round trip
Net elevation gain — 3,070 feet
Difficulty — Moderate to strenuous

321

mine road over part of the distance. The round trip distance is 7 miles, gaining 3,070 feet of elevation to the high elevation point at the plateau just below and west of Rabbit Ears, a distinctive set of granite towers that are one of the better-known landmarks on the mountain. The trail is easy to follow over the first part, but is rough and obscure in places on the upper part and involves some steep scrambling for an overall difficulty rating of moderate to strenuous. There are many scenic rock formations on the upper part of the trail, and also a number of old mine shafts that have some potential for danger for the unwary or overly curious. Also keep in mind that some of the land in the vicinity of the mine shafts is privately owned.

The trailhead is located on the Baylor Canyon Road, south of the Baylor Pass Trailhead and 3.8 miles south of Highway 70. There is a cattleguard on the east side of the Baylor Canyon Road at a gravel road that comes in from the east. This is the road along which the hike proceeds, and although the road can currently be driven part of the way in, it quickly becomes very rough, and you may as well do the whole thing on foot, as it isn't that long a hike. Begin by hiking the jeep road, which meanders generally east, passing a rock hut a little less than a mile from the start, which originally was a dormitory for miners who worked the mine that is encountered farther up the road. The road becomes increasingly rough and continues to climb through heavier vegetation and larger boulders. The road soon passes a large, open area to the right and terminates at an arroyo. A bank of mine tailings is immediately in front of you, with mine openings in the arroyo to the right, as well as old mine equipment, the remains of a rock building, and a tower. The mine shaft is dangerous and had best be left alone.

On the north bank of the arroyo, a trail climbs up, then turns east, crossing a caved-in shaft on a bridge of solid earth, and proceeds to a junction with a trail that comes in from the left, or north. Turn on to this trail, which leads across into Rabbit Ears Canyon. There are a number of mine-shaft openings in this general vicinity, which make it advisable not to be off trail here in the dark. Continuing on the northerly trail, it rises gently and curves east before dropping down into the canyon. At this point the trail becomes more obscure as it crosses boulders, but it heads into the mouth of the canyon, into an area of small trees, and to the bottom of the canyon. From here, the hike becomes something of a boulder-scrambling exercise, and you should generally stay low, avoiding the rock face to the left and heavier brush to the right. But there are spectacular visual rewards; vegetation in the canyon bottom is far more extensive than one would expect after hiking in off the desert, the huge North Rabbit Ear is visible up the canyon to the east, and many other interesting rock formations, most with climbing routes on them, can be seen. The canyon ultimately turns south, still climbing, and what trail there is passes through two alligator junipers and climbs a steep several hundred feet to a saddle between the South Rabbit Ear on the left and the Rabbit Ears massif, or plateau, on the right. Enroute to the high point of the saddle, you will pass both North and Middle Rabbit Ears on the left. Another short, steep climb up to the small plateau to the west leads to a nice area with good views all around.

The retreat from Rabbit Ears Canyon is to retrace the approach route, but care should be taken to leave with plenty of daylight remaining, both to ensure finding the trail out of the mouth of the canyon and to avoid the potentially

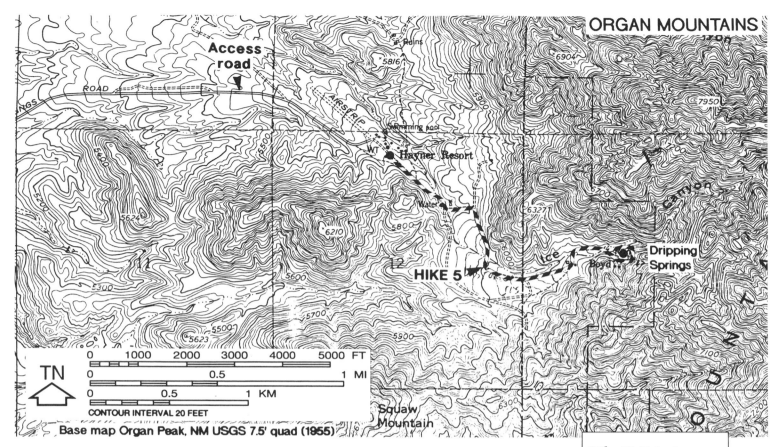

Access road

Hayner Resort

HIKE 5

Dripping Springs

Squaw Mountain

Base map Organ Peak, NM USGS 7.5' quad (1955)

TN

CONTOUR INTERVAL 20 FEET

dangerous mine openings farther on. Once back on the jeep road, it is an easy hike back to the trailhead.

Hike #5. Dripping Springs Trail

Dripping Springs Trail is an easy and popular hike of 3 miles round trip and 550 feet of elevation gain that begins at the Visitor Center for the Cox Ranch and leads to the nearby ruins of the Dripping Springs Resort. The Dripping Springs Resort was built in the 1870s by Col. Eugene Van Patten, a Confederate Civil War veteran and participant of the Battle of Glorieta Pass near Santa Fe. The resort was very popular around the turn of the century and saw many famous visitors, including Pat Garret and Pancho Villa. It eventually passed into the hands of A. B. Cox, who also purchased the nearby Hayner Ranch and developed it into a successful ranching operation. The Cox Ranch and Dripping Springs Resort included unique biotic communities where a number of rare, threatened, and endangered plants could still be found, and realizing the opportunity, the Nature Conservancy purchased the property from the Cox family and transferred the title to the BLM, in exchange for other BLM lands that could be sold to recover the cost of the purchase. Another interesting feature of the area is La Cueva ("the cave"), a large rock monolith containing a shelter cave just west of the Cox Ranch Headquarters and the site of the La Cueva Picnic Area. The cave has been excavated and found to have been occupied from about 5000 b.c. through the historic period, but the most famous occupant was probably Giovanni (Juan) Maria Agostini—the Hermit. He was a religious

Hike #5. Dripping Springs Trail

Distance — 3.0 miles
Net elevation gain — 550 feet
Difficulty — Easy

mystic from Italy, who spent most of his life tramping around Europe, then North and South America. In the early 1860s, when he was already 62 years of age, he drifted down into New Mexico and spent four years living alone in a cave atop a mountain near Las Vegas still known as Hermit's Peak. Perhaps he got tired of the cold winters, for he then drifted into the southern part of the state, ending up at Mesilla and deciding again to do the hermit thing, this time in the Organ Mountains. Although warned about Apaches lurking in the area who might not be inclined to indulge his ascetic piety, he was resolute in his quest to get away from people—and if they were the same then as they are now, who could blame him? So Agostini began to inhabit La Cueva, but was persuaded to light a signal fire at night to indicate to his friends in town that he was safe. However, the signal fires may have attracted other unwanted visitors, for when the fire was not lit one night, a search party was organized, which found his body, apparently killed by Indians. And thus was extinguished one of the truly interesting, though not one of the most sociable, characters ever to set foot in the state.

The trailhead for the Dripping Springs Trail is at the south end of the parking area for the Cox Ranch Visitor Center. The gate to the area closes at 8 p.m. from April through September and 6 p.m. from October through March, and the sign at the trailhead asks that you not start on the trail after 3 p.m., as all visitors are required to vacate the premises by closing time. You are also asked to register at the Visitor Center before starting the hike, and this is a good opportunity to get questions answered if you have as yet generated any.

Begin the hike by walking through the pedestrian gate at the trailhead and following the well-marked trail east toward the mountains. About 0.4 miles up the trail is the junction with the Filmore Canyon Trail, which connects to the trail that leads up Filmore Canyon to the base of the mountains and back down the canyon to the La Cueva Picnic Area. This is a good alternative loop route to take on your return back down the Dripping Springs Trail; there is a trail leading from the picnic area back to the Visitor Center. Meanwhile, the Dripping Springs Trail continues to follow a drainage system, and in addition to the Apache plume, mountain mahogany, and other desert-type plants commonly seen, there are others, such as netleaf hackberry and wright silktassle, which are often seen along an intermittent watercourse such as this. In just over a mile, you will encounter the ruins of the Dripping Springs Resort, including the Boyd Sanitorium and the Van Patten Mountain Camp, with informative signs to help explain the history of the area. There are also several small picnic areas and pit toilets. And, of course, the namesake of the area, Dripping Springs. Complete the hike by walking back the way you came or by adding the Filmore Canyon/La Cueva Trail variation.

For Further Information:

Bureau of Land
    Management
Mimbres Resource
    Area
1800 Marquess Street
Las Cruces, NM 88005
(505) 528-8228

A. B. Cox Visitor Center
(505) 522-1219

A Hiking Guide to Doña Ana County, New Mexico, by Greg S. Magee, published by Naturescapes, Box 3574, Las Cruces, NM 88003, 1989.

Robledo Mountains

GENERAL DESCRIPTION

The Robledo Mountains are a localized mountain range about 10 miles in length, situated along the west bank of the Rio Grande, 8 miles northwest of the town of Las Cruces, in the south-central part of the state. The mountains are named after Pedro Robledo, the first person in the Oñate expedition to die in New Mexico, who was buried nearby on May 21, 1598. The name is also associated with Doña Ana Robledo, the legendary 17th-century lady for whom Doña Ana County is named. The lower elevation parts of the range start at about 4,300 feet, with the high point of the range being the summit of Robledo Mountain at 5,876 feet. The other prominent peak in the range is the slightly lower summit of Lookout Peak, just over a mile farther to the northwest. Lookout Mountain gained notoriety in the Apache wars of the late 1800s as a heliograph station for the U.S. Army. The Army was experiencing such futility in locating and keeping track of the elusive Apaches that a series of heliograph stations were situated through the region to quickly transmit information on the movements of the Apaches across a wide area. Today, the summit of the peak continues to be used as a communications facility. These mountains form the heart of the Robledo Mountains Wilderness Study Area (WSA), a BLM-administered area of 12,811 acres cloaked mainly in the sparse plant life typical of the Lower Sonoran and Chihuahuan life zones, including desert grasses, scattered juniper trees, sotol, ocotillo and prickly pear cacti, creosote bush, acacia, and mesquite. The geology of the mountains involves igneous basalts and rhyolite of the Tertiary Period and various sedimentary rocks dating from the Late Paleozoic era. These sedimentary rocks, particularly in the southern part of the range, have long been known for containing a rich concentration of fossils, and have lately been found to contain some of the most complete sets of fossilized trackways, made by ancient reptiles, that have been found anywhere.

No system of trails has been established in the Robledo Mountains, but a swarm of jeep roads winds about in the lower-elevation parts of the range, particularly on the south and west sides. A jeep road runs all the way to the top of Lookout Peak to the communications facility, but the rugged higher-elevation parts of the mountains are basically free of roads and trails, and don't appear to get much hiking attention, despite the close proximity of Las Cruces and El Paso. Water is essentially nonexistent in the Robledos, and off-trail hiking can be rough, but once away from the main access roads, there is a high degree of solitude to be found. The best time of year to visit is from fall through spring. Winter can get cold but is usually pleasant; summer is uncomfortably hot much of the time. Since some of the access roads travel through normally dry arroyo bottoms, thunderstorm season is a time for caution.

Map Coverage

The best topo map to get, if you can still find it, is the USGS 15-minute scale Las Cruces map. Otherwise, most of the area of interest is shown on the 7.5-minute scale Leasburg and Picacho Mountain quad maps.

Access

Access to the Robledo Mountains is commonly made from jeep roads branching off of Highway 430 on the south end, and from variations off County Road D59 at the north end. As a logical introductory trip into the Robledo Mountains, the road to the top of Lookout Peak is a good starting point, as it leads into the center of the Wilderness, within striking distance to the highest part of the range, and gives access to the lower parts of the mountain as well. Take Interstate 25 to the Radium Springs exit (Exit 19) a few miles north of Las Cruces, and drive west at the exit on Highway 157 for 1.5 miles to an intersection with Highway 185. Go north on Highway 185 about 1 mile to Radium Springs, and continue 0.5 miles past the Blue Moon Bar (located at the far north end of town) to the junction with County Road D59. Turn left on D59, which is a well-maintained gravel road, and continue 3.8 miles past the Highway 185 turnoff, to a major fork in the canyon bottom. Drive 0.1 miles up the right fork, and then take the rough dirt road that climbs up the bank to the left out of the canyon bottom and loops back around to join the left branch of the fork above the rock outcrop that blocks the route farther down. By now, the road that started out over the first 3 miles as a well-graded

gravel road, will have deteriorated into an arroyo bed that will call for a high clearance vehicle. Driving south from the turnoff at the fork in the canyon, continue for 1.2 miles to another place where the arroyo bed splits into two major forks, not far before reaching a windmill on the east side of the road; take the left fork, then turn left on the road that immediately climbs out of the arroyo bed to the east. There is a WSA boundary marker at the entrance to this road, but the entrance is narrow and easy to miss if you aren't paying attention. After turning off from the arroyo bed, the road follows a ridge system east, climbing a steep grade at the 0.4-mile point, which may require four wheel drive, and forks at the 2.2-mile point, with the right fork running south along the west base of Robledo Mountain and the left fork continuing on to Lookout Peak. If you take the Lookout Peak branch, the road drops down into a canyon and runs 0.7 miles to the base of a steep rocky grade that climbs up on a contour to the north. Park at the base of this final stretch of road, which climbs a little over a mile to the summit of Lookout Peak; this is a very punishing stretch of road, and you won't want to try driving it in anything short of a Humvee. A short hike up the road puts you on a saddle atop the crest of the range and in position to continue toward Lookout Peak to the north, or Robledo Mountain to the south.

Hiking Trails

As previously stated, no designated trails exist in the Robledo Mountains, other than the jeep trails that run through the area. Under the WSA designation, driving is permitted on existing roads and trails; if the WSA is upgraded to Wilderness status, those trails within the Wilderness boundary will be closed to vehicular traffic, except for the road to Lookout Peak, which will be "cherry-stemmed"

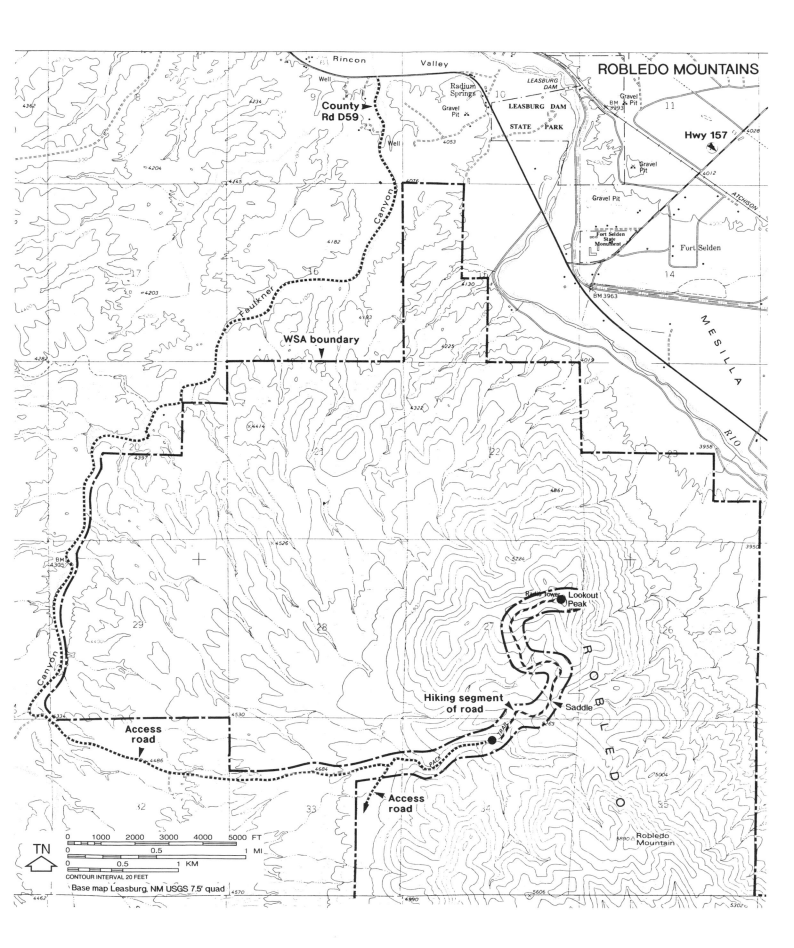

ROBLEDO MOUNTAINS

County
Rd D59

Rincon   Valley

Well

Radium
Springs

LEASBURG
DAM

LEASBURG DAM

STATE   PARK

Gravel
Pit

Gravel
Pit

BM 3993

Hwy 157

ATCHISON

Gravel Pit

Fort Selden
State
Monument

Fort Selden

BM 3963

WSA boundary

Faulkner

Canyon

MESILLA

RIO

Canyon

BM
4305

Radio Tower

Lookout
Peak

R
O
B
L
E
D
O

Hiking segment
of road

Saddle

Access
road

TRAIL

PACK

Access
road

Robledo
Mountain

TN

0	1000	2000	3000	4000	5000 FT

0   0.5   1 MI

0   0.5   1 KM

CONTOUR INTERVAL 20 FEET

Base map Leasburg, NM USGS 7.5' quad

out of the Wilderness. In this case, the quality of hiking in the lower-elevation parts of the range should improve. The most popular hiking destination will probably continue to be Robledo Mountain and Lookout Peak and vicinity. Robledo Mountain can be climbed via a route beginning with the south branch of the last road fork mentioned under the "Access" directions above, or from the saddle along the ridge to the north. And Lookout Peak is accessible from the same ridge approach as well. From the top of the range, the views are outstanding in every direction, including a close-up of the Rio Grande and the agriculturally rich Mesilla Valley through which it flows. It is interesting to note that in ancient times, the river ran south from Hatch along the west side of the range, between the Robledo Mountains and Sleeping Lady Hills. The flora along the high part of the range is also picturesque, with some nice specimens of sotol, agave, and barrel cactus.

For Further Information:

Bureau of Land Management Las Cruces District Office 1800 Marquess Street Las Cruces, NM 88005 (505) 528-8228

A Hiking Guide to Doña Ana County, New Mexico, by Greg S. Magee, published by Naturescapes, Box 3574, Las Cruces, NM 88003, 1989.

Florida Mountains

GENERAL DESCRIPTION

The Florida Mountains include the main range, which is located about 10 miles southeast of the town of Deming, and a smaller subrange, called the Little Floridas, several miles to the north. Currently, a 22,336-acre BLM Wilderness Study Area (WSA) is in effect, which includes much of the federal lands containing the Floridas, but the area is probably not destined to achieve Wilderness designation due to a negative recommendation by the BLM because of the many access roads, mining claims, and other privately-owned land parcels that carve up the area, in addition to the potential for future mining developments. Regardless of what its eventual wilderness status may officially be, it is clear that the main bulk of the mountains are wild in nature and will probably will remain so indefinitely. The range rises abruptly over 2,800 feet from the surrounding landscape and dominates the entire area. The steep relief and broken volcanic rock make the Floridas some of the most rugged and difficult-to-hike mountains of any in the state. The mountains are accessible to hiking virtually year round, but lack of shade and hot temperatures, combined with lack of water, make summer hiking suitable only for the determined. The maximum temperatures typically occur during the month of July, and a fairly regular pattern of thunderstorms is seen from July through mid-September. The arid climate produces a ground cover that

The Florida Mountains, Looking South

is mostly treeless, except for scattered junipers, and suggestive of the Upper Chihuahuan zone at the lower elevations, but somewhat more forested higher up. No designated trails are maintained in the WSA, but for those who are willing to climb up through the strenuous terrain of the main range, there is a possibility of viewing some of the Persian ibex, an introduced species that is apparently thriving in the environment. There are also indigenous populations of mule deer and mountain lion. For those interested in collecting mineral specimens, Rock Hound State Park in the Little Florida Mountains is worth visiting. These mountains were created as an extrusive formation, made mostly of a volcanic mud called rhyolite, which is laced with deposits of variously colored jaspers, geodes and other nodules, opal, agate, quartz crystals, perlite, and manganese minerals. You are allowed to take rock specimens (officially 15 to 20 pounds per person) from the collecting areas inside the Park. Both Rock Hound State Park and Spring Canyon State Park, the primary entry point for the main Floridas, have picnic and restroom facilities, are accessible by paved roads, and charge a $3.00 entry fee. Rock Hound Park also has a few camping sites, which involve an additional fee. The entrance gates are locked from sundown until 7:30 a.m., and if you arrive after dark there is a wide pullout outside the Park entrance which I found to be a suitable, unimproved car camping spot. As previously indicated, water sources in the Florida Mountains are close to nil, and any hiking trip without a quart or two of drinking water is destined to be a short one.

Map Coverage

USGS 7.5 minute scale map coverage is provided by the Capitol Dome, Florida Gap, South Peak, and Gym Peak maps.

Access

Take Interstate 25 to Las Cruces and take the Interstate 10 exit, or the Highway 70 exit if approaching from the north, and drive west. Highway 70 joins Interstate 10 several miles west of town, and the Interstate is followed all the way to Deming, where you take the Highway 11/Motel Drive exit (Exit 85) and follow Highway 11 south. There are several turns to make as the route passes through town, and part of the route is marked as Highway 427, but if make the right turns, you will end up on the south side of town on Highway 11 pointed south toward Columbus. About 4 miles south of Deming is a sign directing you east on Highway 141 toward Rock Hound State Park. This leads to a "T" intersection 6 miles east of the turnoff, where you turn right and continue another 2 miles to the Park entrance. Follow the same route to reach Spring Canyon State Park, except take a right turn on to Highway 198 several hundred yards before you reach the entrance to Rock Hound State Park, and follow Highway 198 about 3 miles more to reach Spring Canyon State Park. The access roads are paved all the way to the park entrances. Typical travel times to reach the Florida Mountains are 5 hours from Albuquerque, 1.5 hours from Las Cruces, and 2.5 hours from El Paso.

Hiking Trails

No maintained trails are present in the Floridas, although there are a number of entry points around the range, many on private land, with rough trails or old roads leading into the foothills. The best legal access to the main range is on the north side from Spring Canyon State Park. At the south end of the Park is a paved parking area with a path that is well worn initially, leading up the canyon. A series of slopes and ridges can be followed as far up into the range as you wish to go.

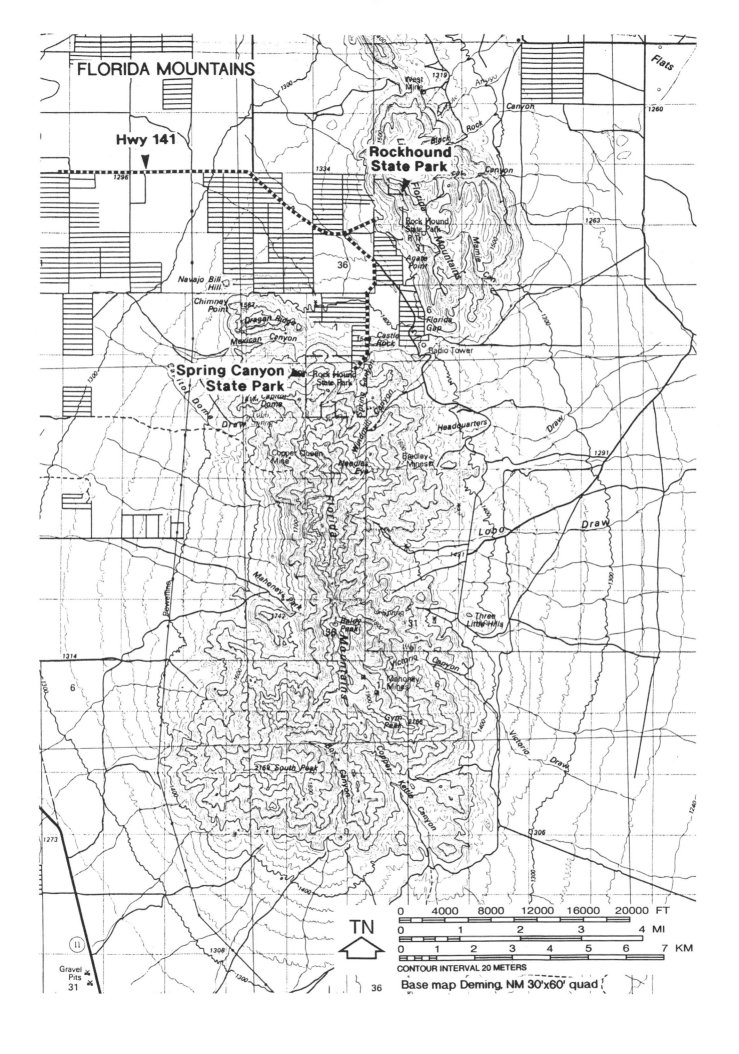

FLORIDA MOUNTAINS

Hwy 141

Rockhound State Park

Spring Canyon State Park

TN

| 0 | 4000 | 8000 | 12000 | 16000 | 20000 FT |

| 0 | 1 | 2 | 3 | 4 MI |

| 0 | 1 | 2 | 3 | 4 | 5 | 6 | 7 KM |

CONTOUR INTERVAL 20 METERS

Base map Deming, NM 30'x60' quad

From Rock Hound State Park on the southwest slopes of the Little Florida Mountains, a swarm of trails lead up the side of the mountain to the mineral collecting areas several hundred feet up. The trail(s) starts at the paved loop on the east side of the Park and braids out into numerous paths that travel up through the same general vicinity, and you can obtain a crude map at the Park Headquarters to help you locate the collecting areas. If you continue on up above the collecting areas, there is a decent-sized area of the mountain that can be explored without the probability of encountering many, if any, other people; they will mostly all be farther down whacking away at the rock with rock hammers.

For Further Information:

Bureau of Land
 Management
 Las Cruces District
 Office
 1800 Marquess Street
 Las Cruces, NM 88005
 (505) 525-8228

*New Mexico Statewide
 Wilderness Summary,
 Volume 3: Appendices,
 Wilderness Analysis
 Reports,* U.S. Depart-
 ment of the Interior,
 Bureau of Land
 Management, New
 Mexico State Office,
 Santa Fe, NM, May
 1985.

Rock Hound/Spring
 Canyon State Parks
 P.O. Box 1064
 Deming, NM 88030
 (505) 546-6182

Mount Riley and the West Portillo Mountains

Mt. Cox, Looking South from the Summit of Mt. Riley

GENERAL DESCRIPTION

Mount Riley is one of three separate peaks clustered closely together at the eastern edge of the West Portillo Mountains, a broad but low volcanic range that includes over 150 separate cinder cones, along with associated lava and basalt flows covering hundreds of square miles. The Mount Riley group makes up a 7,400-acre BLM Wilderness Study Area (WSA), and the West Portillo Mountains contain a 149,785-acre WSA, which is easily the largest in the state. Because the two areas are contiguous, they are discussed together in this section. In addition, the 25,287-acre Aden Lava Flow WSA is located a few miles to the northeast, and all or most of the aforementioned WSA acreage has a good chance of eventually achieving Wilderness designation. Mount Riley and the West Portillo Mountains are located about 30 miles southwest of Las Cruces, 50 miles northwest of El Paso, and less than a mile north of the Mexican border. This is an arid climate, averaging about 8 inches in annual precipitation, in one of the most remote parts of the state. The summers are hot, with daytime temperatures frequently exceeding 100 degrees F., while the winters are mild with nighttime temperatures below freezing but comfortable daytime temperatures. Spring brings gusty afternoon winds with occasional dust storms, and late summer is the thunderstorm season. Water is generally not to be found, except for water that is standing or flowing from recent rains, and the native vegetation in the area reflects the arid makeup of the climate. The most dominant plant seems to be the creosote bush, with snakeweed, mesquite, sotol, mixed grasses, and various cacti, including some wonderful examples of barrel cactus, also common. The only real trees are a few widely scattered junipers. This is rugged and remote country, and except for a few ranchers and a few hunters during quail or deer season, there is very little human traffic through the area, especially off the roads; there are probably acres of land in the West Portillo Mountains that have seen very few footprints since prehistoric times. If solitude is what you want, this is an extreme example of it.

Map Coverage

The Mount Riley group is shown on the USGS 15 minute scale Mount Riley

quad map. If you can't find the 15 minute
map, the 7.5 minute scale alternatives are
the Mount Riley and Mount Riley SE
quads. For the West Portillo Mountains,
the USGS 15 minute scale Mount Riley
and Aden quad maps are needed, in
addition to the 7.5 minute scale X-7
Ranch, POL Ranch, and Camel Mountain
maps. If you are unable to obtain the two
15 minute maps, get, in addition to the
other 7.5 minute scale maps specified, the
Aden Crater, Mount Riley, Mt. Aden, Mt.
Aden SW, Portillo Peak, and Guzmans
Lookout Mountain maps. For large-scale
topographic coverage of the entire area,
the 1:100,000-scale Deming and Columbus maps are the ones to get.

Access

There seems to be no straightforward,
easy-to-describe route for reaching
Mount Riley and the Portillos, but the
following description works and is as good
as any other. Begin by traveling south to
the Community of La Union on Highway
28. You can drive all the way on Highway
28 from Las Cruces (about 26 miles south
of the Interstate 10 overpass), or catch
Highway 28 at numerous points by
driving west from Highway 478. As you
come to La Union, you will pass the
Highway 182 junction (turns off to the
east), and 0.1 miles farther south you
come to the Highway 183 junction. Turn
west on Highway 183 and travel 1 mile to
Alvarez Avenue (the next street past the
La Union Community Center), and take a
right on Alvarez Avenue heading west.
After 0.3 miles the pavement ends, and
the main road continues on out of town,
passing several side streets, and continues
as a county road west, past the town
landfill and (6.9 miles past the end of the
pavement in La Union) to a railroad
crossing and a "T" intersection, with a
gravel road paralleling the tracks on the
west side. Turn right, or northwest, on the

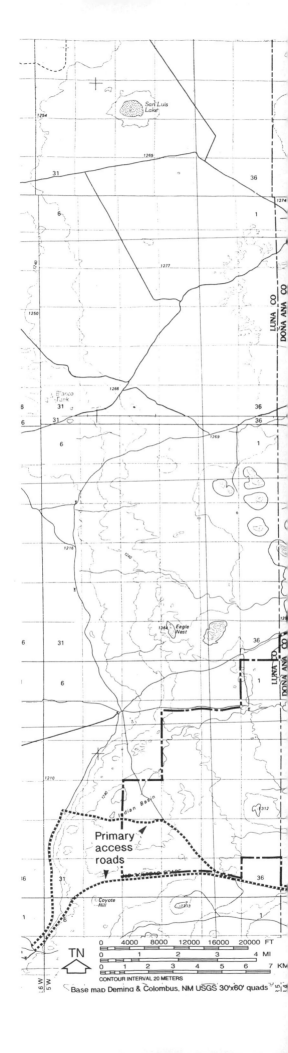

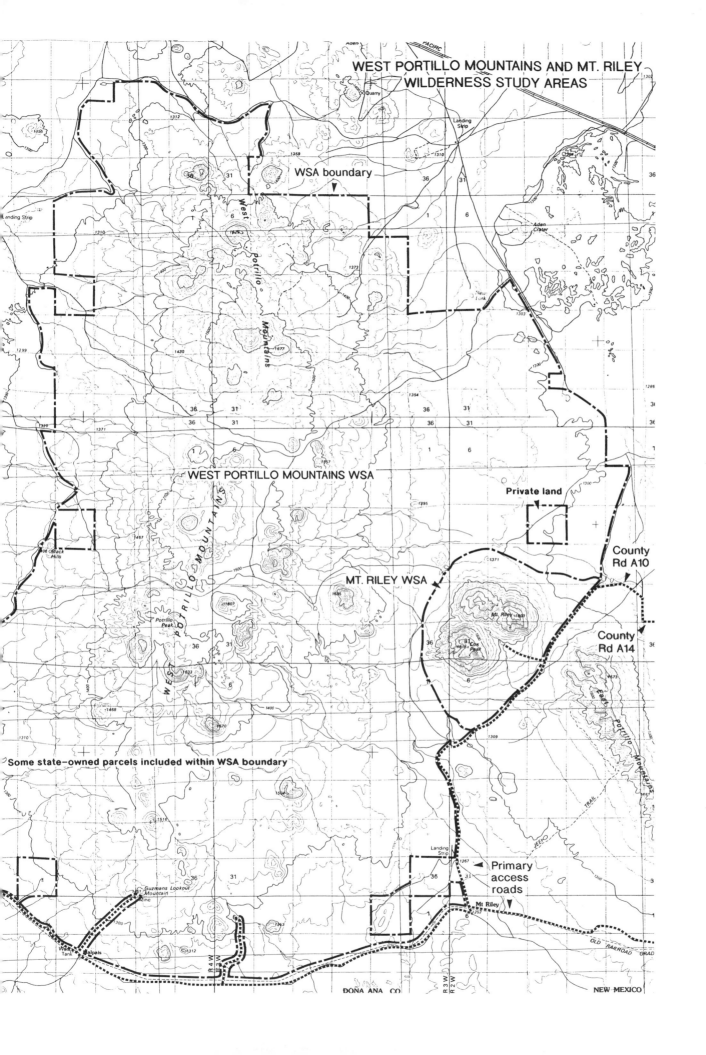

WEST PORTILLO MOUNTAINS AND MT. RILEY WILDERNESS STUDY AREAS

WSA boundary

WEST PORTILLO MOUNTAINS WSA

Private land

MT. RILEY WSA

County Rd A10

County Rd A14

Some state-owned parcels included within WSA boundary

Primary access roads

Mt Riley

DOÑA ANA CO

NEW MEXICO

road, and go 0.4 miles just on the other side of a cattle guard to the junction with County Road A14, which heads west. Drive west on A14 for 13.3 miles until it runs into another "T" intersection. Turn north and follow the road 1 mile (if you pass the Tee Pee Ranch, you are on the right route), where it makes a 90-degree turn back to the west, and goes for another mile to a 90-degree turn back to the north. Another 0.5 miles north from the last turn is a fork in the road, where you take the left fork that becomes County Road A10. You are heading west over a route that deteriorates somewhat, as it begins to negotiate areas that obviously run with water when the rain happens. (Continuing north at the road fork leads past the Lagrimas de Oro, or "golden tears," Ranch, which evidently refers to the pistachio nuts that the fledgling orchards are intended to produce, and a couple of miles farther, to the south rim of the Kilbourne Hole. This impressive feature is a mile across and several hundred feet deep, and is the largest of several explosion craters in the area that were produced when lava flows mixed with ground water beneath the surface of the earth.) Driving west from the road fork on County Road A10, the ridge that forms the East Portillo Mountains and the group of peaks that form the Mount Riley group are evident off to the southwest, as the road bends to the south and heads between the two small ranges. After passing through a gate, at a point 4.2 miles past the previous road fork, a rough but fairly prominent road turns off to the west and heads for the gap between Mount Riley to the north and Cox Peak to the south. This is the best access for the Mount Riley group of peaks, which includes Mount Riley, Cox Peak, and the unnamed peak west of Mount Riley. Continuing south on A10 from the Mount Riley turnoff another 7 miles

leads to an intersection with what is known as the Columbus-Anapra Road, which runs along just north of the Mexican border and provides an alternate access route into the area, if you happen to be coming from El Paso. Turn west on this road and travel about 8 miles to reach the crest of the West Portillo Range and the bottom edge of the WSA.

This whole network of access roads is, for the most part, well graded and suitable for passenger cars, although there are enough rough stretches to justify a high clearance vehicle. I have not driven these roads in wet weather, but with muddy conditions I can imagine the roads changing dramatically for the worse.

Hiking Trails

No trails other than a few ranch roads and jeep roads exist in either the Mount Riley WSA or the West Portillo Mountains WSA. Probably the most common hiking objective in the area is the summit of either Mount Riley (5,915 feet) or Cox Peak (5,957 feet). The best approach is the road mentioned above that turns west off County Road A10 and heads west toward the gap between the two peaks. Should the WSA become a designated Wilderness Area, you will have to hike the road, but presently it can be driven without any trouble if you have a high clearance vehicle. After about 1 mile up the road, you can go cross country and head for the peak of your choice; either way makes about a 2- or 3-mile round-trip hike. The east ridge of both peaks makes the best ascent route; there is plenty of loose rock on the way up, and you will want to take the lowest-angle approach. The net elevation gain for these peaks is in the range of 1,400 to 1,500 feet. The view from the top includes many of the surrounding mountain ranges, including the nearby East and West Portillo Mountains, and also a dramatic view of

Kilbourne Hole and the other explosion craters to the northeast.

The most visited part of the West Portillo Mountains WSA is probably Indian Basin, another low crater on the southwest edge of the range. This large depression, rimmed with sand dunes, drops about 75 feet below the surrounding desert floor and collects water during wet periods, harboring temporary populations of migratory bird life. To reach Indian Basin, drive 8.5 miles west from the crest of the West Portillo Mountains on the Columbus-Anapra Road and take the short spur road leading northwest. The main West Portillo Range is penetrated by old ranch roads in the lower elevations from all directions, but the cinder cones, lava flows, and basalt ridges of the higher interior are unmarked by roads and are even relatively free of the ubiquitous cow. In any hiking trips to this area, it is very important not to underestimate the requirement for drinking water, particularly in hot weather; for any kind of extended trip into the West Portillo Mountains, the amount of water you can carry along will be the factor that limits the length of your outing. It is also important to have map and compass along and to be proficient in their use.

For Further Information:

Bureau of Land
    Management
    Las Cruces District
    Office
    1800 Marquess Street
    Las Cruces, NM 88005
    (505) 528-8228

*New Mexico Statewide
    Wilderness Study:
    Volume 4, Appendices,
    Wilderness Analysis
    Reports*, U.S. Department of the Interior,
    Bureau of Land
    Management, New
    Mexico State Office,
    Santa Fe, NM,
    September 1986.

Guadalupe Mountains

GENERAL DESCRIPTION

The Guadalupe Mountains are a steep, rugged range that is located in southeast New Mexico, extending into Texas, and includes the area administered by the Guadalupe District of the Lincoln National Forest and Carlsbad Caverns National Park in New Mexico, and Guadalupe Mountains National Park in Texas. These mountains are part of one of the most interesting and unique geological areas in the world. The story of the Guadalupes began about 250 million years ago during the Permian geologic period, at the time immediately predating the dinosaurs when the first mammal-like reptiles began to appear. During this time, a vast tropical ocean covered much of the southern part of the continent, including portions of New Mexico and Texas. Over millions of years, an enormously thick layer of limestone sediments, including untold billions of tiny marine organisms, limey precipitates, and gypsum salts, gradually formed below the shallow seas, but of particular interest is the great barrier reef, now called the Capitan Reef, that formed along the edge of the Delaware Basin embayment—one of the large bays at the margin of the sea. This 400-mile-long horseshoe-shaped reef, which in many ways resembles the Great Barrier Reef of Australia, developed under just the right mix of conditions to produce a fertile growth of reef organisms. Calcareous algae and sponges, bryozoans,

corals, crinoids, clams, snails, and other lime-secreting plants and animals proliferated in a population explosion and were cemented together as the great reef grew upward and outward, until the increasing salinity of the nearly land-locked basin halted further growth. Eventually, the sea evaporated and the reef and associated limestone layers were further blanketed under salts and thick ocean sediments until a mountain-building uplift in this region that began about 12 million years ago exposed portions of thick limestone deposits, including the great fossil reef, which now towers above the surrounding desert floor. During the uplift process, the combination of dissolving agents in the water draining down through the limestone, and of gases rising up through it, have produced a vast labyrinth of the deepest and longest-known underground caves to exist in the world. These caves, particularly those in the Carlsbad Caverns National Park, provide one of the country's great tourist attractions, and similarly, the ancient marine fossil reef draw geologists from all over the world to study this natural wonder.

Plant species typical of the Chihuahuan Desert zone dominate the arid lowlands surrounding the Guadalupe Mountains, and give way to alligator and one-seed juniper, oaks, piñon pine, ponderosa pine, and several species of broadleaf trees, as the steep cliffs and ridges of the range are ascended. Water sources are rare, but when encountered in the deep canyons, they result in improbable oases that refresh the landscape. One especially interesting tree is the Texas madrone, found in New Mexico only in the Guadalupes; it is an evergreen tree up to about 20 feet in height with dark green, lance-shaped leaves, dark red berries, and smooth, reddish-colored bark. Another interesting plant, common in this region but not found in most of the rest of the state, is the yucca-like agave, or century, plant. This attractive succulent grows for as long as 10 to 20 years before producing a large central woody stalk with seed pods clustered at the top in a final, life-consuming act of species propagation.

The trails described in this section are in the portion of the Lincoln National Forest sandwiched between the Guadalupe Mountains National Park at the south tip of the range and Carlsbad Caverns National Park, located along the northeast end of the Capitan Reef. These mountains never attracted much in the way of permanent settlement and were one of the primary sanctuaries of the warlike Apache Indians, until they were finally driven out in about 1880. Before the Apaches, were the shadowy tribes that existed many thousands of years before recorded history, and some of the better-known archaeological sites of the Folsom and Clovis paleocultures have been found nearby. These early cultures also camped in some of the many caves that honeycomb the area, some of which undoubtedly await rediscovery. There are legends of buried gold and loot, left by hostile Indians and bandit gangs that operated in the area, which may have some basis in truth, but the rugged terrain of the mountains are faithful guardians of lost secrets. The weather in the Guadalupes is notoriously unsettled during parts of the year, particularly during spring, when

Agave Plant

unusually strong winds often rake the area, and during late summer when thunderstorms can spring up in the afternoons. The summers can be hot but tolerable, and the winters can be either pleasant or cold and snowbound. The best times to visit are likely to be during the fall or during mild stretches of weather in winter, when the weather conditions are pleasant and the trails are empty, although one exception to this time frame would be deer-hunting season, currently the first week of November. I cannot recall another area where I have encountered more deer on the trails and roads, and I would extrapolate from this fact to conclude that there must be plenty of rifle-toting folks combing the place when the season opens. Since Guadalupe Mountains National Park and Carlsbad Caverns National Park are both closed to hunting, these would be good hiking alternatives during this time of year. In addition to mule deer, there are also populations of black bear, mountain lion, and bighorn sheep. For car camping, there are campgrounds at Dog Canyon and Pine Springs in Guadalupe Mountains National Park (camping fee; no campfires allowed) and several commercial campgrounds in the Carlsbad area. Primitive campsites can be found on National Forest land along several forest roads off Highway 137, near the south end of Forest Road 540, and along Forest Trail 201.

Map Coverage

The USGS 7.5-minute scale El Paso Gap and Gunsight Canyon maps work best for the Lonesome Ridge hike, while the El Paso Gap map is adequate for the Camp Wilderness Ridge hike, with the addition of the Guadalupe Peak (Texas) map if you want to continue the hike on down to the lower trailhead in Guadalupe Mountains National Park. For the Sitting Bull Falls Trail, get the 7.5-minute scale Queen map. Good overall coverage of the area, including most of Carlsbad National Park, is shown on the USGS 15-minute scale El Paso Gap and Carlsbad Caverns West maps, although these are now out of print. The Lincoln National Forest map for the Guadalupe Ranger District is also useful for locating roads and trails. If you want to do some hiking in Guadalupe Mountains National Park, there is a special map and guide for that area available at the Visitor Center and major trailheads.

Access

Drive south on Highway 285 to the junction with Highway 137, about 12 miles north of Carlsbad. Turn west on Highway 137, and drive 24 miles to the County Road 409 intersection, where a north turn leads 8 miles to Sitting Bull Falls Picnic Area. To reach the Camp Wilderness Ridge and Lonesome Ridge hikes, continue on Highway 137, west past the County Road 409/Sitting Bull Falls turnoff. Drive for 17 miles (the junction with Forest Trail 68, which is the upper trailhead for the Sitting Bull Falls hike, is reached at the 11.7-mile point) to a road sign for Guadalupe Ridge and Forest Road 540. Turn south here on to Forest Road 540, a good-quality gravel road that continues for 11.7 miles, past some scenic vistas looking west from the sheer Guadalupe Ridge escarpment, to a broad turnaround where the road ends. Forest Trail 201, a rough jeep road, leads off both to the north and the south from this point, providing the start for the two ridge hikes. There are good, unimproved campsites in the treeline bordering the turnaround.

Hiking Trails

The trails described in this section are all in the south part of the Lincoln National Forest, on or near the Capitan Reef. The distinction between trails and jeep roads is blurred in this region, with the general rule of thumb being that you are allowed to drive any of the trails where physically possible, in which case the trail becomes in effect a jeep road, and where the terrain prohibits vehicular access, the trail becomes a single-track path. However, the distinction is often not clear by looking at the map, and some of the double-track sections are so rough that only the most determined four wheelers would want to drive them. This Forest Service "anything goes" policy has both advantages and disadvantages: on the one hand, you stand to encounter motor vehicles on the trails; on the other hand, you can hike and camp anywhere you want, anytime you want, without paying a fee. The Forest Service has established a Wilderness Study Area to look into Wilderness designation for part of this area, but local opposition has apparently doomed the idea. In the adjacent National Parks, motor vehicles and pets are restricted on the trails, but a fee is required to car camp, hiking requires a permit, camping must be done in designated areas, campfires are prohibited, and you are not allowed to hike off-trail. Although not covered in this book, the National Parks have numerous trails through some beautiful country that you may also want to try, some of which are quite popular. For all the trails in the region, it is necessary to take along ample drinking water, particularly in the summer, and someone in the group should have a topo map. Campfires require extra caution during dry periods, and you should be aware that there are rattlesnakes and scorpions in the area, and remember that a high ridge is no place to be when lightning threatens. But despite the potential hazards, this is wonderful hiking country; there are spacious vistas across dramatic landscapes, interesting plants and fossils, plentiful wildlife, and lots of solitude.

TRAIL DESCRIPTIONS

Hike #1. Sitting Bull Falls Trail (#68)

This trail is located to the north of the Capitan Reef near Sitting Bull Falls, a popular warm-weather attraction near the base of the Guadalupe uplift, with a large picnic area nearby. There are actually two separate trails—a short path to the base of the falls, and the main trail, which climbs up past the top of the falls and continues on to Highway 137. The trails in the vicinity of the falls are probably the most heavily hiked of any in the region. The falls are fed by a large spring located 0.5 miles up the canyon and provide a picturesque shower of sparkling droplets down a sheer limestone band over 100

feet in height. The water is highly mineralized and has produced, over many hundreds of years, a substantial travertine formation that overlies the limestone band all across the lip of the falls. The travertine, which appears to be many feet thick in places, is the mineral deposition left by evaporating water, and crystal-clear pools have been eroded into the substance both above and below the falls, providing an irresistible attraction for the nearby picnickers. The trail above the falls continues along the stream to the spring, then climbs out of the canyon to the mesa above, and finishes on a jeep trail through oak and juniper woodlands to an intersection with Highway 137.

The total round-trip trail length is 7.2 miles to the highway, with 1,065 feet of net elevation gained. The round-trip hike to the top of the falls is 1 mile, with 140 feet of net elevation gain. The trail below the spring is heavily hiked, but from the spring to the highway, there isn't much traffic. If you can talk a friend into driving around and picking you up at the upper trailhead, a one-way hike is a good way to go. During cooler weather, the water around the falls won't be as appealing to get into, but the crowds will be gone and the weather will be more comfortable for hiking.

Locate the lower trailhead by approaching via Highway 137 and County Road 409, as described under "Access." The trail begins just to the right of the road as you enter the picnic area. As you top out on the first major limestone shelf, a short walk will lead to a trail junction, with the left fork leading to the falls and the other fork continuing straight toward Highway 137. If you have children along on the branch leading to the falls, watch them around the head of the falls—its a long way down. If you are continuing past the falls, the trail leads along the stream, with juniper, oak, big tooth maple, and an

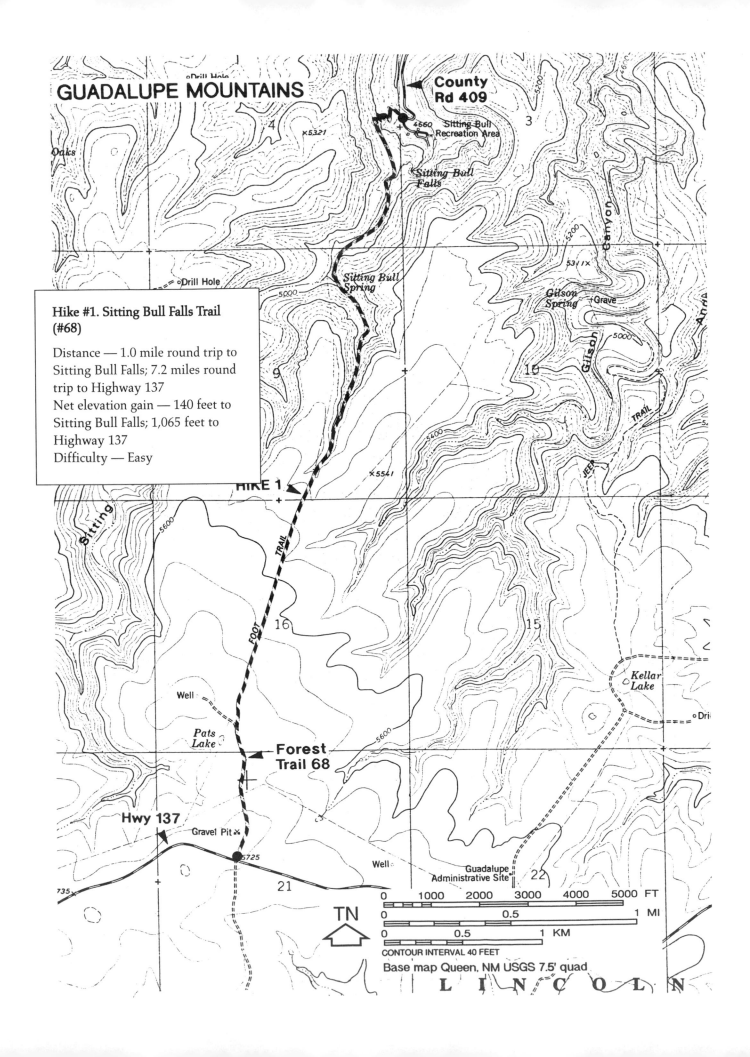

GUADALUPE MOUNTAINS

County Rd 409

Sitting Bull Recreation Area

Sitting Bull Falls

Sitting Bull Spring

Gilson Spring +Grave

Gilson Canyon

Hike #1. Sitting Bull Falls Trail (#68)

Distance — 1.0 mile round trip to Sitting Bull Falls; 7.2 miles round trip to Highway 137
Net elevation gain — 140 feet to Sitting Bull Falls; 1,065 feet to Highway 137
Difficulty — Easy

HIKE 1

Sitting

FOOT TRAIL

Well

Pats Lake

Forest Trail 68

Kellar Lake

Hwy 137

Gravel Pit

5725

Well

Guadalupe Administrative Site

| 0 | 1000 | 2000 | 3000 | 4000 | 5000 FT |

| 0 | 0.5 | 1 MI |

| 0 | 0.5 | 1 KM |

TN

CONTOUR INTERVAL 40 FEET
Base map Queen, NM USGS 7.5' quad

L I N C O L N

occasional Texas madrone along the way, to Sitting Bull Spring. The trail is well marked and easy to follow all the way. Above the spring, the trail begins to climb sharply on a 0.9-mile path to the rim above the canyon. Another 1.7 miles of level trail and jeep road leads the final distance to Highway 137. If you are approaching from the top, the upper trailhead is located by driving 11.7 miles west on Highway 137 past the County Road 409 turnoff to a road sign for Sitting Bull Falls and Trail #68. The trail, which turns north at this intersection, starts out as a dirt road that can be driven for about 0.5 miles before it gets unreasonably rough. Take a right at the first major fork, and continue along the rough road that follows the fence line. About 0.9 miles past the road fork, you will pass through two gates in quick succession, with a sign for Trail #68 at the second gate. The foot trail veers off to the right at an angle here and continues toward the falls. If you want to car camp in the vicinity, there are a number of potential unimproved campsites along the upper end of the road part of Trail #68.

Hike #2. Camp Wilderness Ridge Trail

Along the southeast face of the Capitan Reef escarpment, millions of years of stream erosion produced by water running down from the Guadalupe Mountains has produced great canyons, which cleave the face of the escarpment and run back toward the center of the range. These canyons, some of which are nearly 2,000 feet deep, are separated by ridges that run out to the edge of the reef and that often have trails running along the ridgeline with spectacular views of the majestically eroded spires, ridges, and canyons. One such ridge is Camp Wilderness Ridge, which has the upper trailhead in the Lincoln National Forest of New Mexico and the lower trailhead in the Guadalupe

Mountains National Monument of Texas. The trail, as described here, runs from the upper trailhead to the edge of the escarpment about a mile into the National Monument, for a round-trip hiking distance of 10.2 miles and 210 feet of net elevation differential, although the total elevation gained and lost walking along the ridge is much greater. If the entire trail is hiked from either end, the distance is increased several miles each way, along with another 2,000 feet or so of elevation. The Texas side of the trail is sometimes referred to as the Permian Reef Geology Trail and is a popular field trip for geology students because of the rich fossil history displayed on the ascent up the reef escarpment, although the trail that runs along the top is also well blessed with fossils to observe. There is no water along the trail, and camping on the National Monument side is prohibited except by permit.

The trailhead is reached, as described in the "Access" section, by driving to the south end of Forest Road 540. At the turnaround, there is a section of the Guadalupe Ridge Road, or Trail #201, that continues south. The road is unimproved, but unless road conditions are especially bad, most any vehicle within reason can readily drive the 0.4-mile distance to the first road fork. Park here; the branch that turns off to the right is the route you want to take, and it is a punishing four wheel drive jeep road but a level, easy walk (the branch that continues to the left goes to a short trail/road that runs along Big Canyon Ridge, which is another hike you may want to try if you have some extra time to spend in the area). Hike south from the above road fork for about a mile until you reach the rim of McKittrick Canyon, at which point the trail turns to the east and begins to follow the rim of the canyon down toward the entrance. The trail is easy to follow all the

Hike #2. Camp Wilderness Ridge Trail

Distance — 10.2 miles round trip
Net elevation gain — 210 feet
Difficulty — Easy to moderate

way, and you will be drawn to the edge of the rim at numerous points to admire the views. About 1.6 miles after reaching the canyon rim, the jeep road ends (incredibly enough, you can see where people have driven all the way down this thing) and becomes a single-track trail. The next 2.2 miles leads through some interesting fossil beds, into the National Monument (note the various restricted activities posted at the boundary), and to the east edge of the escarpment, where the trail begins a sharp descent. The scenery is fantastic. Complete the hike by returning along the approach route, or continue to the bottom if you have a car shuttle in place. Either way makes a nice moderate day hike, but the entire trail done from top to bottom and back in a day would be too extreme to enjoy.

Hike #3. Lonesome Ridge Trail

You have got to like the name of this ridge even if you don't know anything about the place. But the name fits. Lonesome Ridge is another of the big ridges that lead to the southeast rim of the Capitan Reef escarpment, with deep canyons on either side and splendid views across stupendous voids of space. The setting is similar to Camp Wilderness Ridge, but is more remote, and although slightly lower in elevation, has more of a feeling of isolation and vertical displacement. The trail, which includes a section of jeep-road hiking on the first part, is 14.2 miles round trip in length, with a net elevation differential of 590 feet. The elevation differential is misleading, since the total elevation gained with all the ups and downs along the ridge is more like 2,500 feet, resulting in a rather strenuous day hike that takes 8 to 12 hours to complete. This trail does not appear to get a lot of traffic, and parts of the trail on the eastern side are obscure, or even nonexistent, in places, with little or nothing in

Part of the Great Barrier Reef Escarpment along the Camp Wilderness Ridge Trail. Note the hiker standing on the far overlook.

the way of trail markers or trail signs. However, the obscure sections are along parts of the ridge where the route is obvious, and if you have a topo map along, the route finding is very straightforward. The rim of the Capitan Reef overlooking the vast plains below marks the east end of the hike as described here, although there are several steep but feasible routes that can be picked out to descend the southeast escarpment. The only route down on the east side that is shown on the map is the Golden Stairway Trail, a circuitous path evidently meant to accommodate horse traffic, that is so faint it is not worth trying to describe. As with the Camp Wilderness Ridge Hike, there are extensive reef fossils on top of the ridge, which are fun to examine. Under normal conditions, there is no water to be found along the hike, and this would be a particularly bad route to be on during a lightning storm. Also, the pervasive scrubby vegetation along the ridge suggests that the hike be done in long pants rather than shorts.

See the "Access" section to locate Forest Road 540, and follow it all the way to the turnaround at the south end of the road. The hike starts at the entrance to Forest Trail #201, which enters the forest at the north side of the turnaround. This Trail is also called the Guadalupe Ridge Road, a jeep road that runs all the way along the top of the ridge above the Capitan Reef, ending 24 miles or so to the northeast. It can be driven in a four wheel drive vehicle, but there are stretches of road that are extremely rough, and since it makes an easy hiking trail, it seems less nerve-wracking and physically punishing to just walk it. The first several miles of the hike go along this road and you have the choice of hiking it, driving it, or some combination of the two.

From the turnaround at the south end of Forest Road 540, go north on Forest

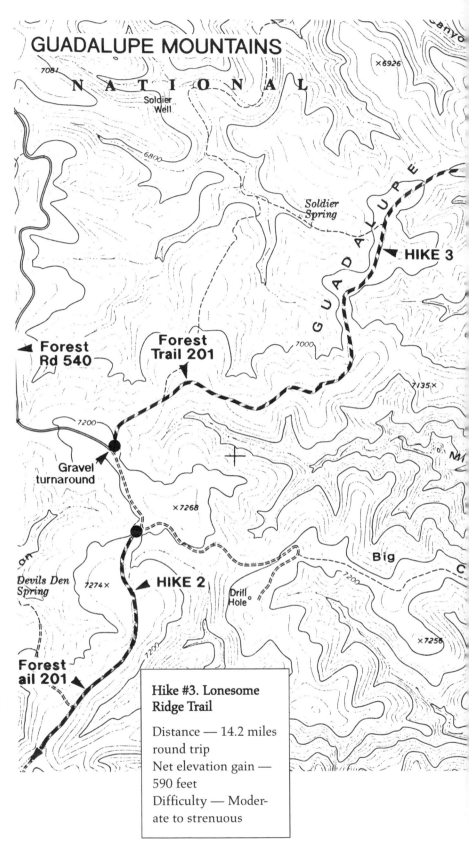

GUADALUPE MOUNTAINS

N A T I O N A L

Soldier Well

Soldier Spring

HIKE 3

Forest Rd 540

Forest Trail 201

Gravel turnaround

Devils Den Spring

HIKE 2

Drill Hole

Big

Forest ail 201

Hike #3. Lonesome Ridge Trail

Distance — 14.2 miles round trip
Net elevation gain — 590 feet
Difficulty — Moderate to strenuous

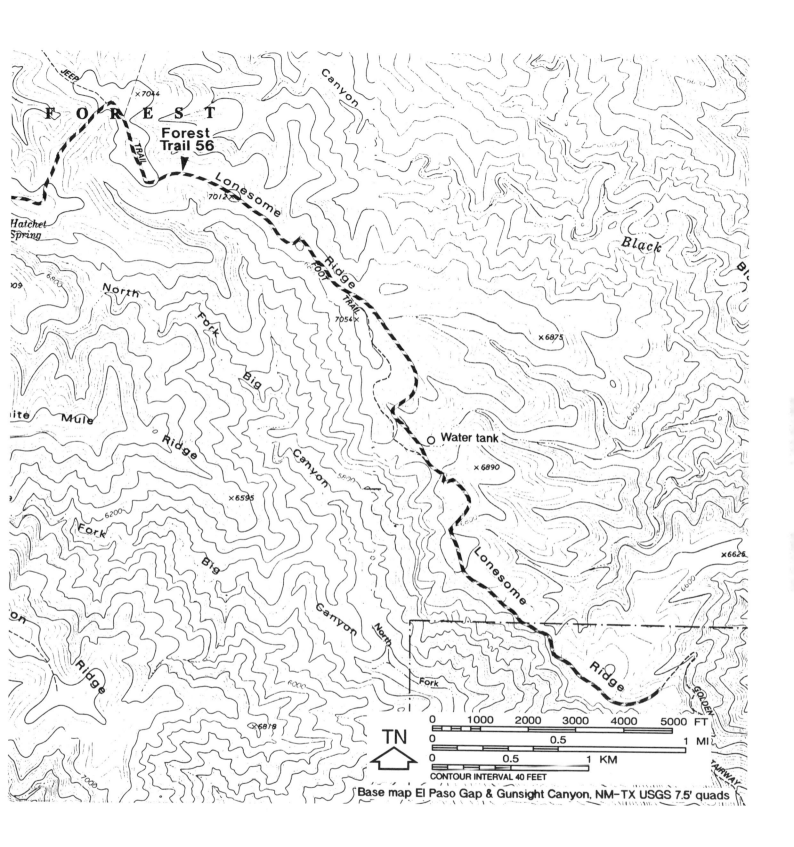

Looking East across the Mouth of Big Canyon on the Lonesome Ridge Hike

Trail #201 for just over 3 miles to a major road junction, where Forest Trail #56 turns off to the right. This is the Lonesome Ridge Trail, and a small road marker identifies the trail number. Walk southeast on Trail #56, which continues as a four wheel drive road for another 1.2 miles, until you come to a narrow limestone ridge at a saddle between two high points on the ridge. From this saddle, you can look down into the deep canyons on either side, and the trail becomes a single track for the remainder of the hike. This is the beginning of the most scenic part of the hike, as the trail basically continues along the north rim of the North Fork of Big Canyon another 2.9 miles to the edge of the Capitan Reef escarpment. The actual trail enters the forest of small, fire-blackened conifers at the far side of the narrow limestone ridge and runs along for about a mile through the woods on the north side of and below the ridge, but if it is a nice day, you may want to keep to the north rim of Big Canyon, where the views will be uninterrupted at the expense of slightly more strenuous hiking, and you will rejoin the trail farther down the canyon rim. Eventually, the trail becomes impossible to locate as it crosses the limestone surface, but you have only to make a route which keeps the canyon in view off to your right. As you near the mouth of Big Canyon, there is a juniper snag wedged in the blocks at the top of a steep, rocky chute that will provide access down into the canyon, and there are several more possibilities to descend at the southeast face of the escarpment, down Calamity Cove or the next canyon to the south. However, it looks like a steep scramble, and unless you have a shuttle vehicle in place, there doesn't seem to be much point. Complete the hike by returning back the way you came. This is a good hike—good exercise, good fresh air, good scenery, and one you'll remember.

For Further Information:

Lincoln National Forest
   Guadalupe Ranger
   District
   Federal Building, Room
   159
   Carlsbad, NM 88220
   (505) 885-4181

Carlsbad Caverns National
   Park
   3225 National Parks
   Highway
   Carlsbad, NM 88220
   (505) 885-8884

Guadalupe Mountains
   National Park
   HC60, Box 400
   Salt Flat, TX 79847
   (915) 828-3251

Hiking Equipment Checklist

The Essentials

* Water bottle (at least one quart)
* Lunch or trail snacks
* Topo map and compass
* Pocket knife/Swiss army knife
* Toilet paper
* Sunglasses
* Sunscreen
* Blister protection (moleskin, adhesive tape, duct tape)
* Rain protection (rain jacket, poncho, large plastic bag, lightweight plastic tarp, rain pants)
* Extra insulation (sweater, insulated vest, synthetic pile jacket, wool shirt)
* Cap with brim or bill
* Insect repellent
* Matches or butane lighter
* Daypack to carry it all
* Hiking boots

Other Stuff You May Want

* Additional drinking water and/or water purification system
* First-aid kit (moleskin, adhesive tape, chapstick, needle, tweezers, aspirin, antacid, antibiotic, vaseline, vitamins, prescription medicine, Band-Aids, sterile dressings, nail clippers, "Second Skin" for blisters)
* Extra prescription glasses

* Croakies (eyeglass retainers)
* Signal mirror
* Whistle for signaling
* Camera and film, extra lenses, lens paper, tripod or monopod
* Binoculars
* Fire starters (candle, paraffin, fire ribbon)
* Nylon cord (lightweight, 20 to 50 feet)
* Flashlight (lightweight, with spare bulb and batteries)
* Tweezers (can be included in first-aid kit or Swiss army knife)
* Bandanna
* Plant and wildlife identification guides
* Insulated hat and gloves
* Wind shell (parka or pullover)
* Paper and pencil, sketchbook, notebook
* Feminine hygiene products
* Running shoes (lightweight, for footwear change or river wading)
* Plastic trowel
* Fishing gear and license
* Altimeter

Additional Stuff for Backpacking

* Backpack
* Lashing straps (to secure tent, pad, etc.)
* Sleeping bag with waterproof stuff sack
* Waterproof pack cover
* Foam pad, Thermarest
* Tent or nylon tarp
* Collapsible water container
* Extra pants, shorts, shirts, underwear

* Extra socks (at least two pair)
* Skin cream
* Camp stove with extra fuel
* Stove repair/maintenance kit
* Kitchen gear (pots, pot gripper or hot pad, cup, spoon and fork, salt and spices, can opener, paper towels or dish towel, scouring pad)
* Food (lightweight and easy to prepare)
* Biodegradable soap
* Toothbrush, shampoo
* Small towel
* Hammock
* Space blanket or plastic tarp
* Snakebite kit
* Candle lantern, extra candles
* Plastic water basin
* Small repair kit (pliers, screwdriver, wire, sewing awl, duct tape, needle and thread, safety pins, spare clevis pins)
* Large plastic garbage bag (for trash, emergency shelter, pack cover)
* Thermometer
* Hiking staff
* Air pillow
* Patch kit for air mattress or Thermarest
* Deck of cards, paperback book, star chart, hacky sack, frisbee
* Zip-lock bags (for food, leftovers, trail map, plant and rock specimens, etc.)

Vocabulary of Spanish Placenames

Azul—blue
Abajo—down; below
Abeja—bee
Abrigo—overcoat
Agua—water
Aguila—eagle
Alamo—cottonwood tree
Alcalde—mayor
Alma—soul; spirit
Almagre—red ocher
Alto, alta—tall; high
Amarillo—yellow
Amole—soapweed
Ancho, ancha—wide
Angostura—narrows
Arroyo—eroded streambed
Azabache—jet trinkets

Bajada—descent; slope
Banco—earthen bench; a narrow
    mesa
Barranca—gorge; ravine
Blanco, blanca—white
Boca—mouth
Boleta—a permit or pass
Bonito, bonita—pretty
Borrego—sheep; fleecy cloud
Bosque—riparian woodland or
    forest
Brazo—arm
Bueno, buena—good

Caballo—horse
Cabra—goat

Cabresto—rope
Caja—box; chest
Cal—lime(mineral)
Calabaza—gourd; pumpkin
Calavera—skull
Caliente—hot
Camino—road
Campana—bell
Canjilon—ram's horn
Cañada—dry riverbed; small
    canyon
Cañoncito—small canyon
Capilla—hood; cap
Capulin—chokecherry
Casa—house
Cebolla—onion
Cedro—cedar
Ceja—eyebrow; edge; rim
Chamisa—rabbit bush
Chato, chata—flat; blunt
Chimayo—obsidian flake;
    indian blanket
Chiquito, chiquita—small; little
Chivato—kid; young goat
Cholla—a common cactus
Chupadero—cattle tick; sinkhole
Cíbola—derivative of indian
    term for bison
Cielo—sky
Cimarron—wild; untamed
Cobre—copper
Colorado, colorada—red; reddish
Concha—shell
Conejo—rabbit

corona—summit
Cortada—wood cut; clearing
Costilla—rib (landform)
Crestón—crest
Cristo—Christ
Cristóbal—christopher
Cuate—twin
Cuchillo—knife
Cuervo—raven
Cuesta—slope; grade
Cueva—cave

Dado—die (dice)
Diablo—devil
Diente—tooth
Dulce—sweet

Embudo—funnel
Encino—evergreen oak
Escabosa—broomgrass
Escoba—broom
Escondido, escondida—hidden

Florido, florida—flowery
Frijole—bean
Frío, fría—cold
Fuego—fire
Fuerte—strong

Gallina—hen
Gallo—rooster
Garita—one—seat privy
Garrapata—tick
Gato—cat

Gigante—giant
Golondrino—swallow;
    brownish color
Gordo, gorda—fat
Grande—large
Grulla—sandhill crane
Guaje—gourd

Hermano—brother
Hermoso, hermosa—
    beautiful
Hondo, honda—deep
Horno—beehive—style
    oven
Huerfano—orphan;
    isolated rock outcrop
Hueso—bone

Indio—indian

Jara—willow shrub
Jornada—journey
Joya—jewel; river basin
Juan—john
Junta—junction; union

Ladera—hillside
Lago—lake
Laguna—lagoon
Lama—moss
Largo, larga—long
Latir—to annoy, bore,
    molest
Leche—milk
Lemita—squawbush

Lindo, linda—pretty
Liso, lisa—smooth
Llano—plain (noun)
Lobo—wolf
Loma—hill
Lugar—a place
Lumbre—light; brightness
Luz—light

Madera—wood
Madre—mother
malpais—badlands
Manga—sleeve
Mano—hand; hand—held
   grindstone
Manzano—apple
Medio, media—middle
Mesita—small mesa
Miel—honey
Miga—small amount; crumb
Milagro—miracle
Mofeta—skunk
Mogote—knoll; hillock
Montañoso, montañosa—
   mountainous
Monte—mountain
Mora—berry; strawberry
Morro—knoll; outcrop
Mosca—fly (insect)
Muerte—death
Mujer—woman
Mula—mule

Nacimiento—birth; origin;
   beginning
Naranjo—orange
Negro, negra—black
Nogal—walnut
Norte—north
Novillo—young bull
Nuevo, nueva—new
Nutria—beaver

Ojito—small spring
Ojo—eye; spring
Olla—indian—style pot

Orilla—border; edge
Oro—gold
Oscuro—obscure; dark; gloomy
Osha—wild, medicinal herb
Oso—bear

Padre—father
Pajarito—small bird
Palacio—palace; mansion
Palo—stick; pole
Paloma—dove
Pardo, parda—gray
Paso—pass
Pavo—turkey
Pedernal—flint
Pedregoso, pedregosa—stony;
   rocky
Pelada—pelt; sheepskin
Pelado—bare; bald
Pelo—hair
Pelon—bald
Peñasco—craggy rock spire
Perro—dog
Petaca—trunk for clothes
Picacho—peak
Piedra—rock
Pilar—basin; bowl; pillar
Pino—pine
Pintado, pintada—painted,
   spotted, mottled
Placita—settlement; plaza
Plata—silver
Playa—beach; shore; dry lake
Polvadera—cloud of dust
Posada—inn; lodging
Poso—sediment; dregs
Potrero—pasture; ridge of lava
   rock
Presa—capture; dam; ditch
Prieto, prieta—dark; blackish
Pueblo—town
Puente—bridge
Puerco—hog
Puerta—door; gateway
Puerto—port; mountain pass;
   haven

Punche—native tobacco
Punta—point; tip

Quemado, quemada—burned
Questa—hillside; grade

Ratón—mouse
Redondo, redonda—round
Relampago—lightning
Rey—king
Rincon—corner; cul de sac
Rinconada—lacking corners
Rio—river
Rito—small river
Robledo—oak—covered
Rociada—sprinkling; dew
Rojo—red
Rosillo—shrubby cinquefoil (a
   common shrub)
Ruidoso, ruidosa—loud;
   sensational

Sacramento—sacrament
Salado, salada—unlucky
Salida—start; exit
Sangre—blood
Sarco—clear blue
Seco, seca—dry
Seguro, segura—certain;
   unfailing
Seis—six
Sierra—saw; sawtooth
   mountain ridge
Silla—chair; saddle between
   two peaks
Socorro—aid; help
Soldado—soldier
Soledad—solitude
Sombra—shadow
Sur—south

Talpa—knob of land rising
   above the mesa
Tapia—adobe wall (also a
   surname)
Techado—roof

Tecolote—owl
Tejano—texan
Tejón—badger
Tetilla—nipple
Tierra—earth
Tijeras—scissors
Todo, toda—all; every-
   thing
Toro—bull
Torreon—turret
Trampas—traps
Tres—three
Trigo—wheat
Truchas—trout
Tularosa—reddish reeds or
   willows

Uno—one
Uva—grape; berry

Vaca—cow
Vado—a river ford
Valle—valley
Vara—pole; rod; staff
Vega—fertile plain;
   grassland
Venado—deer
Verde—green
Vermejo—red
Vida—life; livelihood
Viejo, vieja—old; old man/
   woman
Viento—wind
Volcán—volcano

Yegua—mare
Yerba—grass
Yeso—gypsum

Zorro—fox

Bibliography

Backpacking One Step At A Time, 4th edition, by Harvey Manning, Vintage Books, New York, 1986.

Be Expert With Map And Compass, by Bjorn Kjellstrom, Chas. Scribner's Sons, New York, NY, 1976.

Chaco Canyon, Archaeology and Archaeologists, by Robert H. Lister and Florence C. Lister, University of New Mexico Press, Albuquerque, NM, 1981.

Day Hikes in the Santa Fe Area, by the Santa Fe Group of the Sierra Club, The National Education Association Press, Santa Fe, NM, 1981.

A Dictionary of New Mexico And Southern Colorado Spanish, by Ruben Cobos, Museum of New Mexico Press, Santa Fe, NM, 1983.

Edible Native Plants of the Rocky Mountains, by H. D. Harrington, University of New Mexico Press, Albuquerque, NM, 1967.

Exploring the Jemez Country, by Roland A. Pettitt, revisions by Dorothy Hoard, published by Los Alamos Historical Society, Los Alamos, NM, 1990.

Gem Trails of New Mexico, by James R. Mitchell, published by Gem Guides Book Company, Pico Rivera, CA, 1987.

Geology of Sandia Mountains and Vicinity, New Mexico, by Vincent C. Kelly and Stuart A. Northrup, New Mexico Bureau of Mines and Mineral Resources, Socorro, NM, 1975.

The Gila Wilderness, A Hiking Guide, by John A. Murray, University of New Mexico Press, Albuquerque, NM, 1988.

Glimpses of the Ancient Southwest, by David E. Stuart, Ancient City Press, Santa Fe, NM, 1984.

A Guide to Bandelier National Monument, by Dorothy Hoard, Los Alamos Historical Society, Los Alamos, NM, 1989.

Guide to the New Mexico Mountains, by Herbert E. Ungnade, University of New Mexico Press, Albuquerque, NM, 1965.

Highroad Map Series, Highroad Publications, Albuquerque, NM.

Hiker's and Climber's Guide to the Sandia Mountains, by Mike Hill, University of New Mexico Press, Albuquerque, NM, 1983.

A Hiking Guide to Doña Ana County, New Mexico, by Greg S. Magee, published by Naturescapes, Las Cruces, NM, 1989.

Hypothermia: Killer of the Unprepared, published by the Mazamas, Portland, OR, 1975.

Mountaineering First Aid, 3rd edition, by Martha J. Lentz, Steven C. MacDonald, and Jan D. Carline, The Mountaineers, Seattle, WA, 1985.

The Navajo, revised edition, by Clyde Kluckhohn and Dorothea Leighton, Harvard University Press, Cambridge, MA and London, England, 1946, renewed 1974.

New Light on Chaco Canyon, edited by David Grant Noble, School of American Research Press, Santa Fe, NM, 1984.

New Mexico Handbook, by Stephen Metzger, Moon Publications, Chico, CA, 1989.

New Mexico in Maps, edited by Jerry L. Williams and Paul E. McAllister, University of New Mexico Press, Albuquerque, NM, 1979.

The New Mexico Mountain Bike Guide, by Brant Hayenga and Chris Shaw, Big Ring Press, Albuquerque, NM, 1991.

New Mexico Place Names; A Geographical Dictionary, edited by T. M. Pearce, published by University of New Mexico Press, Albuquerque, NM, 1965.

New Mexico Statewide Wilderness Study, U.S. Department of the interior, Bureau of Land Management, New Mexico State Office, Santa Fe, NM, 1985.

New Mexico Trailheads, prepared by N.M. State Park and Recreation Division: Energy, Minerals and Natural Resources Department, 1989.

101 Trips in the Land of Enchantment, by Betty Woods, edited by George Fitzpatrick, published by *New Mexico Magazine,* Santa Fe, NM, 1969.

Pecos Wilderness Trail Guide, edited by Stephen G. Maurer, in cooperation with Patty Cohn and the Staff of the Santa Fe National Forest, published by Southwest Natural and Cultural Heritage Association, Albuquerque, NM, 1991.

Pecos Wilderness Trails for Day Walkers, by Carl Overcharge, William Gannon Press, Santa Fe, NM, 1984.

Recreation Sites in Southwestern National Forests, prepared by the Forest Service, Southwestern Region, U.S. Department of Agriculture, 1989.

The Roads of New Mexico, published by Shearer Publishing, Fredericksburg, TX, 1990.

Roadside Geology of Mew Mexico, by Halka Chronic, Mountain Press Publishing Co., Missoula, MT, 1987.

Roadside History of New Mexico, by Francis L. and Roberta B. Fugate, published by Mountain Press Publishing Company, Missoula, MT, 1989.

Shrubs and Trees of the Southwest Uplands, by Francis H. Elmore, published by Southwest Parks and Monuments Association, Tucson, AZ, 1976.

Ski touring in Northern New Mexico, by Sam Beard, Adobe Press, Albuquerque, NM, 1988.

The Southwestern Journals Of Adolph Bandelier, 1889–1892, edited and annotated by Charles H. Lange, Carroll L. Riley, and Elizabeth M. Lange, University of New Mexico Press, Albuquerque, NM, and the School of American Research, Santa Fe, NM, 1984.

Southwestern Trees, A Guide to the Native Species of New Mexico and Arizona, Agriculture Handbook #9, by Elbert L. Little Jr., U.S. Department of Agriculture, 1950.

The State Parks of New Mexico, by John V. Young, published by University of New Mexico Press, Albuquerque, NM, 1984.

Trail Guide to the Upper Pecos, by Arthur Montgomery and Patrick K. Sutherland, New Mexico Bureau of Mines and Mineral Resources, Socorro, NM, 1967.

Walking Softly in the Wilderness, by John Hart, Sierra Club Books, San Francisco, CA, 1977.

Wilderness—A New Mexico Legacy, by Corry McDonald, Sunstone Press, Santa Fe, NM, 1985.

Wildernesses in Southwestern National Forests, prepared by the Forest Service, Southwestern Region, U.S. Department of Agriculture, 1986.

Wildlands: A New Mexico BLM Wilderness Coalition Statewide Proposal, edited by Jim D. Fish, published by New Mexico BLM Wilderness Coalition, Placitas, NM, 1987.

Index

Index to Maps

N.B.: Alphabetical listing of topographical maps is arranged in three groups